Praise for PassPorter®

"A nifty travel guide that works overtime as a planner, organizer and journal ..."

— Jacky Runice
Daily Herald–Chicago

"[PassPorter] is a brilliant travel aid ... the most practical, sanity-saving guide you could take along"

— Stephanie Gold,
Amazon.com

"A great resource for anyone visiting Southern California and wondering how to fit everything into one vacation."

— Shoshana Lewin,
MousePlanet.com

"Vacationers who want to enjoy all that Disney has to offer should make sure they take along this PassPorter guide."

— ForeWord Reviews

PassPorter is incredibly easy to use! I loved the sections devoted to each park with the maps right there! Genius!

— Misti Simpson
in South Dakota

I love the wealth of information in PassPorter. Almost every question I've ever had was answered.

— Jonni Ngo
in California

I think PassPorter is the most amazing book ever. I wish I'd had a PassPorter to prepare for my first Disneyland trip.

— Denise Graham
in Alabama

I LOVE IT, I LOVE IT, I LOVE IT! PassPorter is wonderful! It's everything you ever wanted to know in a nice, compact book.

— Julienne Scheibe
in Illinois

Awards for the PassPorter Guide Series:

Silver Award Winner
Guide Book Category
1999 Lowell Thomas
Travel Journalism Competition
Society of American Travel Writers Foundation

FOREWORD MAGAZINE
Book of the Year
AWARD WINNER

-1-

What's Unique in PassPorter

- **Comprehensive yet concise information** is packed into our pages—PassPorter is information rich and padding-free!
- **Full color** brings life and clarity to our maps and photos.
- **Blending of personal experience** from your authors and the collective wisdom from tens of thousands of readers means a guidebook that's full of heart and soul.
- **Well-organized chapters and pages** make it easy to find what you need. We edit our information carefully so that new sections begin at the top of a page.
- **Worksheets** to jot notes and make travel arrangements.
- **Our famous organizer PassPockets** to plan your trip, store your maps and papers, and record your vacation memories.
- **Coverage of the most recent changes** throughout Disneyland—thanks to our later production schedule, this is the most up-to-date 2006 guidebook available!
- **Floorplans of Disney resort hotel rooms** to give you a better sense of the layout.
- **Fold-out maps** of the Disneyland theme parks, printed in full color on heavy paper to stand up to rugged use.
- **Custom-designed attraction charts** provide all the information you need at a glance.
- **Alexander's A-OK! ratings** offer advice for fellow little ones.
- **Color, self-stick tabs** to mark your chapters in whatever way you prefer for quick and easy reference.
- **Original color photos**—many of which include your authors in the picture, too. No stock photos here!
- **Personalization labels and fun stickers** to custom-design your PassPockets to your own vacation.
- **Magical memories** from fellow vacationers to convey the spirit and wonder of Disneyland and Southern California.
- **Contributing writers** to add further depth and a wider range of experiences.
- **Expert peer reviewers** to ensure accuracy and thoroughness.

Visit us at http://www.passporter.com *for a complete list of what's unique in PassPorter Disneyland Resort and Southern California Attractions.*

PassPorter®
Disneyland® Resort and Southern California Attractions
First Edition

The unique travel guide, planner, organizer, journal, and keepsake

Jennifer Marx

Dave Marx

With contributions by
Barbara Baker, Rebecca Oberg,
LauraBelle Hime, and Courtney Fontana

PassPorter Travel Press

An imprint of MediaMarx, Inc.
P.O. Box 3880, Ann Arbor, Michigan 48106
877-WAYFARER
http://www.passporter.com

PassPorter® Disneyland® Resort and Southern California Attractions

by Jennifer Marx and Dave Marx

© 2006 by PassPorter Travel Press, an imprint of MediaMarx, Inc.

P.O. Box 3880, Ann Arbor, Michigan 48106
877-WAYFARER or 877-929-3273 (toll-free)
Visit us on the World Wide Web at http://www.passporter.com

Special Sales: PassPorter Travel Press publications are available at special discounts for bulk purchases for sales premiums or promotions. Special editions, including personalized covers and excerpts of existing guides, can be created in large quantities. For information, write to Special Sales, P.O. Box 3880, Ann Arbor, Michigan, 48106.

Distributed by Publishers Group West

ISBN-10: 1-58771-004-8
ISBN-13: 978-1-58771-004-9

10 9 8 7 6 5 4 3 2 1

Printed and bound in Hong Kong

About the Authors

Name: Jennifer Marx
Date of birth: 10/09/68
Residence: Ann Arbor, MI
Signature: *Jennifer Marx*

Jennifer Marx discovered Disneyland while playing hooky from a writers conference in the mid-'90s. Her solo explorations took her to the Disneyland Park and the Disneyland Hotel (that's essentially all there was back then) and she was amazed to find a place so richly steeped in magic. She'd been to Walt Disney World countless times by this point, but it was only at Disneyland that she felt the presence of Walt Disney himself and sensed a deeper connection to the people that adored him. Since that fateful visit, she's returned many times with her husband Dave and later with their son Alexander. They've added many other Southern California attractions to their itineraries over the years, too. Jennifer is the author of more than 30 titles, almost half of which have been travel guides to various Disney destinations. Jennifer lives in Ann Arbor, Michigan, where she makes her home with Dave and Alexander.

Dave Marx is the co-author of PassPorter Walt Disney World and PassPorter's Field Guide to the Disney Cruise Line. After a lifetime of "not knowing what I want to be when I grow up," he has finally found a satisfying answer. He has a broad professional background in print and electronic media, photography and music, and enjoys bringing nearly all his talents to bear at PassPorter. A "foodie" since his pre-teen days and a "techie" in the performing arts for many years, he takes special joy in reviewing eateries and reporting on the brilliance of Disney's Imagineers. Like so many of us, Dave has been inspired by Walt Disney and his creations since birth. A "Jersey Boy," he first visited Disneyland in the mid-1970s and envies Southern Californians their "home court advantage," but he'd rather live right where he is now, in Ann Arbor, Michigan. Dave is an adoring father to teenager Allison and toddler Alexander and loving partner to Jennifer, and all of this makes him a very happy camper.

Name: Dave Marx
Date of birth: 04/07/55
Residence: Ann Arbor, MI
Signature: *Dave Marx*

Together, Jennifer and Dave created **PassPorter Travel Press** in the '90s to realize their dreams of a unique series of travel guidebooks. Their independent publishing company has far exceeded their expectations, and the acceptance of their efforts by fellow travelers frequently astounds them. PassPorter Travel Press has been honored with nine national awards and honors over the years, including three prestigious Benjamin Franklin Awards, the Lowell Thomas Travel Journalism Award, and two ForeWord Magazine "Book of the Year" awards. Their original title, "PassPorter Walt Disney World Resort," quickly became a bestseller in its first edition and remains so today. By far the best part of PassPorter, however, is the amazing community of readers it has brought together through the guidebooks and the web site. We feel very fortunate that so many readers entrust their precious vacations to our guidebooks and advice, and we take our mission seriously.

PassPorter Contributors

Our Contributors—These four experienced and talented writers shared their Disneyland and Southern California experience through valuable contributions to this edition. Each of these individuals also acted as an expert peer reviewer for this guidebook.

Barbara Baker was addicted to the Disneyland magic after her first terrifying plunge on Pirates of the Caribbean as a six-year-old. Growing up in the San Francisco Bay Area, her annual family trips to visit her Aunt Barbie and Uncle Jack in Southern California nearly always included a trip to Disneyland. Now she lives in Sacramento, a day's drive from the Happiest Place on Earth. Fortunately, her sweetheart, Louis, enjoys visiting the Disneyland Resort as much she does and they make several trips each year. When she's not visiting a Disney theme park or planning the next trip, she spends her time working for California State Parks, motorcycling, knitting, and writing.

Courtney Fontana and her husband Frank are lifelong Disney fans—they even got married with the Mouse in 2003! They have a one-year-old daughter, Taylor, who has already made her first visit to see Mickey. As a former San Diego resident, Courtney has spent a lot of time exploring the area and regularly took her laptop and cell phone to the beach or Balboa Park, rather than working indoors. Her favorite place in San Diego is the Wgasa Bush Line Railway at the Wild Animal Park, and she never visits Disneyland without a stop at Alice in Wonderland. Courtney is co-owner of Grand Getaways Travel and enjoys helping families plan trips to make memories that will last a lifetime.

LauraBelle Hime enjoys traveling to Disney any time of the year with family, friends, or solo, but especially with her grandchildren Alexis, Olivia, Jacob, Caleb, and Samantha. Disneyland Resort has become her favorite Disney vacation spot. She's spent many happy times at Disneyland and at many Southern California attractions, including the Queen Mary, Catalina, Hollywood, Aquarium of the Pacific, Pantages Theatre, Old Town Temecula, Rodeo Drive, Santa Monica Pier, Balboa, and various beaches and communities up and down the coast. She finds great satisfaction sharing information and stories at PassPorter.com as a message board guide (moderator) for The Sunroom and The Family Room forums.

Rebecca Oberg's fondest childhood memory of Disneyland was spotting the Matterhorn from the family car from the freeway. Rebecca has been a fan of Disneyland since her early childhood. She made trips several times a year until moving out of state. She now visits at least once yearly, so her children can enjoy the magic. While she aspires to work on the Storybook Land Canal Boats ride, she currently spends her time teaching second grade and raising three wonderful children. Rebecca's contribution to this book would not have been possible without the loving support of her husband of 14 years, and lifelong encouragement from her mom.

PassPorter Expert Peer Reviewers

Our Expert Peer Reviewers and Researchers—These experts painstakingly checked our text and maps and helped us ensure PassPorter's accuracy, readability, and thoroughness. Thank you for helping to make PassPorter the best it can be!

Dianne Cook and husband Tom had a Disney honeymoon and now travel to a Disney park twice a year since their sons Andrew and Matthew were born. A Disney Vacation Club member since 1996, Dianne is a PassPorter Guide for "Getting There and Back" forum.

 Joanne and Tim Ernest are message board guides at PassPorter, where they enjoy discussing the magic of Disney. They have two boys, David and Andrew, and are veterans of 25+ trips to Disney, three cruises, and a recent Disneyland visit.

Debbie Hendrickson has visited Disneyland eight times, savoring the wide variety of experiences she's acquired there. Debbie is married to Lee and is a PassPorter message board guide for the Disneyland forum.

 Denise Lang and her family love the magic of Disney! Denise, a PassPorter message board guide, loves sharing Disney experiences. She is married to Jason and has two children. They honeymooned at Disney and can't wait to take their children.

Bruce Metcalf has loved and studied Disneyland since his first visit in 1958. Now employed at a major Central Florida theme park, he makes regular pilgrimages to The Original. He also co-writes "Iago & Zazu's Attraction of the Week" at http://aotw.figzu.com.

 Rebekah Moseley grew up in S. California enjoying all its attractions with Disneyland as her favorite. Alongside her husband (they met at Disneyland), she founded LaughingPlace.com, which connects Disney fans across the world with daily updates on all things Disney.

Cheryl Pendry is a PassPorter message board guide and Disney Vacation Club member. She and her husband are regular Disney vacationers even though they live in England, and she recently made a return trip to Disneyland, nearly 20 years after her first visit.

 Tina Peterson has taken an annual trip to Disneyland each year since 2001. She lives in Michigan with her two children, Kylor and Jalen. She is also a PassPorter message board guide for the Globetrotting forum.

Jennifer Sanborn is a frequent visitor to Disney and enjoys helping others plan their vacations to best experience the magic. Jennifer, a PassPorter message board guide, has been married for two years to her husband, John.

 Michelle Smith is past President of the Orlando chapter of the NFFC. She served on the first Disneyland Creative Advisory Council and wrote for Disney sites such as MousePlanet, LaughingPlace.com, MouseInfo.com, and JimHillMedia.com before starting FabRocks.net.

Lani Teshima is a travel writer/editor for MousePlanet and a technical writer for a California software company. She also publishes The Travelite FAQ on how to travel with just carry-on bags. Lani also runs Disney half-marathons annually.

 Marnie Urmaza and her family are avid Disney fans. They have enjoyed five trips to Walt Disney World over the past two years. Alas, they have not made it to Disneyland yet, but that is sure to change! Marnie is also a PassPorter Message Board Guide. [Note: Marnie reviewed our guidebook for the benefit of our readers who are newcomers.]

A very special thank you to our in-house research wizards and office managers, **Nicole Larner and Chad Larner**—this phenomenal brother-and-sister team unearthed tidbits of new and updated information, checked the accuracy of prices, addresses, and phone numbers, assisted in the peer review process, and researched and classified various attraction information. Their essential position on the team enables PassPorter to grow and thrive! Nikki and Chad are both Disney fans, having made numerous trips to Disney World in recent years.

Acknowledgments

A "world" of thanks to our readers, who've contributed loads of tips and stories since PassPorter's debut. A special thanks to those who generously allowed us to include their contributions in this edition:

Misti Simpson, Jonni Ngo, Denise Graham, and Julienne Scheibe (page i); Dianne Cook, Ilisa Oman, and Brad Randall (page 12); Jeff Rosenzweig (page 17); Laura Gilbreath, LauraBelle Hime, Margo Verikas, and Debbie Hendrickson (page 28); Heather Berube (page 78); Katie Gilbert and Kristen Lamb (page 190); Tina Peterson, Susan Billings, Keith Burrus, and Nicola Winkel (page 226); Kristine Chase, Debbie Mekler, Mary Karlo, and Jane Peters (page 246). May each of you receive a new magical memory for every reader your words touch.

PassPorter would not be where it is today without the help and support of the many members of the Internet Disneyland fan community. Our thanks to the friendly folks below and to all who we didn't have room to include!

- AllEarsNet.com (http://www.allearsnet.com). Thanks, Deb and Deb!
- DIS—Unofficial Disney Information Station (http://www.wdwinfo.com). Thanks, Pete!
- Hidden Mickeys of Disney (http://www.hiddenmickeys.org). Thanks, Tom!
- Intercot (http://www.intercot.com). Thank you, John!
- LaughingPlace.com (http://www.laughingplace.com). Thanks, Doobie and Rebekah!
- MousePlanet.com (http://www.mouseplanet.com). Thanks, Mike, Lani, and Shoshana!
- MouseSavers.com (http://www.mousesavers.com). Thanks, Mary!

A big thanks to the Guides (moderators) of our own message boards: Maureen Austin, Kelley Baker, Kelly Charles, Michelle Clark, Dianne Cook, Joanne and Tim Ernest, Kristin Grey, Debbie Hendrickson, LauraBelle Hime, Christina Holland-Radvon, Robin Krening-Capra, Susan Kulick, Marcie LaCava, Denise Lang, Nicole Larner, Tara McCusker, Bill Myers, Michelle Nash, Allison Palmer-Gleicher, Cheryl Pendry, Tina Peterson, Susan Rannestad, Jennifer Sanborn, Ann Smith, Donna Sonmor, Nate Stokes, Suzanne Torrey, Marnie Urmaza, Sara Varney, Margo Verikas, Dave Walsh, Suzi Waters, Brant Wigginton, and Debbie Wright, plus the 11,000+ readers in our amazing community at http://www.passporterboards.com.

A heartfelt thank you to our family and friends for their patience while we were away on trips or cloistered at our computers, and for their support of our dream: Allison Cerel Marx, Alexander Marx; Carolyn Tody; Tom Anderson; Fred and Adele Marx; Megan and Natalie Larner; Dan, Jeannie, Kayleigh, Melanie, and Nina Marx; Gale Cerel; Jeanne and David Beroza; Robert and Sharon Larner; and Marta Metcalf.

A special thanks to these very important folks "behind the scenes" at PassPorter:
Office Managers and Research Wizards: Nicole Larner and Chad Larner
Proofreader: Sandy Zilka
Printer: Magnum Printing, Ltd., Hong Kong (thank you, Anita Lam!)
Online Promotions and Newsletter Editor: Sara Varney
Indexing: Jennifer Marx, Kimberly Larner, and Nicole Larner
Visibility Specialists: Kate and Doug Bandos, KSB Promotions
Assorted Pixies: Tom Anderson, Mariska Elia, Dave Hunter, Carolyn Tody, Dirk Uhlenbrock

Last but not least, we thank Walter Elias Disney for his dream.

Contents

List of
Maps, Worksheets, and Charts

Contents
(continued)

Contents
(continued)

– xi –

Contents
(continued)

Bonus Features...

Southern California Area Map and Mileage Chart
.... front cover flap

2006/2007 Planning Calendars and Planning Timeline
.... under front cover flap

Bookplate for personalization
.... under front cover flap

Fold-out, full-color maps for Disneyland's theme parks
.... pages 90 and 112

Labels and tabs to customize your PassPorter .... in front of pockets

Disneyland Property Map
.... back cover flap

Important Telephone Numbers, Reminders, and Addresses
.... under back cover flap

Page Protector and Marker
.... fold along score on back flap

An elastic band to keep your book securely closed
.... under back cover flap

You're Going to Disneyland!

"Disneyland is like Alice stepping through the Looking Glass; to step through the portals of Disneyland will be like entering another world."

These words, spoken by Walt Disney himself, are as true today as when they were uttered. The Disneyland Resort is a world unto itself, full of magical wonder and imaginative details. Yet the very fact that it is so expansive and surrounded by so many other wonders can make a visit to Disneyland and Southern California seem more like falling down the rabbit hole than a relaxed vacation. And worse yet, pleasant memories of a great vacation may disappear beneath the stress and worries that accompanied it.

Happily, after many trips to Disneyland, we've learned to dispel our stress with one simple and enjoyable task: **planning ahead**. In fact, it is no task at all—planning is as much fun as the vacation itself. Planning gave birth to the PassPorter concept. Originally, Jennifer made itineraries on her computer and placed them in a binder. During the trip, she kept the binder handy, using it to store passes, brochures, and receipts. After the vacation, these organizers had turned into scrapbooks, full of pixie-dusted memories and goofy smiles. When Jennifer's writing career took off, she didn't have the time to create binders for every trip. She wished for a simpler version that she could use each trip without a lot of fuss. It was on a trip to Walt Disney World that the idea came to her. She could make an easy-to-use, book-based version and offer it as a resource to fellow vacationers!

After much work, you hold PassPorter in your hands. The first PassPorter (created for Walt Disney World) debuted in 1999, creating a sensation in the Disney fan community, winning nine national awards, and helping tens of thousands of vacationers plan great vacations. This edition is our first for the Disneyland Resort and Southern California!

It is our greatest hope that PassPorter helps you "discover the magic" through your own eyes, as it did for us. To get you in the spirit, read "Disney Dreaming" on the next page and prepare for your adventure!

Smiles and laughter,

Jennifer and *Dave*

We'd love to hear from you! Visit us on the Internet (http://www.passporter.com) or drop us a postcard from fabulous Southern California!

P.S. For the latest changes and updates, be sure to consult our updates at http://www.passporter.com/customs/bookupdates.htm

Disney Dreaming

A good part of the fun of going to the Disneyland Resort is the anticipation before your trip! To really get you into "Disney Dreaming," we present some of our favorite tips to feed your excitement and prepare you for the adventure that lies ahead. This is magical stuff—don't blame us if you get the urge to hop on the next plane to California.

Watch a Movie
Disney movies—animations and live action alike—capture the Disney spirit wonderfully. Rent your favorite from the local video store and settle in for a cozy evening. (Alas, Disneyland does not offer a free vacation planning video like other Disney properties do.)

Read a Book
Several excellent Disneyland books exist and make for great pre-trip, armchair travel. See pages 243-244 for a list of our favorites.

Go Shopping
You may enjoy a visit to The Disney Store—while many of these closed over the last few years and the chain was recently sold, plenty are still found in major shopping malls. The stores continue to offer delightful theming and foot-tapping music. You can buy park admission at a discount, and special offers may be had with the Disney Visa (see page 10).

Reminisce
If you've visited Disneyland before, think back to your vacation and the things you enjoyed most about it. Dig out your souvenirs, photos, and home movies and view them with fresh eyes. If you haven't gone to Disneyland before, talk to all your friends and family members who have gone and get their impressions, tips, and stories.

Network With Others
Disney fans tend to gravitate toward online services and the Internet. If you've got an Internet connection, you'll find many Disney sites—even one for PassPorter planners! (See page 7 for more information.) No access to the Internet? Look to your communities for other vacationers who'd like to swap ideas and plans—try your workplace and school.

Plan, Plan, Plan
Few things are better than planning your own trip to the Disneyland Resort. Cuddle up with your PassPorter, read it through, and use it to the fullest—it makes planning fun and easy. PassPorter really is the ultimate in Disney Dreaming!

Planning Your Adventure

Planning is the secret to a successful vacation, especially when you're headed for a playground the size of Southern California. You can't see it all or do it all, and you'll experience even less if you arrive without a plan. Your reward for planning is a much more magical vacation experience. And gosh darn it, planning is also wonderful fun. It increases anticipation and starts the excitement months before your vacation begins.

Your plan begins by learning about your destination. While no single guidebook can do justice to a topic like Southern California, your PassPorter has all the information a theme park lover can want, and then some. Written to be complete yet compact, your PassPorter may be all the guidebook you need. It's a great companion to other guidebooks—its unique PassPockets and worksheets will keep all your trip information together, no matter how many sources you use to make your plans. You can use your PassPorter in a variety of ways: as a travel guide, a vacation planner, an organizer, a trip journal, and a keepsake. We designed it for heavy use—you can take it with you and revisit it after your trip is a fond memory. Personalize it with your plans, notes, souvenirs, and memories. We even crafted it with extra room in the binding to hold the things you'll squeeze and jam into the pockets along the way. The PassPorter is the ultimate vacation guide—before, during, and after your vacation.

This first chapter helps you with the initial planning stage: gathering information and budgeting. Your PassPorter then continues through the planning stages in order of priority. Sprinkled throughout are ways to personalize your trip, little-known tips, and magical vacation memories.

Above all else, have fun with your plans. Don't get so bogged down with planning and recording that you miss the spontaneous magic of your vacation. And as Robert Burns so appropriately said, "The best laid plans of mice and men go oft awry." Use your PassPorter to plan ahead and "learn the lay of the land." Then relax and enjoy your Southern California vacation, no matter what it brings.

Planning · Getting There · Staying in Style · Touring · Feasting · Making Magic · Index · Notes & More

Planning With Your PassPorter

Each important aspect of your vacation—budgeting, traveling, packing, touring, lodging, and eating—has a **special dedicated worksheet** in your PassPorter. Don't be shy; we designed these worksheets to be scribbled upon at will. Not only do they take the place of easy-to-lose scraps of paper, they are structured specifically for your vacation.

When you start planning your trip in your PassPorter, **use a pencil** so you can erase and make changes. Use a permanent pen once your plans are definite to avoid smudging. You can **keep a pen** with your PassPorter, too! Slip it inside the book's spiral binding. The pen's pocket clip holds it in place.

Your PassPorter is most useful when you keep it handy before and during your vacation. It fits compactly into backpacks and shoulder bags. Or tuck your PassPorter into a **waist pack** (at least 6.5" x 9" or 17 x 23 cm).

Your PassPorter loves to go on rides with you, but try to **keep it dry** on Splash Mountain and Grizzly River Run. The heavy cover offers good protection, but a simple resealable plastic bag (gallon size) is a big help.

Personalize your PassPorter! **Write your name** under the front cover flap, along with other information you feel comfortable listing. Your hotel name, trip dates, and phone number help if you misplace your PassPorter. Under the back cover flap are places for your important **phone numbers**, **reminders**, and **addresses**. Use the checkboxes to mark items when done. The **label page** at the end of the text is a fun feature—use the labels to personalize your PassPockets and attach the tabs to mark your chapters.

Two tools you may find helpful for planning include a **highlighter** (to mark "must-sees") and those sticky **page flags** (to mark favorite pages).

It's normal for the **handy spiral binding** in your PassPorter to rotate as you flip pages. If this causes your binding to creep up, you can easily rotate it back—just twist the binding while holding the pages securely.

Your PassPorter's **sturdy cover** wraps around your book for protection, and you can fold it back and leave the book open to any page. The binding is a bit bigger than necessary to accommodate the stuff you accumulate in the pockets. We crafted a pocket for each day of your trip (up to eleven days), plus special ones for your journey, lodging, and memories. Read more about these pockets (we call them "PassPockets") on the next page.

Note: Most of the tips on these two pages apply to the regular edition (spiral-bound); if you have a deluxe edition (ring-bound), visit http://www.passporter.com/deluxe.htm.

Using Your PassPockets

In the back of your PassPorter are fourteen unique "PassPockets" to help you plan before you go, keep items handy while you're traveling, and save memories for your return. Just record your trip information and itinerary on the front of each one, store brochures, maps, receipts, and such inside them, and jot down impressions, memories, expenses, and notes on the back. Use the PassPockets in any way that suits you, filling in as much or as little information as you like. Here's how they work:

Read the advice or tip.

Write your itinerary here, including times, names, and confirmation numbers. Or you can just record what you actually did if you like.

Jot down things you want to remember, do, or visit. Check them off as you go.

Make notes before you go or add notes during your trip.

Store items you want to have on hand during your trip, or things you collect along the way, in this roomy pocket. Guidemaps, brochures, and envelopes all fit inside.

Slip small items in this smaller slot, such as receipts, claim tags, and ticket stubs.

Write the day of the week and the date for quick reference.

Record memories of your vacation to share with others or to keep for yourself. You can jot these down as you go or reminisce at the end of the day.

Keep track of photos taken so you can find them later.

Watch your expenses to stay within a budget or to track your hotel charge account balance.

Remember all those great (or not so great) meals and snacks by noting them here. You can even include the price of the meal or snack, too.

What did you forget? What do you want to do again? What would you like to try next time? What wouldn't you touch again with a ten-foot pole? Make a note of it here.

Use the Vacation-at-a-Glance page just before your PassPockets to record park hours, showtimes, meals, or anything that helps you plan your trip. And if you prefer to travel light, don't be shy about removing a PassPocket and carrying it around for the day instead of your entire PassPorter. Just tuck it back in here at the end of the day! (If you have the spiral-bound version and feel uncomfortable about removing a PassPocket, you may prefer our ring-bound Deluxe Edition with looseleaf pockets—see page 280).

Planning · Getting There · Staying in Style · Touring · Feasting · Making Magic · Index · Notes & More

Planning

Getting There

Staying in Style

Touring

Feasting

Making Magic

Index

Notes & More

Finding Disney Information

Your PassPorter can act as your **first source** of information for the Disneyland Resort and Southern California attractions. It can also be a companion to other guides you may already own or buy later. Either way, we like to think it packs a lot of detail into a small package. Everything you need to know to plan a wonderful vacation is found within these pages.

Do keep in mind that the Disneyland Resort is constantly changing. We've taken every step to ensure that your PassPorter is as up-to-date as possible, but we cannot foresee the future. So, to help your PassPorter stay current, we make **free updates** available to you at our web site (http://www.passporter.com/dl/updates.htm). If you have suggestions, questions, or corrections, please contact us—see page 246 for details.

Oodles of **travel guidebooks** are available if you have a hankering for second opinions. We highly recommend these guidebooks: "The Unofficial Guide to Disneyland" (for irreverence and detailed info), "Birnbaum's Disneyland" (for the official line), and "Disneyland and Southern California with Kids" (for a great kid-friendly view). You'll find something different in each guidebook.

Call the **Disneyland Resort** at 714-781-4565 for recorded information, or call 714-781-7290 when you need to speak to a live person (7:00 am to 10:00 pm Pacific Time). Their representatives are very friendly, but they rarely volunteer information and won't offer opinions. Prepare questions in advance. If the person you reach doesn't have an answer, call back at a later time.

Travel agents you know and trust can be an excellent source of information. Also check with membership organizations that arrange travel, such as AAA (see page 11).

Magazines and newsletters about Disney are also available. Annual Passholders (see page 10) also receive a quarterly newsletter. A few unofficial newsletters are available, including our own popular PassPorter News (subscribe at http://www.passporter.com/news.htm), Mouse Ears (http://www.mouseinfo.com/index.php?page=newsletter) and LaughingPlace Daily News (http://www.laughingplace.com). Finally, three paper-based magazines are available: Tales from the Laughing Place Magazine (http://www.laughingplace.com/product-9000.asp), Persistence of Vision (http://venus.aros.net/~pov/) and The "E" Ticket Magazine (http://www.the-e-ticket.com).

Exploring a Whole New World Wide Web

The ultimate source of information, in our opinion, is the **Internet**. Of course, this requires a personal computer with a modem, a network connection, or "WebTV," but with this you can connect to millions of vacationers happy to share their Disney knowledge.

The web offers hundreds of Disney-related sites. In fact, **PassPorter** has its own web site with updates, tips, ideas, articles, forums, and links. Visit us at http://www.passporter.com. More details are on page 277.

As you might expect, Disneyland, and virtually every Southern California attraction, has an **official web site**. You can get official Disneyland Resort information at http://www.disneyland.com—it's an excellent source for basic information, including operating hours, rates, and maps. Late changes to operating hours are best verified at 714-781-4565. Other Southern California park and attraction web sites are provided with their corresponding descriptions later in this guidebook.

We also highly recommend several **unofficial web sites**, which we frequent ourselves when planning a trip. We introduce these web sites as appropriate throughout the book (check pages 244-245 and 260-264 for more), but here are the major players that you should visit at least once:

MousePlanet—http://www.mouseplanet.com/guide.php?pg=A00000
DIS (Disney Information Station)—http://www.wdwinfo.com/disneyland
Disneylandian—http://www.disneylandian.com
MiceAge.com—http://www.miceage.com
Intercot West—http://www.intercotwest.com
LaughingPlace.com—http://www.laughingplace.com
MouseInfo.com—http://www.mouseinfo.com
AllEarsNet—http://www.allearsnet.com/dlr/tp/dl/dl.htm
Yesterland—http://www.yesterland.com
MouseSavers.com—http://www.mousesavers.com

Another source of information (and camaraderie) are **discussion groups**. PassPorter has its own set of message boards with an active, supportive community of vacationers at http://www.passporterboards.com—come chat and ask your questions. Fans also gather at these discussion boards:

DIS (Disney Information Station)—http://www.disboards.com
Intercot West—http://www.intercotwest.com/boards
LaughingPlace.com—http://www.laughingplace.com/MsgBoard.asp
MouseInfo.com—http://www.mouseinfo.com/mousetalk
MousePlanet—http://mousepad.mouseplanet.com
Parks Discussion—http://groups.yahoo.com/group/Disneyland_Park_and_Attractions
alt.disney.disneyland newsgroup—news://alt.disney.disneyland

Planning

Getting There

Staying in Style

Touring

Feasting

Making Magic

Index

Notes & More

Budgeting for Your Vacation

There's nothing magical about depleting your nest egg to finance a vacation. Too many vacationers can tell you that their money worries overshadowed all the fun. Yet you can avoid both the realities and fear of overspending by planning within a budget. Budgeting ahead of time not only keeps you from spending too much, it encourages you to seek out ways to save money. With just a little bit of research, you can often get **more for less**, resulting in a much better, more relaxed vacation.

If you purchase a **vacation package**, you have the advantage of covering most of your major expenses right up front and you can get a deal if you pay close attention. Learn about vacation packages on page 30 and inquire into prices with the Walt Disney Travel Company at 714-520-5060 or on the web at http://www.disneytravel.com. You can also get the scoop on available packages at http://www.mousesavers.com.

Your **vacation expenses** usually fall into six categories: planning, transportation, lodging, admission, food, and extras. How you budget for each depends upon the total amount you have available to spend and your priorities. Planning, transportation, lodging, and admission are the easiest to factor ahead of time, since costs are fixed. The final two—food and extras—are harder to control, but can usually be estimated based on your tastes and habits.

Begin your vacation budgeting with the **worksheet** on the following page. Enter the minimum you prefer to spend and the maximum you can afford in the topmost row. Establish as many of these ranges as possible before you delve into the other chapters of this book. Your excitement may grow as you read more about the Disneyland Resort and surrounding attractions, but it is doubtful your bank account will.

As you uncover costs and ways to save money later, return to this worksheet and **update it**. Think of your budget as a work-in-progress. Flexibility within your minimum and maximum figures is important. As plans begin to crystallize, write the amount you expect to pay (and can afford) in the Estimated Costs column.

Finally, when you are satisfied with your budget, **transfer the amounts** from the Estimated Costs column on the worksheet to the back of each PassPocket. Note that each PassPocket also provides space to record actual expenses, which helps you stay within your budget.

Chapter 1: Planning Your Adventure **Topic: Budgeting for Your Vacation** 9

Planning
Getting There
Staying in Style
Touring
Feasting
Making Magic
Index
Notes & More

Budget Worksheet

Use this worksheet to identify your resources, record estimated costs, and create a budget for your vacation. When complete, transfer the figures from the Estimated Costs column to the back of each PassPocket.

	Minimum	Maximum	Est. Costs
Total Projected Expenses	$	$	$
Planning:			
🕮 Phone Calls/Faxes:			
📓 Guides/Magazines:			
Transportation:	*(transfer to your Journey PassPocket)*		
🎫 Rental Car:			
🎫 Fuel/Maintenance/Tolls:			
🎫 Airfare/Travel Tickets:			
🎫 Shuttle/Taxi/Limo:			
🎫 Wheelchair/ECV:			
🎫 Stroller:			
🎫 Parking:			
Lodging:	*(transfer to your Rooms PassPocket)*		
🛏 Enroute Motel/Other:			
🏨 Onsite Resort/Hotel:			
Admission:	*(transfer to appropriate PassPocket)*		
🎟 Theme Park Passes:			
🎟 Other Passes:			
🎟 Other Passes:			
🎟 Other Passes:			
🎟 Guided Tours/Other:			

Food:	Daily	Total	Daily	Total	Daily	Total
🍳 Breakfast:						
🍱 Lunch:						
🍽 Dinner:						
🍿 Snacks:						
🛒 Groceries/Other:						

	Minimum	Maximum	Est. Costs
	(transfer to each daily PassPocket)		
Extras:			
🎀 Souvenirs/Clothing:			
✉ Gratuities:			
👕 Vacation Wardrobe:			
📷 Photos:			
📋 Other:			
Total Budgeted Expenses	$	$	$

Money-Saving Programs

You can save real money on a Disneyland Resort and Southern California vacation by taking advantage of these money-saving programs. Some require a membership fee, but they often pay for themselves quite quickly.

Disney Visa Card—This credit card from Chase gives cardholders special discounts on Disney resorts and packages and onboard credits on the Disney Cruise Line. The card has no annual fee and earns "Disney Rewards" equal to 1% or more of your purchases. You can redeem your dollars for Disney travel, entertainment, and merchandise. Another perk is the "pay no interest for 6 months" offer on select Disney packages and cruises. And during Disneyland's 50th anniversary celebration, the Disney Visa card is offering 10% off merchandise purchases of $50 or more, 10% off at select dining locations, 20% off select tours, a toll-free phone line for making Disney travel arrangements (866-844-9382), and an exclusive vacation package with preferred parade viewing and show seating. Disney Visa is available to U.S. residents only. For more information, visit http://disney.go.com/visa, http://www.disneyvisa50th.com, or call 877-252-6576.

Annual Pass (AP)—An Annual Pass (deluxe, premium, and SoCal residents) saves money on admission if you plan to visit for more than eight or 13 days in a one-year period (depending on the pass), at which point it becomes less expensive than conventional admission. It can also deliver great discounts at Disneyland resorts, restaurants, and shops. The discounts alone may be worth it! For example, you can get 10–20% off at many eateries and stores at Downtown Disney and 10% off at selected Disneyland eateries. We note these discounts in our Feasting & Snacking chapter when they are available. An annual pass also offers savings on parking. See pages 83–83 for details and call 714-956-6425 for prices.

Disney "Postcard" Specials and Advertisements—Disney frequently offers lodging discounts in direct mail and mass media advertisements. These offers may be sent to previous Disney guests or may appear in newspaper or TV ads. These offers usually have eligibility requirements, such as residence in Southern California, or can only be used by the person who received the mailing. If you receive an offer, be sure to save it. You'll need the "coupon code" and perhaps an ID number to make your reservation. Be sure you are eligible for the offer—if you show up at Disney and can't prove eligibility, you'll lose your "deal." Visit http://www.mousesavers.com for a listing of current offers.

Southern California CityPass—This special pass allows you to visit four Southern California attractions: Disneyland Resort (3-Day Park Hopper Bonus Ticket), Universal Studios Hollywood (1 day), SeaWorld (1 day), and the San Diego Zoo (1 day). At press time, prices are $199/adult and $159/child ages 3–9—a savings of 30%. This is an excellent deal if you plan to visit each of these attractions! There's also a $49/adult and $35/child pass for five Hollywood attractions, including the Kodak Theatre, Starline Tours, Hollywod Entertainment Museum, Red Line Tours, and the Hollywood Museum. Discounted CityPass tickets may be available through outlets like Costco (http://www.costco.com). For more details on CityPass, call 888-330-5008 or visit http://citypass.net.

California Fun Spots Card—This free card from California's Division of Tourism offers discounts on admission to Universal Studios, Legoland, SeaWorld, San Diego Zoo, and other area attractions. To download your coupons, visit http://www.cafunspots.com.

More Money-Saving Programs

Entertainment Book—This coupon book offers discounts on area attractions, restaurants, and services. Disneyland isn't currently among them (though some eateries within driving distance are), but the Orange Country edition does have discounts for LEGOLAND, Six Flags Magic Mountain, Knott's Soak City, etc. Price is $40–$45/year, but discounts may be available at their web site. For details, call 888-231-SAVE (888-231-7283) or visit http://www.entertainment.com.

American Automobile Association (AAA)—AAA members can book Disneyland vacation packages with special perks, but the prices aren't generally discounted. Discounts on Disneyland admission are available only through Southern California AAA offices—check with your local office for details. AAA members do receive 20% off select guided tours. Call 800-222-6424 or visit http://www.aaa.com.

ARES Travel—A Southern California-based travel planning service and ticketing agency that offers excellent discounts on lodging and attraction passes, including Disneyland Park Hopper passes. For information call 800-680-0977 or visit http://www.arestravel.com.

Downtown Disney Customer Clubs—Several Downtown Disney tenants have "clubs" that you can join and get discounts. ESPN Zone has the ESPN Zone MVP Club (free membership) which gives you some great gifts! Sign up within 30 days of your visit at http://www.mvpclub.espnzone.com. The AMC Theater has the AMC Moviewatcher Club (free membership) which allows you to accrue points for various benefits—sign up at http://www.moviewatcher.com/index.html. And the Rainforest Cafe has its Safari Club ($15 membership fee) with a variety of discounts—sign up at http://www.rainforestcafe.com.

Money-Saving Tips

✔ MouseSavers.com is a web site dedicated to cataloging available discounts, coupons, and deals on all things Disney. Webmaster Mary Waring has built a huge, loyal following, both at http://www.mousesavers.com and through her free monthly newsletter. MouseSavers.com is a must-visit site!

✔ If you are flying, check the newspapers and the Internet for fare sales—they occur more frequently than you might think and offer savings. Expedia.com (http://www.expedia.com) and Travelocity (http://www.travelocity.com) also have great deals on fares and hotel rooms!

✔ Keep watching for deals. You can often rebook hotels without penalty. Some travel agents will even monitor prices and rebook automatically.

✔ Visit in the off-season for better discounts on lodging. See page 14 for a chart indicating typical vacation seasons.

✔ You can save money on meals by eating only two meals a day, as restaurant portions tend to be quite large. Bring quick breakfast foods and snacks from home to quell the munchies and keep your energy up.

✔ Always ask about discounts when you make reservations, dine, or shop. You may discover little-known specials for AAA, the Disney Visa Card, Southern California residents, Annual Passholders, or simply vacationers in the right place at the right time.

✔ Join The Mouse For Less community for more money-saving tips—you can subscribe for free at http://www.themouseforless.com.

Planning

Getting There

Staying in Style

Touring

Feasting

Making Magic

Index

Notes & More

Plan It Up!

Use these tips to make planning your vacation fun and rewarding:

 "A big part of that **'Disney Magic' is in the planning** of our trips. My boys are getting older, so we each plan different days of our trip. For each day, the planner decides on which park we will go to, which attractions to see and where we will eat. We always try to include something each day that we haven't done before."
– Contributed by Dianne Cook, winner of our Planning Tip Contest

 Invent new vacation **traditions**. Do a special dinner on the first night, or take turns picking the first ride of the day.

 If you have access to the **Internet**, make it a point to get online once a week for the latest dish on Disneyland. MousePlanet's Disney Trip Reports web site offers a huge collection of trip reports (fun reading!) as well as room to include your own. The site is located at http://www.mouseplanet.com/dtp/trip.rpt.

 "Do not go without purchasing the **Southern California CityPass** (see page 10). This pass gets you a 3-day park hopper pass into Disneyland, admission to Universal Studios Hollywood, SeaWorld, and either the San Diego Zoo or Wild Animal Park. Initial comparisons had us saving a total of about $50 over paying individual admissions (we were two adults and two kids). We then purchased the passes at Costco.com, which saved us another $50 or so. We didn't visit Knott's Berry Farm. Even so, the savings is well worth it."
– Contributed by Ilisa Oman, winner of our Planning Tip Contest

Magical Memory

 "Disneyland was where I first caught the magic of Disney. Growing up in a Denver suburb, Disney parks were well out of range for me, and I grew up visiting some good local parks that had a bunch of wild roller coasters and other shake-you-up kind of rides. In 1982, as a recent high school graduate, I had the opportunity to visit Disneyland for the first time on a church choir tour to California. I went with high expectations—if my local theme parks had good rides, Disney's must be incredibly wild! Wrong attitude. I spent the first half of my visit wondering what the big deal was—none of the rides were scary to me at all. But sometime around midday it hit me—they weren't trying to SCARE me with wild rides. Disney was trying to make me smile! From that time on the cynical teenager in me gave way and the magic of Disney enveloped me. For the rest of the day I enjoyed myself tremendously—and I still smile at the memory!"

...as told by Disney vacationer Brad Randall

Getting There (and Back!)

So, you've promised your family a trip to "The Happiest Place on Earth!" Now, all you can think of is the accident-prone road trip endured by the Griswold family in that classic comedy, "National Lampoon's Vacation." (And if you aren't convinced you need to plan your vacation, go rent that movie!) With that troubling thought in mind, just how are you going to get there?

Traveling in this age of tightened security requires more planning and patience, but there are still few vacation destinations as easy to reach as Southern California. It's a path well-traveled by vacationers, businesspeople, immigrants, and the occasional swallow, and it's served by countless airlines, superhighways, trains, and tour groups. With all these choices, you can probably use some help. So here we are!

In this chapter, we walk you through the process of making your travel arrangements. We brief you on weather, attendance levels, and rates so you can pick the best time to go or make the most of the dates you've already chosen. You'll find descriptions of each major path to Southern California and a worksheet to help you pick a route and make your reservations. Then it's time to get packing, with the help of our special packing lists. Finally, we help you smile and enjoy your journey with tips for having fun along the way.

What we can't do is take up space with the phone number of every airline and car rental company, or provide travel directions from every city. You can find that easily in your phone book and on the Internet. Just jot down numbers and notes on the worksheet, and transfer the winners to the appropriate PassPocket in the back.

It's useful to note that traveling is generally less flexible than lodging, which is in turn more costly. We find it works much better to make travel decisions before finalizing hotel arrangements. However, you may prefer to skip to the next chapter and shop for your lodging first. Just return here to tailor your travel plans to your lodging choice.

The Best of Times

Most Southern California vacation veterans can tell you that some times are much better to visit than others. We wholeheartedly agree, but there's more to it. While there are certainly times of the year that are less crowded or more temperate, no one but you can decide the best time to visit. To help you decide, we charted the **fluctuating factors** for each month. Still, if you ask us, the best times to visit are the first half of May, mid-September through mid-November, and the period between Thanksgiving and Christmas week. Do your best to avoid the holidays, when the crowds swell. The latter half of January, all of February (except Presidents Week), March, and early December are also uncrowded, though you'll have cooler temperatures and more rain to contend with. For links to current temperature and rainfall data, visit http://www.passporter.com/dl/bestoftimes.htm.

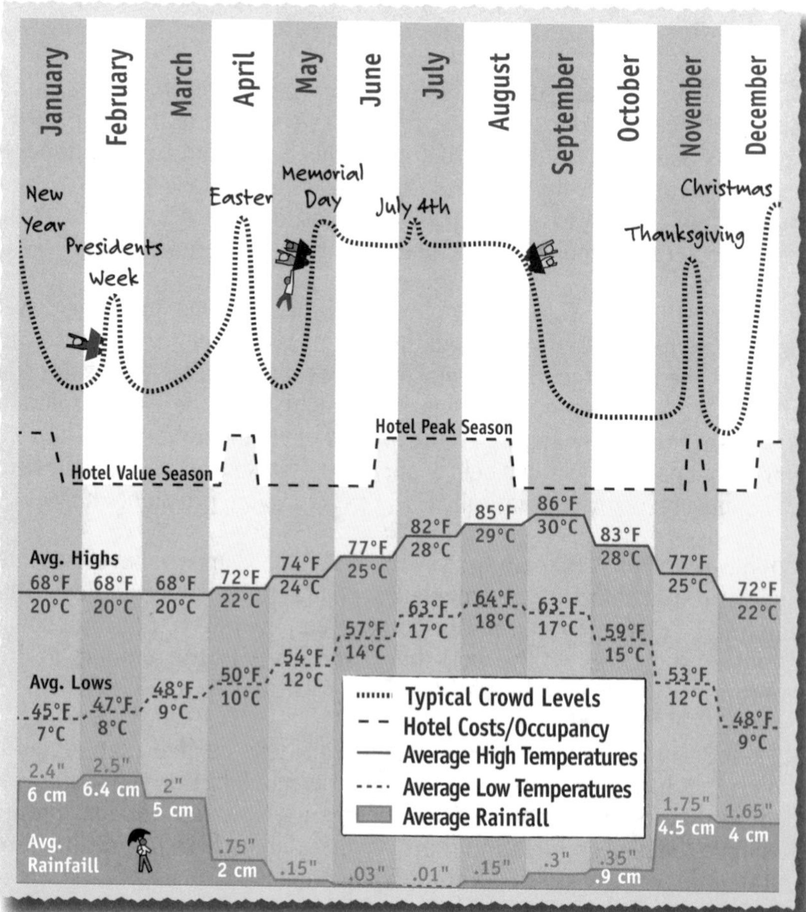
January
February
March
April
May
June
July
August
September
October
November
December
New Year
Presidents Week
Easter
Memorial Day
July 4th
Thanksgiving
Christmas
Hotel Peak Season
Hotel Value Season
Avg. Highs
68°F 20°C
68°F 20°C
68°F 20°C
72°F 22°C
74°F 24°C
77°F 25°C
82°F 28°C
85°F 29°C
86°F 30°C
83°F 28°C
77°F 25°C
72°F 22°C
Avg. Lows
45°F 7°C
47°F 8°C
48°F 9°C
50°F 10°C
54°F 12°C
57°F 14°C
63°F 17°C
64°F 18°C
63°F 17°C
59°F 15°C
53°F 12°C
48°F 9°C
Avg. Rainfall
2.4" 6 cm
2.5" 6.4 cm
2" 5 cm
.75" 2 cm
.15"
.03"
.01"
.15"
.3"
.35" .9 cm
1.75" 4.5 cm
1.65" 4 cm
Typical Crowd Levels
Hotel Costs/Occupancy
Average High Temperatures
Average Low Temperatures
Average Rainfall

Getting There

One of the major obstacles to a Southern California vacation is figuring out how to get there in the first place. Many of us think along the traditional (and expensive) lines first, and become discouraged. It doesn't have to be like that. There are **more ways** to get to Southern California than you probably realize. Below we describe each, beginning with the most popular. At the end of the list, on pages 24–25, a worksheet gives you space to make notes, jot down prices, and note reservation numbers. When your travel plans are finalized, record them on the first PassPocket.

By Car, Van, Truck, or Motorcycle

Most vacationers still arrive at Disneyland and other Southern California attractions in their own vehicle. The **rising sense of excitement** as you draw closer is hard to beat, and it's great to have the freedom of your own wheels upon arrival. Driving may also eliminate the concerns you may have with air travel, and it can be less expensive than air travel, especially with large families. On the down side, you may spend long hours or even days on the road, which cuts deeply into your time with Mickey.

If you opt to drive, carefully **map your course** ahead of time. You can do this with a AAA TripTik—a strip map that guides you to your destination. You must be a AAA member (see page 11) to get a TripTik, but you can easily join for $70/year. You can also try a trip routing service, such as AutoPilot at http://www.freetrip.com. We also recommend you get a good map or atlas of the Southern California area. You can request a free Anaheim/Orange County map at http://www.anaheimoc.org.

If you live more than 500 miles away, **spread out your drive** over more than one day, allotting one day for every 500 miles. Arriving overly road-weary is no way to begin a vacation. If your journey spans more than one day, decide in advance where to stop each night and make reservations accordingly. Sleeping in your vehicle because you cannot find a vacant motel is neither relaxing nor safe. Check that your air-conditioning is in good order. Be sure to compare the price of driving versus flying, too.

Drivers unfamiliar with Southern California laws and freeways should visit **California Driving: A Survival Guide** at http://www.caldrive.com. This web site provides an excellent introduction to the "car culture" of California. Pages 21–22 offer more tips on getting around by car, too.

Planning

Getting There

Staying in Style

Touring

Feasting

Making Magic

Index

Notes & More

By Airplane

Air travel is the best way for many to get to Southern California—and it's a great way to strengthen the air travel industry and the U.S. economy. Plus, air travel may be less expensive than you think if you know the tricks to getting an **affordable flight**.

First, be flexible on the day and time of departure and return—fares differ greatly depending on when you fly and how long you stay. Second, take advantage of the many "fare sales." To learn more, visit airlines' web sites or travel sites like Expedia (http://www.expedia.com), Orbitz (http://www.orbitz.com), or Travelocity (http://www.travelocity.com). Third, try alternate airports when researching fares—Los Angeles International Airport (see below) is the most popular, but Ontario airport (see next page) and John Wayne Airport (see page 18) are actually closer to Anaheim, and Long Beach Airport is another possibility (see page 18). Fourth, be persistent. Ask for the lowest fare and work from there. When you find a good deal, put it on hold immediately (if possible), note your reservation number on page 25, and cancel later if necessary. Finally, don't stop shopping. If your airline offers a cheaper fare later, you may be able to rebook at the lower rate (watch out for penalties), or you may be able to receive credit toward a future flight on that airline.

Consider researching fares on your **airline's web site**—you can experiment with different flights and may get a discount for booking online. Priceline (http://www.priceline.com) is another option where you name your own price for a round-trip ticket, but you cannot pick your specific flight times, and once your price is met, you can't cancel.

Once you reserve a flight, **make a note** of the reservation numbers, flight numbers, seat assignments, and layovers on your first PassPocket. To arrange **ground transportation** from the airport, see page 20. For help getting around once you arrive, see pages 22–23.

Getting Around the Los Angeles International Airport (LAX)

The **granddaddy of California airports**, Los Angeles International Airport is the third busiest airport in the entire world. It's located about 30 miles from either Disneyland or Universal Studios, but you should allow 60 minutes of driving time. When you arrive, your plane docks at one of the eight domestic terminals or the international terminal (see map at right). From there, follow signs to baggage claim. Most ground transportation, including rental cars, is located on the Lower/Arrival Level. Details are on pages 20–21.

Alas, Los Angeles International is **not always user-friendly**. Some airlines require a $10 fee for curbside check-in (inquire with your airline). Security lines can stretch out of the terminal, so arrive early. If you set off the detector, security personnel can be less than friendly—make sure you've got all metal items off. Some airline personnel will require that you match your luggage to your claim tickets before you leave baggage claim, so make sure you know where your claim tickets are (they are often stapled to your ticket jacket).

Meeting up at this sprawling airport can be troublesome, as most of the terminals are not connected. If you must meet another traveling party at the airport before taking ground transportation, check which terminal you'll each be arriving at and decide on one for your meeting location. It's easiest to meet in baggage claim. You can move from terminal to terminal via the free shuttles—go to the Lower/Arrival Level, stand under the blue Shuttle and Airline Connections sign, and watch for the Airline Connections "A" Shuttle. Shuttles arrive every 12–15 minutes. Tip: The "Encounter" restaurant in the round Landmark building was themed by Walt Disney Imagineering! If you've got the time and deep pockets, have a meal there—call 310-215-5151 or visit http://www.encounterrestaurant.com.

For **details** on Los Angeles International, call 310-646-5252 or visit http://www.lawa.org and click the "LAX" tab. Airport address: 1 World Way, Los Angeles, CA 90045.

Getting Around the Los Angeles Intl. Airport (LAX) *(continued)*

Los Angeles International (LAX) Airport

Partial List of Airlines—<u>Terminal 1</u>: America West, Southwest, USAirways; <u>Terminal 2</u>: Northwest, KLM, Air Canada, Air China, American Trans Air, Miami Air, Virgin Atlantic; <u>Terminal 3</u>: Alaska, Frontier, Horizon, Midwest Airlines, American Airlines (CA, AZ, NV, Colorado Springs, Orlando), TWA; <u>Terminal 4</u>: American Airlines, American Eagle; <u>Terminal 5</u>: Delta, Spirit; <u>Terminal 6</u>: Continental, National, Skywest; <u>Terminal 7</u>: United

Getting Around the Ontario International Airport (ONT)

Ontario International Aiport is about the same distance away from Disneyland Resort as Los Angeles International, but thanks to traffic, it's only about a 30–40 minute drive away and it offers **fewer hassles and frustrations than LAX**. Ontario International is served by 12 major airlines (Alaska, American, America West, Continental, Delta, jetBlue, Northwest, Southwest, United/Ted, and United Express Airlines) and eight major car rental agencies (Alamo, Avis, Budget, Dollar, Enterprise, Hertz, National, and Thrifty). The airport is very modern and user-friendly.

Reader Tip: "Most guidebooks I've seen overlook Ontario International, but having grown up in Southern California and being a cast member commuting from this area, I know the airport is a well-kept secret." — contributed by reader Jeff Rosenzweig

For **more details** on the Ontario International Airport, call 909-937-2700 or visit http://www.lawa.org and click the "ONT" tab. Airport address: 2900 East Airport Drive, Ontario, CA 91761.

Ontario (ONT) Airport

Terminal Way
Ground Transportation

Terminal #2
Gates 201–203
Gates 204–208
Gates 209–212

(Alaska, Continental, Delta, jetBlue, Northwest, United, United Express/Ted)

Terminal #4
Gates 401–404
Gates 405–410
Gates 411–414

(America West, American, and Southwest)

Getting Around the John Wayne/Orange County Airport (SNA)

Yes, John Wayne Airport really is named after the famous actor, though the airport's abbreviation (SNA) is due to its location in <u>S</u>anta <u>A</u>na. (If you have extra time, see the huge bronze statue of John Wayne located near the front of the airport!) This medium-sized, modern airport is the **closest airport** to Disneyland. Its two terminals (A and B) are connected to form one long corridor. Ticketing and gates are on the upper level, while baggage claim and ground transportation are on the lower level. For more information, call 949-252-5200 or visit http://www.ocair.com. Airport address: 18601 Airport Way, Santa Ana, CA 92707.

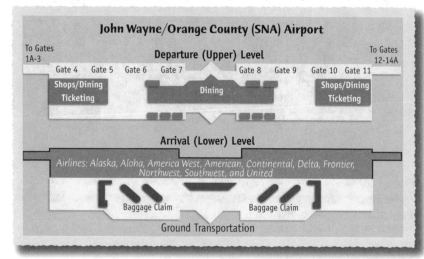

John Wayne/Orange County (SNA) Airport

To Gates 1A-3

Departure (Upper) Level

To Gates 12-14A

Gate 4 Gate 5 Gate 6 Gate 7 Gate 8 Gate 9 Gate 10 Gate 11

Shops/Dining Ticketing

Dining

Shops/Dining Ticketing

Arrival (Lower) Level

Airlines: Alaska, Aloha, America West, American, Continental, Delta, Frontier, Northwest, Southwest, and United

Baggage Claim

Baggage Claim

Ground Transportation

Getting Around the Long Beach Airport (LGB)

Long Beach Airport is a small airport about 20 miles from Disneyland. It serves just four commercial airlines: America West/USAirways, American Airlines, jetBlue, and Horizon. The terminal has two boarding lounges—south (for jetBlue) and north (for the rest). Thanks to its size, this is an easy airport to move about—just follow the signs. Note that the north and south wings have their own baggage claim areas. For details on the Long Beach Airport, call 562-570-2600 (recording), 562-570-2619 (live person), or visit http://www.lgb.org. Airport address: 4100 Donald Douglas Drive, Long Beach, CA 90808.

Long Beach (LGB) Airport

South Boarding Lounge
Gates 1-9 (JetBlue)

North Boarding Lounge
Gates 21-23

(American Airlines, America West Horizon Air)

Ticketing

Terminal

Ground Transportation

Our Top Flying Tips, Reminders, and Warnings

1. Check the status of your flight before departing for the airport.
2. Pack (or pick up) a meal for the flight.
3. Pack sharp or potentially dangerous items in checked luggage (or just leave them at home). If you must bring needles or syringes, also bring a doctor's note.
4. Limit your carry-ons to one bag and one personal item.
5. Plan to arrive at the airport two hours prior to departure.
6. E-Ticket holders should bring a confirmation and/or boarding pass.

By Train, Bus, Tour, and Boat

By Train

The train is a uniquely relaxing way to get to the Disneyland Resort and Southern California. **Amtrak** (call 800-USA-RAIL or visit their web site at http://www.amtrak.com/stations/index.html and search "Anaheim") serves the Los Angeles area daily with passenger trains. Train station stops are plentiful, and there's even an Anaheim train station (station code: ANA) next to the baseball stadium—while it's just about a mile from the Disneyland Resort, you'll need to call a cab to get anywhere. For travelers coming from or going to San Diego, the Pacific Surfliner makes 11 daily trips along the coast between San Diego and Los Angeles, stopping at the Anaheim station along the way. At the time of writing, one adult fare is $40 for an Anaheim–San Diego roundtrip, and discounts are available for additional passengers and kids ages 2 to 15. Taxis are available at the Anaheim train station, and Hertz serves the station with a shuttle to its rental car office. The Anaheim station is located at 2150 E. Katella Ave. For more details, visit http://www.amtrak.com and search for "Anaheim."

By Bus

Buses make good economic and environmental sense if you're traveling a short distance. **Greyhound** (800-231-222, http://www.greyhound.com) serves Anaheim with direct buses from both Los Angeles and San Diego. The Greyhound Anaheim station is located at 100 W. Winston Road (714-999-1256), which is about one mile from the Disneyland Resort. Taxis are available from the bus station. Keep in mind that bus fares are lowest if you live within ten hours of your destination.

By Tour

A number of **special tours** go to the Disneyland Resort, which you may want to consider if you prefer to go with a large group or with like-minded folks. Check with the associations, organizations, and societies you belong to, or contact a travel agent.

By Boat

In summer 2005, the Disney Cruise Line sailed from Florida to Los Angeles, then between Los Angeles and the Mexican Riviera for three months, and finally back to Florida. While there are no current plans for a Disney cruise ship to return, it's always a possibility, especially in light of the popularity of the West Coast cruises. To check on availability, call 888-DCL-2500, visit http://www.disneycruise.com, or see our Disney Cruise Line guidebook (details on page 281) for any information.

By Everything Else!

The list of ways to get to Disneyland is really endless. Consider traveling under your own power—bicycles! Or combine business with pleasure.

Planning
Getting There
Staying in Style
Touring
Feasting
Making Magic
Index
Notes & More

Planning

Getting There

Staying in Style

Touring

Feasting

Making Magic

Index

Notes & More

Are We There Yet?

Once you reach Southern California, you need to continue on to Anaheim or another outlying area to reach your destination. Here are your options:

Taking a Bus

Travelers flying to the LAX or the John Wayne Airport can get scheduled bus service via the Disneyland Resort Express, a service from Southern California Gray Line (800-938-8933, http://www.airportbus.com). Disneyland Resort Express goes to Disneyland and Knott's Berry Farm. From LAX, follow the signs to the Lower/Arrival Level island in the front of each terminal and stand under the green bus sign in the center island—a one-way fare is $19/adult ($28 roundtrip) and $16/kids 3–11 ($20 roundtrip). From the John Wayne Airport, follow the signs to baggage claim, pick up your luggage, and cross the street to the Disneyland Express/Airport Bus ticket booth at the Ground Transportation Center—a roundtrip fare is $24/adult and $16/kids. Disneyland Express buses are identified as such, and may even be emblazoned with Disneyland art. Bus time schedules are available via phone or their web site. Keep in mind that buses can make several stops along the way to drop off other passengers, taking up to an hour and a half to reach your destination. Note that you can take a Metro Bus from LAX to Disneyland also, but the price is the same and it's harder to transport lots of luggage—for more information, visit http://www.mta.net.

Using a Shared-Ride Van Service or Shuttle

Another ground transportation option available from all three airports, L.A.'s Amtrak Union Station, and L.A.'s Greyhound Terminal are shared-ride vans, also known as shuttles. SuperShuttle (714-517-6600 or 800-BLUE-VAN, http://www.supershuttle.com) and Prime Time Shuttle (310-356-7922 or 800-RED-VANS, http://www.primetimeshuttle.com) will take you nearly anywhere in the greater Los Angeles vicinity. From LAX, follow the signs to the Lower/Arrival Level island and request a pickup under the Shared-Ride Vans sign. From other locations, call or go online to make reservations at least 24 hours in advance—upon arrival, you may also need to use a courtesy phone to request pickup. At press time, a one-way fare from LAX to Disneyland is $15/person (SuperShuttle) or $15/person (Prime Time Shuttle). Kids ride free under age 3 (on SuperShuttle) and under age 2 (on Prime Time Shuttle). These shuttles tend to carry fewer people than the Airport Bus, meaning they'll probably make fewer stops before reaching your destination. Parents take note: If you're traveling with a child under 6 years of age or under 60 lbs. (27 kg.), you must bring an approved child safety seat to use on the shuttle. Accessible vans for travelers with special needs are also available upon request. What about hotel shuttles? Hotels near Disneyland and most other attractions are just too far away from airports to offer shuttles. If you're staying in a hotel within 5–10 miles of an airport, inquire with that hotel directly.

Using a Car Service, Towncar, or Limo

Both SuperShuttle and Prime Time Shuttle offer car services, though they're pricey—about $85 for a one-way trip from LAX to Disneyland for up to three adults. We've found better rates through Airport Towncar Limo (800-794-2794, http://www.airportsupercar.com), which offers a $69/one-way fare between LAX and Disneyland for up to four adults. They also have a stretch limo for $65/hour (minimum 3 hours). Reservations are required.

Taking a Taxi

Figure about $74 plus tip for one-way cab fare from LAX to Disneyland. **Large parties may be able to ride in a taxi mini-van economically, however.** From LAX, follow the signs to the Lower/Arrival Level and look for a yellow taxi sign. If you need a taxi from within the Disneyland Resort, call the Anaheim Yellow Cab Company (http://www.yellowcab.com, 714-535-2211)—they're the only licensed taxi approved to serve Disneyland.

Renting a Car

If you are planning a visit to Disneyland Resort exclusively, you probably don't need to rent a car—use the Disneyland Resort Express, SuperShuttle, or Prime Time Shuttle mentioned on the previous page. On the other hand, if you are one of the many vacationers whose plans include visits to other Southern California attractions, you'll find a car **very handy** and the most economical method of travel. Driving in Southern California can be confusing to first-time visitors, so if possible we suggest taking a shuttle to your hotel and then renting a car once there. Many car rental agencies have offices in or near hotels. In fact, Alamo has a new car rental office in Downtown Disney near the AMC Movie Theaters. Within walking distance of Disneyland are many agencies: Hertz has an office at 221 W. Katella Ave., just a couple of blocks from the parks, as well as one in the Anaheim Marriott (see page 58). National and Alamo have at office on 711 W. Katella Ave. Avis is on 200 W. Katella Ave., as well as at the Park Vue Hotel on 1570 S. Harbor Blvd. (across the street from Disneyland Resort). Budget is at 2132 S. Harbor Blvd. (a few blocks south of Disneyland). Enterprise is at 231 W. Katella Ave. Thrifty is at 1855 S. Harbor Blvd.

If renting a car near your hotel is not an option, **all three airports offer rental cars** through most of the major rental companies. LAX has about 40 rental car companies, all of which are located off-site and provide free shuttles to the rental car offices. Just follow the signs to the Lower/Arrival Level and wait under the purple rental car signs for the appropriate rental car company shuttle. At John Wayne Airport, seven major companies are on-site (Alamo, Avis, Budget, Enterprise, Hertz, National, and Thrifty), with eight more companies located off-site. Rental car counters are located in the Ground Transportation Center across the street from baggage claim. At Long Beach Airport it works similarly, with its rental car counters (Avis, Budget, Enterprise, Hertz, and National) located across the street from the terminal.

Thanks to the huge numbers of car rental companies, **rates** are competitive and cars are plentiful. Expect to pay at least $20/day or $100/week for an economy car rented from LAX (rates were higher elsewhere). Note that California imposes a $1.95/day fee + 8% sales tax on top of quoted rates for car rentals. To get the best rates, visit travel reservations sites such as Travelocity (http://www.travelocity.com), Expedia (http://www.expedia.com), and Orbitz (http://www.orbitz.com). You can also contact the car rental agencies directly via phone or their web site. We recommend you reserve a car before you leave home—if you change your mind later, there is no penalty.

The above rates do not include collision damage waiver **insurance**, which can be expensive at $9–$12/day. Before you accept the insurance, check with your credit card companies— some may offer free coverage when you charge the rental car cost to the credit card. At the time of writing, the Disney Visa card offers this protection if you use the card to initiate and complete the entire rental transaction and decline the agency's insurance. See your credit card benefits booklet for more information, or call their customer service.

If you opt for a rental car, you'll need to **consider parking**—at your hotel, the parks, and in parking garages (it's difficult to find street parking in Los Angeles). You'll find parking rates in both our "Staying in Style" chapter and our "Touring the Lands" chapter. Disneyland Resort parking is detailed on page 85.

Tip: It can be difficult to **spot an unfamiliar rental car** in a large parking lot at the end of a long day. Be sure to note your parking location on one of your PassPockets when you park it. If you have a digital camera or a camera phone, take a picture of your parking location (including signage) in the event you need a refresher at the end of the day. We also recommend you bring something to attach to the car's radio antenna, such as a brightly-colored ribbon (note that Disney antenna balls are common around here).

Getting Around Town

If you're planning to visit to Disneyland Resort, getting around is easy—walk or take the monorail! Other Southern California attractions aren't within walking distance of Disneyland, however. Most folks will drive, but there are a few other options if you prefer public transportation.

Driving Around

Whether you're driving your own car or a rental, you should get to know the "lay of the land" before you arrive. California is the **land of the freeways**, with up to 12 lanes of concrete criss-crossing and connecting you to the places you want to be. Study the maps on the front and back flaps of this guidebook, and pick up a good driving map of the area. The two main north-south freeways are Interstate 405 (San Diego Freeway) and Interstate 5 (Santa Ana Freeway). I-5 passes right through the northeast corner of the Disneyland Resort. Several freeways go east-west, including Route 22 (Garden Grove Freeway), Route 91 (Artesia/Riverside Freeway) and I-10 (Santa Monica Freeway). Learn both their numbers and names so you can recognize them as you're zipping along the highway.

Local streets around the Disneyland Resort are well-marked. The major streets to know are Harbor Blvd. along the east perimeter of the Disneyland Resort, Katella Ave. along the south, Disneyland Drive along the west, and Ball Road along the north.

L.A. traffic is notoriously bad, and it's worse during rush-hour or in rain. Always leave plenty of time for travel. Tip: Tune in to traffic reports on your car radio— try 1070 AM (Los Angeles) or 1670 AM (Anaheim). Or visit http://sigalert.com before you leave. Watch for overhead road displays which alert you to delays.

Driving laws are straightforward. All passengers must wear a seatbelt. You can turn right on a red light and make U-turns unless otherwise posted. Kids under 6 years of age or under 60 lbs. must use an approved child safety seat.

Mileage/Travel Times from Disneyland Resort

Destination	Miles	Time
Hollywood	35	55 min.
John Wayne Airport	15	25 min.
Knott's Berry Farm	7	15 min.
Long Beach Airport	20	30 min.
Los Angeles/LAX	35	60 min.
Ontario Airport	33	40 min.
San Diego	95	110 min.
Six Flags	60	90 min.
Universal Studios	35	55 min.

Get **driving directions** before you depart. Use MapQuest (http://www.mapquest.com) for point-to-point directions and maps. We provide general directions for the airports below and directions for each park or attraction later in this guidebook. Disneyland Resort's web site also provides customized driving directions to the Disneyland Resort—go to http://www.disneyland.com and search on "driving directions."

Driving Directions from the Airport to Disneyland

From LAX: Take I-405 (San Diego Freeway) south to Route 22 (Garden Grove Freeway), then take the Harbor Blvd. exit and go north 3 miles, following the Disneyland Resort signs. About 35 miles.

From Ontario Airport: Take CA-60 West for 12 miles, merge onto CA-57 South for 14 miles, take the Ball Rd. exit (#3) and follow signs. About 33 miles.

From John Wayne Airport: Take I-405 (San Diego Freeway) north to I-5 (Santa Ana Freeway) north, then take the Katella Ave. exit, go straight to Disney Way, and follow the signs. About 14 miles.

From Long Beach Airport: Take CA-19 (N. Lakewood Blvd.) north to CA-91 east, merge onto I-5 south, then take the Disneyland Drive exit and follow signs.

Planning
Getting There
Staying in Style
Touring
Feasting
Making Magic
Index
Notes & More

Taking the Monorail

The Disneyland Monorail is more of an attraction than a serious transportation system. The monorail makes two stops along its $2\frac{1}{2}$-mile-long route—one at Tomorrowland (inside the Disneyland Park) and one at Downtown Disney. See page 85 for more details.

Taking a Bus

Hop one of three convenient bus systems to get around Anaheim and Southern California! The **Anaheim Resort Transit (ART)** system offers fun, colorful "trolley" buses—most of which are all-electric—to many points within the Anaheim Resort district. There are eight different routes throughout the area, stopping at the Disneyland Resort, the Anaheim Convention Center, and non-Disney hotels in the resort area (see page 52 for participating hotels). The buses are clean and quiet—and they're accessible to the differently abled. All-day passes are available from your hotel's front desk for $2/day for adults (ages 9 and up)—kids under 9 are free. Three-day passes are $5, and five-day passes are $8. You can also get passes from the Anaheim Convention Center and the Anaheim Resort Tourist Information Center located at 1500 S. Harbor Blvd. across from the Disneyland Resort entrance. The trolleys begin operating one hour prior to park opening and end 30 minutes after park closing. Look for them every 10 minutes during the morning and evening, and every 30 minutes the rest of the day. For more information, call 888-364-ARTS.

Going further afield? **Southern California Gray Line/Coach USA** (see Disneyland Resort Express on page 20) offers bus service from Disneyland to Knott's Berry Farm and Universal Studios. You may even be able to catch the bus across from Disneyland in the Howard Johnson parking lot (see page 63), but you should confirm this when you call to make reservations in advance. Fares are $5/person for a roundtrip to Knott's Berry Farm and $20/adult ($15/kids 3–11) for a roundtrip to Universal Studios.

A third option is the **Metro Bus** system (http://www.mta.net). For example, you can get from Disneyland to Knott's Berry Farm by walking to to the southeast corner of Harbor Blvd. and Manchester Ave. (right across the street from Disneyland), catch the MTA Bus #460 (Los Angeles), and get off at the Knott's Berry Farm stop. The bus trip takes about 25 minutes and costs $1.85. Visit their web site for routes and details, or call 800-COMMUTE. Tip: You can use a handy trip planner to learn how to get from point A to point B in the Los Angeles area at http://www.socaltransit.org.

Taking the Train

The Metro Rail is a relatively new, underground subway system and a good option for travel to or from Universal Studios, Hollywood, and downtown Los Angeles attractions. Alas, while there is an Anaheim station on the subway line, it's not convenient from the Disneyland Resort area. For information, call 800-266-6883 or visit http://www.mta.net.

Going to San Diego? Amtrak offers daily trips to and from Anaheim and San Diego for a very reasonable price. See page 19 for more information.

Taking a Taxi

We've said it before, we'll say it again—this is our least recommended option, as it's pricey (about $85 from LAX to Anaheim). But if you want a taxi, just ask your hotel's bell staff.

Walking

Believe it or not, you can use your own power to get around—but only a bit. You can walk anywhere within the Disneyland Resort for starters. You can also reach many of the restaurants, hotels, and services surrounding Disneyland on Katella Ave. and Harbor Blvd. (see maps on page 51 and on back flap). In fact, the motels across the street from Disneyland on South Harbor Blvd. are actually closer in distance to the park entrances than any of the official Disneyland hotels. If you're walking from one of these streets, use the pedestrian walkway from Harbor Blvd. to reach the parks or Downtown Disney.

Travel Worksheet

Use this worksheet to jot down preferences, scribble information during phone calls, and keep all your discoveries together. Don't worry about being neat—just be thorough! When everything is confirmed, transfer it to your first PassPocket in the back of the book. ✎ Circle the names and numbers once you decide to go with them to avoid confusion.

Arrival date: _____ Alternate: _____

Return date: _____ Alternate: _____

We plan to travel by: ❑ Car/Van ❑ Airplane ❑ Train ❑ Bus ❑ Tour
❑ Other: _____

For Drivers:

Miles to get to Anaheim: _____ ÷ 500 = _____ # days on the road

We need to stay at a motel on: _____

_____

Tune-up scheduled for: _____

Rental car info: _____

_____

For Riders:

Train/Bus phone numbers: _____

Ride preferences: _____

Ride availabilities: _____

Reserved ride times and numbers: _____

Routes: _____

For Tour-Takers:

Tour company phone numbers: _____

Tour preferences: _____

Tour availabilities: _____

Reserved tour times and numbers: _____

Routes: _____

For Flyers:

Airline phone numbers: _____

Flight preferences: _____

Flight availabilities: _____

_____

_____

_____

Reserved flight times and numbers: _____

_____

For Ground Transportation:

Town car/shuttle/rental car phone numbers: _____

_____

Town car/shuttle/rental car reservations: _____

_____

Package ground transportation details: _____

_____

Additional Notes:

Reminder: Don't forget to confirm holds or cancel reservations (whenever possible) within the allotted time frame.

Planning

Getting There

Staying in Style

Touring

Feasting

Making Magic

Index

Notes & More

Packing List

Packing for a vacation is fun when you feel confident you're packing the right things. Over the years, we've compiled this packing list for a great vacation. Just note the quantity you plan to bring and check items off as you pack. Consider carrying items in **magenta** on a daily basis as you tour.

The Essentials

❑ Casual clothing you can layer—the dress code nearly everywhere at Disney is casual, even at dinner. One "nice" outfit is usually enough.

___ Shorts/skirts	___ Pants/jeans	___ Shirts	___ Sweaters
___ Underwear	___ Socks	___ Pajamas	___ _____

❑ Jacket and/or sweatshirt (light ones for the warmer months)

___ **Jackets**	___ Sweatshirts	___ Sweaters	___ Vests

❑ Comfortable, well-broken-in shoes ... plus a second pair, just in case!

___ Walking shoes	___ Sandals	___ Sneakers

❑ Swim gear (bring one-piece suits for water slides)

___ Suits/trunks	___ Cover-ups/towels	___ Water shoes	___ Goggles

❑ Sun protection (the California sun can be brutal)

___ **Sunblock**	___ **Lip balm**	___ **Sunburn relief**	___ Body lotion
___ **Hats w/brims**	___ **Caps/visors**	___ **Sunglasses**	___ _____

❑ Rain gear (compact and light so you don't mind carrying it)

___ Raincoat	___ **Poncho**	___ Umbrella	___ **Extra socks**

❑ Comfortable bags with padded straps to carry items during the day

___ **Backpacks**	___ **Waist packs**	___ Shoulder bags	___ **Camera bag**

❑ Toiletries (in a bag or bathroom kit to keep them organized)

___ **Brush/comb**	___ Toothbrush	___ Toothpaste	___ Dental floss
___ Favorite soap, shampoo, and conditioner	___ Deodorant	___ **Baby wipes**	
___ **Aspirin/acetaminophen/ibuprofen**	___ **Band aids**	___ **First aid kit**	
___ **Prescriptions** (in original containers)	___ Vitamins	___ Fem. hygiene	
___ Hair dryer/iron	___ **Anti-blister tape**	___ Makeup	___ Hair spray
___ Razors	___ Shaving cream	___ Cotton buds	___ Lotion
___ Nail clippers	___ Spare eyeglasses	___ Lens solution	___ **Bug repellent**
___ Mending kit	___ Small scissors	___ Safety pins	___ **Insect sting kit**

❑ Camera/camcorder and more film/tape than you think you need

___ **Camera**	___ **Camcorder**	___ **Film/tapes**	___ **Storage cards**
___ **Batteries**	___ Chargers	___ **Camera case**	___ _____

❑ Money in various forms and various places

___ **Charge cards**	___ **Traveler's checks**	___ **Bank cards**	___ **Cash**

❑ Personal identification, passes, and membership cards

___ Driver's license	___ **Other photo ID**	___ **Passport**	___ Birth certificate
___ **AAA card**	___ **Discount cards**	___ Air miles card	___ _____
___ **Tickets/passes**	___ **Insurance cards**	___ **Calling cards**	___ _____

Tip: Label everything with your name, cell phone, and hotel to help reunite you with your stuff if lost. Every bag should have this info on a luggage tag as well as on a slip of paper inside it. Use our Luggage Tag Maker at http://www.passporter.com/wdw/luggagelog.htm.

Planning | Getting There | Staying in Style | Touring | Feasting | Making Magic | Index | Notes & More

For Your Carry-On

- ❏ Your **PassPorter**, **tickets**, **maps**, **guides**, and a **pen** or pencil! ✎ Remember to pack any sharp or potentially dangerous items in your checked luggage, not your carry-on.
- ❏ **Camera** and/or **camcorder**, along with **film**, **memory cards**, **tapes**, and **batteries**
- ❏ Any **prescriptions**, important toiletries, **sunblock**, **sunglasses**, **hats**, **bug repellent**
- ❏ Change of clothes appropriate to your destination's weather, jewelry, and valuables
- ❏ **Snacks**, 🥤 **water bottle**, **juice boxes**, gum, favorite books, **toys**, **games**, blankets

For Families

- ❏ Snacks and juice boxes
- ❏ Books, toys, 🎲 and games
- ❏ Stroller, carrier, and accessories 🚼
- ❏ **Autograph books** and **fat pens**
- ❏ EarPlanes (http://www.earplanes.com)

For Couples

- ❏ Corkscrew and wine glasses 🍷
- ❏ Candles and matches
- ❏ Evening wear for nights out
- ❏ Portable music player and tunes
- ❏ Massage oil

For Connected Travelers

- ❏ Laptop and power supply
- ❏ Extension cord/surge suppressor
- ❏ Phone/network cables, coupler, splitter
- ❏ Security cable with lock
- ❏ **Cell phones** and chargers
- ❏ **Two-way radios**
- ❏ Local access numbers 📟
- ❏ **Handheld/Palm organizer**

For Heat-Sensitive Travelers

- ❏ **Personal fans/water misters**
- ❏ **Water bottles** (frozen, if possible)
- ❏ **Washcloth** to cool off face and neck
- ❏ Loose, breezy clothing
- ❏ **Hats** with wide brims
- ❏ **Sunshades** (for baby strollers)
- ❏ **Elastics** to keep long hair off neck
- ❏ **Sweatbands**

Everyone Should Consider

- ❏ Big beach towels (for pools and water parks)
- ❏ **Penlight** or flashlight (for reading/writing in dark places and to alleviate kids' fears)
- ❏ **Water bottles** and personal **fan/water misters**
- ❏ **Snacks** for any time of the day (plus gum, if you chew it)
- ❏ Plastic cutlery for snacks or leftovers ✐
- ❏ **Quarters** and **pennies** (and a way to hold them) for the coin presses and/or laundry
- ❏ Plastic storage bags that seal (large and small), plus trash bags
- ❏ Address book, stamps, and envelopes ✉
- ❏ Laundry detergent/tablets, bleach, dryer sheets, stain stick, and a laundry tote
- ❏ **Binoculars**
- ❏ Collapsible bag or suitcase inside another suitcase to hold souvenirs on your return

Your Personal Packing List

❏ _____	❏ _____
❏ _____	❏ _____
❏ _____	❏ _____
❏ _____	❏ _____
❏ _____	❏ _____
❏ _____	❏ _____
❏ _____	❏ _____
❏ _____	❏ _____

Tip: If you forget something, try Target (8 am–10 pm) at 12100 Harbor Blvd. (714-971-4826)—just about 3 miles from Disneyland. There's also a Wal-Mart (8 am–11 pm) at 440 N. Euclid Ave. (714-491-0744). From Disneyland, get on I-5 north and exit at Euclid (#112).

Planning | Getting There | Staying in Style | Touring | Feasting | Making Magic | Index | Notes & More

Adventuring!

Your journey is more pleasant when you consider it an adventure rather than a tiring trek. Here are our tried-and-true adventuring tips:

 "As the song says, 'It never rains in southern California...' but sometimes it pours. **Rainy days are great days** to visit Disneyland because the locals stay away in droves. Some attractions, like the Mad Tea Party and Alice in Wonderland, are closed when it rains, but most are running and the lines are short." — *Contributed by Laura Gilbreath*

 "Remember that S. California can have **very chilly** evenings. If you are not staying at the Disneyland Resort and you are day-tripping instead, be sure to bring something warm and layer! Plan on getting a locker and storing your warmer items during the day. The lockers in both parks are very accessible." — *Contributed by LauraBelle Hime*

 "To get as much fun out of our vacation as possible, I like to surprise the kids with a **homemade activity book for the long drive** to L.A. I include things like Disney coloring pages, free printable puzzles with all Disney words (http://puzzlemaker.school.discovery.com), crosswords/puzzles/mazes/ bingo (http://www.kidprintables.com), a page of jokes (kids like to show off how funny they are), ideas/ rules for car games (http://www.momsminivan.com/bigkids.html), a calendar with the days of our vacation marked, and our itinerary. I top it off with a personalized cover with a picture of their favorite Disney ride. Planning ahead puts my family in the mood for Disney magic long before we even get there." — *Contributed by anonymous*

 "I visited California every April from 1992 until 1998 and I highly recommend flying into **Orange County Airport** (also known as John Wayne Airport) if it is financially feasible for you. It is a small, quiet airport and easy to get around. It is also closer to Disneyland than Los Angeles Airport (LAX)." — *Contributed by Margo Verikas*

Magical Memory

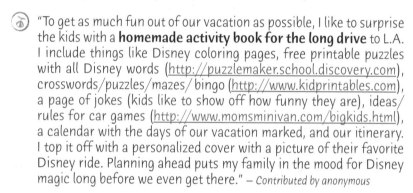 *"My husband Lee and I traveled to Disneyland in 1980 with my family. Until that time, Lee had never been on a vacation. We arrived at Disneyland and parked way out in the parking lot. Lee began walking toward the gate. He walked faster and faster, the distance between us and him getting larger and larger. Finally, he could stand the excitement no longer. Turning back to us, he waved his arm in a large arc and yelled, "Well, COME ON!" He then broke out into a run, leaving the rest of us with no choice but to follow. It is one of my favorite memories!"*

...as told by vacationer Debbie Hendrickson

Staying in Style

There are hundreds of thousands of hotel rooms in Southern California, which makes "where do we stay?" a very bewildering question indeed! We don't pretend to be experts on every hotel and motel in the region. That would be a full-time occupation. But we certainly can help point you toward a good selection of hotels, especially near Disneyland. You can use these listings as a jumping-off point, you may find they're enough to meet your needs. Use as many lodging resources as you can. The ratings provided by AAA and Mobil can be a big help, and there's a wealth of detail on web sites and in other reputable guidebooks. And if you start by bargain-hunting at travel web sites, our listings can refine your choices.

Naturally, our focus is on the Disneyland Resort. We dedicate our most detailed coverage to Disney's three, "on-property" resort hotels, where you're only a short walk from the parks. We're big fans of Disney hotels (if only we could live at Disney's Grand Californian!). If it's within your budget, we highly recommend a stay "on property," where you can leave the world behind and spend your days and nights immersed in Disney magic. We'll show you all the "inns" and outs of Disney lodging, including how to get the best deals. You can find nearly as much magic (and often, far more affordable prices) at Disney's "Good Neighbor" hotels. We deliver reports on every one of them, too! We don't stop there, though. We list budget (non-Good Neighbor) lodging near Disneyland, and hotels of all sorts near the other attractions covered in this guide. We even toss in some enticing recommendations for Los Angeles and San Diego!

If you plan to stay a week or more in this sprawling area, we suggest that you "hotel hop." Some Californians are willing to commute across the region, but your vacation will be less stressful (and you'll have more time to tour) if you move your home base at least once. When you've decided which attractions you'll visit, return here to choose lodging that fits your plans.

So turn the page, and dive in! You may spend your days playing, but for a relaxing vacation, you need a good place to rest your head.

Planning
Getting There
Staying in Style
Touring
Feasting
Making Magic
Index
Notes & More

Choosing a Hotel

The Disneyland Resort boasts three Disney-owned and operated hotels: The Disneyland Hotel, Paradise Pier, and the more recently built Grand Californian. These are supplemented by about three dozen "Good Neighbor" hotels—they're "off property," but very close to the magic. And there are more **motels and hotels** near the Disneyland Resort, as well as many near other Southern California attractions.

To help you choose the **right hotel for you**, we divide this chapter into three sections: Disney Resorts, Good Neighbor hotels, and Nearby Attraction Hotels. We introduce each section with a helpful hotel comparison chart filled with facts, amenities, and services. This is followed by general information, reservation tips, and detailed descriptions of each hotel. We devote a generous amount of space to Disney hotels—we even include room layouts, maps, and photos. This isn't necessarily because Disney resorts are our favorites (though we confess they tend to be). Rather, the Disney hotels are generally of the most interest to our readers and there's much to say about them. Alas, we just can't devote so much space to the other hotels, but we always give you web links to find more information on your own.

Start with the helpful **Hotel Checklist** on the next page. Compare it with your preferences to uncover the hotel category that meets your needs. You may find the sidebar below helpful in deciding whether to stay "on property" (at a Disney hotel) or "off-property." Then carefully read the hotel descriptions, beginning on page 39. When you're ready, use the Lodging Worksheet on pages 76–77 to record your dates, preferences, and reservation options.

To Stay On Property or Off

For most, the decision to stay on property or off depends on budget. It's generally less expensive to stay off property, as prices are often lower and there may be more discounts. On the other hand, the on-property hotels may offer more bang for your buck and, in the end, save you money. If you stay on property, you're always within walking distance of the parks, you get guaranteed admission on busy days (with a ticket), room charging privileges, package delivery, on-site character meals, and that delightful Disney magic. Personally, we prefer to stay on property—for us, time is money, so the ability to walk anywhere within the resort is important. Besides, being immersed in the magic is what it is all about for us.

Hotel Category Checklist

Feature/Amenity	Disney Resort Hotel	Good Neighbor Hotel	Other Motels and Hotels
Located on Disney property	✔		
Least expensive		some	✔
Guaranteed admission to parks	✔		
Transportation to parks	walk or monorail	most	some
Room charging privileges at Disney's parks	✔		
Package delivery to bell desk	✔		
Wake-up calls from Mickey	✔		
Disney vacation packages	✔	✔	
Pool with water slide	✔	some	some
Suite accommodations standard		some	some
Kids Suites available		some	
Free continental breakfast		some	some
Inexpensive meal options nearby		most	most
Refrigerator in room	✔	some	some
Microwave in room		some	some
Pets allowed		some	some
Free parking	✔	most	most
High-speed Internet access	✔	some	some
PlayStation or other video games		some	
View of fireworks	some	some	some
On-site restaurant(s)	✔	most	
Fitness center	✔	most	some
Game arcade	✔	most	some
Guest laundry	most	most	some

Planning

Getting There

Staying in Style

Touring

Feasting

Making Magic

Index

Notes & More

The Disney Hotels

When Disney claims you can "**stay in the middle of the magic**," they're not kidding around. The three official Disney resort hotels are smack dab inside the Disneyland Resort—one is even inside a park! You can't sleep this close to the parks at even the more expansive Walt Disney World Resort in Orlando, Florida. We've stayed at each of the three Disney resort hotels, and we love each one for its own unique qualities.

All three Disney hotels—the original Disneyland Hotel, Disney's Paradise Pier Hotel, and the new Disney's Grand Californian—are all within walking distance of the Disneyland Resort theme parks, with the Grand Californian being the closest. Each hotel offers deluxe accommodations equivalent to a 3- or 4-star hotel. You can expect a basic level of service regardless of which one you choose—these amenities and features are described on the next three pages. Better yet, guests of any of the three Disney resort hotels are entitled to exclusive benefits, described below. To reserve a room, see page 38.

✓ **Room Charging Privileges**—If you put down a credit card at check-in, you can charge almost any expense at the Disney theme parks or a Disney hotel. You must present the special charging authorization slip, which you are handed during check-in, and valid photo identification. Your room account is valid for charging up to 11:00 am on departure day. Note that most Downtown Disney establishments and a few in-park locations do not accept the room charge yet, however.

✓ **Package Express Delivery**—Buy something in the parks but don't want to lug it back to your room? No problem! Inquire about package delivery to your hotel's bell desk at the time of purchase. Note: Packages are not delivered until day's end.

✓ **Guaranteed Admission**—Disney hotel guests with a ticket are guaranteed admission into the parks even if the parks reach capacity.

✓ **Monorail Transportation**—Disney hotel guests can board the monorail in Downtown Disney and ride it into the Disneyland Park. Just show your hotel ID and admission.

✓ **Wake-Up Calls From Mickey**—When you set a wake-up call at your Disney hotel, your old pal Mickey Mouse greets you with a cheerful hello! Tip: If your phone has a speakerphone, use it for your wake-up call so everyone in the room can hear it.

✓ **Packages**—The Walt Disney Travel Company and AAA offer several packages that include a Disney hotel stay, plus special perks. At press time, there are four Disneyland packages—see page 37 for the details.

✓ **Proximity**—Walk less, play more when you stay at a Disney hotel. Disney's hotels are closer to the theme parks than most, and the monorail is an added bonus.

✓ **Service**—Disney is famous for its service, and one of the best places to experience it is at a Disney hotel. They're friendly, helpful, and accommodating. If you ever have a question, touch Guest Services on your in-room phone or visit the Guest Services desk in the lobby.

Disney Hotel Features and Amenities

Special Feature Comparison Chart	Total Rooms	Year Built	Restaurants	Quick-Service Cafe	Themed Pool	Regular Pool(s)	Water Slide	Whirlpool Spa	Recreation on Site	Rollaway/Sofa Beds	Bunk Beds/Trundles	In-Room Safe	Two-Line Phone	Robes/Triple Sheeting	Park Views	Childcare Center	Special Park Entrance	Starting Rates
Disneyland Hotel	990	'55	3	1	1	2	✓	1	✓	✓	–	✓	✓	–	–	–	–	$205+
Grand Californian	751	'01	2	1	1	1	✓	2	✓	–	✓	✓	✓	✓	✓	✓	✓	$265+
Paradise Pier	502	'83	2	–	–	1	✓	1	–	✓	–	✓	–	–	✓	–	–	$160+

Use the chart above to see the differences in amenities and features among the three hotels. Beyond these, features are pretty standard. Here are the details:

Amenities—All rooms have the basics: television with remote control, phone, drawers, clothing rod with hangers, small desk or table, chairs, alarm clock, iron/ironing board, as well as simple toiletries. A few additional amenities—such as in-room safes or two-line phones—differ from resort to resort and are detailed in the appropriate hotel description.

Check-In Time—Check-in time is 3:00 pm at all three Disney hotels, although rooms may be available earlier if you inquire upon your arrival. If your room is not available, you can register, leave your luggage, and go play in the parks while your room is being prepared.

Check-Out Time—Check-out time is 11:00 am. If you need to check out an hour or two later, ask the Front Desk the morning of check-out. If the resort isn't busy, they may grant your request at no extra cost. Extended check-out may also be available for an extra fee. You can also leave your bags with Bell Services and go play in the parks.

Childcare—A children's "club" for ages 5–12—Pinocchio's Workshop—is available at the Grand Californian. In-room childcare is also available at all Disney hotels—contact Guest Services at your hotel or call the Fullerton Child Care Agency at 714-528-1640. See page 237 for rates, details, and more childcare agencies.

Concierge—All three Disney hotels offer a concierge level with extra perks like upgraded amenities, access to a concierge lounge with a continental breakfast, all-day snacks, and twilight wine and cheese. Concierge services are associated with certain rooms within a resort (often the higher floors) and come at a higher rate.

Convention Centers—All Disney hotels are popular among convention-goers due to their excellent meeting facilities and business centers. For more details on convention facilities, call 714-956-6510 or visit http://www.disneyland.com and click on Meetings.

Data Services—In-room local calls, in-room high-speed Internet access, and wireless Internet access in public areas are "free" when you pay the $10/day + 15% tax resort access fee (see page 35). The front desk will also receive your faxes for a fee.

Disabled Access—The Disney hotels offer access for differently-abled guests, including two types of ADA-compliant accommodations. Inquire at reservation time on availability and specifics, and be sure to ask that "Special Needs" be noted on your reservation. Our hotel descriptions indicate the number of barrier-free rooms in each Disney hotel.

Planning
Getting There
Staying in Style
Touring
Feasting
Making Magic
Index
Notes & More

Disney Hotel Amenities: Food to Pools

Food—Every Disney hotel offers eateries, including quick-service cafes, full-service restaurants, and room service. All hotel eateries are noted in each hotel's dining section later in this chapter. Details on the table-service restaurants start on page 197. If you are looking for snack food or groceries, each hotel has a gift shop with a small selection of foodstuffs and drinks. You could also go to Wal-Mart or Target—see bottom of page 27.

Guest Services—Each Disney hotel has a Guest Services desk where you can purchase park passes, make dining arrangements, and find answers to just about any question. You can also connect to Guest Services through a button on your in-room phone.

Housekeeping Services—Every Disney hotel has daily "mousekeeping" services, and provides you with extra towels, pillows, and blankets upon request, as well as a hair dryer if one isn't provided in your room. If you need extra toiletries, don't hesitate to ask.

Ice and Soda—All hotels have ice machines. Most, but not all, also have soda machines. If soda is important, pick some up at a grocery store before you arrive (it's cheaper).

Information—Check the Disneyland information channel on your in-room TV. This channel offers a nice introduction for newcomers, plus a peek at what's new for veterans.

Laundry—The Disneyland Hotel and the Grand Californian have laundry rooms on their premises—Paradise Pier Hotel guests can use the laundry room at the Disneyland Hotel. Expect each washer load and each dryer load to cost about four quarters ($1.00) each. Laundry bags and forms are available in your hotel room for same-day laundering (but it's very expensive). Tip: Store your dirty laundry in the laundry bags.

Mail and Packages—Purchase stamps at Guest Services and in many shops; mail can be dropped off at Guest Services or placed in mailboxes in the hotel lobbies. Federal Express also picks up and drops off packages. A full-service Post Office (Holiday Station) is at 1180 West Ball Rd., about $1/2$ mile northwest of the Disneyland Resort.

Money—Cash, Disney Dollars, Disney gift cards, traveler's checks, MasterCard, Visa, American Express, Discover, Diner's Club, and JCB are accepted, as well as personal checks with proper ID. ATMs are located near the hotel's front desk. Make your room deposit over the phone or fax with the above credit cards or by mail with a check.

Parking—Secured, gated parking lots are available at all Disney hotels—it is included in the $10/day resort access fee. Non-hotel guests pay $6/hour for parking at the Disney hotels. Valet parking is $12/day for all. Show your resort ID at the security gate for entry.

Pets—Pets are not allowed in the hotels unless you travel with a companion (guide) animal. Guests can leave pets for $15/day in the Disneyland Kennel, just east of the main Disneyland entrance. No overnight facilities are available. You may want to consider one of the Good Neighbor hotels that accepts pets (see chart on page 52).

Pools—Every Disney hotel has at least one swimming pool and water slide, and both the Grand Californian Hotel and the Disneyland Hotel have an additional themed pool complex. Paradise Pier's pool area is recently updated as well. Please note that only guests staying at a hotel can use its pool. Towels are available at the pool, as are flotation vests for kids. See hotel details later in this chapter for pool descriptions.

Never Land Pool at Disneyland Hotel

Disney Hotel Amenities: Rates to Wheelchairs

Rates—Starting "rack" rates are listed in each hotel's description. There is no charge for kids or extra adults (more than two) in a room. Rollaway beds, sleeping bags, and cribs may be used free of charge.

Recreation—You can visit another hotel to use its recreational facilities (with the exception of swimming pools). Be sure to note the operating hours upon arrival or by phoning ahead.

Resort Access Fee—All Disney hotels charge an additional mandatory fee of $10/night + 15% hotel tax (so figure $11.50) on top of your daily room rate for a group of services they term "resort access." This fee covers self-parking for guests with a vehicle (one vehicle per room), in-room local phone service, in-room high-speed Internet access, wi-fi Internet access in certain public areas of the hotels, and unlimited fitness center usage. The fee does not cover in-room incidentals (such as games, movies, or the mini-bar), gratuities, laundry, non-local phone calls, or other expenses not listed in the rates or as a part of your package. Some non-Disney hotels may charge a similar resort fee, but rates and services vary.

Room Locations—You can request room locations such as a tower or room number, but these are not guaranteed. Note your preferences when you make your reservation, via phone about three days before arrival, and again when you check in. If you don't like the particular room you've been assigned, politely request another room.

Room Service—All Disney hotels offer room service.

Security—Security at the Disneyland Resort has always been good, and since 9/11, security has visibly heightened. A gatehouse guards entry into every parking lot, and virtually everyone who drives through the gates is questioned. Show your photo ID and resort ID, or explain why you are visiting the hotel. All resort rooms have electronic locks that open with your resort ID for added security. You can store small valuables in your in-room safe.

Spa (Hot Tub)—Disney-speak for a hot tub. There's at least one spa at every Disney hotel. Traditional spa facilities (massages and manicures) are available at the Grand Californian.

Smoking—All three Disney hotels are entirely smoke-free as of March 1, 2006.

Telephones—All rooms have a phone and usage information. Local calls within a 12-mile radius of the hotel are free when you pay the $10/night resort access fee. Toll-free and credit card calls are also free of access charges. Long-distance calls are $1.50 + 155% of the cost of the call. Use calling cards instead. Incoming calls are free. All major carriers have coverage for cell phones at Disneyland, but the coverage can be spotty due to all the structures.

Tipping—You may tip valet parking attendants $1-$2, bell services $1-$2/bag upon delivery and pick up, and housekeeping $1/person/day (leave tip in room on a daily basis).

Transportation—As the hotels are within walking distance, transportation is not provided. You can request taxis or shuttles to go to other destinations, however. Tip: To save time, use the Grand Californian park exit (see map on page 46) when leaving Disney's California Adventure; cast members restrict entrance to Grand Californian guests, but not exits.

Voice Mail—Every hotel offers free voice mail that can be retrieved from your room or any other phone in or outside of the Disneyland Resort up to 24 hours after checkout. If you are on the phone when a call comes in, the voice mail system takes your caller's message. See the Telephone Information card in your room for usage instructions.

Wheelchairs—Wheelchairs may be rented from each of the Disney hotels for $10/day—ask at Bell Services, or call 714-956-6833 before arriving. Wheelchairs and motorized wheelchairs (ECVs) may also be rented at the parks (availability is limited and you can only use them in the parks). You may find it more helpful to rent from B&R Medical Equipment (714-850-9326), who will deliver to Disney hotels. For stroller rentals, see pages 81 and 97.

Finding the Best Disney Hotel Rates

If you're anything like us, you want to see the **best rates** you can get on hotels before deciding where to stay. You can use the rack rates we list later in this chapter as a guideline, but it's pretty safe to say that you should be able to find better rates if you look around. Below are our top five tips to find the best rates on Disney hotels (you can use these tips to find the best rates for Good Neighbor hotels, too.)

1. **Check the available rates** for your vacation dates by calling Disney at 714-956-MICKEY (714-956-6425). This gives you a baseline at which to begin. Now inquire about discounts or specials—if you have a Disney Visa card or an annual pass, if you are age 60 or older, live in Southern California, and/or are active or retired military, be sure to mention this and ask about special rates. Repeat this process with the Walt Disney Travel Co. at 800-854-3104 to get available package rates.

2. Visit **MouseSavers.com** (http://www.mousesavers.com) to get the latest list of deals.

3. Visit **Expedia.com** (http://www.expedia.com), which often beats other rates. Check MouseSavers.com for great tips and helpful links to Expedia. In general, remember that the best deals are found closest to your vacation dates. You may want to compare the rates at Expedia.com to those at Travelocity.com (http://www.travelocity.com).

4. You may be tempted to use **Priceline.com** to bid on a Disney hotel, but don't bother—at the time of writing, the three official Disney hotels didn't participate in the Priceline system. Some Good Neighbor hotels do participate, however. You'll find Priceline.com tips at MouseSavers.com and also at http://www.biddingfortravel.com.

5. Consider an **annual pass**. Annual passholders are often entitled to Disney hotel discounts of 40% to 50%. You can inquire about annual passholder rates prior to purchasing an annual pass, but you will need to have it (or a voucher from the Disney Store) in hand at check-in time.

Disney Hotel Ratings Explained

In each of the Disney hotel descriptions that follow, we offer ratings to help you make the best decisions. We recommend you use these ratings as a guide, not gospel. **Value Ratings** range from 1 (poor) to 10 (excellent) and are based on quality (cleanliness, maintenance, and freshness); accessibility (how fast and easy it is to get to parks); and affordability (rates for the standard rooms)—overall value represents an average of the above three values. **Magic Ratings** are based on theme (execution and sense of immersion); amenities (guest perks and luxuries); and fun factor (number and quality of hotel activities)—overall magic represents an average of the above three values. We use a point accumulation method to determine value and magic ratings. **Readers' Ratings** are calculated from surveys submitted by experienced vacationers at the PassPorter site (http://www.passporter.com/dl/rate.htm). **Guest satisfaction** is based on our and our readers' experiences with how different types of vacationers enjoy the Disney hotel: ♥♥♥♥♥=love it ♥♥♥♥=enjoy it ♥♥♥=like it ♥♥=tolerate it ♥=don't like it

Choosing a Disney Hotel Package

Disney's vacation packages offer the promise of simplicity, peace of mind, and an air of luxury to the bewildered vacation planner. Even better news: Disney package **rates can be lower** than the total list price for each package component, particularly on the seasonal and special packages offered. Prices vary considerably—be sure you price out the components of the package at full price to be sure you're getting a good deal. You may book a minimum of two nights and a maximum of 14 nights for most packages. At press time, these are the available Disney packages:

Resort Magic 2006

Available year-round, you get two nights or more at a Disney hotel, free self-parking, fitness center access, a Park Hopper ticket for the length of your stay, one Early Entry pass for Fantasyland, one Mickey's Toontown Morning Madness (an enhanced character experience one hour before park opening), 50th aniversary guidemap, preferred seating to select shows in Disney's California Adventure, one trading pin and lanyard, one luggage tag, and one California Fun Book. Prices start at $339 per person (based on double occupancy).

Good Neighbor Magic

Everything in the Resort Magic package described above, but accommodations are at one of the three dozen Good Neighbor hotels instead. See pages 51–64 for descriptions of Disney's Good Neighbor hotels. Prices start at $209 per person (based on double occupancy).

Disneyland 50th Celebration Package

Everything in the Resort Magic package described above, but accommodations are for three or more nights and you get a 50th Anniversary certificate. Offered through Dec. 2006.

Disney Visa Resort Dream Vacation Package

Available exclusively to Disney Visa cardholders. This package offers two nights or more at a Disney hotel, free self-parking, fitness center access, a Park Hopper ticket for the length of your stay, entry to Mickey's Toontown Morning Madness (an enhanced character experience one hour before park opening), one trading pin and lanyard, one California Fun Book, preferred seating at a show, preferred parade viewing area, and a totebag. More information at http://disney.go.com/visa/disneyland50th.

In addition to the above, **seasonal packages** may be offered. For example, in the past there have been a number of packages that offered a free fourth night if you stayed three. And at press time, an "Everyone Plays at the Kids Price" and "Kids Play FREE" specials are available until 4/25/2006. These packages are offered for Disney and Good Neighbor hotels.

Note that the **Grand Plan package** is not being offered at press time.

Book packages through the **Walt Disney Travel Co.** at 800-854-3104 or 714-520-5060, at http://www.disneyland.com (click "Hotels" then "Packages"), or through a travel agent.

Many **outside organizations** offer Disneyland packages, too. Organizations include AAA (http://www.aaa.com), Amtrak (http://www.amtrak.com), Southwest Airlines (http://www.southwest.com), United Vacations (http://www.unitedvacations.com), and Delta Vacations (http://www.deltavacations.com).

Planning

Getting There

Staying in Style

Touring

Feasting

Making Magic

Index

Notes & More

Planning

Getting There

Staying in Style

Touring

Feasting

Making Magic

Index

Notes & More

Reserving a Disney Hotel Room

Making reservations for a Disney hotel is **simple**. A travel agent is not needed, but if you have a great travel agent, by all means consult him or her—they do not generally charge extra fees for their services and they may have access to special deals. Here's the lowdown on reservations:

Before you make your reservations, read the **hotel descriptions** on the following pages and use the worksheet on pages 76–77 to jot down the dates you prefer to visit along with any alternates. Even a one-day change in your travel dates can open the door to a great deal. Be familiar with all resorts in your price range.

Reservations for all Disney hotels can be made at **714-956-MICKEY (714-956-6425)**. Disney representatives can offer assistance in English, Spanish, Japanese, French, and many other languages. If you have Internet access or prefer to use mail, use the resources described on page 36. You may be able to hold more than one reservation for the same date, but eventually you have to put down a deposit or lose the reservation. Most reservations can be cancelled for full credit up to 72 hours prior to arrival (or up to 30 days prior to arrival for packages). Disney sends a confirmation of your reservation by mail.

Ask about **special deals or packages** when you call. If your dates aren't available, ask about alternates. Sometimes you can get a discount for part of your stay. Lock in whatever discount you can get, and book at full price for the rest. Keep calling back, as cancellations are released every morning. If a lower rate comes out later, ask if it can be applied.

Make any **special requests** at the time of reservation and again at check-in. If you need a non-smoking or barrier-free room, a rollaway bed or a crib, request this now. If you have a particular location or room in mind (we make many suggestions later on), make sure to tell the reservations agent. Disney will not guarantee a particular room or view, but if your request is "in the system," they will try their best to make your wish come true. Call your resort about three days before arrival to confirm any requests you made.

Finalize Disney hotel reservations after you make your **flight reservations**. Room reservations can usually be changed or cancelled without penalty, whereas flight changes often incur a fee. If you wish to cancel your Disney hotel reservations without penalty, cancel no later than 72 hours prior to your arrival (or no later than 30 days for packages).

Once you've made reservations, **record the information** on your Lodging PassPocket, including the name of the hotel, dates, type of room, price, reservation number, and any special information you want to note. This is also an ideal place to note any special requests you want to verify at check-in. Use a pencil if your plans aren't final.

Typically, Disney hotel reservations are held for 21 days without confirmation. Confirmation requires a **deposit** equal to one night's stay plus the 15% hotel tax (packages require a deposit of $200, due in 10 days). Be sure to pay your deposit before midnight Pacific Time on the 21st day (if you are calling, note that the phone lines close at 10:00 pm PT). Your deposit can be made over the phone with the Disney Visa, American Express, MasterCard, Visa, Discover, JCB, Diner's Club, or through mail or fax with the same credit cards or a personal check. If you pay your deposit over the phone, your credit card is not charged until check-in. The Lodging Worksheet at the end of the chapter (pages 76–77) has spaces to check off confirmations and deposits made, too!

Disneyland Hotel

The original "official hotel of the Magic Kingdom" is the Disneyland Hotel. Located just west of the Disney parks, the Disneyland Hotel captivates guests with its own brand of Disney magic, fun, and convenience. Of the three Disney resort hotels, the Disneyland Hotel is mid-range in price.

A stay at the Disneyland Hotel feels like **visiting your favorite Uncle Walt**. Even on Jennifer's first visit years ago, she was delighted by the sense of history and the familiar Disney characters cavorting throughout the hotel's decor and grounds. While the Disneyland Hotel was built in 1955—the same year that Disneyland opened—it was actually built and operated by Walt's friend Jack Wrather. The Wrather Corp. expanded the resort from its original structure by adding the three towers—in fact, the Bonita Tower is named after Jack's wife. In the '80s, the Disney Company purchased the entire corporation, thereby becoming the hotel's owners as well. The hotel was then completely renovated to evoke the magic of Fantasia. The monorail originally connected to the Disneyland Hotel, but after hotel renovations the monorail stop is now a 5-minute walk away inside Downtown Disney. The hotel isn't themed like the Grand Californian, but its recent renovation gives it an upscale, almost Victorian feel. Of the three Disney resorts, the Disneyland Hotel feels the most magical ... you almost expect to see Walt himself walk around the corner.

The 990 guest rooms at the Disneyland hotel are housed in **three towers**: Marina (north) is 11 stories, Sierra (east) is also 11 stories, and Bonita (south) is 14 stories. Visitors to the hotel prior to 1999 may remember garden villas, but these were removed during the resort expansion. Guest rooms were recently renovated with whimsical decor, including a glow-in-the-dark Tinker Bell border, Mickey light fixtures, and light maple furnishings with Herb Ryman sketches. The armoire has a historic 1953 concept drawing of Disneyland (the one that sold bankers on the whole idea) and the headboard has a drawing of Sleeping Beauty Castle (so you can say you "slept under the castle"). Standard rooms range from 364 to 415 sq. ft. and have two queens or one king poster bed, plus either a sofa bed or a comfy chair and footstool. All rooms sleep up to five guests. Other features include a desk, a small refrigerator in the armoire, two-line phone, an in-room safe, and a makeup mirror. Room layouts differ (see two typical floor plans below), but all rooms have sliding glass doors with narrow, step-out balconies. Standard rooms have three views: standard city view, lower-level resort/pool view, and upper-level resort/pool view. The Sierra Tower has 79 concierge rooms offering upgraded amenities, light snacks, and views of the pool or Downtown Disney. 62 suites, from one-bedroom and up, range in size from 740 to 3400 sq. ft. All rooms are non-smoking as of March 1, 2006. 30 barrier-free rooms are also available.

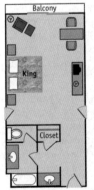
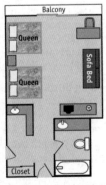

Planning

Getting There

Staying in Style

Touring

Feasting

Making Magic

Index

Notes & More

EATING & DRINKING

PLAYING & RELAXING

ACCESS

Using the Amenities at the Disneyland Hotel

Disneyland Hotel edges out other hotels in the sheer **number of eatery choices**, including three full-service restaurants (all described in detail on pages 207-208). Goofy's Kitchen offers a character meal for breakfast, lunch, and dinner—you can chow down at the buffet while Chef Goofy and Disney friends cavort around. Hook's Pointe & Wine Cellar serves lunch and dinner. The best restaurant is Granville's Steak

Our pool-view, king-bed room in the Marina Tower

House, open for breakfast and dinner (closed Sundays and Mondays). Several places to get a quick bite are available. Croc's Bits 'n' Bites is the poolside snack stand with burgers and ice cream. Captain's Galley is a popular breakfast spot with coffee and pastries, but it also has boxed lunches and snacks. The Coffee House is also great in the mornings with espresso, bagels, and fruit. The Lost Bar and Top Brass are popular lounges in the evenings, often with live guitar music. Room service is available from 5:00 am to 1:00 am. Earlier visitors may remember the Monorail Cafe, Neon Cactus, Grandma Maize's, and Stromboli's, but these are now gone.

For Athletes: Team Mickey's Workout offers exercise equipment and weight machines. Fitness center access is included in the $10/day resort access fee.

For Children: A small playground is back by the Cove Pool. Kids love the water slides, wading pool, and Jungle Cruise-themed remote-control boats, too.

For Gamers: A large arcade is located behind the Euro Gifts shop. The Safari Adventure remote-control boat lagoon near the Bonita Tower is fun, too—pay $2 to manuever one of 20 boats, each a replica of the Jungle Cruise boats.

For Shoppers: A Fantasia-themed shop in the lobby of Marina Tower offers Disney logowear and gifts. The nearby Marina Lobby Shop offers film, newspapers, and sundries. Euro Gifts and Collectibles (formerly Tinker Bell's Treasures) in the courtyard features crystal and glass by Arribas Brothers.

For Swimmers: The Never Land Pool area sports a fun Peter Pan theme, complete with a 5,000-sq.-ft. heated pool, a 110-ft. water slide, a pirate ship, and a "mermaid lagoon" whirlpool spa. Typically open from 10:00 am to 9:00 pm. The quieter, shallower Cove Pools in the back of the courtyard are open from 7:00 am to 7:00 pm—there's also a shady beach area and a volleyball court.

All Disney-owned hotels are within **walking distance** of the Disney parks. The monorail station in nearby Downtown Disney can zip you into the Disneyland Park—be sure to bring your hotel ID card and park admission. Hotel guest parking is nearby—cost is included in the $10/night resort access fee (see page 35). Valet parking is available for $12/day. Airport buses stop just outside the Marina Tower (the home of Guest Services, check-in, and the gift shop). Shuttles and other buses are also nearby.

Making the Most
of the Disneyland Hotel

When you arrive, you **check in** at the front desk in the Marina (north) Tower. This is also where you'll find Guest Services and an ATM (cash machine).

Take time to stroll the acres of **beautiful grounds**. You can't miss the roaring waters of Horseshoe Falls, a 165-foot-wide cascade of water. Look for the pools filled with more than 200 koi fish, too. Other fun spots include the pretty wedding gazebo near the South Lawn, and the huge Sorcerer Mickey Hat near Downtown Disney.

Fantasy Waters, a Disneyland Hotel tradition, performs nightly. It delights guests with a 15-minute synchronized light, music, and water show—it's not sophisticated, but it's good Disney fun. Performances are free, and open to everyone. Shows are typically held three times a night. Located in the back of the courtyard.

Look for the **Photo Hall of Fame** near Goofy's Kitchen—it's a floor-to-ceiling collage documenting the colorful history of the Disneyland Resort.

The **concierge level** is popular at this hotel. For the extra money, you get priority check-in, an upper-level room in the Sierra Tower, a concierge lounge with a breakfast bar, afternoon snacks, and twilight wine and cheese reception, turndown service (upon request), and access to Team Mickey's Workout fitness center.

Rollaway beds and cribs are available for use free of charge. Request when you make your reservation or upon check-in.

Disneyland Hotel has the largest **convention center** of the three Disney hotels. It flanks the west side of the courtyard and offers 136,000 sq. ft. of meeting space. For more info, visit: http://www.disney.com/vacations/meetings/disneyland.

A small **laundry room** is tucked away in the back of the courtyard near the Cove Pools. Washers and dryers are $1 each—a change machine is available. Bring your own laundry soap and dryer sheets from home, or buy from the front desk.

The hotel was updated in 2004, during which time the registration areas got a facelift. There was also a **$50 million renovation** in 2001.

We have it on good authority that a **"Where the Magic Began" hotel tour** may begin here soon. It should be free to hotel guests. Inquire with the front desk.

Check-in time is 3:00 pm. Check-out time is 11:00 am. If you arrive before 3:00 pm, you can register and store your luggage until your room is ready.

Ratings are explained on page 36.

Our Value Ratings:		Our Magic Ratings:		Readers' Ratings:
Quality:	7/10	Theme:	5/10	52% fell in love with it
Accessibility:	9/10	Amenities:	8/10	30% liked it well enough
Affordability:	7/10	Fun Factor:	8/10	12% had mixed feelings
Overall Value:	**8/10**	**Overall Magic:**	**7/10**	6% were disappointed

The Disneyland Hotel is enjoyed by...	(rated by authors and readers)	
Younger Kids: ❤❤❤❤❤	Young Adults: ❤❤❤❤	Families: ❤❤❤❤❤
Older Kids: ❤❤❤❤❤	Mid Adults: ❤❤❤	Couples: ❤❤
Teenagers: ❤❤❤❤	Mature Adults: ❤❤	Singles: ❤❤❤

TIPS

NOTES

RATINGS

Planning

Getting There

Staying in Style

Touring

Feasting

Making Magic

Index

Notes & More

Finding Your Place
at the Disneyland Hotel

ESPN Zone

To Downtown Disney & Disney Parks

Disneyland Hotel

To Paradise Pier Hotel & Grand Californian

Disneyland Drive

Rose Court Garden

Sierra Tower

Captain's Galley

Hook's Pointe

Croc's Bits 'n' Bites

★ Check-In & Guest Services

Never Land Pool

The Lost Bar

Bonita Tower

Entry Plaza

Marina Tower

Remote Control Boats

Horseshoe Falls

Koi Pond

Arcade

Parking

The Coffee House

Never Land Glen

Waterfall Garden

Parking

Goofy's Kitchen

Cove Pools

Conference Center

Granville's Steak House

Laundry / Team Mickey's Workout

Fantasy Waters Show

Offices

Many guests prefer the **Sierra Tower** because it's a bit closer to the parks. An upper-level view of Downtown Disney from Sierra Tower tends to be a guest favorite, and a pool view is also delightful. Guests report that the rooms in Sierra Tower tend to be a bit larger, too. **Marina Tower** offers views of the pool or the city—we loved our view of the Never Land Pool from the ninth floor and our convenient access to Guest Services in the lobby. **Bonita Tower** is a few more steps away, but the splashing from the waterfall is soothing and drowns out pool noise. Parties with five guests should request a room with a sofa bed, which is more comfy than a rollaway bed. If you're looking for **extra space** and considering a one-bedroom suite, keep in mind that they're just two standard rooms, one of which has a small kitchenette instead of a bathroom and a fold-out sofa in place of beds. Thus, you may get a better deal and more comfortable accommodations by booking two connecting standard rooms instead of a one-bedroom suite.

2006 Sample Room Rates

Rack rates—prices change by season

Room Type	Rate	Room Type	Rate
City Standard View	$205	One-Bedroom Suite	$460
Premium View	$236	Two-Bedroom Suite	$595
Concierge	$385	Three-Bedroom Suite	$720

The above rates do not include 15% hotel tax or the $10/night resort access fee. Rates vary by season—see chart on page 14 for seasons.

Disneyland Hotel

✉ 1150 Magic Way, Anaheim, CA 92802

☎ Phone: 714-778-6600   ✎ Fax: 714-956-6597

📋 For reservations, call 714-956-MICKEY (714-956-6425)

Disney's Grand Californian Hotel

Planning

Getting There

Location, location, location. The recently built Grand Californian Hotel is in the best possible location, straddling the Downtown Disney shopping district and Disney's California Adventure park (with direct entrances to both). This is Disneyland's most luxurious (and expensive) hotel.

AMBIENCE

To enter Disney's Grand Californian Hotel is to take a step back in time to the spirit and splendor of early, turn-of-the-century California. Built as a living tribute to the **Arts and Crafts movement**, the soaring, six-story Great Hall lobby blends the simplicity of California's redwood forests with the romance of rustic yet elegant charm. A great hearth warms the travelers who linger about the fire for storytelling or sink into the comfortable arms of an oversized chair. Built by Peter Dominick in 2001, this grand hotel pays special attention to architecture, art, landscape, and the decorative arts of the Craftsman movement. Display cabinets throughout the Great Hall are filled with authentic period and reproduction art, and cast members wear quaint period costumes. Disney's Grand Californian Hotel is the first Disneyland hotel to be built by Disney from the ground up, and the attention to detail and theme is awe-inspiring. Those familiar with Walt Disney World will recognize this hotel as a cross between the Wilderness Lodge Resort and the Grand Floridian Resort & Spa, both celebrated favorites among Walt Disney World guests.

Staying in Style

Touring

LAYOUT & ROOMS

This 751-room resort hotel offers **deluxe accommodations** for all guests. Most guest rooms offer views of Downtown Disney and Disney's California Adventure. In fact, the rooms overlooking the park are so close to the action you may feel like you're really there—and that's because you are! The hotel is technically located within the park, affording stunning panoramas of the Golden State and Paradise Pier districts. The back-to-nature Arts and Crafts theme is carried to the guest rooms, with dark redwood-hued armoires carved with stylized trees, tall headboards with individual, mica-style lamps, a signature Napa Rose border around the ceiling, and bedspreads inspired by the intricate lines of stained glass. Disney touches are evident in the Bambi characters that frolic across the shower curtains. The 713 standard guest rooms are 353 sq. ft. (see floor plans below) and come with two queen beds, though about 80 rooms have one king bed and 160 rooms have one queen and a bunk bed with a trundle bed underneath it to sleep up to five guests! Note: The bunk bed isn't very long and is really intended for kids under 48". All guest rooms come

Feasting

equipped with an armoire with a 27" TV and a mini-bar/refrigerator, a large in-room safe, a desk with chairs and a 2-line phone, a lighted wardrobe, an iron and ironing board, hair dryer, coffeemaker, makeup mirror, and crib. You can request sleeping bags and cushions, too. Luxurious features include comfy robes to wear during your stay, dimmer-controlled lighting, Italian marble double vanities, and signature toiletries. Concierge rooms are available, offering upgraded amenities and access to the concierge lounge. 38 suites are available, including 34 one-bedroom suites.

Making Magic

Index

Notes & More

Using the Amenities
at Disney's Grand Californian Hotel

DINING

Disney's Grand Californian offers an **excellent cross-section** of dining options (see page 209 for details). Napa Rose is an upscale, dinner-only restaurant offering fresh California cuisine. Storyteller's Cafe is a family favorite serving breakfast (with characters), lunch, and dinner. Hearthstone Lounge is a coffee shop with baked goods in the morning and cocktails throughout the day. White Water Snacks is a quick-service cafe. Room service is available 24 hours.

Turndown at the Grand Californian

PLAYING & RELAXING

For Athletes: Keep in shape in the new Mandara Spa, which is slated to replace the Eureka Springs Spa in 2006. A variety of exercise equipment is available, along with massage treatments, dry and steam saunas, and lockers. You can also swim laps in the Fountain Pool.

For Children: Pinocchio's Workshop is a supervised childcare club for kids ages 5–12, open from 5:00 pm to midnight. Licensed caregivers supervise children while they do arts and crafts, watch videos, and play games. Cost is $13/hour per child. Grand Californian hotel guests may make reservations up to two months in advance (call 714-635-2300 or extension 7301); Disneyland Hotel and Paradise Pier Hotel guests may make same-day reservations only. A children's pool is also available, as is a playground. Kids should also ask how they can learn to draw Mickey.

For Gamers: Grizzly's Game Arcade lets you play video games to your heart's content. Or hop over to Downtown Disney's ESPN Zone for more games.

For Shoppers: The charming Acorns Gifts & Goods shop outfits you with sundries, foodstuffs, books, clothing, and Arts & Crafts-style gifts. And let's not forget that the entire Downtown Disney shopping district is just a few steps away.

For Swimmers: Soak in the Redwood Pool, a large pool with a playful theme that matches the Redwood Creek Challenge Trail attraction just visible in the park. The 100-ft. water slide masquerades as the stump of a fallen redwood tree. A Mickey-shaped wading pool is also here for the kids. The quiet Fountain Pool is a haven of relaxation, as are the two whirlpool spas. Towels are available at the pool.

For Weddings: A Wedding Garden and Bridal Salon are on the premises. For more information on getting married here, call 714-956-6527.

For the Young At Heart: Stop by the Great Hall for "Tales From the Hearth," an imaginative storytelling session for young and old alike. It's generally held three times a day in the afternoons and evenings.

ACCESS

Disney's Grand Californian Hotel guests are right in the middle of the action, with **easy access to everything**. To enter Disney's California Adventure, use the exclusive entrance on the east side of the hotel (just follow the signs or check our map on page 46). Guests bound for Disneyland Park can follow the signs to the Downtown Disney entrance and either board the monorail or simply walk (5–10 minutes). The other Disneyland hotels are right across the street to the west. Hotel guest parking is free (included in the $10 resort access fee); valet parking is $12.

Making the Most
of Disney's Grand Californian Hotel

Watch your room for a daily "Grand Adventures" sheet with daily activities, such as The Grand Quest (a free family treasure hunt). Of particular interest is the free **"Art of the Craft" guided tour**. This daily walking tour points out the delightful details of the Arts & Crafts decor, as well as a few Hidden Mickeys. We recommend you do it early in your stay as it will help you appreciate the architecture and decor that much more. You can call 714-635-2300 in advance of your visit to get details.

Take the time to **fully explore** this magnificent resort hotel. Look for the intricate Sun Gate (it leads to the pool) and the Moon Gate (which leads to Downtown Disney). The Brisa Courtyard (see map on next page) is a quiet retreat on a busy day—look up and you'll see that the monorail passes above and through the hotel. Inside there are delightful sitting areas all over the place. And be sure to catch some storytelling at the hearth or listen to the pianist in the Great Hall.

Ask about a **refillable mug** at White Water Snacks. If available, this $8–$10 mug gives you free refills on soda, coffee, and tea during your stay.

Doing business? There's 20,000 sq. ft. of meeting space, a full-service business center (8:00 am–5:00 pm), and wireless Internet access in the Great Hall lobby.

Concierge-level guests have access to a staffed concierge lounge on the sixth floor, which offers a continental breakfast in the morning, wines and cheeses in the afternoon, and goodies throughout the day. You can view the fireworks from the concierge lounge, and the music is piped in. Concierge guest rooms also sport DVD players, and you can borrow DVD titles from the lounge.

The **Presidential and Vice Presidential suites** are truly breathtaking. If we had the money, this is the first place we'd stay. If you can afford it, go for it.

No rollaway beds; instead request **sleeping bags** with pads from housekeeping.

The **mini-bar** has motion sensors—if you even move an item, you may be charged for it. You can ask to have the mini-bar locked if you don't intend to use it.

The **guest laundry room** is located above the Napa Rose restaurant. The only way to reach it is via the elevators located next to the restaurant.

This is a **completely non-smoking hotel**—you can't even smoke at the pool.

Check-in time is 3:00 pm. Check-out time is 11:00 am.

Ratings are explained on page 36.

Our Value Ratings:		Our Magic Ratings:		Readers' Ratings:
Quality:	9/10	Theme:	10/10	65% fell in love with it
Accessibility:	10/10	Amenities:	9/10	15% liked it well enough
Affordability:	3/10	Fun Factor:	8/10	15% had mixed feelings
Overall Value:	**7/10**	**Overall Magic:**	**9/10**	5% were disappointed

Disney's Grand Californian is enjoyed by... *(rated by both authors and readers)*		
Younger Kids: ❤❤❤❤	Young Adults: ❤❤❤❤❤	Families: ❤❤❤❤❤
Older Kids: ❤❤❤❤	Mid Adults: ❤❤❤❤❤	Couples: ❤❤❤❤❤
Teenagers: ❤❤❤	Mature Adults: ❤❤❤❤	Singles: ❤❤❤

Planning

Getting There

Staying in Style

Touring

Feasting

Making Magic

Index

Notes & More

TIPS

NOTES

RATINGS

Finding Your Place
at Disney's Grand Californian Hotel

GRAND CALIFORNIAN MAP

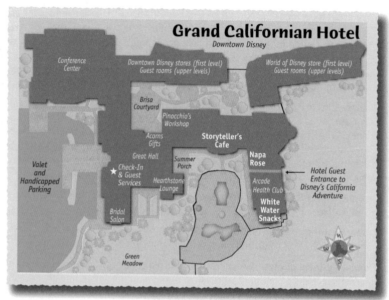

BEST LOCATIONS

Standard rooms are located on floors 2–5 and come in three different views: standard city view, Downtown Disney view, and theme park/pool view. If the theme park view is your main draw, be sure to reserve a park/pool view room and then specifically request a park view. We had a Downtown Disney view and loved it—we could even see the Disneyland fireworks in the evenings. We also had a "city standard" (read: parking lot) view which suited us just fine as we spent little time in our room. Note also that the bunk bed rooms are popular—if this is your preference, be sure to request it at the time your reserve your room and again when you check in. **Concierge rooms** are on floor 6, which is also key-protected. Note that there are only two sets of elevators, both of which are centrally located—if you get a guest room at the far end of one of the wings, you may have a long walk. If this is an issue, request a room near an elevator.

RATES

2006 Sample Room Rates

Rack rates—prices change by season

Room Type	Rate	Room Type	Rate
City Standard View	$265	Concierge Courtyard View	$470
Downtown Disney View	$295	Concierge Theme Park View	$490
Theme Park/Pool View	$325	One-Bedroom Suite	$655

The above rates do not include 15% hotel tax or the $10/night resort access fee. Rates vary by season—see chart on page 14 for seasons.

INFO

Disney's Grand Californian Hotel
✉ 1600 South Disneyland Drive, Anaheim, CA 92803
☎ Phone: 714-635-2300   📠 Fax: 714-300-7300
📱 For reservations, call 714-956-MICKEY (714-956-6425)

Disney's Paradise Pier Hotel

Planning · Getting There · Staying in Style · Touring · Feasting · Making Magic · Index · Notes & More

Located across the street from the Paradise Pier district of Disney's California Adventure theme park, this hotel offers delightful views and a low-key atmosphere. Of the three Disney hotels, Disney's Paradise Pier is the **least expensive** and often the one with the most availability.

AMBIENCE

Disney's Paradise Pier Hotel reflects the laid-back, carefree culture of California, evoking a subtle **seaside pier atmosphere**. Fewer rooms mean a more intimate scene and a smaller hotel. Although not as themed as its sister hotels, Paradise Pier does have its own charms: a relaxed and quiet setting, breathtaking views of Disney's California Adventure, and a large rooftop pool and new water slide. Mickey is also evident in the large lobby statue, the artwork, and the upholstery. Rooms were renovated in 2004 with a fresh, seaside resort decor. Previously this hotel was known as Disney's Pacific Hotel—remnants of its Japanese theme can be seen in the simple architectural styling and the Yamabuki restaurant and sushi bar. It was originally built as the Emerald Hotel in 1983 and renamed the Pan Pacific Hotel before being acquired in 1996 by The Walt Disney Company.

LAYOUT & ROOMS

The 489 guest rooms at Paradise Pier Hotel are situated in **two high-rise towers**, painted in sunny yellow and framed by towering palm trees. The two 14- and 15-story towers meet to form a lobby atrium. Guest rooms are upscale and contemporary, with warm woods, breezy colors, and soft lighting. Most rooms are moderately sized at 364 sq. ft., and all standard rooms hold up to five guests (up to four adults). Choose from two queens or one king bed. Other features include a sofa with a foldover twin bed, table, armoire with TV and refrigerator, coffeemaker, and a lifeguard Mickey lamp. While there are no balconies, rooms do have a large picture window—these offer spectacular views for the rooms that overlook Disney's California Adventure (see photo on next page). Rooms now have in-room safes, thanks to the 2004 renovations. Rooms come in two views: city view (pool and parking lot) and DCA Resort theme park view. The standard rooms have two different layouts (see floor plans below). You'll notice that one layout has a shower instead of a tub—if a tub is important to you, request it. A limited number of Family Suites are available offering a sitting area, two bathrooms, and a bedroom—all have theme park views. Concierge rooms with DVD players, upgraded amenities, and daily snacks and beverages are also available on the 3rd, 14th, and

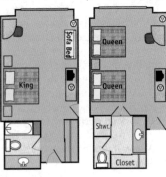

15th floors—rooms on the 3rd floor facing the pool are known as "cabana" rooms and have large patios with direct access to the pool. Among the concierge-level rooms are 12 suites ranging in size from 792 sq. ft. (one-bedroom suites for up to 4 guests) to 1,245 sq. ft. (Laguna Suite for up to 8 guests). There are also 14 barrier-free rooms, all of which are non-smoking. Cribs and rollaway beds are available upon request. All guest rooms are non-smoking as of March 1, 2006.

Using the Amenities at Disney's Paradise Pier Hotel

DINING & LOUNGING

Paradise Pier is Californian, right down to its dining choices (all are described in detail on page 210). The **PCH Grill** offers a character breakfast with Lilo and Stitch every morning, and California cuisine for lunch and dinner. **Yamabuki** is a Japanese restaurant serving sushi, a la carte dishes, and set menus—open for dinner only. **The Coffee Bar** offers coffee specialties, juice, soda, and pastries. Tip: Look

Our park-view, queen-bed room

here for a refillable mug for about $6–$7 each—it gives you free refills of coffee, tea, or soda. A pool bar on the pool deck (third floor) is open in the summer only. The Practically Perfect Tea was held here on the second floor, but it closed its doors in 2002. Room service is available from 6:30 am to 1:00 am.

PLAYING & RELAXING

For Athletes: Mickey's Team Workout II Fitness Center on the second floor offers exercise equipment and weight machines. Access is available to all hotel guests (it is included in your mandatory $10/night resort access fee). You can also swim laps in the rooftop pool, and walk/jog on the nearby Disneyland Hotel grounds.

For Children: Alas, there is no playground at this hotel. Families may use the playground at the nearby Disneyland Hotel, however.

For Gamers: A small arcade is near the back of the hotel on the first floor.

For Shoppers: Mickey in Paradise (formerly Disney Touch) is a Disney theme shop with logowear, gifts, and collectibles. The Boardwalk Boutique has closed.

For Swimmers: The terraced rooftop—accessible via the 3rd floor—is the home of a large heated pool, wading pool, whirlpool spa (hot tub), and water slide. The pool area was renovated in 2004, at which time the splashdown waterslide was added. The pool is open until 11:00 pm. A whirlpool spa (hot tub) is nearby.

GETTING ABOUT

Previously, one of the best features of the Paradise Pier Hotel was its **easy access** to Disney's California Adventure—there was a Disney's California Adventure park entrance for the "exclusive use" of Paradise Pier Hotel guests. The gate was closed when Disney found guests weren't using it and instead were cutting through the Grand Californian's lobby to get to Disney's California Adventure, Disneyland Park, and Downtown Disney. We found it fastest to cut through the Grand Californian's lobby, exit on the Downtown Disney side, and walk the rest of the way. The monorail at Downtown Disney is always an option, too. Note that a double-decker jitney used to stop at the hotel to shuttle guests to the parks, but we've since learned it closed after September 11 due to security issues. Parking is available in a multi-level lot behind the hotel, and it's included in the $10/night resort access fee (see page 35). Valet parking is available for $12/day. Airport buses stop just outside the hotel. Ask at Guest Services about shuttles to other parks.

Making the Most
of Disney's Paradise Pier Hotel

Guests with park views may enjoy watching **Disney's Electrical Parade** from their window in the evenings. Check the park schedule for dates and times. Also check your room TV for a channel with parade music! If you're lucky, you may even get to see the Disneyland fireworks from your room.

Guests with **concierge-level rooms** receive a special check-in, access to a lounge on the second floor with snacks and drinks, and turndown service. Concierge rooms also have DVD players—ask at check-in about borrowing DVDs during your stay.

Rollaway beds and cribs may be requested free of charge. Keep in mind that the sofa in your room folds over into a twin-size bed.

Don't be shy about going over to the **Disneyland Hotel** to use their facilities, such as the restaurants and the Fantasy Waters show. Unfortunately this does not include the Never Land Pool complex (unless the Paradise Pier pool is closed).

Good deals can be found here through online hotel clearinghouses like Expedia (http://www.expedia.com). The least expensive rates show up in their system only about three months to 10 days in advance of your arrival date, so this is an excellent option if your trip is arranged at the last minute. You'll find some helpful tips on booking a room through Expedia at http://www.mousesavers.com/dlresorts.html.

Some guests (like us) prefer to stay here before **moving up** to a pricier hotel later in the trip. If you do this, just ask the bell staff to transfer your luggage to your new Disney hotel and allow a few hours for it to arrive.

There is no **guest laundry** at Paradise Pier Hotel, but you can walk over to the Disneyland Hotel and use their laundry (see map on page 42).

Paradise Pier doesn't have quite the **same charm** as the Disneyland Hotel or the Grand Californian, except for its wonderful park views. This is an excellent choice for those who want a good deal but still want to stay "on property," as well as those who prefer peace and quiet after a long day. We really enjoyed it!

This hotel is "on property," but you must **cross a city street** to get to the parks.

The hotel has 30,000 sq. ft. of **meeting space**, plus a business center.

Check-in time is 3:00 pm. Check-out time is 11:00 am.

Ratings are explained on page 36.

Our Value Ratings:		Our Magic Ratings:		Readers' Ratings:
Quality:	8/10	Theme:	5/10	24% fell in love with it
Accessibility:	8/10	Amenities:	5/10	51% liked it well enough
Affordability:	8/10	Fun Factor:	5/10	12% had mixed feelings
Overall Value:	**8/10**	**Overall Magic:**	**5/10**	13% were disappointed

Paradise Pier Hotel is enjoyed by...	(rated by both authors and readers)	
Younger Kids: ❤❤	Young Adults: ❤❤❤	Families: ❤❤❤
Older Kids: ❤❤❤	Mid Adults: ❤❤❤❤❤	Couples: ❤❤❤❤❤
Teenagers: ❤❤❤❤	Mature Adults: ❤❤❤❤❤	Singles: ❤❤❤❤

Sidebar: Planning · Getting There · Staying in Style · Touring · Feasting · Making Magic · Index · Notes & More · TIPS · NOTES · RATINGS

Planning

Getting There

Staying in Style

Touring

Feasting

Making Magic

Index

Notes & More

Finding Your Place at Disney's Paradise Pier Hotel

PARADISE PIER HOTEL MAP

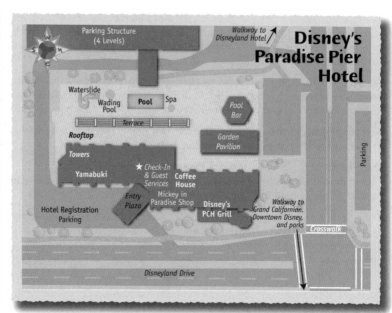

BEST LOCATIONS

In our opinion, the rooms with views of Disney's California Adventure are well worth the extra money. The day and night views of Disney's California Adventure are the most magical of any Disney hotel. Otherwise, you just end up overlooking the no-frills pool and the city smog. **Upper-level park views** are the best—we loved our room on the ninth floor (see photo on page 48). If you can't afford the extra up front for the park view, inquire about an upgrade when you check in. If you expect to use the pool often, consider one of the **concierge rooms with a patio** on the third floor. These are the only rooms with patios and they're great when you're hanging out at the pool. Like the Disneyland Hotel, Paradise Pier has one-bedroom suites—if you're just looking for extra space for the kids, consider getting two connecting rooms instead and save some money. The concierge rooms on the fourteenth and fifteenth floors offer the best views—you can see for miles on a clear day.

RATES

2006 Sample Room Rates

Rack rates—prices change by season

Room Type	Rate	Room Type	Rate
Standard City/Pool View	$160	Concierge City/Pool View	$260
Theme Park View	$210	Concierge Park View	$280
One-Bedroom Family Suite	$445	Two-Bedroom Suite	$570

The above rates do not include 15% hotel tax or the $10/night resort access fee. Rates vary by season—see chart on page 14 for seasons.

INFO

Disney's Paradise Pier Hotel

✉ 1717 Disneyland Drive, Anaheim, CA 92802

📞 Phone: 714-999-0990 📠 Fax: 714-776-5763

📋 For reservations, call 714-956-MICKEY (714-956-6425)

Good Neighbor Hotels

As you can imagine, the three official Disney hotels just can't hold all of the overnight guests. So Disney created a "Good Neighbor" program for area hotels to help guests decide where to stay among the hundreds of choices. At last count, 43 hotels **met Disney's standards** and received the "Good Neighbor" stamp of approval. These range from motels and "value" hotels to all-suite and deluxe resorts. Most are very close to Disneyland; some are even closer than Disney's hotels. All are available through Walt Disney Travel Co. packages (see page 37).

While the Good Neighbor hotels are "off property" and generally lacking in Disney magic, many of them offer **unique features**. For example, several allow pets, offer complimentary breakfasts, evening receptions, or Kids Suites. Plus, they're often less expensive than the Disney hotels. Alas, the Good Neighbor hotels do not offer the special perks that Disney hotel guests get (as described on page 32), unless you purchase a Disney package.

On the following 13 pages, we offer **detailed descriptions** of each of these 43 Good Neighbor hotels. This is still a long list, so to help you hone in on the one that's right for you, we've created a feature comparison chart on the next page. You'll also find the map below helpful if you're looking for a particular location (the locator codes in the colored circles on the map correspond to the codes on the following pages).

Please note that each year, the list of Good Neighbor hotels changes a bit—some drop out of the program, others are added, but most stay. To check the latest list, call 714-956-6425 or check http://www.disneyland.com and do a search for "Good Neighbor hotels."

Note: Sample hotel rates were obtained at Expedia (http://www.expedia.com).

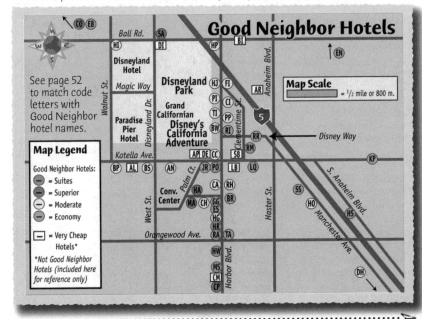

Good Neighbor Hotels

See page 52 to match code letters with Good Neighbor hotel names.

Map Scale = ½ mile or 800 m.

Map Legend

Good Neighbor Hotels:
- = Suites
- = Superior
- = Moderate
- = Economy
- = Very Cheap Hotels*

*Not Good Neighbor Hotels (included here for reference only)

Planning

Getting There

Staying in Style

Touring

Feasting

Making Magic

Index

Notes & More

Good Neighbor Hotel Comparisons

Name Color Codes:
Suite Hotel
Superior Hotel
Moderate Hotel
Economy Hotel

Name	Map code	Page number	Total rooms	Refrigerator [s=some]	Microwave [s=some]	On-site restaurants	Free breakfast	Room service	Swimming pools	Whirlpool spa	Pets accepted	Self parking	Valet parking	Shuttle to Disney	Starting rates
Anabella	AN	59	359	✓	–	1	–	✓	2	✓	–	Free	–	$3	$79
Best Western Anaheim Inn	BW	59	88	✓	✓	–	–	–	1	✓	–	Free	–	$3	$89
Best Western Park Place Inn	PP	59	199	✓	✓	–	✓	–	1	✓	–	Free	–	$3	$84
Best Western Pavilions	BP	59	99	s	–	–	–	–	1	✓	–	Free	–	$3	$78
Best Western Raffles Inn	BR	64	108	✓	–	✓	–	–	1	✓	–	Free	–	$3	$110
Best Western Stovall's Inn	BS	60	199	s	s	–	–	–	1	✓	–	Free	–	$3	$90
Candy Cane Inn	CC	60	172	✓	s	–	✓	–	1	✓	–	Free	–	Free	$82
Carousel Inn & Suites	CI	60	131	✓	✓	–	–	–	1	✓	–	Free	–	–	$59
Clarion Hotel Anaheim Resort	CH	61	284	✓	s	2	✓	–	1	–	✓	$10	–	$3	$82
Coast Anaheim Hotel	CA	61	499	s	–	2	–	✓	1	✓	✓	$8	$13	$3	$79
Courtyard Anaheim Buena Park	CO	57	145	✓	–	2	–	–	1	✓	–	Free	–	Free	$114
Crowne Plaza Resort Anaheim	CP	57	384	✓	–	1	–	✓	1	✓	–	Free	$10	Free	$103
Doubletree Hotel	DH	61	454	s	–	1	–	✓	1	✓	–	Free	$10	Free	$125
Embassy Suites Anaheim–North	EN	53	222	✓	✓	1	✓	✓	1	✓	✓	Free	–	Free	$129
Embassy Suites Anaheim–South	ES	53	375	✓	✓	1	✓	✓	1	✓	–	Free	–	$3	$119
Embassy Suites Buena Park	EB	53	199	✓	✓	1	✓	–	1	✓	–	Free	–	Free	$105
Fairfield Inn Anaheim	FI	61	467	✓	–	2	–	–	1	✓	–	Free	–	Free	$107
Hampton Inn Suites Garden Grove	GG	54	172	✓	✓	–	✓	–	1	✓	–	Free	–	$3	$79
Hilton Anaheim	HA	57	1572	–	–	4	–	✓	2	✓	✓	$11	17	$3	$149
Hilton Garden Inn	HG	62	169	✓	✓	1	–	✓	1	✓	–	Free	–	$3	$105
Hilton Suites Anaheim-Orange	HS	54	230	✓	✓	1	✓	✓	2	✓	–	Free	–	Free	$119
Holiday Inn Anaheim Resort	HO	62	264	✓	–	1	–	✓	1	✓	–	Free	–	$3	$75
Holiday Inn at the Park	HP	62	235	s	–	1	–	✓	1	✓	–	Free	–	$3	$61
Holiday Inn Hotel & Suites	HI	62	255	s	s	1	–	✓	1	✓	–	Free	–	$3	$67
Homewood Suites by Hilton	HW	54	165	✓	✓	–	✓	–	1	✓	–	Free	–	Free	$159
Howard Johnson Hotel	HJ	63	318	✓	–	1	–	–	1	✓	–	Free	–	$3	$99
Hyatt Regency Orange County	HR	54	654	✓	✓	4	–	✓	2	✓	✓	$12	$15	Free	$89
Jolly Roger Hotel	JR	64	58	s	–	1	–	–	1	–	–	Free	–	$3	$83
Katella Palms Hotel	KP	64	234	s	–	1	–	–	1	✓	–	Free	–	Free	$69
La Quinta Inn & Suites	LQ	55	130	✓	✓	–	✓	–	1	✓	–	Free	–	$3	$78
Marriott Anaheim	MA	58	1000	s	s	4	–	✓	2	✓	✓	$13	$20	$3	$159
Marriott Anaheim Suites	MS	55	371	✓	✓	2	–	✓	1	✓	✓	Free	$12	$3	$149
Park Inn & Suites	PI	63	121	✓	✓	–	–	–	1	✓	–	Free	–	–	$91
Portofino Inn & Suites	PO	55	190	s	s	–	–	–	1	✓	–	Free	–	$3	$70
Radisson Hotel Maingate	RH	63	314	–	–	1	–	✓	1	✓	–	$10	–	$3	$117
Ramada Inn Maingate	RI	64	185	–	–	–	–	✓	1	✓	–	Free	–	$3	$69
Red Roof Inn Anaheim	RR	64	235	s	s	–	–	–	1	✓	–	Free	–	$3	$49
Residence Inn Anaheim Resort	RA	56	200	✓	✓	–	✓	–	2	✓	–	Free	–	Free	$112
Residence Inn Maingate	RM	56	200	✓	✓	–	✓	–	2	✓	–	Free	–	$3	$149
Sheraton Anaheim	SA	58	489	–	–	2	–	✓	1	✓	–	$10	–	Free	$125
Staybridge Suites	SS	56	143	✓	✓	–	✓	–	–	✓	–	Free	–	$3	$89
Travelodge Intl. Inn Anaheim	TA	64	120	✓	–	s	–	–	1	✓	–	Free	–	$3	$77
Tropicana Inn & Suites	TI	63	194	✓	✓	–	✓	–	1	✓	–	Free	–	–	$89

Good Neighbor Suite Hotels

Code	Hotel Name	Rates	Distance	Shuttle	Year Built	Renovated
EN	Embassy Suites Anaheim–North	$129+	6 mi.	Free	1987	1996

Lushly tropical, seven-story hotel with 222 suites. Enter via a garden atrium with waterfalls, koi fish ponds, and quaint bridges. All suites feature a living room with a sofa bed, a separate bedroom with a king bed (see floor plan) or two double beds, two 2-line telephones, two 25" TVs, refrigerator, microwave, wet bar, table and chairs, hair dryer, iron, and coffeemaker. High-speed Internet access available for $10/night. Hotel features a free, cooked-to-order breakfast in the atrium, cocktail reception nightly, fitness center, indoor pool, whirlpool spa, sundeck, dry sauna, and room service. An on-site restaurant, Gregory's, is open for lunch and dinner. Check-in time: 3:00 pm/check-out: 12:00 pm. Pets allowed ($50 non-ref. deposit). Self-parking (free). Disneyland is 15 minutes away via the free hourly shuttle (reservations needed). Address: 3100 E. Frontera, Anaheim, CA 92806. Phone: 714-632-1221. Web: http://www.esanaheim.com.

Code	Hotel Name	Rates	Distance	Shuttle	Year Built	Renovated
ES	Embassy Suites Anaheim–South	$119+	1 1/2 mi.	$3	2001	n/a

Closer to Disneyland than its northern cousin (see above), this newly built, 14-story hotel has an "exotic jungle" theme. All 375 suites open to a lush atrium in the center of the hotel and feature a living room with a sofa bed and a private bedroom. Three suites are available: one king bed (4 adults) is 442 sq. ft. (see above floor plan), two doubles (see floor plan on the right), or one double/one queen (6 adults) is 481 sq. ft.. Additional guest amenities include two telephones, two TVs, refrigerator, microwave, table and chairs, coffeemaker, complimentary cooked-to-order breakfast, evening manager's reception, room service, fitness center, arcade, outdoor pool, and whirlpool spa. High-speed Internet access available for $10/night. Free shuttle bus departs every 30 minutes. The Serengeti Grill is the on-site restaurant (11:00 am–11:00 pm). Check-in time: 3:00 pm/check-out: 12:00 pm. No pets allowed. Self-parking is free (no valet parking). Address: 11767 Harbor Blvd., Garden Grove, CA 92840. Phone: 714-539-3300. Web: http://www.embassysuites.com.

Code	Hotel Name	Rates	Distance	Shuttle	Year Built	Renovated
EB	Embassy Suites Buena Park	$105	6 mi.	Free	1982	1997

If you expect to spend a lot of time at Knott's Berry Farm, this all-suite hotel is within walking distance. The 199 suites are arranged around a four-story, open-air courtyard. Guest rooms feature a living room with a sofa bed and a private bedroom with either one king or two doubles. Amenities include table and chairs, two telephones, two TVs, Sony PlayStation, refrigerator, microwave, coffeemaker, free breakfast, evening reception, room service, fitness center, arcade, outdoor pool, and a whirlpool spa. Le Bistro is the on-site restaurant, open for lunch and dinner. Free hourly shuttle bus to Disneyland. Check-in time: 3:00 pm/check-out: 12:00 pm. Free parking. Address: 7762 Beach Blvd., Buena Park, CA 90620. Phone: 714-739-5600. Web: http://www.embassysuites.com.

Planning

Getting There

Staying in Style

Touring

Feasting

Making Magic

Index

Notes & More

Good Neighbor Suite Hotels *(continued)*

Code Hotel Name	Rates	Distance	Shuttle	Year Built	Renovated

GG Hampton Inn Suites Garden Grove $79 1 1/2 mi. $3 1999 n/a

This comfortable, modern hotel has bright, clean rooms and suites. In addition to a free hot breakfast buffet, every room has refrigerator, microwave, and coffeemaker for convenient, quick meals. In-room entertainment includes cable TV, pay-per-view movies, and Sony Playstation. And if you need to get online, there is free high-speed Internet in the rooms and wireless Internet in the public areas. With an outdoor heated pool and spa, fitness center, guest laundry, and convenience store, there is plenty to do when away from the parks. Free parking. Check-in time: 3:00 pm/check-out: 12:00 pm. Address: 11747 Harbor Blvd., Garden Grove, CA 92840. Phone: 714-703-8800. Web: http://www.hamptoninn.com.

HS Hilton Suites Anaheim-Orange $119 2 1/2 mi. Free 1989 2000

A full-service, 230-suite hotel with a 10-story atrium. The two-room suites offer a living room with sofa bed, table and chairs, wet bar, refrigerator, microwave, and coffeemaker, plus a separate bedroom with either one king bed or two doubles. All suites have 2-line phones, two TVs, VCR, Sony PlayStation, hair dryer, and iron. The hotel features two pools (indoor and outdoor), sauna, sundeck, whirlpool spa, fitness center, and room service. The Great American Grill is on-site. No free breakfast. Check-in time: 4:00 pm/check-out: 11:00 am. Parking is free. Address: 400 N. State College Blvd., Orange, CA 92868. Phone: 714-938-1111. Web: http://www.hilton.com.

HW Homewood Suites by Hilton $159 2 mi. Free 2000 n/a

This modern, 7-story hotel's 165 spacious suites have separate living rooms and full kitchens and sleep up to six people. Relax after a long day in the parks with HBO, the Disney Channel, pay-per-view movies, and video games. Or stay connected with Web TV and free high-speed Internet access. Enjoy social hour by the fireplace in the lodge (Monday-Thursday 5:00-7:00 pm) and relax in the guest library. The on-site exercise facility, large pool, and wading pool for children are great for working off the complimentary hot breakfast buffet. Check-in time: 3:00 pm/check-out: 12:00 pm. Address: 12005 Harbor Blvd., Garden Grove, CA 92840. Phone: 714-740-1800. Web: http://homewoodsuites.hilton.com.

HR Hyatt Regency Orange County $89 1 1/4 mi. Free 1986 2004

Rows of towering palm trees and a 17-story atrium welcome you to this resort with a wide variety of accommodations (654 guest rooms), including Kids Suites with bunk beds and two-bedroom suites that sleep up to eight. Rooms feature pillowtop mattresses, TV, desk, coffeemaker, hair dryer, iron, ironing board, and voice mail, plus turndown service and bathrobes (on request). Enjoy your time away from the parks with cable movie channels, pay-per-view movies, two pools, tennis courts, fitness center, video arcade, and game room. Walk next door and practice your swing at the driving range. Dine in several restaurants, including the California Grill, Networks Lounge, Starbucks, and Pizza Hut Express. Guest laundry facilities are not available. Pets are allowed (restrictions and deposit may apply). Self-parking is $12/night, valet is $15/night. Check-in time: 3:00 pm/check-out: 12:00 pm. Address: 11999 Harbor Blvd., Garden Grove, CA 92840. Phone: 714-750-1234 or 800-809-1956. Web: http://orangecounty.hyatt.com.

Good Neighbor Suite Hotels *(continued)*

Code	Hotel Name	Rates	Distance	Shuttle	Year Built	Renovated
LQ	**La Quinta Inn & Suites**	**$78**	**1 mi.**	**$3**	**1992**	**2004**

Located just four blocks from Disneyland, this 130-suite, 5-story hotel has a retro California feel. Each spacious suite (350 sq. ft.) has a private bedroom with either one king bed or two double beds, French doors, queen sofa bed, two armchairs, two TVs, microwave, refrigerator, 2-line phones, in-room safe (extra fee applies), and complimentary high-speed Internet access. Kids Suites are also available with one king bed in the first bedroom, one bunk bed and an activity table in the second bedroom. There's also a Family Suite option at 450 sq. ft. with two bathrooms. Hotel amenities include a covered, heated, outdoor pool, whirlpool spa, 24-hour fitness center, guest laundry, and complimentary continental breakfast. No restaurant on property, but several are in walking distance. The 4th-floor gift shop sells Disney merchandise at good discounts. Pets up to 50 lbs. are accepted (no fee/deposit). Self-parking is free. Check-in time: 3:00 pm/check-out: 12:00 pm. Address: 1752 Clementine St., Anaheim, CA 92802. Phone: 714-635-5000 or 800-725-1661. Web: http://www.laquinta.com.

Code	Hotel Name	Rates	Distance	Shuttle	Year Built	Renovated
MS	**Marriott Anaheim Suites**	**$149**	**2 mi.**	**$3**	**2002**	**n/a**

This elegant, all-suite hotel opened in November 2002. The 371 suites come in three layouts: King suites have a king bed, hold four persons, and are 440 sq. ft (see floor plan). Family suites have two doubles, hold six persons, and are 600 sq. ft. Executive suites have a king, hold four persons, and are 600+ sq. ft. All suites have a living room with a sofa bed, down comforters, feather pillows, wet bar, desk, two 2-line speakerphones, two TVs, in-room safe, iron, high-speed Internet access ($9.95/day), and, available on request, coffeemaker, refrigerator, and microwave. The 14-story, luxury hotel features a free, cook-to-order breakfast, fitness center, outdoor pool, whirlpool spa, and room service. The on-site restaurants, Five Feet (California cuisine) and Starbucks (coffeehouse), are open all day. Pets allowed ($15 each). Self-parking (free), plus valet parking ($12). The Disneyland Resort is 5 minutes away via the ART shuttle (every 30 minutes). Check-in time: 4:00 pm/check-out: 12:00 pm. Address: 12015 Harbor Blvd., P.O. Box 61009, Anaheim, CA 92803. Phone: 714-750-1000. Web: http://www.marriott.com/snaas.

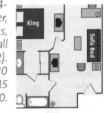

Code	Hotel Name	Rates	Distance	Shuttle	Year Built	Renovated
PO	**Portofino Inn & Suites**	**$70**	**³⁄₄ mi.**	**$3**	**2000**	**n/a**

This popular hotel is smack-dab across from Disneyland. The Italian-themed hotel offers 78 deluxe rooms and 112 suites, each with a 2-line phone, iron and ironing board, hair dryer, and cable TV. The suites add a sofa bed, microwave, refrigerator, two vanity areas, shower massager, French doors, and king beds. Kid Suites (see floor plan) have bunk beds and activity tables, too. Hotel amenities include heated outdoor pool, whirlpool spa, arcade, fitness center, guest laundry, and complimentary parking. High-speed Internet access is $10/day. The Jolly Roger Cafe is next door (kids eat free with paying adults). Disney packages with tickets are available. Conference facilities are available, and this hotel specializes in youth groups (which could lead to crowded conditions). Check-in time: 3:00 pm/check-out: 12:00 pm. Address: 1831 South Harbor Blvd., Anaheim, CA 92802. Phone: 714-782-7600 or 800-398-3963. Web: http://www.portofinoinnanaheim.com.

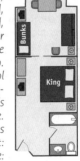

Planning

Getting There

Staying in Style

Touring

Feasting

Making Magic

Index

Notes & More

Good Neighbor Suite Hotels *(continued)*

Code Hotel Name	Rates	Distance	Shuttle	Year Built	Renovated
RM Residence Inn Maingate	**$149**	**1 blk.**	**$3**	**1988**	**2004**

© MediaMarx, Inc.

Upon entering through the Gatehouse you are greeted by a roaring fire, colorful aquarium, and friendly front desk staff. The 200 suites vary from one-room studios to two-bedroom/two-bath options. Each suite offers a private entrance, sofa bed, fully equipped kitchens including full-size stove, microwave, refrigerator, dishwasher, garbage disposal, toaster, and coffeemaker. Each suite also offers 1–2 televisions with cable and pay-per-view or Nintendo 64 options, data ports (may incur extra charge), ironing boards, and hair dryers. Each morning the serene setting of the Tea Garden features a free continental breakfast and then it's Social Hour in the afternoons (5:00–7:00 pm, Monday–Thursday). Other features are a regular and toddler pool, two whirlpool spas, sport court, free daily newspaper, free self-parking, and a "First Nighter Kit" (coffee, popcorn, fire log, etc.). Check-in time: 4:00 pm/check-out: 12:00 pm. Small pets allowed for $10/day ($40–$60 fee); only one pet per room. Address: 1700 S. Clementine, Anaheim, CA 92802. Phone: 714-533-3555. Web: http://www.residenceinn.com.

RA Residence Inn Anaheim Resort	**$112**	**1 ¼ mi.**	**Free**	**2003**	**n/a**

© MediaMarx, Inc.

Bright colors and light woods decorate the studio, one-, and two-bedroom suites at this hotel. Enjoy the full kitchen, free high-speed Internet, morning newspaper, and cable TV with CNN, ESPN, and HBO. Kids suites have bunk beds. Start your day with the free hot breakfast buffet, and end it with snacks and drinks on Monday–Thursday evenings. Splash in the pools, relax in the whirlpool spa, and play on the sport court or in the video game room. Books, newspapers, and board games are available at the front desk. Free self-parking. Pets allowed for a $75 fee. Valet service and guest laundry facilities available. Check-in time: 3:00 pm/check-out: 12:00 pm. Address: 11931 Harbor Blvd., Anaheim, CA 92840. Phone: 714-591-4000 or 800-308-5440. Web: http://www.residenceinnanaheim.com.

SS Staybridge Suites	**$89**	**1 ¾ mi.**	**$3**	**2001**	**n/a**

© MediaMarx, Inc.

A flagstone fireplace and dark woods provide a warm welcome to this 143-suite hotel with rooms that sleep up to eight people. Every room has fully equipped kitchens, cable TV, DVD/VCR player, coffeemaker, hair dryer, iron, ironing board, and complimentary high-speed Internet access. Start your morning with the free hot breakfast buffet, then relax at the evening sundowner socials with hors d'oeuvres and beverages (Tuesday–Thursday, 5:30–7:30 pm). Put some hot dogs on the barbecue and enjoy the outdoor pool and spa. The American Brasserie Restaurant is adjacent to the hotel. Fitness buffs enjoy the fitness center and sports court, and free guest laundry facilities let you pack light. Note that the $3 ART shuttle pick-up/drop-off location is next door at the Holiday Inn. Pets permitted for a $150 nonrefundable fee. Check-in time: 3:00 pm/check-out: 12:00 pm. Address: 1855 S. Manchester Ave., Anaheim, CA 92802. Phone: 714-748-7700 or 1-800-238-8000. Web: http://www.staybridge.com.

Good Neighbor Superior Hotels

Code	Hotel Name	Rates	Distance	Shuttle	Year Built	Renovated
CO	**Courtyard Anaheim Buena Park**	$114	6 mi.	Free	1986	2003

Near Knott's Berry Farm, this recently renovated, two-story hotel has 145 spacious and comfortable rooms. After a long day in the parks, enjoy free in-room high-speed Internet access, and cable TV including CNN, ESPN, HBO, and pay-per-view movies. There's also a coffeemaker, iron, ironing board, hair dryer, 2-line phone, and refrigerator. Then work off extra energy at the fitness center, splash in the heated outdoor pool, and soothe stiff muscles in the whirlpool spa. The Courtyard Café serves breakfast and The Market is open 24 hours for breakfast, lunch, and dinner. Several restaurants are nearby. Complimentary coffee and newspapers are found in the lobby. Coin laundry facilities and valet laundry services are available. Free parking; no pets are allowed. Complimentary, limited shuttle has morning pick-up at 8:00, 9:00, and 10:00 am with a 5:00, 6:00, or 7:00 pm return. Check-in time: 3:00 pm/check-out: 1:00 pm. Address: 7621 Beach Blvd., Buena Park, CA 90620. Phone: 714-670-6600 or 800-321-2211. Web: http://www.marriott.com/courtyard.

Code	Hotel Name	Rates	Distance	Shuttle	Year Built	Renovated
CP	**Crowne Plaza Resort Anaheim**	$103	2½ mi.	Free	2000	n/a

Palm trees and fountains accent the grounds of this Mediterranean-style resort. It's easy to relax in one of the 384 rooms with Spanish-style furnishings of natural woods, terra cotta, and wrought iron along with marble accents. Each room has a coffeemaker, mini-bar, 2-line phone, in-room safe, iron, ironing board, hair dryer, and Sony PlayStation. Check e-mail with in-room high-speed T-1 Internet access (included in $7/day/person resort access fee), access Wi-Fi in the lobby, and watch cable TV with CNN, ESPN, HBO, and pay per view movies. Kids like playing in the game room and in the heated outdoor pool, while adults can relax sore feet in the whirlpool spa and work out in the fitness center. The Copa de Oro Restaurant serves a Mexican buffet and room service is available. Guest laundry facilities available. Self-parking included in $9 daily resort access fee; valet parking is $10/day and $12/overnight. Check-in time: 4:00 pm/check-out: 12:00 pm. Address: 12021 Harbor Blvd., Garden Grove, CA 92840. Phone: 714-867-5555 or 866-888-8891. Web: http://anaheim-crowne-plaza.com.

Code	Hotel Name	Rates	Distance	Shuttle	Year Built	Renovated
HA	**Hilton Anaheim**	$149	1½ mi.	$3	1984	1997

Cheerful colors and modern art decorate this high-rise hotel adjacent to the Anaheim Convention Center. Popular with conventioneers, this hotel offers many amenities including several restaurants, an award-winning health club and spa, and a year-round children's program. The 1,572 guest rooms feature floor-to-ceiling windows, hair dryer, iron, and voice mail. If the in-room coffeemaker isn't enough, get your espresso at Starbucks in the lobby. Play in the outdoor and indoor swimming pools or on the putting green, then relax in one of the four whirlpool spas on three garden decks. There's also an indoor basketball court. In-room entertainment includes high-speed Internet access (fee), cable TV, and pay-per-view movies. The on-site restaurant, Pavla, serves Northern Italian cuisine for dinner only. Other dining options include Cafe Oasis (all day), The Sushi Bar (dinner), The Gazebo (the poolside cafe for lunch), and room service. We tried this hotel in August 2005 and found it adequate, though it did have a large, impersonal feeling. A $55 million renovation begins spring 2006. Small pets allowed (no charge; 25 lbs. or less). Self-parking is $11/day; valet parking is $17/day. Check-in time: 3:00 pm/check-out: 11:00 am. Address: 777 Convention Way, Anaheim, CA 92802. Phone: 714-750-4321 or 800-932-3322. Web: http://www.hilton.com/hotels/SNAAHHH.

Planning

Getting There

Staying in Style

Touring

Feasting

Making Magic

Index

Notes & More

Good Neighbor Superior Hotels (continued)

Code Hotel Name	Rates	Distance	Shuttle	Year Built	Renovated
MA Marriott Anaheim	**$159**	**1 ½ mi.**	**$3**	**1981**	**2006**

© MediaMarx, Inc.

Adjacent to the Anaheim Convention Center, this large, 19-story high-rise hotel with more than 1,000 rooms is popular with convention travelers. All rooms have a coffeemaker, iron, ironing board, hair dryer, in-room safe, 2-line phone. You can also request a small refrigerator and microwave for your room. There is plenty of in-room entertainment, including cable TV with CNN, ESPN, HBO, pay-per-view movies and video games, plus high-speed Internet access for an extra fee. With four family-friendly restaurants including Café del Sol (breakfast buffet, plus lunch and dinner), Pizza Hut (lunch and dinner), JW's Steakhouse (dinner only), and Starbucks Marketplace (all day), everyone can find something to eat. Play in the two swimming pools (one indoor, one outdoor), two whirlpool spas, arcade, fitness center, and sauna. Small pets allowed ($50 deposit). Self-parking is $13/day; valet parking is $20/day. There's also a Hertz rental car desk here. Note that guest rooms and corridors are scheduled for renovation Aug.–Dec. 2006. Check-in time: 4:00 pm/check-out: 12:00 pm. Address: 700 W. Convention Way, Anaheim, CA 92802. Phone: 714-750-8000 or 800-228-9290. Web: http://marriottanaheim.com.

Code Hotel Name	Rates	Distance	Shuttle	Year Built	Renovated
SA Sheraton Anaheim	**$125**	**¾ mi.**	**Free**	**1969**	**2003**

© MediaMarx, Inc.

After spending the day visiting Sleeping Beauty's castle, spend the night at this unique castle-themed hotel with a stone turret and a stream filled with koi fish meandering through the lobby. Some of the 489 guest rooms at this 13-acre property even have views of the park. Standard guest rooms here are very large at about 500 sq. ft. and each offers one king or two queen beds, a coffeemaker, and a hair dryer. Watch cable TV and pay-per-view movies. If you want to get online, be sure to request a room that offers high-speed Internet access. Eateries on site include the popular, indoor/outdoor Garden Court Bistro, the California Deli, and 24-hour room service. Additional facilities include a sunny outdoor pool, whirlpool spa, fitness center, room service, and arcade. Parking is $10/day. Dogs under 20 lbs. are accepted for a $25/day fee. The complimentary shuttle picks up every half hour. Note that this hotel is scheduled for a complete renovation to be finished by mid-2006. Check-in time: 3:00 pm/check-out: 12:00 pm. Address: 900 S. Disneyland Dr., Anaheim, CA 92802. Phone: 714-778-1700. Web: http://www.sheraton.com.

Hotels Offering $3 ART Shuttles

Most of the hotels we've listed having a $3 shuttle are using ART, described in detail on page 23. Some (but not all) of those hotels that offer a "free" shuttle are including the price of an ART pass into your room rate. And plenty of other hotels that aren't Disney "Good Neighbor hotels" are near ART stops, too—you should be able to buy ART passes at your hotel's front desk. When in doubt, call the hotel and ask them what type of shuttle service they offer. You can also find ART route maps at http://www.rideart.org or 888-364-ARTS.

© MediaMarx, Inc.

Good Neighbor Moderate Hotels

Code Hotel Name	Rates	Distance	Shuttle	Year Built	Renovated
AN Anabella	$79	1 mi.	$3	2001	n/a

© MediaMarx, Inc.

Splashing fountains, towering palm trees, and tile patios create a lush oasis at this mission-style hotel. From standard rooms to deluxe Kids Suites, each room has a private patio, granite bathroom, refrigerator, tea/coffeemaker, and safe. Be aware that there are a handful of extra-small rooms at this hotel, however. Relax in the room with pay-per-view movies and video games, high-speed Internet access (fee) plus free HBO, CNN, and Disney Channels. Travelers without kids appreciate the adults-only pool, and there is a second pool for families. Get pampered at the Bella Nail Salon & Spa gift shop, then try the whirlpool spa, fitness center, and patio bar. Dine at the Tangerine Grill & Patio Restaurant. Small guest laundry available.
Check-in time: 3:00 pm/check-out: 11:00 am. Address: 1030 W. Katella Ave., Anaheim, CA 92802. Phone: 714-905-1050 or 800-863-4888. Web: http://www.anabellahotel.com.

BW Best Western Anaheim Inn	$89	½ mi.	$3	1983	1999

© MediaMarx, Inc.

Palm trees and tile roofs create a tropical atmosphere at this hotel. Skip the shuttle and take a short walk down the block and across the street to Disneyland Resort. Each of the 88 rooms has a refrigerator, microwave, and coffee/tea maker for convenient snacks. In-room entertainment includes cable TV with HBO, ESPN, Disney, CNN, and MTV. For larger groups, kitchenettes and two-room family suites are available. Relax outside in the heated pool, sauna, and spa. Many restaurants are nearby, and there is a guest laundry. Free parking.
Check-in time: 3:00/check-out: 12:00 pm. Address: 1630 S. Harbor Blvd., Anaheim, CA 92802. Phone: 714-774-1050 or 800-854-8177 ext. 1. Web: http://www.anaheiminn.com.

PP Best Western Park Place Inn	$84	¼ mi.	$3	1987	2001

© MediaMarx, Inc.

This hotel is the closest you can get to Disneyland without staying on property. The crosswalk is right outside your hotel room door, and the free continental breakfast buffet is great for a quick bite on your way out. Every one of the 199 rooms is a mini-suite, featuring a separate sitting area with sofa bed, a microwave, refrigerator and coffee/tea maker. In-room entertainment includes cable TV and pay-per-view movies. Enjoy the outdoor heated pool, whirlpool spa, and sauna. Guest laundry facilities available. Free parking. Check-in
time: 3:00 pm/check-out: 12:00 pm. Address: 1544 S. Harbor Blvd. Anaheim, CA 92802. Phone: 714-776-4800 or 800-854-8177 ext. 4. Web: http://www.parkplaceinnandminisuites.com.

BP Best Western Pavilions	$78	1 mi.	$3	1963	2000

© MediaMarx, Inc.

Tropical landscaping creates a palm tree oasis at this 99-room hotel. The outdoor heated pool, whirlpool spa, and sauna are perfect for relaxing after a long day at the parks. Sit under the palms with your laptop and enjoy the free wireless Internet access, available in all public areas and in some rooms. Bright rooms have cable TV with premium channels, hair dryers, irons, and coffeemakers—refrigerators are available for $8/night. Parking is free, and kids eat free at the Denny's Restaurant next door. No pets. Check-in time: 3:00 pm/check-out: 12:00 pm. Address: 1176 W. Katella Ave., Anaheim, CA 92802. Phone: 714-776-0140 or 800-854-8175. Web: http://www.pavilionshotel.com.

Planning

Getting There

Staying in Style

Touring

Feasting

Making Magic

Index

Notes & More

Good Neighbor Moderate Hotels *(continued)*

Code Hotel Name | Rates | Distance | Shuttle | Year Built | Renovated

| BS | **Best Western Stovall's Inn** | **$90** | **³/₄ mi.** | **$3** | **1969** | **2000** |

The grounds of this hotel feature whimsical topiary animals that rival those at "it's a small world" at Disneyland Park. Fuel up each morning with the free continental breakfast and relax in the afternoon in one of two pools, two whirlpool spas, or the wading pool. Every room has cable TV with CNN, ESPN, and Disney Channel. Microwaves and refrigerators are available for an extra charge. Work out in the fitness room, get online with free high-speed Internet access, and get last-minute shopping done at the gift shop. Free parking. No pets. Check-in time: 3:00 pm/check-out: 12:00 pm. Authors Jennifer and Dave stayed at this resort in June 2003 and found it clean and cheerful. Address: 1110 W. Katella Ave., Anaheim, CA 92802. Phone: 714-778-1880. Web: http://www.stovallsinn.com.

| CC | **Candy Cane Inn** | **$82** | **³/₄ mi.** | **Free** | **1957** | **1999** |

Built just two years after Disneyland opened, this 172-room hotel is known for the beautifully landscaped grounds and clean, sunny guest rooms with plantation shutters. Each room has a mini refrigerator, cozy down comforters, coffeemaker, hair dryer, iron, ironing board, and cable TV with Showtime and the Disney Channel. Splurge for an upgraded room and you'll get a microwave, video player with free video rentals, in-room breakfast, and late check-out (2:00 pm). All guests enjoy a complimentary continental breakfast buffet served poolside. Cool off in the outdoor pool, wading pool, and whirlpool spa. Free parking. Even though this hotel is within walking distance, the free shuttle is a welcome amenity at the end of a long day (you'll need your Candy Cane Inn room card to board the shuttle). Check-in time: 3:00 pm/check-out: 11:00 am. Address: 1747 S. Harbor Blvd., Anaheim, CA 92802. Phone: 714-774-5284 or 800-345-7057. Web: http://www.candycaneinn.net.

| CI | **Carousel Inn & Suites** | **$59** | **¹/₄ mi.** | **None** | **1985** | **2002** |

Start the day with a complimentary continental breakfast buffet in the Parkview Room, with a great panoramic view of the park. Then end it swimming in the rooftop, outdoor pool with a great view of the fireworks or spending quarters in the video game room. Each of the 131 guest rooms has a refrigerator, microwave, coffeemaker, and cable TV. Guest laundry facilities and valet service are available. Families wanting some extra space can reserve a two- or three-bedroom suite with two bathrooms. Free parking. Note: This hotel is undergoing some renovations at press time and is scheduled to be completed early spring 2006—the renovations will add a Quizno's eatery. Check-in time: 3:00 pm/check-out: 11:00 am. Address: 1530 S. Harbor Blvd., Anaheim, CA 92802. Phone: 714-758-0444 or 800-854-6767. Web: http://www.carouselinnandsuites.com.

Good Neighbor Moderate Hotels *(continued)*

Code	Hotel Name	Rates	Distance	Shuttle	Year Built	Renovated
CH	**Clarion Hotel Anaheim Resort**	$82	1½ mi.	$3	1972	1999

© MediaMarx, Inc.

An aquarium tank full of tropical fish greets you as you enter this 9-story hotel. Each of the 284 rooms offers a refrigerator, coffeemaker, hair dryer, iron, and ironing board. Both standard rooms and family suites are offered. Hotel amenities include a heated outdoor pool, sundeck, gift shop, arcade, and guest laundry. Two restaurants are on premises—Tivoli Gardens serves breakfast and lunch, and The Clubhouse Grill and Tavern offers dinner nightly. An Internet kiosk is located in the lobby. Check-in time: 4:00 pm/check-out: 11:00 am. Address: 616 W Convention Way, Anaheim, CA 92802. Phone: 714-750-3131 or 877-424-6423. Web: http://www.clarioninn.com.

Code	Hotel Name	Rates	Distance	Shuttle	Year Built	Renovated
CA	**Coast Anaheim Hotel**	$79	1 mi.	$3	1973	2006

© MediaMarx, Inc.

Relax on your private balcony overlooking a lush tropical pool and spa, or even the Disneyland Resort. Each of the 499 rooms has cable TV, pay-per-view movies, Sony PlayStation, refrigerator, and a coffeemaker. Refrigerators are available for a fee. Stay connected with wireless Internet service ($9.95/24 hours). After your workout in the fitness center, dine at one of two restaurants and enjoy cocktails in the lobby bar or poolside. Self-parking is $8/day; valet parking is $13/day. Pets are allowed for a $25 cleaning fee. Check-in time: 4:00 pm/check-out: 12:00 pm. Authors Jennifer and Dave stayed at this hotel and enjoyed a glorious view of Disney's California Adventure (see photo). Following its $32 million renovation in spring 2006, this hotel's name changes to "Sheraton Park Hotel." Address: 1855 S. Harbor Blvd., Anaheim, CA 92802 Phone: 714-750-1811 or 800-716-6199. Web: http://www.coasthotels.com/home/sites/anaheim.

© MediaMarx, Inc.

Code	Hotel Name	Rates	Distance	Shuttle	Year Built	Renovated
DH	**Doubletree Hotel**	$125	3 mi.	Free	1984	1997

The best thing about this hotel is the warm chocolate chip cookies everyone gets when checking in! The lobby has cascading waterfalls and there is a koi-filled private lagoon. The rooms offer standard amenities, including cable TV with CNN, ESPN, HBO, pay-per-view movies, and video games. All rooms have coffeemakers, and refrigerators are available for a fee. Relax at the outdoor pool and in the whirlpool spa, or get in shape on one of two lighted tennis courts and in the fitness center. Casual meals are served at the Café from 6:00 am to 10:00 pm. Parking is $8/day; valet parking is $10. Check-in time: 3:00 pm/check-out: 12:00 pm. Address: 100 The City Dr., Orange, CA 92868. Phone: 714-634-4500. Web: http://doubletree.hilton.com.

Code	Hotel Name	Rates	Distance	Shuttle	Year Built	Renovated
FI	**Fairfield Inn Anaheim**	$107	½ mi.	Free	1988	1998

© MediaMarx, Inc.

This hotel offers rooms within sight of the park, so be sure to ask for a room with a view! All of the 467 rooms have mini-refrigerators and coffeemakers. Entertainment includes cable TV, pay-per-view movies, and video games. After a day in the parks, swim in the heated outdoor pool or rest on the palm-shaded sun deck. Relax in the spa while the kids play in the game room. Free parking. Guest laundry facilities on site. Dining options include the Cafasia snack shop and Millie's Restaurant (see page 218). Check-in time: 4:00 pm/check-out: 12:00 pm. Address: 1460 S. Harbor Blvd., Anaheim, CA 92802. Phone: 714-772-6777 or 800-228-2800. Web: http://www.marriott.com.

Planning · Getting There · Staying in Style · Touring · Feasting · Making Magic · Index · Notes & More

Good Neighbor Moderate Hotels (continued)

Code Hotel Name	Rates	Distance	Shuttle	Year Built	Renovated
HG Hilton Garden Inn	**$105**	1 ¼ mi.	**$3**	1999	n/a

© MediaMarx, Inc.

Tropical plants and a fountain by the swimming pool provide a relaxing atmosphere at this 10-story hotel. Each of the 169 rooms has a refrigerator, microwave, and coffeemaker so it's easy to fix quick meals and snacks. In-room entertainment includes cable TV plus pay-per-view movies and video games. Complimentary in-room high-speed Internet access is available. In addition to the heated outdoor pool, there is a whirlpool spa, fitness center, guest laundry, 24-hour convenience store, business center, and the Great American Grill restaurant and lounge. Free parking. Check-in time: 3:00 pm/check-out: 12:00 pm. Address: 11777 Harbor Blvd., Garden Grove, CA 92840. Phone: 714-703-9100. Web: http://www.hiltongardeninn.com.

Code Hotel Name	Rates	Distance	Shuttle	Year Built	Renovated
HO Holiday Inn Anaheim Resort	**$75**	1 ¾ mi.	**$3**	2001	n/a

This recently built, 264-room resort is a full-service, "prototype" Holiday Inn sporting upgraded amenities and a resort feel. So if relaxing by the pool is in the vacation plans, consider this resort with a large outdoor heated pool shaped like mouse ears, a whirlpool spa, and the seasonal Cabana Bar. There is also a game room, fitness center, and sports court, along with the American Brasserie Restaurant for casual dining. Guest rooms include refrigerators, coffeemakers, cable TV with free CNN, ESPN, Disney, and HBO, and pay-per-view movies. In-room wi-fi Internet access is available. For midnight snacks and emergencies, there is a 24-hour convenience store. Check-in time: 3:00 pm/check-out: 12:00 pm. Address: 1915 S. Manchester Ave., Anaheim, CA 92802 Phone: 714-748-7777. Web: http://www.holiday-inn.com.

Code Hotel Name	Rates	Distance	Shuttle	Year Built	Renovated
HP Holiday Inn at the Park	**$61**	¾ mi.	**$3**	1984	1998

© MediaMarx, Inc.

If swimming is your favorite vacation pastime, this hotel has the only pool open 24 hours a day in the Anaheim resort area. Fiber-optic lighting, a cascading fountain, a children's play fountain, a whirlpool spa, and lush, tropical landscaping make this outdoor pool special. The 235 rooms have a coffeemaker, cable TV, and in-room pay-per-view movies. Suites and kids suites with bunk beds are available. There is also a full-service restaurant, fitness center, and a guest laundry on-site. Free parking. No pets. Check-in: 3:00 pm/check-out: 12:00 pm. Address: 1221 S. Harbor Blvd., Anaheim, CA 92805. Phone: 714-758-0900. Web: http://www.holiday-inn.com. Note: This hotel's name is changing to "Anaheim Palms Resort" in February 2006.

Code Hotel Name	Rates	Distance	Shuttle	Year Built	Renovated
HI Holiday Inn Hotel & Suites	**$67**	1 ¼ mi.	**$3**	1979	2001

The rhythmic splashing of an antique water wheel provides a relaxing backdrop to this 6-story hotel with old-fashioned western charm. The outdoor pool and whirlpool spa, fitness center, video arcade, and cowboy-themed lounge (The Silver Saloon) provide for relaxing afternoons. In-room amenities for the 255 guest rooms include a coffeemaker, cable TV, pay-per-view movies, video games, and high-speed Internet access. Suites sleep up to four and include kitchenettes. Guest laundry facilities are available and you can dine on-site at the Chaparral Café. Free parking. No pets are allowed. Check-in time: 3:00 pm/check-out: 11:00 am. Formerly the Conestoga Hotel. Address: 1240 S. Walnut, Anaheim, CA 92802. Phone: 714-535-0300. Web: http://www.holiday-inn.com.

Planning
Getting There
Staying in Style
Touring
Feasting
Making Magic
Index
Notes & More

Good Neighbor Moderate Hotels (continued)

Code Hotel Name	Rates	Distance	Shuttle	Year Built	Renovated
HJ **Howard Johnson Hotel**	**$99**	**¹/₂ mi.**	**$3**	**1965**	**2000**

This popular hotel is on seven acres of beautifully landscaped grounds, with a garden courtyard, two outdoor heated swimming pools, whirlpool spa, wading pool and a "Sprayground." Every colorful, contemporary room has free in-room high-speed Internet access, cable TV, pay-per-view movies and Sony PlayStation, a refrigerator, and a coffee/tea maker. Some rooms have vaulted ceilings, skylights, and large balconies, and suites are available. Enjoy the convenience of a gift shop, game room, tour desk, guest laundry, and Mimi's Café. Free parking. Check-in time: 3:00 pm/check-out: 12:00 pm. Address: 1380 S. Harbor Blvd., Anaheim, CA 92802. Phone: 714-776-6120. Web: http://www.hojoanaheim.com.

PI **Park Inn & Suites**	**$91**	**¹/₂ mi.**	**None**	**1994**	**2006**

One look at this English Tudor-style hotel and it feels like you're in Fantasyland. Wing chairs, dark woods, and Queen Anne furnishings add to the atmosphere. A free continental breakfast is served in the hospitality room. All rooms have refrigerators, coffeemakers, cable TV, and pay-per-view movies. Relax at the terrace-level pool and spa, and play in the game room. Several restaurants are nearby. Guest rooms are undergoing renovations and will be complete in summer 2006. Guest laundry. Free parking. Check-in time: 3:00 pm/Check-out: 11:00 am. Address: 1520 S. Harbor Blvd., Anaheim, CA 92802. Phone: 714-635-7275 or 800-670-7275. Web: http://www.parkinn.com.

RH **Radisson Hotel Maingate**	**$117**	**1 mi.**	**$3**	**1968**	**1998**

All the modern amenities available at this hotel make it popular with business people and families. The concierge tour desk will help you make your vacation memorable, and when you aren't at the parks you can enjoy the pool, fitness center, and video arcade. There is a restaurant and pub on-site, as well as self-laundry facilities. Every room has a coffeemaker, cable TV, plus pay-per-view movies and high-speed Internet access (fee). Parking is $10/day. Check-in time: 3:00 pm/check-out: 12:00 pm. Address: 1850 S. Harbor Blvd., Anaheim, CA 92802. Phone: 714-750-2801 or 800-624-6855. Web: http://www.radisson.com/anaheimca_maingate.

TI **Tropicana Inn & Suites**	**$89**	**¹/₄ mi.**	**None**	**1955**	**2004**

Built the same year that Disneyland opened, this two-story Mediterranean-style hotel is adjacent to the pedestrian walkway into the Disneyland Resort itself. The 194 recently renovated guest rooms offer a choice of one king, two queens, or suites with kitchens. All rooms have a refrigerator and microwave. Enjoy an Olympic-style pool with oversized whirlpool spa or just relax and soak up the sun. Free parking and complimentary continental breakfast. There is no restaurant at the hotel, but an International House of Pancakes is nearby, as are many other eateries (see page 218). Check-in time: 3:00 pm/check-out: 11:00 am. Pets are not allowed. Address: 1540 S. Harbor Blvd., Anaheim, CA 92802. Phone: 714-635-4082 or 800-828-4898. Web: http://www.tropicanainn-anaheim.com.

Planning · Getting There · Staying in Style · Touring · Feasting · Making Magic · Index · Notes & More

Good Neighbor Economy Hotels

Code	Hotel Name	Rates	Distance	Shuttle	Year Built	Renovated
BR	**Best Western Raffles Inn**	$108	1 mi.	$3	1985	2002

© MediaMarx, Inc.

This 108-room hotel offers both standard rooms and suites with granite vanities and Spanish tile bathrooms. All rooms have a microwave, refrigerator, coffeemaker, hair dryer, iron, ironing board, and cable TV. Complimentary continental breakfast is served daily. Amenities include an outdoor heated pool, whirlpool spa, free parking, guest laundry, and high-speed Internet access (for an extra fee). Check-in time: 3:00 pm/check-out: 11:00 am. Address: 2040 S. Harbor Blvd., Anaheim, CA 92802. Phone: 714-750-6100 or 800-654-0196. Web: http://www.bestwestern.com.

Code	Hotel Name	Rates	Distance	Shuttle	Year Built	Renovated
JR	**Jolly Roger Hotel**	$80	3/4 mi.	$3	1955	1997

Another 1955 classic! This popular hotel has a large heated outdoor pool and sundeck, gift shop, and fitness center next door. Each of the 58 rooms has cable TV and coffeemakers. Refrigerators on request. Check out the pirate ship model in the Jolly Roger Café (breakfast, lunch, and dinner; kids 10 and under eat free with each adult entree). Guest laundry. Free parking. $3 daily resort fee. Check-in time: 3:00 pm/check-out: 11:00 am. Address: 640 W. Katella Ave., Anaheim, CA 92802. Phone: 714-782-7500 or 888-296-5986. Web: http://www.jollyrogerhotel.com.

Code	Hotel Name	Rates	Distance	Shuttle	Year Built	Renovated
KP	**Katella Palms Hotel**	$69	2 mi.	Free	1975	2000

Formerly the Ramada Anaheim. Sharky, the friendly shark, lives in a 1,900-gallon aquarium in the lobby of this two-story hotel. Be sure to ask about the feeding schedule at the front desk! Rooms feature Thomasville furnishings and have wireless Internet access (extra fee), cable TV, and pay-per-view movies. Microwaves and refrigerators are available for a fee. There aren't any sharks in the outdoor pool and whirlpool spa, and there is a restaurant and sports bar on-site. Free parking. Check-in time: 3:00 pm/check-out: 11:00 am. Address: 1331 E. Katella Ave., Anaheim, CA 92805. Phone: 800-228-0586. Web: http://www.katellapalms.com.

Code	Hotel Name	Rates	Distance	Shuttle	Year Built	Renovated
RI	**Ramada Inn Maingate**	$69	1/2 mi.	$3	1974	1997

This hotel features a free continental breakfast daily and a large outdoor pool with a whirlpool spa. Each of the 185 guest rooms has a coffeemaker, hair dryer, iron, and ironing board. Pizza and Chinese food, as well as gift and specialty shops, are located on premises. Tony Roma's Restaurant is located next door. Includes continental breakfast daily. Guest laundry. Check-in time: 3:00 pm/check-out: 12:00 pm. Address: 1650 S. Harbor Blvd., Anaheim, CA 92802. Phone: 800-854-6097. Web: http://ramadamaingate.com.

Code	Hotel Name	Rates	Distance	Shuttle	Year Built	Renovated
RR	**Red Roof Inn Anaheim**	$49	1 mi.	$3	1984	2001

This 235-room, 4-story hotel offers an outdoor heated pool, whirlpool spa, guest laundry, and gift shop. Some rooms have a refrigerator and microwave for an extra fee; all rooms are recently renovated with new bathrooms, granite countertops, and easy chairs. One pet per room is allowed. Check-in time: 1:00 pm/check-out: 12:00 pm (yes, those times are correct). Address: 100 Disney Way, Anaheim, CA 92802. Phone: 714-520-9696. Web: http://www.redroof.com.

Code	Hotel Name	Rates	Distance	Shuttle	Year Built	Renovated
TA	**Travelodge Intl. Inn Anaheim**	$77	1 1/2 mi.	$3	1982	2001

While the 120 rooms are basic at this hotel, the extras like free continental breakfast, free wireless high-speed Internet access, and the 10% discount for guests at the Denny's Restaurant next door make this hotel a good value. All rooms have cable TV, refrigerators, and coffeemakers—microwaves are available for an extra fee. Relax in the outdoor heated pool and whirlpool spa, and with guest laundry facilities, you can leave room in your suitcase for souvenirs. No pets are allowed. Free parking. Check-in time: 3:00 pm/check-out: 11:00 am. Address: 2060 S. Harbor Blvd., Anaheim, CA 92802. Phone: 714-971-9393. Web: http://www.anaheimresorttravelodge.com.

Very Cheap Hotels Near Disneyland

For those of you on a very limited budget who want to stay close to the parks, here are a few of the least expensive Disneyland-area motels. Please note that these are not Disney Good Neighbor hotels, which means either they didn't qualify or they chose not to participate in the Good Neighbor program. Use them at your own risk.

Code	Hotel Name	Rates	Distance	Shuttle	Year Built	Renovated
AL	Alamo Inn and Suites	$45	1 mi.	$3	1980	1990

This 86-room motel has a Tudor-style exterior and cozy lobby filled with sunlight, wicker furniture, and plants. Standard rooms feature one king, one queen, or two double beds plus a small refrigerator, microwave, cable TV, iron, ironing board, and hair dryer. Complimentary continental breakfast served daily. Relax in the outdoor pool and indoor whirlpool spa. Free parking. No restaurant on-site, but Denny's is nearby, as is all of Downtown Disney. No pets allowed. No elevator, but doorways are wide for wheelchair access. Check-in time: 2:00 pm/check-out: 11:00 am. Address: 1140 W. Katella Ave., Anaheim, CA 92802. Phone: 714-635-8070 or 800-378-9696. Web: http://www.alamoinnandsuites.com.

AP	Alpine Inn	$50	1 mi.	$3	1960	2001

With a snow-covered roof and Swiss Alps theme, this hotel would fit right in at the base of Disneyland's Matterhorn. A short walk from Disneyland Resort makes it easy to take an afternoon break at the heated outdoor pool. Rooms have cable TV with HBO, ESPN, and CNN, and refrigerators and microwaves are available for an extra fee. The free daily continental breakfast is a great time- and money-saver. High speed wireless Internet and guest laundry available. Free parking. Check-in time: 2:00 pm/check-out: 11:00 am. Address: 715 W. Katella Ave., Anaheim, CA 92802. Phone: 800-772-4422. Web: http://www.alpineinnanaheim.com.

BI	Best Inn	$49	1 mi.	$3	Unknown	–

This colorful motel has just 26 guest rooms, each with one king or two queen beds, refrigerator, microwave, satellite TV with HBO, iron, ironing board, and hair dryer. Free parking. Free continental breakfast. Some rooms offer a view of fireworks (when shown). Small outdoor pool is available. Check-in time: 1:00 pm/check-out: 11:00 am. Address: 414 W. Ball Rd., Anaheim, CA 92802. Phone: 1-800-999-1367. Web: http://www.bestinnanaheim.com.

CM	Comfort Inn Maingate	$73	2 mi.	$3	Unknown	1999

This 128-room hotel has a charming mission-inspired décor. Guest rooms have light wood furniture and soothing colors, each overlooking the landscaped courtyard. Kids Suites with bunk beds sleep up to eight guests. Bathrooms have granite vanity tops and Spanish tiled floors. A refrigerator and coffeemaker are in every room. Free wireless Internet access, too. Start your morning with the free deluxe continental breakfast and morning newspaper, heated outdoor pool, and whirlpool spa. Guest laundry facilities available. Free parking. Formerly Days Inn Park South. Check-in time: 3:00 pm/check-out: 11:00 am. Address: 2171 S. Harbor Blvd., Anaheim, CA 92802. Phone: 714-703-1220. Web: http://www.comfortinnmaingate.com.

Very Cheap Hotels Near Disneyland
(continued)

Code	Hotel Name	Rates	Distance	Shuttle	Year Built	Renovated
DI	**Anaheim Days Inn West**	**$55**	**1/2 mi.**	**$3**	**1985**	**1999**

© MediaMarx, Inc.

Each of the 44 rooms have a microwave, refrigerator, coffeemaker, iron, ironing board, hair dryer, and cable TV. Some rooms offer a view of fireworks (in season), and some rooms have whirlpool tubs. Complimentary continental breakfast is served from 7:00 am to 9:00 am. Small outdoor heated pool and spa. Free parking. Note that one of the Disneyland parking lots is behind the hotel—you may want to use the Disneyland parking lot tram as transportation between the hotel and the park. Check-in time: 3:00 pm/check-out: 11:00 am. Address: 1030 W. Ball Rd., Anaheim, CA. 92802. Phone: 714-520-0101 or 800-331-0055. Web: http://www.daysinn.com.

Code	Hotel Name	Rates	Distance	Shuttle	Year Built	Renovated
DE	**Desert Inn & Suites**	**$79**	**1/2 mi.**	**–**	**1991**	**2001**

© MediaMarx, Inc.

This convenient hotel is located directly across from the Disneyland Main Entry Plaza. The 144 guest rooms come in five floor plans: deluxe (standard room with a king or two queen beds), Parlor Suite (separate living room), Family Suite (two bedrooms), and two different Parlor Family Suites (one that sleeps up to eight, the other up to ten). All rooms have refrigerators and microwaves. Hotel amenities include an indoor pool and whirlpool spa, arcade, laundry, gift shop, and complimentary breakfast. There's even a rooftop viewing deck to see the fireworks (in season). Free parking. Check-in time: 3:00 pm/check-out: 11:00 am. Note that this hotel claims to be a Good Neighbor hotel although they were not on Disney's list at press time. Address: 1600 S. Harbor Blvd., Anaheim, CA 92802. Phone: 714-772-5050 or 800-433-5270. Web: http://www.anaheimdesertinn.com.

Code	Hotel Name	Rates	Distance	Shuttle	Year Built	Renovated
LB	**Little Boy Blue Motel**	**$39**	**1/2 mi.**	**–**	**Unknown**	**1998**

© MediaMarx, Inc.

This very basic, 2-story motel has 19 rooms, each with two queen beds, microwave, refrigerator, cable TV, and pay-per-view movies. A complimentary continental breakfast (coffee and danish) is served. Outdoor heated pool. Free parking. We've heard reports that the guest rooms are not well cleaned and the decor is out of date. This is one of the cheapest motels—remember, you get what you pay for. Check-in time: 2:00 pm/check-out: 11:00 am. Address: 416 W. Katella Ave., Anaheim, CA 92802. Phone: 714-635-2781 or 800-284-3804. Web: http://www.anaheim-littleboyblue.com.

Code	Hotel Name	Rates	Distance	Shuttle	Year Built	Renovated
S8	**Super 8 Motel**	**$48**	**1/2 mi.**	**$3**	**1972**	**1999**

For a clean and inexpensive place to stay, this motel offers all the basic amenities including cable TV and pay-per-view movies, an outdoor pool and whirlpool spa, and a complimentary continental breakfast. High-speed Internet access in public areas, and guest laundry is on-site. Free parking. No pets allowed. Check-in time: 3:00 pm/check-out: 11:00 am. Address: 415 W. Katella Ave. Anaheim, CA 92802. Phone: 714-778-6900. Web: http://www.super8.com.

Code	Hotel Name	Rates	Distance	Shuttle	Year Built	Renovated
AR	**Anaheim Resort RV Park**	**$44**	**1 mi.**	**Free**	**1956**	**2004**

While this isn't a hotel, it is a 150-site RV park with good rates and in close proximity to Disneyland. All sites have full hookups and cable TV. The park also has showers, heated pool, whirlpool, guest laundry, and wireless high-speed Internet access available. Pets allowed. Check-in time: 3:00 pm/check-out: 11:00 am. Address: 200 W. Midway Drive, Anaheim, CA 92805. Phone: 714-774-3860. Web: http://www.anaheimresortrvpark.com.

Hotels Near Other Attractions

If you plan to make forays to other parks or attractions, you'll find it's often **easier to move your lodgings**. This is particularly true for destinations like Universal Studios Hollywood, which is a good 45-minute drive from Anaheim, and San Diego. And, of course, we don't want to assume that everyone's first priority is Disneyland. While we can't offer an exhaustive look at all Southern California hotels, we can give you a good cross-section of recommended lodging in areas popular among our readers. Below is a map showing the general locations of the hotels detailed in the following pages.

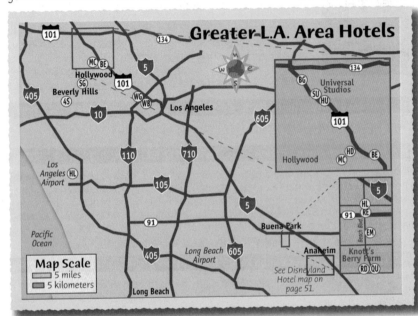

Getting a Deal with Priceline.com

Priceline.com (http://www.priceline.com) is a "name your own price" travel dealer. If you're flexible and willing to take a chance, Priceline can offer great deals on Southern California lodging. Before you try Priceline, however, we recommend you do some research into the type of lodging you want, typical prices for it, and other vacationers' experiences using Priceline. The best place to do this is at BiddingForTravel.com (http://www.biddingfortravel.com). Just navigate down to the California forums (there are several for each of the various cities/regions). Read these forums carefully for invaluable advice on how (and how much) to bid on Priceline lodging to get the best price. Pay attention to what others have successfully bid for lodging in your range. Also visit http://www.passporter.com/articles/priceline.htm for our own Priceline experiences and tips on making the most of it.

Knott's Berry Farm Hotels

These hotels are all within walking distance of Knott's Berry Farm, located either to the north of it along Beach Boulevard or to the south along Crescent Avenue. Distances indicated are to Knott's Berry Farm.

Code	Hotel Name	Rates	Distance	Shuttle	Year Built	Renovated
RE	**Knott's Berry Farm Resort**	**$89**	**0 mi.**	**Free**	**1973**	**1999**

This is the only hotel located at Knott's Berry Farm itself. When it's time to relax, guests will find a lush pool area with sundeck, whirlpool, and children's activity area. Hotel amenities include a full-service fitness center with saunas and showers, lit tennis and sports courts, and a golf pro shop that can arrange tee times at six local golf courses. Guests can get a free 10-minute shuttle ride to Disneyland. Dining options include two full-service restaurants. High-speed Internet access and suites are available. Parking is $9 for your stay. Check-in time: 3:00 pm/check-out: 12:00 pm. Address: 7675 Crescent Ave., Buena Park, CA 90620. Phone: 714-995-1111 or 866-752-2444. Web: http://www.knottshotel.com.

| **EM** | **Embassy Suites Buena Park** | **$105** | **1/2 mi.** | **Free** | **1982** | **1997** |

This is a Disney Good Neighbor hotel—see full description on page 53.

| **HL** | **Holiday Inn Buena Park** | **$89** | **1/2 mi.** | **Free** | **1972** | **2003** |

This 248-room hotel boasts the area's largest outdoor heated pool and whirlpool spa. Newly renovated guest rooms feature free wireless high-speed Internet access, coffeemaker, iron, ironing board, and hair dryer. Kids Suites are available, too. Hotel amenities include a fitness center, lounge (open for lunch and drinks), and an on-site restaurant (for breakfast and dinner). Free parking. No pets. Check-in time: 3:00 pm/check-out: 12:00 pm. 7000 Beach Blvd., Buena Park, CA 90620. Phone: 714-522-7000. Web: http://www.holidayinnbuenapark.com.

| **QU** | **Quality Inn & Suites Buena Park** | **$80** | **1 mi.** | **–** | **1985** | **1997** |

Located directly across from Knott's Berry Farm, this basic motel is clean and quiet. Each of the 90 guest rooms is spacious with one king or two queen beds, cable TV, free high-speed Internet access, iron, ironing board, hair dryer, microwave, and a coffeemaker. Some rooms have a refrigerator. Hotel amenities include a heated outdoor pool and whirlpool spa. Pets are allowed for $20/night/pet plus a $75 deposit. Free parking. Formerly the Colony Inn. Check-in time: 2:00 pm/checkout: 11:00 am. Address: 7800 Crescent Ave., Buena Park, CA 90620. Phone: 714-527-2201. Web: http://www.qualityinnbuenapark.com.

| **RD** | **Red Roof Inn Buena Park** | **$49** | **2 mi.** | **–** | **Unknown** | **–** |

This 122-room, 4-story hotel offers an outdoor heated pool and whirlpool spa, plus high-speed wireless Internet access in all guest rooms. Some rooms have a microwave and small refrigerator. A guest laundry is also available. One well-behaved family pet per room is welcome. Free parking. Check-in time: 1:00 pm/check-out: 12:00 pm. Address: 7121 Beach Blvd., Buena Park, CA 90620. Phone: 714-670-9000. Web: http://www.redroof.com.

Also: Courtyard Anaheim Buena Park (see full description on page 57) is nearby.

Universal Studios Hollywood Hotels

There are a slew of hotels and motels near Universal Studios Hollywood—the following are Univeral's "partner hotels." Distance and shuttles indicated are for Universal Studios.

Code	Hotel Name	Rates	Distance	Shuttle	Year Built	Renovated
SU	**Sheraton Universal**	$160	1/2 mi.	Free	1969	1999

Located on the back lot of Universal Studios, this 436-room hotel has hosted many distinguished guests and has been called the "Hotel of the Stars." Take the shuttle or walk to Universal Studios and Universal CityWalk. Guest rooms have Sweet Sleeper beds, mini-bar, coffeemaker, iron, ironing board, hair dryer, safe, bathrobes, and high-speed Internet access. There's even a special "Shrek Suite" with green sheets, a twig table, and mud baths—rates start at $500/ night. Amenities include a restaurant, lounge, large outdoor pool, whirlpool, fitness center, and gift shop. Conveniently located just minutes from Melrose Avenue, Hollywood, Beverly Hills, and downtown Los Angeles. Pets allowed (restrictions/fee). Parking fee. Check-in time: 4:00 pm/check-out: 12:00 pm. Address: 333 Universal Hollywood Dr., Universal City, CA 91608. Phone: 818-980-1212. Web: http://www.sheraton.com/universal.

Code	Hotel Name	Rates	Distance	Shuttle	Year Built	Renovated
HU	**Hilton Universal City**	$125	0 mi.	Free	1984	2000

© MediaMarx, Inc.

Situated at the very entrance to Universal Studios Hollywood and CityWalk, high on a hill above Los Angeles. Each of the 483 rooms features oversized beds, large closet, large bath and dressing area, in-room safe, mini-bar, coffeemaker, hairdryer, and a view of either the park, the Valley, or the Hollywood Hills. Rich mahogany and earth tone décor. Amenities include a restaurant, lounge, heated outdoor pool, whirlpool spa, and fitness room. Self-parking is $11/day; valet is $16/day. The MTA Redline Subway is within walking distance. Check-in time: 3:00 pm/check-out: 12:00 pm. Address: 555 Universal Hollywood Dr., Universal City, CA 91608. Phone: 818-506-2500. Web: http://www.hilton.com.

Code	Hotel Name	Rates	Distance	Shuttle	Year Built	Renovated
BG	**Beverly Garland's Holiday Inn**	$129	1 mi.	Free	1971	2003

This 255-room hotel's namesake and owner—Hollywood actress Beverly Garland—starred in 41 feature films and nearly 700 TV shows. All guest rooms have private balconies, cable TV, 2-line phones, wireless high-speed Internet access, iron, ironing board, coffeemaker, and hair dryer. Rooms with king beds and kids suites are also available. Hotel amenities include an on-site restaurant and lounge, room service, heated outdoor pool, lighted tennis courts, fitness center, and gift shop. Parking is $9/day. Seniors get 25% off. Check-in time: 3:00 pm/check-out: 12:00 pm. Address: 4222 Vineland Ave., N. Hollywood, CA 91602. Phone: 818-980-8000 or 800-238-3759. Web: http://www.beverlygarland.com.

Code	Hotel Name	Rates	Distance	Shuttle	Year Built	Renovated
HD	**Holiday Inn Hollywood**	$89	1 mi.	Free	1998	–

Located near Hollywood Boulevard, the Hollywood Bowl, and the new Academy Awards' Kodak Theatre. This 7-story hotel offers 160 guest rooms with two double beds or one king bed. Dine at Hollywood Hills Café located inside the hotel or enjoy a cocktail in the Producer's Lounge. Free morning newspaper. Relax in the tropical setting of the outdoor pool and spa area or enjoy a workout in the fitness center. On-site restaurant and lounge. No pets. Parking/valet parking is $14/day. Check-in time: 3:00 pm/check-out: 12:00 pm. Address: 2005 N. Highland Ave., Hollywood, CA 90068. Phone: 323-876-8600. Web: http://www.holiday-inn.com.

Planning

Getting There

Staying in Style

Touring

Feasting

Making Magic

Index

Notes & More

Los Angeles Hotels

Hundreds of hotels are available in the greater Los Angeles area. While we can't include them all, we do recommend these seven hotels, which we feel represent a good cross-section. The map on page 67 shows each hotel's location in the greater Los Angeles area. Note that seveal of these hotels are centrally located in Los Angeles, making for a good base hotel if you plan to visit several attractions in Southern California. For more L.A. hotels, visit http://www.travelhero.com and search on "Los Angeles."

Code	Hotel Name	Rates	Distance	Shuttle	Year Built	Renovated
BE	**Best Western Hollywood Hills**	$79			1940	2002

Decorated with unique murals of Hollywood scenes, this 82-room hotel is also home to the hip "101 Coffee Shop," where local stars and stars-to-be hang out. Rooms have a collection of photos of some of the greatest Hollywood actors and actresses of years gone by. Relax by the large tiled outdoor pool, surf the net with wireless Internet access, or head to nearby Griffith Park. Guest laundry facilities available. Up to two small pets are allowed ($25 fee/night for each pet). Free covered parking. Check-in time: 3:00 pm/check-out: 11:00 am. Address: 6141 Franklin Ave., Hollywood, CA 90028. Phone: 323-464-5181 or 800-287-1700. Web: http://www.bestwestern.com.

4S	**Four Seasons Hotel**	$350			1897	1997

Close to Beverly Hills and Rodeo Drive, this luxury hotel known for lush floral gardens and impeccable service is in a quiet residential neighborhood. Every guest room has a balcony, down pillows, duvets, fuzzy bathrobes, and a DVD/VCR. Childproofed guest rooms are available. Relax at the pool terrace café and enjoy the outdoor pool, whrlpool spa, poolside cafe, and fitness center. Award-winning restaurant Gardens has indoor/outdoor seating and is open for breakfast, brunch, lunch, afternoon tea, and dinner. Complimentary limo service to Rodeo Drive, and free milk and cookies for children are some of the nice touches. Splurge on a massage from the world-class spa. Small pets welcome (no fee). Free parking; valet is $21/day. Check-in time: 3:00 pm/check-out: 1:00 pm. Address: 300 S. Doheny Dr., Los Angeles, CA 90048. Phone: 310-273-2222. Web: http://www.fourseasons.com/losangeles.

HL	**Hilton Los Angeles Airport**	$109			1983	2003

Close to Los Angeles International Airport with complimentary 24-hour shuttle service, this 1,234-room luxury hotel is popular with business travelers. Guest rooms offer irons, ironing boards, coffeemakers, hair dryer, and 2-line speakerphone. Relax in the gardens, pool, and four whirlpool spas, or work out in the on-site 24-hour fitness center. Wireless Internet access available in the lobby (extra fee). Several dining options are available, including The Café (casual, all-day dining), The Bistro (casual, 24-hour eatery), Andiamo (Italian, dinner), Landings (sports bar), and 24-hour room service. Parking is $13/day, valet is $17/day. Check-in time: 3:00 pm/check-out: 12:00 pm. Pets allowed. Address: 5711 W. Century Blvd., Los Angeles, CA 90045. Phone: 310-410-4000. Web: http://www.hilton.com/hotels/LAXAHHH.

Code	Hotel Name	Rates	Distance	Shuttle	Year Built	Renovated

MC **Magic Castle Hotel** $69   1956   2004

Stay at this 41-room hotel and get an exclusive opportunity to experience the Magic Castle, a private dinner club for magicians with magical entertainment. Enjoy the free turndown service with chocolates and continental breakfast, and walk to the Hollywood Walk of Fame and Grauman's Chinese Theater. Guest rooms in this converted apartment complex have kitchen facilities and are truly spacious. Amenities include an outdoor heated pool, laundry facilities, secure covered parking $8/night. Note that if you want to experience the Magic Castle Club, you'll need to fork over a $15 cover fee plus the cost of dinner ($40–$100/person)—dress is formal and no one under 21 is allowed except during Sunday brunch. Check-in time: 3:00 pm/check-out: 11:00 am. Address: 7025 Franklin Ave., Hollywood, CA 90028. Phone: 323-851-0800 or 800-741-4915. Web: http://www.magiccastlehotel.com.

SG **Secret Garden B&B** $95   1923   –

Feel like a movie star staying in this large pink Mediterranean-style home in the Hollywood Hills, a quiet respite close to all the Hollywood action. The lobby features a Steinway baby grand piano and an 18th century French chandelier, and a friendly cat lives with the owner on premises. Hot cooked breakfasts are a specialty served each morning on an antique stove. There are five guest rooms and one guest cottage—some of the rooms share baths. Two-night minimum stay on weekends, no guest pets allowed. One block from Sunset Strip. Check-in and check-out time is flexible. Address: 8039 Selma Ave., Los Angeles, CA 90046. Phone: 877-732-4736. Web: http://www.secretgardenbnb.com.

WB **Westin Bonaventure** $119   1976   2003

This unique 35-story hotel is made up of four mirrored towers and is in the center of the financial district. Glass elevators rise above the six-level atrium to the revolving lounge and the 35th floor restaurant with fantastic views of the city. Covering a full city block, there are more than 40 restaurants, shops, and services inside the complex, including the plaza pool deck and a fitness center. Each of the 1,354 guest rooms feature floor-to-ceiling city views, two queens or one king bed, a coffeemaker with Starbuck's coffee, and in-room high-speed Internet access ($16/day). At press time, not all rooms were renovated or offer the Westin Heavenly Bed. Parking: $22/night. Check-in time: 3:00 pm/check-out: 12:00 pm. Address: 404 South Figueroa St., Los Angeles, CA 90071. Phone: 213-624-1000 or 800-228-3000. Web: http://www.westin.com/bonaventure.

WG **Wilshire Grand Hotel** $147   1954   2004

This large, 900-room hotel is in the heart of Downtown Los Angeles, surrounded by high-rises, museums, and theaters. The hotel features an espresso bar, 24-hour outdoor pool, fitness center, gift shops, boutiques, florists, salon, travel agency, ticketing agency, car rental, and business center. Large, retro-style rooms have cable TV with pay-per-view movies and free wireless Internet access. Deluxe rooms have a sitting area and some feature two full baths. Authors Jennifer and Dave enjoyed a deluxe, executive-level room on the 15th floor with lots of extra space (see photo). Parking: $30/night, valet available. Check-in time: 3:00 pm/check-out: 12:00 pm. Address: 930 Wilshire Blvd., Los Angeles, CA 90017. Phone: 213-688-7777 or 888-773-2888. Web: http://www.wilshiregrand.com.

Our spacious guest room

San Diego Hotels

Below are seven San Diego hotels located within easy reach of attractions. Each is a "preferred lodging" hotel for SeaWorld and offers reliable accommodations. For additional San Diego hotel information, we recommend you visit http://www.travelhero.com and search on "San Diego." Distances and shuttles indicated are for SeaWorld.

Hotel Name	Rates	Distance	Shuttle	Year Built	Renovated
Bahia Resort Hotel	$169	1 mi.	–	1953	2004

Situated on a private 14-acre Moroccan-inspired oasis with lush tropical gardens and winding walkways, a seal pond (home to an active Harbor seal), a private beach with children's playground, and an Olympic-size swimming pool and whirlpool spa. Each of the 320 guest rooms—from standard rooms to beachfront cottages—offer cable TV, coffeemaker, iron, ironing board, hair dryer, and complimentary high-speed Internet access. Suites with kitchenettes are available. Two 1860s-era sternwheelers, docked at the marina, take guests on cocktail cruises. Café Bahia serves Southern California cuisine for breakfast, lunch, and dinner. Free children's activities Memorial Day through Labor Day. No pets allowed. Free parking. Check-in time: 4:00 pm/check-out: 12:00 pm. Address: 998 West Mission Bay Dr., San Diego, CA 92109. Phone: 800-576-4229. Web: http://www.bahiahotel.com.

Comfort Inn & Suites	$99	3 mi.	–	1996	1999

This 200-room hotel sports a mission-style exterior. Guest rooms come in a variety of configurations: deluxe rooms (two queen beds or one king, some include a whirlpool tub and/or refrigerator), kids suites (king bed and twin-size bunk beds), kids mini suites (bunk beds in room), and two-room suites (two double beds, sofa sleeper, separate rooms). Each of its guest rooms comes with cable TV and a coffeemaker. Free breakfast buffet and morning newspaper. Hotel amenities include an outdoor heated pool and spa, fitness center, guest laundry, video arcade, and free parking. Business services available. All rooms non-smoking. Check-in time: 3:00 pm/check out: 12:00 pm. Address: 2485 Hotel Circle Pl., San Diego, CA 92108. Phone: 619-881-6200 or 800-380-3583. Web: http://www.comfortinnzoo.com.

The Dana on Mission Bay	$109	0 mi.	–	Unknown	2004

Located on 10 acres in Mission Bay Aquatic Park, next door to Sea World. Each of the 270 guest rooms have a light, contemporary decor with granite counter tops, teak and mahogany furniture, and plantation shutters. High-speed Internet access. Rooms offer balconies or patios with views of the bay, marina, pool, or gardens. Surrounded by beautiful landscaping, this resort offers a tropical-style pool with gaming area (ping-pong, shuffleboard, and foosball) and a bayside infinity pool, a family-style restaurant, picnic area, private marina with bicycle, boat, and water-sport rentals, and a 27-mile jogging/biking path. Two whirlpool spas, pool bar, and free shuttle service to San Diego attractions. Two restaurants. Free parking. Formerly the Dana Inn & Marina. Check-in time: 4:00 pm/check-out: 12:00 pm. Address: 1710 Mission Bay Dr., San Diego, CA 92109. Phone: 619-222-6440 or 800-DANA-INN. Web: http://www.thedana.net.

Hotel Name	Rates	Distance	Shuttle	Year Built	Renovated
Days Inn Hotel Circle	**$85**	**5 mi.**	**Free**	**1976**	**2000**

All 280 guest rooms at this hotel have HBO and Disney Channel, pay-per-view movies and Nintendo, mini-refrigerators, and coffeemakers. High-speed Internet access is available in public areas. The hotel's outdoor pool and whirlpool spa are surrounded by towering palm trees and large potted plants, with barbecue grills nearby. Pam Pam Café and Grill is located at the hotel, with many restaurants in walking distance. Free parking. Check-in time: 4:00 pm/check-out: 12:00 pm. Address: 543 Hotel Circle S., San Diego, CA 92108. Phone: 619-297-8800 or 800-227-4743. Web: http://www.daysinnhc.com.

Hotel Del Coronado	**$250**	**12 mi.**	**–**	**1888**	**2001**

A classic historic hotel, the unique design of "The Del" was inspiration for the Grand Floridian Resort in Walt Disney World. Designated a National Historic Landmark, accommodations include historic and contemporary rooms, from quaint with no view to a luxurious two-bedroom beach house. Features include cabanas, poolside dining, and luxury health spa services, including in-room massages complete with candlelight and wine. There's also a fitness room, tennis courts, bicycle, boat, and jet ski rentals, plus special programs for children. Check-in time: 4:00 pm/check-out: 12:00 pm. Address: 1500 Orange Ave., Coronado, CA 92118. Phone: 800-HOTELDEL or 619-435-6611. Web: http://www.hoteldel.com.

Howard Johnson SeaWorld	**$66**	**2 mi.**	**Free**	**Unknown**	**1999**

Howard Johnson Express Inn by Sea World and San Diego Zoo is conveniently located in the heart of Mission Valley in Hotel Circle. Clean, basic décor in its 98 guest rooms, each with in-room refrigerators, microwaves, and cable TV with free HBO. Amenities include a heated outdoor pool, whirlpool spa, complimentary continental breakfast, morning newspaper, guest laundry facility, Internet kiosk in lobby, and free shuttle to airport and SeaWorld. Free parking. Check-in time: 3:00 pm/Check out: 11:00 am. Address: 3330 Rosecrans St., San Diego, CA. 92110. Phone: 619-224-8266. Web: http://www.howardjohnsonsandiego.com.

Ramada Plaza	**$93**	**5 mi.**	**–**	**1972**	**2004**

Light marble in the lobby with large arched windows greets you at this 183-room hotel. Each guest room has two queen or one king bed, cable TV with HBO and pay-per-view movies, in-room safe, coffeemaker, iron, ironing board, hair dryer, room service, and high-speed Internet access. Refrigerators may be available, too. Deluxe Business Class Rooms include free wireless Internet access, a microwave, and new furnishings. Hotel amenities include an outdoor pool, whirlpool spa, free newspaper, fitness center, and free parking. The Tickled Trout restaurant and pub is open for breakfast, lunch, and dinner (ask about a 10% discount and free dessert). Business Center with computer, printer, and fax service. Check-in time: 3:00 pm/Check-out: 12:00 pm. Address: 2151 Hotel Circle S., San Diego, CA 92108. Phone: 619-291-6500 or 800-532-4217. Web: http://www.ramadaplaza-hc.com.

Disney Vacation Club

Disney Vacation Club (DVC) is a Disney-run, Walt Disney World-based **vacation ownership program**. DVC is Disney's kinder, gentler version of a vacation timeshare and offers several enticing twists on the timeshare experience. As with all timeshare offerings, the DVC offers the promise of frequent, reduced-cost Disney vacations in exchange for a significant up-front investment on your part.

While there are no designated hotels for DVC at Disneyland, DVC members **can use their points for Disneyland visits**. In fact, points were lowered in celebration of the 50th anniversary. DVC members also receive $20 off their first purchase of a Disneyland Annual Pass, as well as 10–20% off selected eateries in the parks and at Downtown Disney and 10–20% off merchandise purchases in selected stores in Downtown Disney.

Beyond Disneyland, Disney operates **seven DVC resorts** (with most in Walt Disney World): Old Key West, Boardwalk Villas, Villas at the Wilderness Lodge, Beach Club Villas, Saratoga Springs, Vero Beach (Florida coast), and Hilton Head Island (South Carolina). As with other timeshare programs, "swaps" can be arranged at many resorts worldwide.

With a typical vacation timeshare you buy an annual one-week (or multiple week) stay during a particular time period in a specific size of accommodation. DVC uses a novel point system that adds far **greater flexibility** and complexity to the process. You can use your points however you wish to create several short getaways or a single, grand vacation—at any time of the year and at any DVC or other Disney resort. Here's how it works: You buy a certain number of points at the going rate ($98 per point as of 8/2005). 150 points is the minimum and a typical purchase—so every year you'd have 150 points to apply toward accommodations. You might need 15 points/night for a one-bedroom at Old Key West weeknights during the off-season. 100 points/night may be needed for a two-bedroom at BoardWalk weekends in peak season. Just as with a regular resort room, rates are affected by size, view, location, season, and day. You also pay annual dues based on the number of points purchased. Rates vary, depending on your "home" resort—from about $3 to $5 per point—so dues on a 150-point purchase would be approximately $475–600. If you compare the combined cost of points and annual membership fees to renting comparable resort rooms at non-discounted rates, it could take about five years to recover the value of the points purchased. After that, vacations might cost half the prevailing rental rates. Membership contracts expire in 2054 for Saratoga Springs; all others expire in 2042.

To **learn more** about DVC, visit http://www.mouseplanet.com/dtp/dvc for an excellent overview and review of the DVC experience. You can also visit the information booths while at Disneyland—you'll find them in the Grand Californian, the Disneyland Hotel, Disneyland Park (near the hub), and Disney's California Adventure (near the entrance to California Screamin'). These information booths are recent additions and it's our hope that they are laying the groundwork for a new DVC property near Disneyland.

Disney Vacation Club
✉ 200 Celebration Place, Celebration, FL 34747-9903
📞 Phone: 800-800-9100   📠 Fax: 407-566-3393
💻 http://www.disneyvacationclub.com

Special Places for Special Guests

California culture is diverse and tolerant, accommodating special guests of all walks and talks.

Children—What is Disney without children? Indeed, every resort is kid-friendly to one degree or another. While only the Grand Californian offers a childcare program, all Disney hotels have wading pools, playgrounds, arcades, and fun activities for kids. Even the "adult" Grand Californian goes out of its way to offer wonderful children's activities.

Older Adults—California is a haven for mature travelers, and Disneyland is a popular destination. Good hotels for the senior set include all three Disneyland hotels—you just can't beat the location and convenience.

Business Travelers—Combine business with pleasure and visit Disney the next time you're in town for work. You can often stay at a Disney hotel for the same price as a business hotel. All three Disneyland hotels have full-service business centers and meeting space, and the Grand Californian is specifically designed to be business-friendly. Some of the off-property hotels have guest rooms with features specifically for business travelers, too.

Singles—Whether you travel solo for work or pleasure, Disney is accommodating, as Jennifer discovered on her very first trip to Disneyland. Good resorts for single travelers include the Disneyland Hotel and the Paradise Pier Hotel.

Couples—Celebrating an anniversary, going on your honeymoon, or just enjoying your time together? The Disneyland Hotels, particularly the Grand Californian, can be magical and romantic. Consider a small suite or concierge service for extra magic.

Large Families and Groups—We've organized several family and group trips over the years to various Disney destinations. All the Disneyland hotels offer suites with ample space for your family reunion or group. Adjoining rooms are available at most hotels, too. These are pricey solutions, however, and you may want to consider an off-property hotel or "timeshare" property with larger units. For example, the Dolphin's Cove Resort (719-980-0830) has one- and two-bedroom units within walking distance of Disneyland.

Physically Disabled—The Disneyland Resort is far ahead of the rest of the world in providing access, facilities, and fun for those with different needs. When Jennifer visited in May 2004, well advanced into her pregnancy with some special needs, she found the resort very accessible. All of the Disney hotels, and many of the off-property hotels, offer disabled-accessible guest rooms. Call 714-781-4560 for more details on accessible rooms in the Disney hotels.

Gay and Lesbian—With Disney's famous reputation for tolerance, you'll feel welcomed and accepted here.

International Guests—Los Angeles is one of the best cities an international traveler can visit, thanks to its diverse population and multi-language accommodation.

Bargain Hunters—If you're looking for a bargain, you aren't terribly likely to find it at one of the Disneyland hotels. Rather, look to the off-property hotels near Disneyland or elsewhere in the Southern California area. See the sidebar on Priceline (page 67) for tips on getting great rates on lodging.

Planning

Getting There

Staying in Style

Touring

Feasting

Making Magic

Index

Notes & More

Lodging Worksheet

Use this worksheet to jot down preferences, scribble information during phone calls, and keep all your discoveries together. Don't worry about being neat—just be thorough! Circle your final choices once you decide to go with them (to avoid any confusion) and be sure to transfer them to your Lodging PassPocket.

Arrival date: _____ Alternates: _____

Departure date: _____ Alternates: _____

Total number of nights: _____ Alternates: _____

We prefer to stay at: _____

Alternates: _____

_____

Using your preferences above, call Disney's Reservations phone line at 714-956-6425 (or the phone number for the hotel of your choice) and jot down hotel availabilities in the table on the next page. It works best for us when we write the available days in the far left column, followed by the resort, view/type, special requests, rate, and total cost in the columns to the right. Draw lines between different availabilities. Circle those you decide to use, and then record the reservation numbers, as you'll need them to confirm, cancel, or make changes later. The two columns at the far right let you note confirmations and room deposits so you don't forget and consequently lose your reservation.

Additional Notes:

Collect information on lodging in the table below. We've included some sample notes to show you how we do it, but you're welcome to use this space in any way you please.

Dates	Resort	View/Type/Requests	Rate	Total	Reservation #	Confirm by	Dep.
7/10 - 7/13	Paradise Pier	Standard City/Pool View	$160	$480	DTVZK	7/14/06 ✓	✓
7/11 - 7/14	Howard Johnson	Standard (Two Queens)	$99	$396		7/15/06	

Planning · Getting There · Staying in Style · Touring · Feasting · Making Magic · Index · Notes & More

Planning

Getting There

Staying in Style

Touring

Feasting

Making Magic

Index

Notes & More

The Last Resort

Make resort memories that last a lifetime with these helpful tips!

Get an **extra day** of use of hotel facilities! Plan your flight (or drive) home late in the day. Pack a bag with your travel clothes (include plastic bags for wet swimsuits) and check out at the normal time—you still have use of the pool, etc. for the rest of the day. Swim all day and then change in poolside restrooms. It's like having an extra day, and all we do is relax by the pools and go home feeling refreshed.

Always check back for **discounts** on your hotel rooms. Many readers report they received better discounts when they called back later to inquire about rates.

Stay on track on vacation by continuing to worship or attend your meetings. Many houses of worship are near Disneyland and there are loads in Los Angeles—get a good list at http://www.usachurch.com. Friends of Bill W. (Alcoholics Anonymous) can find local meeting information at http://www.oc-aa.org.

It is easy to eat a **quick breakfast** in your hotel room before a day at the parks. We often plan ahead for this and bring simple breakfast foods from home (they're much cheaper) and pick up anything perishable we may need once we arrive.

Magical Memories

"Our favorite experience in an off-property hotel at Disneyland was a stay at the Howard Johnson's. Request a room on the second floor as these rooms have skylights! Our first night in Anaheim, we arrived tired from our flight, grabbed something to eat, then returned to our room to get some sleep for our big adventure the next day. We had just settled in and turned off the light when we heard 'boom!' and saw the Disneyland fireworks explode overhead! How fun to lay in bed on our first night and watch the fireworks through our skylight!"

...as told by an anonymous Disney vacationer

"My two sons and I spent a delightful, relaxing, low-cost afternoon exploring the Disneyland Hotel. We discovered the tranquil Japanese koi fish pool and the beautifully landscaped Horseshoe Falls. Then we sat near the Never Land Pool and savored every delicious bite of our Mickey ice cream bars from the nearby Captain's Galley. Inside, near the convention area, we found a floor-to-ceiling montage of photos, Disney collectibles, and other memorabilia illustrating the fascinating and colorful history of Disneyland. Next we toured the lobby of Disney's Grand Californian Hotel which offered additional visual treats with its rich wood paneling, inviting colors, and detailed theming. Our unhurried exploration proved to be a refreshing break from the action-packed parks!"

...as told by Disney vacationer Heather Berube

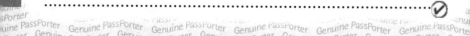

Touring the Lands

Once upon a time, one of the world's greatest filmmakers created the world's first theme park, and the world came to marvel at it. Now, more than 50 years later, Disneyland is still the wondrous house that Walt built, and the industry he created still calls Southern California home. In a region filled with enough sights and sounds to keep a vacationer busy 52 weeks out of the year, millions of visitors come to Southern California for no other reason than to spend a week (or more) visiting Disneyland, other theme parks, and similar destinations. And that's what this chapter is all about. It's time to visit Disneyland!

Closest to our hearts and the hearts of many others is Walt Disney's original Disneyland park. This is the park that Walt dreamed and built, and shared with us on his weekly television shows. The pavement still echoes with his footsteps, and more than 10,000 "cast members" (all employees help put on the "show" and are "on stage" whenever they are in the public eye) carry on Walt's vision with love and devotion. Walt's vision included standards for customer service and imaginative design that still motivate and inspire his cast today. A short stroll away, across a sun-drenched plaza (the esplanade) is the fledgling Disney's California Adventure park (DCA). While it's 45 years younger than its big brother across the plaza, DCA boasts a growing lineup of fabulous attractions and is one of Disney's most beautiful parks—breathtakingly designed vistas open around every bend.

We have no problem spending five or more days at what's now known as Disneyland Resort, so you must excuse us if we devote a good portion of this chapter to Walt Disney's pride and joy. But we haven't left out the other popular parks in Southern California. This chapter covers the ins and outs of admission tickets, detailed descriptions of virtually every park and its attractions, our detailed park maps, tips, tricks, touring plans, and a Touring Worksheet to help you organize your days. We'll show you how to have the most magical Southern California vacation imaginable.

So please keep your hands and feet inside the moving vehicle. It's time to go to the happiest place on earth!

Planning

Getting There

Staying in Style

Touring

Feasting

Making Magic

Index

Notes & More

Disney Park Passwords

Admission Media—Park passes (tickets). See pages 82–83.

Attraction—An individual ride, show, or exhibit.

Baby Services—Special centers are found at both of Disney's parks, as noted on our park maps. All restrooms (men's included) support diaper changing.

Cast Member—All Disneyland employees are "cast members"—they wear nametags with their first names, pinned to the left side of their chest.

Child Switch—Adults with kid(s) too small to ride can take turns waiting with the kid(s) while the other(s) ride. Saves time in line. Ask a cast member for details as you enter the queue.

Disney Dollars—Disney's own currency, good throughout the resort.

Early Entry—Allows guests with Park Hopper Bonus Tickets (see page 82) and some packages (see page 37) to enter a designated park earlier than official opening time on certain days.

ECV—Electric Convenience Vehicle. You can rent these four-wheeled scooters at the parks and elsewhere. See also "wheelchairs" on page 35.

FASTPASS—Disney's popular ride "reservation" system (see below).

Making the Most of Disney's FASTPASS

Tired of waiting in long lines? Disney introduced FASTPASS to reduce the amount of time you spend in line—and it's free to all park guests! Just slip your park pass into a machine near an attraction with FASTPASS. Out pops your pass and a printed ticket (see sample below) that promises you a ride during a particular period some time later in the day. Depending on how many tickets have been issued, you may be able to return in 25 minutes, or hours later. When you receive your FASTPASS, look for the time you can get your next FASTPASS. When your FASTPASS return time arrives, walk up to the attraction's "FASTPASS Return" entrance, show your FASTPASS to the cast member, and walk on in. There's usually still a short wait, and you'll experience most or all "pre-show" activities. Every FASTPASS attraction has a "Standby" line, which is the regular wait-in-line queue—the wait time for the Standby queue is typically half as long as the FASTPASS return time. We highly recommend you get your first FASTPASS early in the day for one of the more popular rides, as FASTPASS tickets can run out on busy days. Our attraction descriptions later in this chapter indicate if an attraction has FASTPASS (look for the **FP** icon), and our touring plans give recommendations on which FASTPASSes to get throughout a day. Note: FASTPASS isn't always available, especially near closing time or during non-peak periods. **Tip #1:** The FASTPASS networks at Disneyland Park and Disney's California Adventure are not connected, so you can get a FASTPASS for Indiana Jones Adventure at Disneyland then walk across the esplanade to get a FASTPASS at Tower of Terror at Disney's California Adventure. **Tip #2:** Enjoy the same ride twice! Get a FASTPASS, then get in the Standby queue. By the time your ride is over, your FASTPASS may be ready to use.

Sample FASTPASS
Enter Any Time Between
9:45 am
and
10:45 am
Another FASTPASS ticket will be available after
11:45 am
07/04/05   9:25

Actual size: 2¼" x 2¾"

First Aid—First aid stations and automatic defibrillators are at every park and are indicated on Disney's park maps.

Guest Relations—An information desk, located inside and outside the front gates of both parks. Guest Services at Disney hotels provide a similar range of services.

Guidemaps—Free maps available at the parks. Times Guides may also be available.

Land—An area of a park organized around a common theme.

Lockers—Automated Smarte® lockers are available in each park for $6–$10, depending on size. Lockers are also just outside the park entrances and at Downtown Disney.

Lost & Found—Lost items or children can be claimed at a central location in each park. Consult a guidemap or a cast member. Also see page 234.

Money—Pay with cash, Disney Dollars, Disney gift cards, travelers checks, Visa, MasterCard, American Express, Discover, JCB, and Diner's Club. Disney Dollars are sold at parks, resorts, and the Disney Store. ATMs are located in the parks, Downtown Disney, and hotel lobbies. Disney resort guests can charge to their room.

Packages—Disney hotel guests can have packages delivered free of charge to their resort for next-day pickup after 7:00 am. Inquire before purchasing. Non-hotel guests who do not want to carry a package around can drop it off at the park entrance and have it held for guest pickup later in the day—drop off packages at The Newsstand (Disneyland Park Main Entrance) or at Greetings from California (under the Golden Gateway in Disney's California Adventure).

Park—Disney's recreational complexes requiring admission, namely Disneyland Park and Disney's California Adventure. Descriptions begin on page 87.

Parking—$10 ($12/oversized vehicles or $17/buses); free to Premium Annual Passholders (Deluxe Annual Passholders and Seasonal Passholders can buy a parking pass for $49). Downtown Disney parking (see map on back flap) is free for the first three hours and $6/hour thereafter, with a maximum fee of $30/day (you can get an additional two hours with validation from AMC Theatres or a Downtown Disney table-service restaurant). Also see page 85.

Queue—A waiting area or line for an attraction or character greeting.

Re-Entry—Guests may exit and re-enter the same park on the same day. Be sure to get your hand stamped as you exit, and hold on to your pass. Guests with Park Hopper Tickets can move between the two Disney parks but should still get a hand stamp upon exiting.

Security—All bags are searched before entering the parks.

Shopping—A variety of shops sell Disney items, themed products, and sundries.

Smoking—Prohibited in most places in parks. See park maps for smoking areas.

Strollers & Wheelchairs—Strollers ($8/day), wheelchairs ($8/day + $20/deposit), and ECVs ($35/day + $20 deposit) can be rented in the esplanade area between the two parks, and inside both parks. Limited availability—arrive early, bring your own, or rent elsewhere (see page 35). Park hopping guests may take their stroller, wheelchair, and/or ECV rental with them to the other park. Wheelchairs are available to Disney hotel guests for $10/day (no deposit). See also page 97.

Tax—Orange County sales tax is 7.75%. Anaheim hotel tax is 15%.

Planning

Getting There

Staying in Style

Touring

Feasting

Making Magic

Index

Notes & More

Disney Park Passes

Disney offers many admission options. It's safest to budget **$59** a day for adults and kids ages 10+ (**$49** for kids 3–9), the single-day price for each park. Most multi-day passes emphasize flexibility over big savings, so you can do more for a slightly lower price. Here's the deal on multi-day passes, based on options at press time (prices include tax). Prices were last increased in January 2006 and will go up again in January 2007.

Park Hopper Passes

Unlimited admission to both Disneyland parks for one or more days—it allows you to move between the parks as often as you like for the duration of your pass. Prices at press time are as follows: one day ($79/$69) or two days ($116/$86). You can puchase these passes in advance, but no savings are available. Note that the pass expires 13 days after your first use.

Park Hopper Bonus Tickets

Unlimited admission to both Disneyland parks for 3–5 days, plus an ESPN Zone Arena Game Card ($10 value) and early entry for Disneyland Park on Monday, Tuesday, Thursday, or Saturday. Main gate prices are: three days ($169/$139), four days ($199/$169), and five days ($219/$189). Buy in advance and save even more! Passes expire 13 days after first use.

CityPass for Southern California Attractions

If you're planning to visit other parks, this is a great deal! For $185/$127 you get a three-day Park Hopper Pass for Disneyland, plus three one-day tickets for Knott's Berry Farm, Sea World, and the San Diego Zoo. (Tip: You can do the San Diego Wild Animal Park instead of the San Diego Zoo.) Pass expires thirteen days after your first use. Purchase at Disneyland (phone, web, or resort), directly at http://www.citypass.net, or at http://www.costco.com.

Deluxe Annual Pass

Unlimited admission to both Disneyland parks for 320 days of the year (holidays and Saturdays in peak season are blocked out). Cost is $229 for all ages, which represents a huge savings over the park hoppers if the blockout dates don't get in the way. If you want to visit on a blackout date, deluxe annual passholders pay just $30 for a single-day ticket. Annual passholders receive extra benefits, such as 10% off select Disneyland Resort restaurants, special rates at the Disneyland hotels, and the option to buy an annual parking pass for $49 (all benefits are subject to availability and restrictions may apply). You cannot share an annual pass. For a list of blackout dates, visit http://www.disneyland.com.

Premium Annual Pass

A Premium Annual Pass ($349/all ages) offers the same privileges as the Deluxe Annual Pass but you get admission for a full year (no blockout dates), free parking in the Mickey and Friends structure, a 10% discount on merchandise at select locations throughout the Disneyland Resort (including many non-Disney shops at Downtown Disney) and more—see page 10 for more information.

Southern California Resident Seasonal Passes

Residents of Southern California can get an annual pass good for non-peak weekdays only ($119) or for 227 pre-selected days ($149). Single-day tickets on blackout days are $30; a parking pass is $49. For a list of blackout dates, visit http://www.disneyland.com.

Upgrades: Apply the unused value of a park pass to a more expensive pass at any time before your pass expires. For example, apply the unused portion of a Park Hopper Pass to the cost of an Annual Pass. Visit Guest Relations in the parks or Guest Services at a resort for details. Tip: If you want to buy a Deluxe Annual Pass but your first day falls on a blockout date, get a Park Hopper Pass and apply it toward the purchase of your Deluxe Annual Pass.

AAA Discount: AAA members (see page 11) can expect a roughly 5% discount on some passes. AAA members must purchase Park Hoppers directly from AAA to get the discount. AAA also offers a "Passport Plus Package" in 6-7 day increments with a Park Hopper Pass, $10 ESPN Zone game card, free parking, and more.

Advance Purchase Discounts: Available if you buy certain multi-day passes from http://www.disneyland.com, The Disney Store (in California), your travel agent, or with resort reservations. Order at least 8 days before your vacation, and check shipping costs.

Unused Disney World Passes Work at Disneyland: Because the value of a Walt Disney World pass is higher than a Disneyland pass, you can use leftover days on a Walt Disney World pass for admission to a Disneyland park. Does not apply to Annual Passes. Inquire at a Guest Services window.

Get a Park Hopper With an Extra Day: If you're already in the area, stop by the Anaheim Visitor Center at 1770 S. Harbor Blvd. (in the McDonald's parking lot) and inquire into their Park Hopper Passes. You may be able to purchase a five-day for the price of a four-day, and a six-day for the price of a five-day! It's still cheaper to purchase Park Hoppers in advance if you're able, however.

Southern California Resident Discounts: It pays to live nearby. S. California Resident Seasonal Passes work like Annual Passes, but with blockout dates on busy days. To qualify as a resident, you must show photo identification with an address in the 90000-93599 zip codes. (Tip: Inquire into other resident discounts—a "2Fer" pass was offered in early 2006 that gave residents in U.S. zip codes 90000-93599 and Mexico zip codes 21000-22999 the option to purchase two tickets (one for each park) for the price of one single-day.)

Special Discounts for Special People: Military personnel, California teachers, college students, and corporate employees may be eligible for discounted admission. Military personnel should inquire with their local ITT or MWR office; teachers inquire with the California Teachers Association; S. California college students inquire with the student union; and corporate employees inquire with the Human Resources department.

Online Ticket Brokers—ARES Travel sells some Park Hopper Passes at a discount, though you'll pay a $5.75 fee/order. Order at http://www.arestravel.com or call 800-434-7894.

Kids Ride Free (Well, Some Do): Kids under 3 are admitted into the parks for free (and get a free ride if the ride allows someone that small). Anyone 10 and over is considered an adult in the eyes of the ticket booth. Passes for kids ages 3-9 cost about 20% less than adults'.

Pass Comparison Chart: Options and prices for your number of days.
(Prices are the 2006 costs of adult, non-discounted passes.)

Pass Type Days:	1	2	3	4	5	6	7	8	9	10	11	12	13	14
Single Day/Single Park	$59	$118	$177											
Park Hopper	$79	$116												
Park Hopper Bonus			$169	$199	$219									
Deluxe Annual Pass					$209									→
Premium Annual Pass						$329								→

Planning
Getting There
Staying in Style
Touring
Feasting
Making Magic
Index
Notes & More

Disney Park Hours

Disneyland Resort's park operating hours vary from day to day and season to season, which can make detailed trip planning a bit of a challenge. While Disney does announce its schedule about three to four months in advance, those **hours can and do change without notice**. They'll even extend park hours on the spot if the day's crowd is larger than expected.

Essentially, Disneyland Resort has **three park seasons**: The Summer schedule runs from Memorial Day Weekend (usually the last weekend in May) through Labor Day (the first Monday in September). The Off-Season picks up where the busy Summer leaves off, running from September through May, with breaks for major holidays. During Holiday weeks and long Holiday weekends, you can expect that the parks will be open later than usual, parades will be more numerous, and the fireworks and Fantasmic! at Disneyland Park will light up nearly every evening after dark.

To help you peer farther into the future, we've prepared a chart that shows typical operating hours during the **various seasons and days of the week**. As we've already noted, these hours can vary. Further, some attractions at Disneyland Park are open early on select days for special guests (see pages 82–83), and both parks may open an hour earlier (and remain open an hour or more later) on busier weekends and holidays. Each of Downtown Disney's shops, restaurants, and entertainment venues sets its own schedule—you can get more information on these in the Downtown Disney section.

Typical Disneyland Resort Theme Park Hours (subject to variation and change)

	Summer Season & Holidays		Off-Season (Sept.–May)	
	Disneyland	DCA	Disneyland	DCA
Monday–Thursday	8:00 am–11:00 pm (some 'til 10:00 pm)	10:00 am–9:00 pm	10:00 am–8:00pm	10:00 am–6:00 pm
Friday	8:00 am–11:00 pm	10:00 am–9:00 pm	9:00 am–11:00pm	10:00 am–9:00 pm
Saturday/Holiday	8:00 am–11:00 pm	10:00 am–9:00 pm	8 or 9 am–11:00 pm	10:00 am–9:00 pm
Sunday	8:00 am–11:00 pm	10:00 am–9:00 pm	9:00 am–10:00 pm	10:00 am–9:00 pm

For the most up-to-date information, phone **Disneyland Guest Relations** at 714-781-7290, or ask at your hotel's front desk. Park guidemaps also list hours and event schedules.

If you have Internet access, **Disneyland Resort's web page** lets you peer as far as 120 days (four months) into the future (http://disneyland.disney.go.com/dlr/calendar). Select the month and date you're interested in from the calendar grid to view park operating hours, parades, entertainment schedules, featured performers, and attractions closed for refurbishment. The listings for Downtown Disney even include movie showtimes for the AMC theater (available about a week in advance).

Mouseplanet.com prepares its own schedule, adjusted to reflect their experience and research—you can access it online at http://www.mouseplanet.com/parkupdates/dlr, or just visit http://www.mouseplanet.com and click on "DLR Park Update").

Hitting the Pavement

Most of you will get to Disneyland in one of two ways: you'll drive and park, or you'll walk from your hotel. And once you're there, you'll walk just about everywhere or ride the "highway in the sky," the monorail. You'll see a lot of pavement. Embrace the pavement. Your feet are your friends.

Parking—Once you've made it to Disneyland (we give driving directions on page 22), you can park right on property. You'll be directed into one of several lots: the relatively new Mickey and Friends parking structure, Pinocchio (near the Disneyland Hotel), Simba (near Paradise Pier Hotel), and Timon (part of the original parking lot located off Harbor Boulevard). Cast members and signs will direct you to the best parking lot—lots do fill up and can become congested, so it's best to allow at least 20-30 minutes extra for parking. Parking fees are $10/day (oversized and recreational vehicles are $12/day and buses are $17/day), but free to Premium Annual PassHolders (other annual passholders can purchase an annual parking pass for $49). Hold on to your parking receipt in case you leave and decide to return later. Lock your car and make a note of where it is parked, including the row number, section letter, and Disney character—jot it down on a PassPocket or your parking receipt, or take a digital photo. Follow signs to the tram pickup point, board the tram (strollers must be folded), and enjoy the brief ride to the parks. At the end of the day, expect the parking lots to be busy, and allow at least 30 minutes to exit.

Walking—Thanks to the proximity of the parks and Downtown Disney, walking is really the quickest way to get to most spots on property. Be sure to wear well-broken-in shoes—blisters are no fun (but if you do get blisters, bandages are available at the First Aid Centers). If you have young kids, you may want to bring your own stroller to help with all the walking you'll do (see page 97 for stroller tips). For those 'who have difficulty walking, wheelchairs and ECVs are available for rent inside the parks. See page 81.

Monorail—The famous monorail runs along one 2½-mile loop through both parks and Downtown Disney. You can only embark and disembark the monorail at two points, alas—in Tomorrowland inside Disneyland Park and beside Rainforest Cafe in Downtown Disney. It's useful transportation if you're near Downtown Disney and want to get to Tomorrowland, or vice versa. Beyond that, it's mostly just a fun attraction (see page 105).

Disneyland Railroad—This is a fun way to travel to certain lands within the Disneyland Park. It may not be much faster than walking, but it gives your feet a rest, offers a cool breeze, and provides fun scenery (see page 94). It's a real time saver during parades!

Finding Your Way Around

Plenty of signs point you in the direction of the parks and such. But once you're in the park, the signs are noticeably absent. At this point, the free park guidemap becomes your best asset. Pick up maps when you enter (grab more than you need) and make sure everyone in your party has a copy. (If you forget to pick them up on the way in, you can usually get copies in the shops or from cast members.) The maps are well done, and you can use buildings and landmarks on them to orient yourself. If you get lost, just ask a cast member for assistance. If a member of your party is lost, report directly to a cast member. Tip: Put contact information on kids in case they get lost, but don't display names. And dress everyone in the same color to easily spot each other in crowds.

Planning
Getting There
Staying in Style
Touring
Feasting
Making Magic
Index
Notes & More

Disney Park Tips and Ratings

Before you arrive, check **park hours** by calling 714-781-4565 or by visiting http://www.disneyland.com. Hotel guests may also consult the park maps and Times Guides on arrival.

Study the descriptions and maps to **familiarize yourself** with the names and themes of the lands before you arrive.

Check the **Tip Board** at the end of the main thoroughfare in each park. These tip boards are continuously updated with wait times and closings—even openings or sneak peeks of new attractions.

Plan your visit around the things that are **most important** to you or require advance planning (like restaurant seatings or show times). If you're just not sure, you can use our favorite touring plans included in each park description as a starting point. Or make your own touring plan based on the "must-see" attractions on your list. In general, though, we feel it is more enjoyable to "go with the flow" from attraction to attraction within each land in a park. Relax and have fun!

Park Ratings

We rate each park to help you make the best decisions. Even so, our ratings may differ from your opinions—use the ratings as a guide only.

Value Ratings range from 1 (poor) to 10 (excellent) and are based on **quality** (cleanliness, maintenance, and freshness); **variety** (different types of thing to do); and **scope** (quantity and size of things to do)—**overall value** represents an average of the above three values. **Magic Ratings** are based on **theme** (execution and sense of immersion); **excitement** (thrills, laughs, and sense of wonder); and **fun factor** (number and quality of entertaining activities)—**overall magic** represents an average of the above three values. We use a point accumulation method to determine value and magic ratings.

Readers' Ratings are calculated from surveys submitted by vacationers at our web site (http://www.passporter.com/dl/rate.htm).

Guest satisfaction is based on our and our readers' experiences with how different types of guests enjoy the park: ♥♥♥♥♥=love it ♥♥♥♥=enjoy it ♥♥♥=like it ♥♥=tolerate it ♥=don't like it

Disneyland Park

You may know it as "Disneyland" or even "The Magic Kingdom," but we're going to bet you do know it in one way or another—Disneyland Park has been part of American culture for more than 50 years. This is quintessential Disney—if you do nothing else in Anaheim, visit this park.

Disneyland Park conjures up fantasy, nostalgia, youth, and most of all, **magic**. This 85-acre playground attracts visitors of all ages to its bygone boulevards, tropical gardens, western saloons, and living cartoons. All roads lead to Sleeping Beauty Castle, the crown of the Kingdom. If you've been to the Magic Kingdom in Walt Disney World, this is the jam-packed, souped-up, and slightly more compact version. More importantly, this is the only park that Walt himself built—and you can see his touch everywhere you go.

Five "lands" radiate like spokes from the hub of **Sleeping Beauty Castle**, located in the center of the park, with three more lands added on for good measure (see the fold-out map on page 90). Below are the lands in clockwise order, along with descriptions and headline attractions. See page 89a&b for an at-a-glance list of attractions and our favorite itineraries, and pages 94–106 for attraction details.

Main Street, U.S.A. *Headline Attractions:*	An early 1900s main street bustles with shops, eateries, vintage vehicles, and the City Hall. *Disneyland Railroad, The First 50 Magical Years*
Adventureland *Headline Attractions:*	Walk to the beat of jungle drums in a paradise filled with parrots, crocs, trees, and temples. *Enchanted Tiki Room, Jungle Cruise, Indiana Jones Adventure*
New Orleans Square *Headline Attractions:*	Jazz it up with a stroll through a lively market street complete with a railroad station. *Haunted Mansion, Pirates of the Caribbean*
Critter Country *Headline Attractions:*	Take an adventure to the backwoods to splash about in logs, paddle canoes, and play with Pooh. *Splash Mountain, Many Adventures of Winnie the Pooh*
Frontierland *Headline Attractions:*	Journey back to the American Frontier, complete with a fort, shootin' range, and saloon. *Big Thunder Mountain Railroad, Tom Sawyer Island*
Fantasyland *Headline Attractions:*	An enchanted, brightly colored "small world" where elephants fly and teacups spin. *Dumbo, "it's a small world," Matterhorn Bobsleds*
Mickey's Toontown *Headline Attractions:*	A cartoon land with Chip & Dale's Treehouse, Mickey and Minnie's homes, and Donald's Boat. *Roger Rabbit's Car Toon Spin, Mickey's House*
Tomorrowland *Headline Attractions:*	The future as imagined in the 1930s, complete with space flights, aliens, and time travel. *Space Mountain, Star Tours, Buzz Lightyear's Astro Blasters*

AMBIENCE

PARK LAYOUT AND HIGHLIGHTS

Planning

Getting There

Staying in Style

Touring

Feasting

Making Magic

Index

Notes & More

ENTERTAINMENT

Entertainment and Shopping at Disneyland Park

Fold out the next page for touring plans and a handy attraction chart

For most of us, Disneyland Park is virtually synonymous with "fun." Live entertainment fills the streets with parades, performers, bands, and, yes, fireworks. Every afternoon the all-new, 20-minute **Parade of Dreams** showcases more than 50 Disney characters on amazing floats (see the parade route on page 90). We like to watch the parade from Fantasyland as it's less crowded than Main Street. Between Thanksgiving and New Year's Day, the **Christmas Fantasy Parade** marches along the same parade route. In peak seasons, the dazzling, 17-minute "**Remember... Dreams Come True**" fireworks show explodes over and around Sleeping Beauty Castle (see page 107 for details and tips). Disney characters make appearances throughout the park, particularly in Fantasyland

© MediaMarx, Inc.

Two classic Disneyland attractions—Mark Twain Riverboat (foreground) and Big Thunder Mountain (background)

and Mickey's Toontown—check your park map for locations and times. Many of the lands offer their own shows and entertainment, too. The chart below lists some of our favorite shows. Performances vary from day to day and season to season—your park map lists the day's shows and times.

Show/Entertainment	Land	What makes it special
Flag Retreat	Main Street, U.S.A.	It's patriotic. See page 91 for info.
Aladdin's StoryTale	Adventureland	Delightful story—includes Jasmine!
Golden Horseshoe Show	Frontierland	It's foot-tappin', foolish fun.
Sword in the Stone	Fantasyland	Your child could be crowned!
Club Buzz Stage	Tomorrowland	Munch lunch while you watch!

You can get a preview of showtimes at http://www.disneyland.com.

SHOPPING

Sure stops for general Disney merchandise include much of Main Street, U.S.A.—shops here are open for half an hour after park closing. Here are some of our **favorite themed shops**:

Shop	Land	What makes it special
Disneyana	Main Street, U.S.A.	Hand-drawn character sketches
Disney Clothiers	Main Street, U.S.A.	Upscale yet casual Disney clothes
The Disney Gallery	New Orleans Square	Amazing art, quaint courtyard
Castle Princess Shop	Fantasyland	Disney costumes and dolls
Mad Hatter	Fantasyland	Hats with embroidered names
Gag Factory	Mickey's Toontown	Silly fun amid the Disney goods
The Star Trader	Tomorrowland	Sci-fi toys and gadgets

Making the Most
of Disneyland Park

TIPS

Main Street, U.S.A. may open **half an hour earlier** than the rest of the park. So arrive early, grab breakfast, and get ready to hit the park.

Is this your first visit to the park? Take a spin around the park when you first arrive by boarding the train at the **Disneyland Railroad** station in Main Street, U.S.A. The 20-minute journey is a great introduction to the park.

Consider a **guided tour**. Disneyland Park offers several guided tours, including "A Walk In Walt's Footsteps," a $3^1/_2$-hour guided tour with delightful historical facts about the park and its founder. For tour details, see pages 228–229.

Make time for the **Flag Retreat** in the Main Street, U.S.A. town square, held daily about 30 minutes before sunset. On some days, a color guard takes down the American flag. Veterans may inquire at City Hall about assisting, too.

Seniors traveling with **grandchildren** should visit the Disneyland Park together. The look in the childrens' eyes alone will be worth the trip.

Delightful details are everywhere in this park. You'll notice several in Main Street, U.S.A. For example, listen for the "voices" coming from upstairs windows along the street, look for Walt's miniature train and an aerial photo of the park in the train station, and an old-time "party line" phone at the Market House shop.

Take a moment out of your busy day to stop by the **Snow White Grotto**, located to the right of the Sleeping Beauty Castle drawbridge. Drop a coin in the well, make a wish, and listen for Snow White's wishing song.

Disneyland Park offers plenty of **dining choices**—see pages 197–200. Keep in mind that you can also pop out to one of the restaurants in Downtown Disney, too.

No alcohol is served here. If you want an adult beverage, go to Downtown Disney, visit one of the hotels, or park hop to Disney's California Adventure.

Need a good **place to meet**? The passageway through Sleeping Beauty Castle is a good choice as it is central and easy to find.

Got a boo-boo or have a baby on board? Both **First Aid** and the **Baby Care Center** are located at the end of Main Street, U.S.A. near the Plaza Inn eatery.

Many **restrooms** in Disneyland Park have automatic flush toilets, which can be frightening to very young kids who are newly acquainted with toilets. Visit "The Happiest Potties on Earth" web site at http://www.mouseplanet.com/potties.

Guests with obvious ambulatory impairments, the legally blind, or those with certain "invisible" disabilities, such as autism or cystic fibrosis, may apply at City Hall on Main Street, U.S.A for a **Guest Assistance Card**. This is the also the spot to pick up the "Services for Guests with Disabilities" guidebook (or download it from http://www.disneyland.com in advance). If you are unable to stand in long lines, you probably won't be able to obtain a Special Assistance Card unless you're also using a brace, cane, or crutch—consider renting a wheelchair or ECV to assist you. Guests with hearing impairments may borrow a **handheld captioning device** that works places where reflective or video captioning is impractical—inquire at City Hall.

Getting the Best
at Disneyland Park

Planning

Getting There

Staying in Style

Touring

Feasting

Making Magic

Index

Notes & More

BEST TIMES TO GO

What are the **best times to go?** The park tends to be the busiest on the weekends, when locals claim the park as their backyard playground—Saturday is the single busiest day while Sunday morning is the most tolerable time of the weekend. Best days to visit are mid-week (Tuesday, Wednesday, and Thursday). Arrive as early as possible—if you're there before the "rope drops," walk through the shops in Main Street, U.S.A. (they're all connected) to get closer to the rope. Popular attractions such as Splash Mountain, Star Tours, Indiana Jones Adventure, and Haunted Mansion are best done first thing in the morning to avoid long lines. Visit lands on the east (right) side of the park earlier in the day, as most folks tend to go in the opposite direction first. Parents of young children are best off doing Fantasyland first as it gets busier later in the day. Take advantage of FASTPASS (see page 80) whenever possible, and check the Tip Board at the end of Main Street, U.S.A. for showtimes and wait times. Shop in the afternoon to avoid crowds. Remember to take breaks regularly throughout the day and drink plenty of water.

BEST SPOTS

For those in need of guidance, here are our **favorite spots** in the park:

Best Places to Cool Off—Main Street Cinema, Pirates of the Caribbean, "Honey, I Shrunk the Audience," Innoventions, Donald's Boat, any shop, the hotel pool

Best Places to Relax—On a wrought-iron bench near the Haunted Mansion, on the Mark Twain Riverboat, Fantasia Gardens, Plaza Gardens

Best Places to Burn Off Energy—Tom Sawyer Island, Chip 'n Dale Treehouse, Tarzan's Treehouse

Best Attractions to Visit During the Holidays—"it's a small world" and Haunted Mansion Holiday (in Nightmare Before Christmas garb)

Best Places to Propose—Snow White's Grotto, Blue Bayou Restaurant

Best Place to Sneak a Kiss—Adventureland in the evening

Best Place to Get a Snack—Tiki Juice Bar in Adventureland (try a Dole Whip)

Best Places for Meals—Plaza Inn, Blue Bayou Restaurant, Rancho del Zocalo

Best Places to Watch the Parade—By Alice in Wonderland or "it's a small world" (in Fantasyland), in front of the Main Street railroad station or on the platform

Best Place to Meet Mickey—Mickey's House in Mickey's Toontown

Ratings are explained on page 86.

RATINGS

Our Value Ratings:		Our Magic Ratings:		Readers' Ratings:
Quality:	7/10	Theme:	7/10	82% fell in love with it
Variety:	9/10	Excitement:	10/10	15% liked it well enough
Scope:	7/10	Fun Factor:	7/10	2% had mixed feelings
Overall Value:	**8/10**	**Overall Magic:**	**8/10**	1% were disappointed

Disneyland Park is enjoyed by...		(rated by both authors and readers)	
Younger Kids: ♥♥♥♥♥	Young Adults: ♥♥♥♥	Families: ♥♥♥♥♥
Older Kids: ♥♥♥♥♥	Mid Adults: ♥♥♥	Couples: ♥♥♥♥
Teenagers: ♥♥♥♥	Mature Adults: ♥♥♥	Singles: ♥♥♥

Understanding and Using the Attraction Descriptions and Ratings

PassPorter's custom-designed attraction charts include background, trivia, tips, restrictions, queues, and accessibility details. We've organized these details into a consistent format so you can find what you need at a glance. Below is a key to our charts, along with notes and details. Enjoy!

Description Key

Icons[4]   Ratings[5]

1 Attraction Name [D-3²] (Bar Color³) FP ẋǏ A-Ok! # # #	
Description offering an overview of the attraction, what to expect (without giving too much away, of course), historical background, trivia and "secrets," our recommendations for the best seating/viewing/riding, tips on getting the most out of the attraction, suggestions on when to visit, waiting/queue conditions (i.e., covered, outdoor, etc.), wheelchair and stroller accessibility, height/age restrictions, and accessibility for the differently abled.	**Type**[6]
	Scope[6]
	Ages[7]
	Thrill Factor[8]
	Avg. Wait[8]
	Duration[8]

[1] Each chart has an empty **checkbox** in the upper left corner—use it to check off the attractions you want to visit (before you go) or those you visited (after you return).

[2] **Map coordinates** are presented as a letter and a number, i.e. B-5. Match up the coordinates on the park's map for the attraction's location within the park.

[3] The **bar color** indicates the attraction's target audience, as follows:

Thrill-Seekers	Family-Friendly	Loved by Little Kids	Everything Else

[4] Icons indicate when an attraction has FASTPASS (**FP**) or a height/age restriction (**ẋǏ**).

[5] Our **ratings** are shown on the far right end. An **A-Ok!** indicates that an attraction is toddler-friendly and Alexander-approved (as rated by our 1-year-old son). The three boxes on the right side show ratings on a scale of 1 (poor) to 10 (don't miss!). The first is **Jennifer's** rating, the second is Dave's, and the third is our **Readers'** ratings. We offer our personal ratings to show how opinions vary, even between two like-minded people. You can also use our ratings as a point of reference—Jennifer appreciates good theming and dislikes sudden spins or drops, while Dave enjoys live performances and thrills. We both appreciate detail-rich attractions where we can learn something new.

[6] The boxes on the right below the numeric ratings give basic information. The first box is **attraction type**. The second box is always **attraction scope**, which we rate as follows:

E-Ticket	Headliner attraction; the ultimate; expect long lines
D-Ticket	Excellent fun, not-to-be-missed
C-Ticket	Solid attraction that pleases most guests
B-Ticket	Good fun, but easily skipped in a pinch
A-Ticket	A simple diversion; often overlooked

[7] **Age-appropriate ratings**. For example, we may say "All Ages" when we feel everyone, from infant on up, will get something out of the experience. More common is "Ages 4 & up" or "Ages 8 & up" for attractions we think will be best appreciated by vacationers who are at least 4 or 8. This is only a guideline from fellow parents and not a rule. On the other hand, it is a Disney rule that 7 is the minimum age to ride any moving attraction alone.

[8] **Thrill/scare factor, average wait**, and **duration** follow the age ratings, though we eliminate these if they don't apply or expand them if deserving. We did our best to format this information so you can understand it without having to check this key, too!

Charting the Attractions
at Main Street, U.S.A.

| | Jennifer's Rating | Dave's Rating | Readers' Rating |

Disneyland Railroad [D-6]   A-ok! | 5 | 5 | 7 |

Circle the Disneyland park on a steam train, with stops at Main Street, U.S.A., New Orleans Square, Mickey's Toontown, and Tomorrowland. You'll catch glimpses of all but Adventureland along the 1.5-mile journey. Ride the full route for fun, or disembark at any stop along the way. Provides glimpses into two otherwise unseen vistas—Grand Canyon Diorama and Primeval World. Personal strollers must be folded before boarding. Replacement rental strollers may be available at other stops (keep your nametag!) but aren't guaranteed. Attraction closed during the fireworks. Must transfer from ECV to wheelchair. Handheld captioning.

Rail Ride
C-Ticket
All ages
A bit loud
Gentle ride
Short waits
20 min. ride (roundtrip)

Main Street Cinema [E-5] | 3 | 5 | 5 |

Many guests overlook this "hole in the wall" showing Disney cartoon shorts like "Steamboat Willie." Most are vintage, silent, and black and white, but it's still fun to watch. Six different "screens" show different short movies continuously throughout the day. Cool off in the air conditioning. No seating available.

Film
A-Ticket
Ages 2 & up
Simple fun

Main Street Vehicles [D-6] | 3 | 2 | 5 |

Catch a one-way ride to the hub of the park in vehicles fashioned after those popular at the turn of the 20th century. We've seen horseless carriages, trolleys pulled by Belgian horses, and even a fire engine. These vehicles are fun to ride in if you're willing to wait in the slow, long lines. No time? Just walk instead. Must transfer from wheelchair. Board at either end of Main Street.

Vehicles
A-Ticket
All ages
Gentle ride
Long waits

Penny Arcade [D-5] | 3 | 3 | 5 |

While Disney doesn't list this fun little spot as an attraction on its guidemaps, we think it's deserving of the title and a few minutes of your time. Bring some coins for the old-fashioned "fortune tellers" and moving picture machines.

Arcade
A-Ticket
Ages 4 & up

Disneyland: The First 50 Magical Years [E-6] | 8 | 7 | 7 |

This is a delightful, all-new attraction showcasing the fun and fascinating history of the first Disney theme park, Disneyland! Held in the Opera House (it's temporarily replacing "Great Moments with Mr. Lincoln"), it begins with a detailed exhibit of attraction models, concept art, photos, and old ticket media, including a new, highly detailed model of what Disneyland looked like on the day it opened. Guests are then invited into the theater for a film highlighting Disneyland's memorable moments, hosted by Steve Martin and Donald Duck. Closed captioning. Assistive listening. Shows every 20 minutes.

Show
C-Ticket
Ages 7 & up
Dark
Short waits
7 min. pre-show
13 min. show

Attraction descriptions and ratings are explained on page 93.

🚱 What Is and Isn't an Attraction?

We defined an "attraction" on page 80 as an individual ride, show, or exhibit. These are the destinations at the park and almost invariably come with a queue. We cover virtually all the attractions that Disney lists in its own guidemaps, plus a few that aren't listed (such as the Penny Arcade). Like Disney, we don't consider things like talking trash cans (yes, they exist!) to be attractions. We also don't consider outdoor shows, parades, or fireworks to be attractions—we cover these in the Entertainment sections of this chapter.

Charting the Attractions
at Adventureland

	Jennifer's Rating	Dave's Rating	Readers' Rating

▢ Aladdin's Oasis [D-5] · 7 · 7 · 8

Enjoy imaginative, improvisational shows featuring the exploits of Aladdin and Jasmine. The kid-friendly story is narrated by Barker Bob and Kazoo, with lots of audience participation. Prior to 1997, this was a dinner show, but food is no longer served here. Before that, it was the Tahitian Terrace restaurant. Check your Times Guide for showtimes. This is a seasonal attraction, but it's typically open on weekends and in the summer. Sit at tables and chairs, or stand.

Live Show
C-Ticket
Ages 2 & up
Lots of stairs
Allow 20–30 min. for show

▢ Enchanted Tiki Room [D-5] · A-ok! · 7 · 7 · 6

A perfectly cool place to sit and rest while 225 Audio-Animatronics birds, flowers, and other creatures sing and cavort above you. The Tiki Room has been a Disney fixture for many childhoods and was the first attraction to feature Audio-Animatronics. This is a fun musical revue, which grew from Walt Disney's notion for an unusual Chinese restaurant called The Bird Cafe. Don't miss the delightful tiki gods in the outdoor garden before the show. Note to Walt Disney World fans: this is the original without Iago and Zazu! Best views are on the left side. Bench seating. Must transfer from wheelchair. Recently renovated.

Show
D-Ticket
Ages 4 & up
Dark, loud, angry gods
Short waits
10 min. intro
16 min. show

▢ Indiana Jones Adventure [C-6] · FP 🚶 · 9 · 8 · 9

Enter the Temple of the Forbbiden Eye for a rollicking, fast-paced adventure, Indiana Jones-style! The very long but delightfully themed queue is mostly indoors and snakes through an archealogical dig—for some fun, push lightly on the spike holding up the ceiling, and pull on the rope going into the well. Eventually you board 12-person "troop transport" vehicles and head off in search of Indiana Jones. Along the way, you'll bounce and jostle, encountering mummies, fires, lava, "poison darts," rats, failing bridges, and, yes, snakes ("oh, why does it have to be snakes?") Height restriction of 46"/117 cm. Kids under the age of 7 must be with accompanied by an adult. Health warning. Must transfer from wheelchair. Video captioning.

Thrill Ride
E-Ticket
Ages 6 & up
Very dark, very loud, scary stuff
FASTPASS or long waits
3½ min. ride

▢ Jungle Cruise [C-5] · A-ok! · 6 · 6 · 7

See the sights along the "rivers of the world" in the company of an intrepid and slightly silly skipper. You and your fellow explorers will go chug-chugging up river in an open-air, awning-covered river boat inspired by the movie, "African Queen." Every skipper tells a slightly different tale. Audio-Animatronics animals and "natives" liven things up. You may get damp. After-dark cruises are particularly fun. Outdoor, covered queue—lines can be deceptively long. Must transfer from wheelchair. Recently renovated—there are now "piranhas" in the water!

Boat Ride
D-Ticket
Ages 3 & up
Corny jokes, animals
Long waits
8 min. ride

▢ Tarzan's Treehouse [C-5] · 5 · 5 · 4

The story of Tarzan unfolds as you climb through the branches of the huge (and very fake) banyan tree, known affectionately as "Disneyodendron Semper Florens." The treehouse has multiple levels which you access via stairs and it can be tiring for some. The line of guests winds through slowly. Prior to 1999, this was home to the shipwrecked family from the Disney classic "Swiss Family Robinson." The lowest level is accessible to wheelchairs and strollers.

Walkthru
B-Ticket
Ages 4 & up
Lots of stairs
Allow 10–20 min. to tour

Side tabs: Planning · Getting There · Staying in Style · Touring · Feasting · Making Magic · Index · Notes & More

Planning

Getting There

Staying in Style

Touring

Feasting

Making Magic

Index

Notes & More

Charting the Attractions at New Orleans Square

Jennifer's Rating
Dave's Rating
Readers' Rating

■ The Disney Gallery [C-5]   8 9 7

Climb the elegant stairs above Pirates of the Caribbean to enter this French Quarter-style gallery of Disney art. This is a real treat for Disney fans, with plenty of concept drawings. Spend a few minutes in the cool courtyard, or watch the boats go by while sitting on the balcony. Ask a cast member for a guided tour. A dessert buffet with Fantasmic! seating is available (see pages 107 and 223). Originally designed as Walt's private apartment. Wheelchair accessible.

Exhibit
B-Ticket
All ages
No waits
Allow 20-40 minutes

■ Haunted Mansion [B-4]   9 8 9

Go for a gore-free ride through a world of 999 grinning ghosts. The spooky visual effects are astounding, but the scares are served up with a wink and lots of chuckles. Keep your eyes wide open (when you can). There's so much delicious detail here that you'll ride again and again. Just be sure to leave room in your two-to-three-person "doom buggy" for hitchhiking ghosts! May be too intense for young kids. Recently renovated—Madame Leota's ball now "floats." Transfer from wheelchair to ride. Look at the upper windows of the mansion in the evenings—is that a ghost? Visit http://www.doombuggies.com for more details. In November and December, this attraction becomes the delightful Haunted Mansion Holiday with characters from "A Nightmare Before Christmas"—we love it!

Track Ride
E-Ticket
Ages 6 & up
Mild scares, very dark
Medium waits
2 min. intro 5½ min. ride

■ Pirates of the Caribbean [C-5] (closed for renovations until 6/24/2006)   8 7 9

"Yo ho, yo ho!" Take a slow, dark cruise through a subterranean world of Audio-Animatronics pirates and the townsfolk they plunder. Your boat drifts past scene after riotous scene and fun special effects, including new Audio-Animatronics appearances by Captains Jack Sparrow and Barbossa. It's not 100% politically correct but still a longtime favorite. Lines can be long but generally move quickly. You aren't likely to get wet. Transfer from wheelchair to ride. Walt Disney World fans should note that this is a better, longer version with two bigger drops.

Boat Ride
E-Ticket
Ages 6 & up
Gentle drop, dark, scary to young kids
13 min. ride

Tip: You can board the train (see page 94) at the New Orleans Square Depot [B-5].

🚩 Club 33

As you wander down New Orleans Square, you may spy a discreet door at 33 Royal Street. This is the private Club 33, only open to members and their guests. Club 33 was designed by Walt as a place to entertain VIPs and continues that tradition today. Both corporate and individual memberships are available, but the price tags are high—we've seen reports as high as $20,000 for a corporate membership or $7,500 for an individual Gold membership. However, membership is limited to just 400 and the waiting list is very long, several years at best. Most folks get in by knowing someone else with a membership. Once inside, you take the French lift to the second floor where you can enjoy an elegant meal in one of two dining rooms. This is the only spot in the Disneyland Park where alcoholic beverages are served. Conceptual sketches line the walls, antiques decorate the various rooms, and French doors lead out to a balcony overlooking the river. Want a look inside? Take "A Walk in Walt's Footsteps" tour (see page 229) for a peek into the club's lobby. You can also view photos and other details on the unofficial Club 33 web site at http://www.disneylandclub33.com.

Charting the Attractions
at Critter Country

(ratings columns: Jennifer's Rating / Dave's Rating / Readers' Rating)

☐ Davy Crockett's Explorer Canoes [B-4]   **2 1 3**

You'll need pioneer spirit to cruise these long canoes along the Rivers of America. Everyone paddles the free-floating fiberglass canoes, which can be fun for some but tiring for others. You'd think this would be one of Dave's favorite attractions considering he was, in part, named after Davy and absolutely adores canoeing, but it doesn't "float his boat." The near ½-mile route around Tom Sawyer Island is long, but the sights are interesting. We think the Mark Twain Riverboat offers more interest. Open seasonally. Closes at dusk. Must transfer from wheelchair.

Boat Ride
B-Ticket
All ages
Paddling, you may get a bit damp
10 min. ride

☐ The Many Adventures of Winnie the Pooh [A-4]   A-OK!   **6 5 7**

Take a gentle ride through the world of that fabulously popular Pooh Bear as he searches for a pot of hunny. Breeze through the 100 Acre Wood in a six-seated "hunny beehive" that moves along an indoor/outdoor track. On the adventure Baby Roo and Piglet are saved from the storm, Heffalumps and Woozles come out to play, and Pooh gets a birthday party from all his friends. The better you know Pooh's tales the more you'll get from your tour through the cartoon cut-out scenery. The uncovered queue winds beside a brook. Sit in the first two rows for best view. This attraction replaced the Country Bear Jamboree in 2003, and you can still see the heads of three Country Bear critters (Max, Melvin, and Buff) in the "Hunny" room. Transfer from ECV to wheelchair.

Track Ride
D-Ticket
All ages
Kid-friendly; dark could be slightly scary
Short waits
3 min. ride

☐ Splash Mountain [A-4]   FP ♿   **4 6 9**

Even bystanders can get soaked when riders slide down this five-story log flume into the Briar Patch. The first nine minutes of this attraction are a gentle ride through an Audio-Animatronics wonderland with all the "brer" creatures from The Song of the South (and even some from "America Sings"). Then, kersplash! The five-person log flume drops down the 52 ft. Chickapin Hill at a 45° angle just as your photo is taken. We do not recommend this for the timid. You will get wet! 40"/102 cm height restriction; guests under 8 years old must be accompanied by an adult. Health warning. Must transfer from wheelchair to ride.

Flume Ride
E-Ticket
Ages 7 & up
Very steep drop at end!
FASTPASS or long waits
10 min. ride

Attraction descriptions and ratings are explained on page 93.

ⓘ Strollers: To Bring or Rent

If you bring your own stroller (a boon for the airport and parking lots), we recommend a compact, umbrella stroller, as it's easy to tote about. You may instead prefer to rent a stroller for $8/day at the park—you can rent them from the ticket booths outside the parks or inside at one of several locations, including the main rental shops just inside both parks on the right. The strollers are "Baby Joggers" (http://www.babyjogger.com) with canvas seats and large rear wheels. Rentals are good for kids who only need an occasional ride. Keep in mind that while you may take the stroller to the other Disney park, it cannot go beyond that—so if you're staying at a hotel within walking distance or plan to spend a lot of time in Downtown Disney, you may want to bring your own stroller instead. If you do rent, keep your rental receipt on you in the event you lose track of your stroller or need to get a stroller in a different location. Note: Wagons aren't allowed in the park. For more tips, visit http://www.mouseplanet.com/akrock.

(margin tabs: Planning · Getting There · Staying in Style · Touring · Feasting · Making Magic · Index · Notes & More)

Charting the Attractions at Frontierland

Jennifer's Rating · Dave's Rating · Readers' Rating

■ Big Thunder Mountain Railroad [C-3] _FP_ 🚶 | 7 | 8 | 9

Be prepared to grin as you ride this not-so-scary '49er roller coaster through a two-acre Wild West landscape. There is plenty of speed and lots of curves, but no fearsome drops on this short, "runaway" mine train ride. You'll tilt, shake, and rattle, though! Look around and enjoy Disney's lovingly built environment, including a "natural" arch bridge, falling rocks, and a flooded bridge. Lines can be long, with only fans and shade to cool you off. 40"/102 cm height restriction, adult supervision required. Guests must transfer from wheelchair. Health warning. This attraction re-opened in 2004 after renovations and repairs following a serious accident in September 2003.

Coaster
E-Ticket
Ages 6 & up
Fast turns, dark caves
FASTPASS or long waits
3½ min. ride

© MediaMarx, Inc.

A "runaway" mine train

■ Little Patch of Heaven Petting Farm [C-2] _A-ok!_ | 5 | 5 | 5

Open again after an eight-year hiatus, this petting zoo is a "little patch of heaven," themed after "Disney's Home on the Range" animated feature. The small enclosure features a horse, turkeys, pygmy goats, baby sheep, and a young Jersey cow, though more animals may be introduced in the future. A small log cabin houses a crafts area for kids. A hand-washing station is provided, as are dispensers of hand-sanitizing gel. The petting farm may get gussied up for the holidays in November and December—in 2005, Santa's Reindeer Round-Up appeared here. Formerly the Festival of Fools show.

Petting Zoo
B-Ticket
All ages
Real animals
Short waits
Allow 15 min.

■ Frontierland Shootin' Exposition [D-4] | 4 | 6 | 3

Have fun shootin' targets on Boot Hill with one of 18 infrared rifles, cuz nobody's keepin' score. Aim at cactus, tombstones, and bits of the landscape—no people or animals at which to shoot, thank goodness! Your reward for hitting a target is a surprise sight gag. Rifles are heavy—Allie couldn't properly hold one until she was nine. Cost is 50 cents for about 25 shots. Until 1987, this was the Frontierland Shooting Gallery with "real bullets" (lead shot).

Arcade
A-Ticket
Ages 8 & up
Guns
Short waits
Allow 10 min.

■ The Golden Horseshoe Stage [C-4] | 5 | 7 | 5

Grab a ringside table for a wild 'n' funny live stage show with Billy Hill and the Hillbillies, bluegrass musicians, and comedians extraordinaire. Be ready to stomp your feet and join in the fun. Not sure you're ready for that much fun? Sit in the balcony to avoid being part of the show. Belly up to the bar for a limited selection of chicken strips, fish & chips, mozzarella sticks, and root beer (see page 198). This is a great way to eat lunch and enjoy a show at the same time. Wheelchair accessible. Assistive listening devices. This attraction used to require reservations, but that went the way of the tumbleweed a few years ago—now it's first-come, first-served. Check your times guide for showtimes.

Live Show
C-Ticket
Ages 3 & up
Corny jokes, audience participation
Short waits
35 min. show

Attraction descriptions and ratings are explained on page 93.

Planning
Getting There
Staying in Style
Touring
Feasting
Making Magic
Index
Notes & More

Charting the Attractions
at Frontierland
(continued)

	Jennifer's Rating	Dave's Rating	Readers' Rating

☐ Mark Twain Riverboat [C-4]   A-OK!   6 6 5

Take a cruise on a steam-driven sternwheeler (see photo on page 90). Mark Twain narrates your spin around Tom Sawyer Island, but the real joy is the attention to detail. The boat and its steam power plant are more interesting than the scenery—be sure to tour the decks. There are a few chairs on the bow of the bottom deck. This is one of the original Disneyland attractions on opening day in 1955. Kids under 10 may have the chance to "steer" the ship in the wheelhouse—ask a cast member for details. Wheelchair accessible. Adult supervision. Cruises depart on the hour and half-hour.	**Boat Ride** C-Ticket All ages Gentle rides Medium waits 20 min. ride

☐ Sailing Ship Columbia [C-4]   A-OK!   7 6 6

This full-scale replica of an 18th century merchant sailing ship offers a sedate cruise around the Rivers of America. The three-masted, ten-gun ship is open to guests both above decks (for a view of the same route you ply with the Mark Twain Riverboat and Davy Crockett Explorer Canoes) and below decks (for a look at the way the ship's crew would have worked and lived in 1787). This attraction only operates on very busy days—we've only encountered it up and running a few times. If it's running, we suggest you choose this over the Mark Twain Riverboat. Must be ambulatory to ride. Adult supervision.

Boat Ride
C-Ticket
All ages
Gentle rides
Short waits
14 min. ride

Alexander inspects the riggin'

☐ Tom Sawyer Island [B-4]   A-OK!   6 7 5

Board a free-floating raft in New Orleans Square to explore the last 2 ½ "undeveloped" acres of Frontierland. Young 'uns enjoy Injun Joe's Cave, Castle Rock Lookout, Tom's Treehouse, and a barrel bridge as they scamper over Tom and Huck's legendary hangout. Oldtimers can wander the winding paths and suspension bridge. This is a great place for a mid-afternoon break. Guests must be ambulatory. The island closes at dusk. This underappreciated attraction reopened in summer 2003 after extensive renovations. Changes include character interactions with Tom Sawyer and Huck Finn, narrower cave entrances (some adults may no longer fit through), and a wonderful treehouse play area. The caves also have some new lighting, making them slightly less scary for young kids.	**Playground** D-Ticket All ages Dark, narrow caves Short waits Allow 1-2 hours

ⓘ Disneyland's Original Attractions

With the 50th anniversary celebration in full bloom, you may like to know which of the original opening day attractions are still operating: Disneyland Railroad, Main Street Cinema, Main Street Vehicles, Penny Arcade, Jungle Cruise, Mark Twain Steamboat, Golden Horseshoe Revue, King Arthur Carrousel, Peter Pan's Flight, Snow White's Scary Adventures, Mad Tea Party, Mr. Toad's Wild Ride, and Autopia.

Charting the Attractions at Fantasyland

	Jennifer's Rating	Dave's Rating	Readers' Rating

☐ Alice in Wonderland [E-3]　　A-OK!

	5	6	6

Hop a ride aboard a four-person caterpillar to go through Alice's rabbit hole and on to her infamous adventures in Wonderland. You'll follow the white rabbit through the dark as you shrink down, meet Tweedle Dum and Tweedle Dee, play with the Queen of Hearts, discover the Cheshire Cat, and enjoy an unbirthday party and a surprise! It's fun to ride this attraction just before going on the Mad Tea Party. Must transfer from wheelchair. May close when it rains.

Track Ride
C-Ticket
All ages
Dark ride
4 min. ride

☐ Casey Jr. Circus Train [D-2]　　A-OK!

	5	4	5

Just chant "I think I can, I think I can" and you'll find yourself climbing inside one of the charming little train cars and chug-chugging around Storybook Land. While you won't get as good a look at the miniatures of Storybook Land as you do on the Canal Boats (see page 102), it is faster. This is a fun ride for the little ones, but adults may find the cars a tight squeeze. Inspired by Disney's animated feature, "Dumbo." Opened July 31, 1955. Must transfer from wheelchair.

Train Ride
C-Ticket
All ages
Little cars
Short waits
3½ min. ride

☐ Dumbo The Flying Elephant [D-3]　　A-OK!

	6	5	6

Every child wants to ride around, up, and down on Dumbo. Two-seater flying elephants take you for a short, fast spin. Show your child how to lift the control lever to go higher. Grownups will enjoy the pachyderm's-eye view of Fantasyland. The lines are long and hot—the queue area has virtually no shade. Adults must ride with small children, and you know the kids will want to ride again. Try to ride early in the day, as the wait is very long the rest of the time. Opened August 16, 1955. Must transfer from wheelchair.

Ride
C-Ticket
All ages
Spins high in the air
Long waits
2 min. flight

☐ Fantasyland Theatre playing "Snow White" [E-2]

	7	7	6

This large outdoor amphitheatre has hosted a variety of stage shows over the years, with "Snow White – An Enchanting New Musical" now playing since February 23, 2004, but set to end in summer 2006. The sets, music, and performances of the new show are excellent, and we consider it a must-see. The story is very similar to that told in the animated feature. Arrive at least 30-45 minutes early to get a seat. While the 2,000-seat theater offers plenty of shade and protection from rain, the queue is uncovered. The nearby "Enchanted Cottage" serves snacks. Wheelchair friendly. Assistive listening devices available.

Live Show
D-Ticket
All ages
Evil witch
28 min. show

Attraction descriptions and ratings are explained on page 93.

ⓘ Meet Your Favorite Characters in Fantasyland

Fantasyland is home to several classic Disney characters you can meet and greet in their "natural environments." Ariel can be found in her grotto in Triton's Garden, which is just south of the Matterhorn Bobsleds. Disney princesses Snow White, Cinderella, Belle, and Aurora (the "Fantastic Four") grace the Sleeping Beauty Castle environs. Merlin makes his magical appearance at the Sword in the Stone Ceremony in front of the King Arthur Carrousel. And there's often a princess on hand to tell a story in Once Upon a Time... The Disney Princess Shoppe. Check your guidemap for character greeting times and locations.

Charting the Attractions
at Fantasyland
(continued)

	Jennifer's Rating	Dave's Rating	Readers' Rating

☐ "it's a small world" [E-2] A-oh! | 5 | 6 | 6 |

"It's a world of laughter, a world of tears..." Yes, these are Disney's famous singing and dancing dolls, who first debuted their act at the 1964-65 New York World's Fair. Their catchy song by the legendary Sherman Brothers adapts to the local surroundings as your boat floats sedately past scenes depicting the world's continents and cultures. You'll be either charmed or bored by the rich costumes and details. This attraction is much improved following a recent makeover. This ride becomes a jolly winter wonderland between Thanksgiving and New Year's. Must transfer from ECV to wheelchair to ride.

Boat Ride
C-Ticket
All ages
That song!
Short to med. waits
11-15 min. cruise

☐ King Arthur Carrousel [D-3] A-oh! | 5 | 5 | 6 |

A colorful, lovingly maintained carrousel painted with scenes from Sleeping Beauty, near the center of Fantasyland. Each of the 72 moveable, antique horses was beautifully carved in Germany in 1875. A bench is available for those who don't want to mount a horse. Disney tunes make it a joy for the ears! Enchanting in the evening. Wheelchair-friendly. Adult supervision of young children required. One of the original attractions available on opening day.

Ride
B-Ticket
Ages 2 & up
High horses
Short waits
2 min. ride

☐ Mad Tea Party [E-3] | 1 | 3 | 6 |

Spin and spin and spin some more inside a giant teacup. Young kids love to get dizzy, so this ride draws them like a magnet. Turn the metal wheel at the center of your teacup to make it spin even faster. You'll be as dizzy as the Mad Hatter. This is one ride that lasts a bit longer than you'd like. Sit this one out if you're prone to dizziness. Uncovered queue. Must transfer from wheelchair.

Ride
C-Ticket
Ages 4 & up
Short waits
2 min. spin

☐ Matterhorn Bobsleds [E-3] | 6 | 5 | 8 |

The 1/100th scale Matterhorn peak houses a rollicking steel roller coaster, circa 1959. Hop in one of the two deceptively long lines for one of two slightly different ride experiences in "the Rock"–thrill-seekers should take the left line on the Tomorrowland side, while those who prefer a smoother, slightly longer ride should take the right line on the Fantasyland side. In both ride experiences, you sit front-to-back in a four-person "bobsled" which winds through dark, alpine tunnels past dripping icicles, misty caves, giant crystals, and an angry Abominable Snowman. Be leery of riding in the rain–while most of the ride is inside the mountain, dirty rain water still collects in the bottom of the bobsleds and gets all over your shoes. This very bumpy, jerky coaster is relatively tame–the dark makes it seem scarier. You may get a bit damp at the "splashdown" finale. Uncovered queue. 38"/89 cm height restriction; guests must be at least 3 years of age. Must transfer from wheelchair. Health warning.

Coaster
E-Ticket
Ages 8 & up
Bumps and rattles
Medium to long waits
(ride early in the day for shorter waits)
2-2½ min. ride

☐ Mr. Toad's Wild Ride [E-3] | 3 | 4 | 7 |

A classic "dark ride" through the bizarre world of Mr. Toad from the 1949 Disney animated feature "The Adventures of Ichabod and Mr. Toad." Board a two-person buggy and careen through slightly cheesy, definitely wacky scenes of Toad's library, the English countryside, and the streets of London, going "nowhere in particular." This attraction is best appreciated by adults and diehard Disney fans–young children will be scared, and the rest will be bored. Indoor/outdoor queue. Must transfer from wheelchair. Young kids must be with an adult.

Track Ride
B-Ticket
Ages 7 & up
Dark, creepy
Medium waits
2 min. ride

Charting the Attractions at Fantasyland
(continued)

	Jennifer's Rating	Dave's Rating	Readers' Rating

☐ Peter Pan's Flight [E-3]   A-oh!   5   6   8

Climb aboard a flying, three-seat pirate galleon that twists and turns sedately through the clouds. Follow Peter Pan and the Darling children from London to Never Land. Aerial scenes featuring the Lost Boys, mermaids, Captain Hook's ship, and the crocodile unfold beneath you before arriving safely home. Covered queue area. Guests must transfer from wheelchair to ride. Ships comfortably seat two adults and two children, or three adults.

Track Ride
C-Ticket
Ages 3 & up
Dark, heights
Long waits
2 min. ride

☐ Pinocchio's Daring Journey [D-3]   A-oh!   4   5   6

Yet another classic "dark ride," this one only slightly better than Mr. Toad's Wild Ride. Jiminy Cricket is your guide through Pinocchio's story, starting in Gepetto's home, then on to scary Pleasure Island, through the stomach of Monstro the Whale, and—with a little help from the Blue Fairy—ending happily back at Gepetto's workshop. The four-person wooden cars travel sedately through the simple, dark attraction with mostly three-dimensional scenes. Must transfer from wheelchair to ride. Young children must be accompanied by an adult.

Track Ride
B-Ticket
Ages 5 & up
Dark, scary for young kids
Short waits
3 min. ride

☐ Sleeping Beauty Castle [D-3]   7   6   6

While it may not be listed on your guidemap as an attraction, we think it qualifies. Sleeping Beauty Castle serves as the focal point of the park and offers the perfect entry point to Fantasyland beyond. The 77 ft. tall castle bears an uncanny resemblance to the Bavarian castle "Neuschwanstein," though

Eye Candy
A-Ticket
All ages

Disney's is made of wood and concrete with 22-karat gold leaf. Look for the brass spike in the pavement behind the castle—rumor has it this was the exact center of the park before Toontown was added. There used to be a walk-through diorama of Sleeping Beauty inside the castle, but it closed indefinitely in 2001 due to security and accessibility issues. Spend some time in the romantic garden on the east end of the castle—this delightful little area is Snow White Grotto, complete with a melodic wishing well and a waterfall fountain. For Disneyland's 50th, the castle is dressed up in gold accents (see cover photo) and lighting effects appear during the fireworks. Note that there is no restaurant in this castle.

☐ Snow White's Scary Adventures [D-3]   5   6   6

Become Snow White and experience her classic story in wooden mining cars that carry you from scene to scene. The Evil Queen/Witch provides the scares, but just when things get too gloomy, you'll be transported into the welcome arms of the Seven Dwarfs and Prince Charming. May be too intense for young children—it's quite dark and the Evil Queen/Witch is everywhere. Watch the large window above the entrance for the Evil Queen. Must transfer from wheelchair to ride. One of the original attractions operating on opening day!

Track Ride
C-Ticket
Ages 5 & up
Dark, scary for kids
Short waits
2½ min. ride

☐ Storybook Land Canal Boats [E-2]   A-oh!   5   6   6

Take a sweet, simple cruise through classic storybook scenes in miniature (1/12th scale). You board one of the large boats—each named after a famous heroine from a classic Disney story—and enter through the mouth of Monstro the whale. You'll see scenes from Three Little Pigs, Alice in Wonderland, Aladdin, The Little Mermaid, Peter Pan, Snow White, and Cinderella. Must transfer from wheelchair to ride.

Boat Ride
B-Ticket
All ages
Medium waits
8 min. cruise

Attraction descriptions and ratings are explained on page 93.

Charting the Attractions at Mickey's Toontown

Jennifer's Rating
Dave's Rating
Readers' Rating

☐ Chip 'n Dale Treehouse [D-1]   A-ok!   3 3 4

Kids can pretend to be chipmunks and scurry up a giant oak tree to frolic and play. Just climb up the spiral staircase and explore. Parents, this is mostly just a gussied-up jungle gym, but it's an easy way for the kids to burn off some energy for a few minutes—if you need to go in after your kids, use the full-size stairs on the left. It used to also have a slide and the Acorn Crawl, a room filled with "acorns" (balls) for the kids to play in, but these were removed a few years ago and there's not really much to do anymore. There's virtually no wait for this attraction, if you can still call it that.

Playground
A-Ticket
Ages 2–6
Allow 10 minutes

© MediaMarx, Inc.

Alexander fancies himself a chipmunk

☐ Disneyland Railroad–Mickey's Toontown Station [E-1]   A-ok!   5 5 7

All out for Toontown and Fantasyland! Next stop, Tomorrowland. See page 94. This is a fun shortcut when you're heading for the exit, though it may be faster to walk. Originally known as the Fantasyland Station when it opened in 1985. ECV must transfer to wheelchair. Handheld captioning.

Train Ride
C-Ticket
All ages
Medium waits

☐ Donald's Boat [D-1]   A-ok!   3 3 5

Your little ducklings will have a hoot exploring Unca Donald's boat, the "S.S. Miss Daisy." Climb up to the pilothouse to sound the ship's horn or take a turn at the wheel. Fountains outside the boat provide atmosphere, but it's not possible to play in them as you can at Walt Disney World. Must be ambulatory.

Playground
A-Ticket
All ages
No wait

☐ Gadget's Go Coaster [D-1]   4 5 6

Finally, a steel roller coaster just for kids! Climb into your two-person "acorn shell" car for a pint-size thrill. Beware grownups: the seats may be too small for big/tall adults. Alas, the ride is over before you know it, making it hardly worth the long wait. By the way, Gadget Hackwrench was the mouse inventor from the short-lived "Chip 'n' Dale's Rescue Rangers" cartoon show on Toon Disney in 1989–1990. Minimum age is 3 and minimum height restriction is 35"/89 cm. Kids must be with an adult. Must transfer from wheelchair to ride.

Coaster
C-Ticket
Ages 5 & up
Simple thrills
Long waits
1 min. ride

☐ Goofy's Bounce House [E-1] [CLOSED] – Future Toddler Playground?   4 5 6

Goofy's Bounce House closed in January 2006. We've heard a rumor it may re-open as a toddler play area similar to Pooh's Playful Spot at Walt Disney World, which has a huge faux tree with a play house, hollow logs to climb through, a not-so-high slide with easy steps to climb, and a water play area to get wet and cool off. The ground in these playgrounds is always padded to prevent skinned knees and there's usually just once entrance to make it easy to keep an eye on wandering toddlers. For more details about the attraction when it re-opens, visit http://www.passporter.com.

Playground
B-Ticket
Ages 3–6
No waits
Simple fun
Allow 15–20 minutes

Sidebar tabs: Planning · Getting There · Staying in Style · Touring · Feasting · Making Magic · Index · Notes & More

Charting the Attractions at Mickey's Toontown
(continued)

	Jennifer's Rating	Dave's Rating	Readers' Rating

☐ Jolly Trolley [E-1] *(Closed at press time)*   *A-ok!*   2   4   5

This attraction appears to be closed at press time and its future is uncertain. When it was open, you could take a one-way trip to silliness on a slow-moving train that bounced, twisted, weaved, and perambuled its way around Mickey's Toontown. The trolley stopped in front of Roger Rabbit's Car Toon Spin and Mickey's House. Must transfer from wheelchair to ride.

Track Ride / B-Ticket / All ages / Allow 20-30 minutes

☐ Mickey's House and Meet Mickey [D-1]   *A-ok!*   6   6   7

Mickey's house is chock-full of chuckles and "tchochkes" (knick-knacks). Look closely at his decorating—there are enough sight gags and delights to turn anyone into a gleeful kid. Long, slow lines snake in the front door, out the back, through his garden, and into Mickey's Movie Barn, because Mickey himself is waiting to greet you in his dressing room. If the house and garden are enough, exit before you meet Mickey. Wheelchair accessible.

Walkthru / C-Ticket / All ages / Long waits / Allow 20 min. to 1 hour

☐ Minnie's House [D-1]   *A-ok!*   5   6   7

Walk through Minnie's pastel home for a fascinating glimpse into the talents of this fabled celebrity. Her living room is "cosmousepolitan," complete with an answering machine (with messages from Mickey) and a computer where you can design her clothes. Minnie's kitchen is a wonder (be sure to look in the fridge). Minnie is sometimes outside to greet you—check your guidemap for character greeting times. Wheelchair accessible.

Walkthru / B-Ticket / All ages / No scares / Med. waits / Allow 20 min.

☐ Roger Rabbit's Car Toon Spin [E-1]   *FP*   6   5   8

Hop aboard a two-person taxi for a spin through the back alleys of Toontown from Disney's animated feature "Who Framed Roger Rabbit." Beware the weasels—their "dip" sends your cab into a 360° "uncontrollable" spin through the dark. Grab the wheel in your cab to slow (or increase) the spinning and save Jessica Rabbit. While you won't spin as fast as you would at the Mad Tea Party, it's just as well—you'll want to pay attention to the colorful sets with their Audio-Animatronics characters. The queue for this attraction is inside and quite delightful—pay attention to the fun details. Must transfer from wheelchair to ride. Children must be accompanied by an adult.

Track Ride / D-Ticket / Ages 5 & up / Motion sickness alert / FASTPASS or medium waits / 3 min. ride

Attraction descriptions and ratings are explained on page 93.

ⓘ Exploring Mickey's Toontown

This colorful, cartoon world is full of sight gags, silly sets, and hidden gags. In the downtown area, check out the talking mailboxes at the Post Office, the "Clockenspiel" atop City Hall (when it chimes, a character emerges for a meet-and-greet), Goofy's Gas Station (what's floating in those gas tanks?), and the phone outside the Power House. Mickey's Fountain marks the beginning of the residential section of Toontown, which has its own "Hollywood"-type sign and Toon Park for romping toddlers. Explore everything, listen carefully, and pay attention to those little details—this is the real fun of Mickey's Toontown. And when you're ready to meet the residents, check your guidemap for times—Mickey, Minnie, Goofy, and Pluto are ready to shake hands and pose for photos.

Charting the Attractions at Tomorrowland

Jennifer's Rating
Dave's Rating
Readers' Rating

Astro Orbitor [E-4]

| | 1 | 3 | 5 |

Go for a short, fast spin in a cozy, two-seat rocket. You'll zip around a colorful, futuristic sculpture in which the fanciful planets go into motion with each launch. Think Fantasyland's Dumbo with small, golden space ships going higher and faster. Pull back on your ship's stick to "soar" high. Get a great view as your ship whirls. Motion sickness warning! Outdoor, uncovered queue. Adults must accompany kids; guests must be at least one year old. Transfer from wheelchair to ride. Originally the Astro-Jets, which opened in 1956.

Ride
C-Ticket
Ages 5 & up
Motion sickness
Long waits
1½ min. flight

Autopia [G-4]

| | 6 | 5 | 6 |

Every kid wants a chance to drive, and when they're tall enough, they can at this popular attraction. Experienced drivers won't be as thrilled. Guide rails, shock-absorbing bumpers, and a low top speed (7 mph/11 kph maximum) make these gas-powered, two-seater cars safe. Three different models of cars are available to drive: a "sports" car, an "off-road" vehicle, and a "VW Bug"-like car. Mostly covered outdoor queue. Must transfer from wheelchair to ride. 52"/132 cm. height restriction to drive solo; minimum age to ride is 1 year. Health warning. Adult supervision required. This attraction was redesigned in 2000, and we think its theming makes it a better attraction than Walt Disney World's version.

Ride
C-Ticket
Ages 4 & up
Cars may bump yours from behind
FASTPASS or long waits
5 min. drive

Buzz Lightyear Astro Blasters [E-4] *FP*

| | 9 | 8 | 9 |

Hey, Space Rangers, this new attraction lets you help Toy Story's Buzz Lightyear defeat the evil Emperor Zurg! Buzz himself briefs new cadets before you're sent into battle in a comic book world. Your two-seat space vehicle (an "XP-37 Space Cruiser") is equipped with a pair of "ion cannons" (laser pointers) on cables. Aim and shoot the electronic targets to accumulate points. Move the joystick to make your vehicle spin and hone in on your targets. Compare your scores at the end. You can also play online at http://www.disneyland.com. Covered queue area is mostly indoors. Must transfer from ECV to wheelchair. Handheld captioning.

Ride
E-Ticket
All ages
Semi-dark
FASTPASS or long waits
4 min. flight

Disneyland Monorail [F-3] *A-ok!*

| | 8 | 8 | 7 |

Ah, who doesn't recognize this classic icon of Disneyland? You can board the monorail here in Tomorrowland to get one-way transportation to Downtown Disney. If you get off at Downtown Disney and plan to return to the park, be sure to get a handstamp. The outdoor queue is both covered and uncovered, and the waits aren't too bad until dinnertime and the last hour or so of the day. Tip: Ask a cast member about sitting in the front nose cone (it fits up to five guests). This was America's first monorail to operate on a daily basis back when it was introduced in 1959. Wheelchair and stroller friendly. For more details, see page 85. Note: The monorail is in "shuttle mode" due to construction and guests cannot currently make round trips; round trips should return in late 2006/early 2007.

Ride
D-Ticket
All ages
Short to medium waits
5 min. one-way trip

Disneyland Railroad–Tomorrowland Station [G-4] *A-ok!*

| | 5 | 5 | 7 |

Next stop, Main Street, U.S.A (with views of the Grand Canyon and Primeval World dioramas along the way). See page 94. This is a fun shortcut when you're heading for the exit, though it may be faster to walk. ECV must transfer to wheelchair to ride. Handheld captioning. This station was built in 1958.

Train Ride
C-Ticket
All ages
Medium waits

Charting the Attractions
at Tomorrowland
(continued)

Jennifer's Rating
Dave's Rating
Readers' Rating

"Honey, I Shrunk the Audience" [F-5]

| | 8 | 8 | 7 |

Get shrunk by Dr. Wayne Szalinski (Rick Moranis) when a demonstration of his world-famous shrinking/enlarging machine goes awry. A funny story and spectacular visual and special 3-D effects make this a must-see show for those who aren't terrified by snakes, mice, and dogs. Everyone wears "protective glasses" (3-D glasses) during the show. There's no need to sit up front. Indoor and outdoor queue, mostly covered. This may be too intense for children and some adults (tip for scared kids: have them take off their 3-D glasses). Wheelchair accessible. Assistive listening. Reflective and closed captioning.

3-D Film
E-Ticket
Ages 8 & up
Loud, intense
Short to medium waits
8 min. intro
18 min. film

Innoventions [F-4]

| | 7 | 7 | 5 |

Those who remember Carousel of Progress will recognize it as the home for Innoventions, a two-level showcase of futuristic demonstrations and exhibits. After a short introduction from an Audio-Animatronics character called Tom Morrow, you're free to explore the high-tech exhibits on your own. There's lots of fun stuff to do here, and it's easy to spend several hours. The floor rotates, so keep an eye on those young kids. No restrooms—make a pit stop beforehand. Wheelchair accessible. Assistive listening. Closed captioning.

Show
D-Ticket
Ages 7 & up
Easy to get lost here
Med. waits
Allow 1-2 hrs.

Space Mountain [F-5]   FP 🚹

| | 10 | 9 | 9 |

Space Mountain "relaunched" in July 2005 with an ultra-smooth ride, more special effects, digital technology, a new soundtrack, and an integrated audio sound system. This fast, indoor, 2/3-mile ride with its sudden turns and short drops in the dark is a real crowd-pleaser. There are no big, stomach-in-your-throat drops—the darkness makes it seem more intense. The revamped indoor queue and loading areas are rich with visual detail. In mid-2006, it may transform into Rockit Mountain, a special evening version of the ride. Must transfer from wheelchair. 40"/102 cm height restriction. Adult supervision. Health warning. Visit http://www.disneyland.com for videos and photos.

Coaster
E-Ticket
Ages 8 & up
Dark and fast
FASTPASS or long waits
3 min. flight

Starcade [F-5]

| | 2 | 2 | 4 |

Play the latest in video games, as well as some old classics, in this large, noisy arcade. Spending money is required. Wheelchair accessible.

Arcade
A-Ticket

Star Tours [B-5]   FP 🚹

| | 8 | 8 | 8 |

Take a flight to a galaxy far, far away in this "must ride" for all Star Wars fans, as space travelers go on a voyage they didn't quite bargain for. Although the flight simulator at the heart of this ride never really goes anywhere, you'll find it hard to believe as your StarSpeeder dives, banks, and speeds towards the Moon of Endor with a rookie pilot at the helm. But that doesn't mean the ride isn't rough. The roughest seats are in the back row. Indoor queue offers many visual delights, including R2-D2 and C-3PO. Overflow queue outdoors is uncovered. 40"/102 cm height restriction. Adult supervision; minimum age is 3. Health warning. Must transfer from wheelchair. Closed captioning.

Thrill Ride
E-Ticket
Ages 7 & up
Rough, rocky
FASTPASS or long waits
3 min. intro
5 min. flight

A new Tomorrowland attraction called **Finding Nemo Sumbarine Voyage** [F-3] debuts in 2007. From what we understand, guests will board subs in which they can see Finding Nemo characters digitally projected into the underwater world.

Evening Entertainment

Fantasmic! is a breathtaking mix of live action, music, and fireworks on the banks of the Rivers of America in Frontierland and New Orleans Square. This 22-minute show is performed nightly on weekends, and twice nightly during holidays and busy seasons (usually at 9:00 pm and 10:30 pm). The best place to watch the show is from the terrace near the river in front of Pirates of the Caribbean—just be sure you can see both Tom Sawyer Island and the water. We recommend you arrive an hour early to get a good spot to watch. If you can afford it, you get an even better view from the balcony of The Disney Gallery, where a reservations-only dessert buffet is held for $56/ages 3+. More premium seating is available elsewhere (the view isn't as good but it doesn't sell out as fast) for the same price—it comes with a boxed dessert and beverages. Details on both of these special Fantasmic! seatings are on page 223.

"Remember ... Dreams Come True" is a brand-new, grand fireworks show over Sleeping Beauty Castle, created for Disneyland's 50th anniversary. The 17-minute show (almost twice as long as the previous show) is held nightly at 9:25 pm (or at park closing). The fireworks begin with a dramatic launch from the peak of the Matterhorn, followed by the flight of Tinker Bell, who dips, glides, and soars overhead at up to 20 mph! More than 80 pieces of music and sound effects from beloved attractions—as well as new lighting effects on the castle and the façade of "it's a small world" and laser effects on Tom Sawyer Island—highlight the "E-Ticket in the Sky" segments. Custom, state-of-the-art pyrotechnics were created just for the show—look for a cube, bull's-eye, happy face, and more shapes. Compressed air lifts the fireworks, virtually eliminating ground-level smoke. Perhaps most amazing are the "perimeter" fireworks which immerse you in the show. The absolutely best place to watch the fireworks are from the hub—just make sure you have a good view of the castle. Other good vantage points include just in front of "it's a small world," Casey Jr. Circus Train, and New Orleans Square, where you'll see the fireworks but miss the castle lighting effects and (possibly) Tinker Bell's flight. Special versions of these fireworks are typically held on 4th of July and during the holiday season.

The new fireworks show is a "star!"

🎵 Dancing at Disneyland

Love to dance? You'll love Disneyland on weekend evenings! In Tomorrowland, the Club Buzz Stage rocks with musical acts and dance parties on most Friday and Saturday nights. The Plaza Gardens Stage (near the Central Plaza) is home to the "Jump, Jive, Boogie Swing Party" on Saturday evenings. Bands and showtimes vary—check your guidemap for the current shows and times. There is no extra charge (other than your regular park admission) for these dance parties, and it's not uncommon to see "regulars" dancing every weekend. Disneyland has held big band dance parties with live music since the '50s. Even if you don't dance, it's worth a visit—there's something infectious about the music and the dancers, and it's really quite entertaining to just watch.

Disneyland's 50th Anniversary Celebration (Happiest Homecoming on Earth)

On July 17, 2005, Disneyland celebrated its 50th anniversary ... but who says the party only has to last just one day? In true Disney style, the big hoopla **began in April 2005 and will last for 18 months**, 'til the end of 2006. That's plenty of time for you to get there and join in the celebration, which Disney is calling (appropriately enough) the "Happiest Homecoming on Earth." And as this is the first time any Disney park has celebrated a golden aniversary, you can expect a spectacular celebration, filled with new attractions, entertainment, and special events. In fact, the party is so big it's been extended to the other Disney theme parks, including Walt Disney World! We were on hand for the celebration kickoff on May 5, 2005, so here's a run-down of new goodies:

New Look for the Crown Jewel—Sleeping Beauty Castle received a makeover with royal-hued banners, gold trim, and five bejeweled tiaras atop the five most prominent spires (see book cover image). Each tiara represents a decade of Disneyland history.

New Attractions—Buzz Lightyear's Astro Blasters is an improved version of the popular attraction in Florida (see page 105). "Disneyland: The First 50 Magical Years" is a heart-warming tribute to this amazing place (see page 94). And, in July 2005, Space Mountain (see page 106) re-opened with new effects and a new soundtrack, along with Turtle Talk with Crush (see page 115) from "Finding Nemo" at Disney's California Adventure.

New Parades—"Walt Disney's Parade of Dreams" highlights more than 50 Disney characters with large, detailed floats that delight and entertain. Plus, your favorite Pixar film pals come out to party in "Block Party Bash" at Disney's California Adventure (see page 122).

New Fireworks—The amazing "Remember ... Dreams Come True" fireworks extravaganza explodes over Sleeping Beauty Castle (see previous page).

New Decorations—The "Happiest Faces on Earth" photo collages create well-known Disney characters and animated scenes out of photos submitted by vacationers and cast members—the collages are all over the resort. Be on the look-out for 50 golden, hidden "50s" on and around attractions in Disneyland park. Disney even honors those attractions that debuted on opening day with "golden" vehicles—these make great photo ops! Last but not least, even cast member badges have a fun, new look!

New Stuff—Let's not forget the special 50th anniversary merchandise, like golden Mickey ears (see photo to right), limited edition pins, mega music collections, and even food and drink, like the "Tinker Bell Twist" beverage (a combination of sour apple and sour watermelon) and an anniversary dessert that you can order with a collectible, gold-rimmed plate. Even the Disney Dollars have a new look! It extends beyond the parks—there's 50th anniversary packaging on several of Disney's corporate sponsors' products, including Coca-Cola.

Sporting our gold ears on the golden carpet for the kick-off

Planning
Getting There
Staying in Style
Touring
Feasting
Making Magic
Index
Notes & More

Disney's California Adventure

Served up with a hearty helping of Hollywood fantasy (including a fantasy Hollywood), this loving evocation of California's scenery and culture brings us the crisp, cool air and flowering meadows of the High Sierra, a taste of Cannery Row, a sip of the Wine Country, a Disney-clean old-time amusement pier, and a bug's-eye view of the Golden State's agricultural bounty. Disney's California Adventure is just to the south of Disneyland Park, a short stroll across the esplanade.

AMBIENCE

While it is too often underrated, we think Disney's California Adventure (DCA) is Disney's most beautiful park. No matter which way you turn, Disney's Imagineers have created a **breathtaking vista**, whether it's the monorail crossing a Lilliputian Golden Gate Bridge, the golden radiance of the Sun-thingy, Grizzly Peak bathed in the glow of sunset, or the carnival lights of Paradise Pier after dusk. Thanks to its proximity to Disneyland Park, park-hopping tickets turn Disney's California Adventure into a glorious extension of its senior sibling. And lest you think this is just a sightseeing tour, consider the first-class thrills and entertainment this park has in store: The Twilight Zone Tower of Terror (shudder), Soarin' Over California, Aladdin the Musical, and California Screamin'. Are you California dreaming yet?

Unlike Disneyland Park, the **layout** of Disney's California Adventure is free-form, much like the personalities of California (see park map on page 112). See pages 111a&b for daily touring itineraries and an attractions-at-a-glance list and pages 115–121 for attractions.

PARK LAYOUT AND HIGHLIGHTS

Sunshine Plaza	Walk under the Golden Gate Bridge and into the bright California "sunshine!" The 50-foot gold titanium sun is lit by reflected light from six heliostats around the plaza.
Hollywood Pictures Backlot *Headline Attractions:*	Explore the glamour of Tinseltown with Hollywood-inspired attractions. The huge entrance gate evokes the classic Babylonian palace movie sets of bygone days. *Tower of Terror, Monsters, Inc., Hyperion Theater*
Golden State *Headline Attractions:*	From the redwood forests to the Bay Area waters, this land is home to several popular rides, the Golden Dreams film, food and wine tastings, and wharfside eateries. *Soarin' Over California, Grizzly River Run*
A Bug's Land *Headline Attractions:*	Become the size of a bug in Flik's Fun Fair! Aside from the fun pint-sized attractions perfect for your little "bug," the attention to detail here is delightful. And the 3-D fun here is guaranteed to make you buggy! *It's Tough to be a Bug!*
Paradise Pier *Headline Attractions:*	Step back in time to the excitement of a seaside park, complete with a boardwalk, "tacky" souvenir shops, silly games, and classic rides like a "wooden" roller coaster, an old-fashioned merry-go-round, and a giant ferris wheel with a California twist. *California Screamin', Sun Wheel, Maliboomer*

Planning

Getting There

Staying in Style

Touring

Feasting

Making Magic

Index

Notes & More

Entertainment and Shopping at Disney's California Adventure

Fold out the next page for touring plans and a handy attraction chart

ENTERTAINMENT

Disney's California Adventure has a fair number of entertainment offerings, though most take the form of **live shows and parades**. The Hyperion Theater in Hollywood Pictures Backlot is home to the magnificent "Disney's Aladdin" broadway-style show. There's also the "Playhouse Disney—Live on Stage!" show that preschoolers just love. Be on the lookout for other special performances, such as "The Magic of Brother Bear" in the Redwood Creek Challenge Trail or the "Ugly Bug Ball" kids' show on the stage in Flik's Fun Fair. On weekend evenings, the Pacific Wharf Stage presents live music. The new Block Party Bash (see page 122) is a high-energy, retro parade that stops along its route three times to invite

© MediaMarx, Inc.

Dave takes Soarin' Over California a little too seriously

guests to play with the "Toys" from Toy Story, scream with the "Monsters" from Monsters, Inc., and dance with the "Bugs" from A Bug's Life. Dancers, acrobats, and jumping stilt-walkers fill the street during the parade. Look for the "Party Zone Banners" along the parade route to help you choose a spot where the Block Party Bash stops to party. At night, Disney's Electrical Parade (see page 122) winds its way through the park on most weekends and during the busy season. The parade's 30 floats, 500,000+ lights, and cast of more than 100 performers make for an unforgettable experience. The parade route for both parades is shown on our park map on page 112—we recommend you find a good viewing spot along the route 20–30 minutes before the start of the parade. For show and parade times, check your park guidemap or visit http://www.disneyland.com before you arrive.

SHOPPING

Disney's California Adventure has **more than a dozen shops** where you can pick up a souvenir or buy a gift. Here are the shops we find particularly interesting:

Shop	Location	What makes it special
Greetings from California	Sunshine Plaza	Disney clothes and souvenirs
Engine-Ears Toys	Sunshine Plaza	Interactive and theme park toys
Off the Page	Hollywood Pictures	Disneyana and collectibles
Studio Store	Hollywood Pictures	Great theme, and Muppets stuff!
Fly 'n' Buy	Golden State	Aviation paraphenalia
Golden Vine Winery	Golden State	Bottles of good wine for sale
Rushin' River Outfitters	Golden State	Fun "adventure" souvenirs
P.T. Flea Market	A Bug's Land	Bug stuff and souvenirs
Sideshow Shirts	Paradise Pier	T-shirts galore
Dinosaur Jack's	Paradise Pier	Lots of sunglasses
Treasures in Paradise	Paradise Pier	Kid stuff, toys, and clothes

Making the Most of Disney's California Adventure

The **Guest Relations** window—which serves the entire Disneyland Resort—is located to the left of the entrance. You can reach it both before you go through the turnstiles and once you're in the park. The outside window is actually behind part of the park entrance's tile mural of Southern California, and it can be hard to spot—as you're facing the entrance to the park, it's on the left side.

Take a moment to admire the **50-foot golden sun** that dominates Sunshine Plaza. It's actually illuminated by solar light from heliostats (reflectors) that follow the sun all day long. This also happens to be an great meeting spot as it's large, easy-to-spot, and centrally located. Live bands also frequently perform here.

As you enter the park and walk through the Sunshine Plaza, look for the **Tip Board** on the right, located in a tall, white replica of the Union Station tower. This Tip Board is updated throughout the day with information on attractions and wait times.

Sunshine Plaza shops are open for 30 minutes after park closing.

Watch for fun "**streetmosphere**" entertainment in the park during the summer—these impromptu shows are always worth the time.

Paradise Pier, with its lights reflecting off the lagoon, is enchanting in the evenings. Be sure to take a stroll around it if time allows.

You can **rent lockers, strollers and wheelchairs** after entering the park by visiting Golden Gateway, just under the Golden Gate Bridge on the right.

Paradise Pier at twilight

First Aid and the Baby Care Center aren't as centrally located as you might think, making them harder to find when you're in a hurry. If you think you'll need these services, find their location now on the park map on the previous page—they are just behind the Mission Tortilla Factory in Golden State.

You may have heard **negative comments** about this park, and claims you only need a half-day to do everything. Don't believe everything you hear. We can't do everthing in a full day ourselves, and we're extremely experienced theme park veterans. The park offers plenty of delightful attractions, shows, and restaurants to completely fill an entire day. We feel the real problem is that Disney's California Adventure round-up of attractions doesn't compare to the packed Disneyland Park across the way—but why would it when it is almost 50 years younger? You really need more than two days to do Disneyland Park, which means at least two days' worth of admission. When you compare that with one days' admission to Disney's California Adventure, you'll find you get your money's worth at both parks, which is just as it should be.

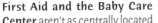

Getting the Best at Disney's California Adventure

Planning

Getting There

Staying in Style

Touring

Feasting

Making Magic

Index

Notes & More

BEST TIMES TO GO

The **best times to visit Disney's California Adventure** are days when Disneyland Park is overly crowded. Seriously, Disney's California Adventure is rarely packed, so plan to visit based on your schedule. It's not uncommon for guests to leave DCA in mid-afternoon and hop over to Disneyland Park, so you'll find DCA is remarkably quiet later in the day (barring special events or shows). If you have park hopping privileges on your park admission, there's no reason you can't hop back and forth between the parks all day if you wish. Do note, however, that as DCA tends to open later and close earlier than Disneyland Park, you'll find DCA busiest around the middle of the day. If you can visit this park at any time of the year, it's always best to avoid school vacations, when kids and their parents throng both parks.

BEST SPOTS

For those in need of guidance, here are our **favorite spots** in the park:

Best Places to Cool Off—Grizzly River Run, S.S. rustworthy, Princess Dot's Puddle Park, and any of the indoor attractions with air conditioning such as Golden Dreams, Disney Animation, and the Hyperion Theater. Soarin' Over California gets points, too—while it isn't long, it does generate a cooling breeze.

Best Place to Relax—On a bench on the boardwalk in Paradise Pier, at a picnic table at Bountiful Valley Farm

Best Places to Burn Off Energy—Redwood Creek Challenge Trail, the midway on Paradise Pier, S.S. rustworthy, Flik's Fun Fair

Best Place to Propose—Sun Wheel, Wine Country area of Golden State

Best Place to Sneak a Kiss—Sun Wheel

Best Places to Get Your Adrenaline Going—Twilight Zone Tower of Terror, California Screamin', and Maliboomer

Best Place to Get a Snack—Bur-r-r Bank Ice Cream in Sunshine Plaza

Best Place to Be in the Evening—Paradise Pier

Best Places for Meals—The Vineyard Room, the Pacific Wharf District

Best Places to Watch the Parade—Sunshine Plaza (near the big Sun), in front of Golden Dreams, or Golden State Park

Best Place to Meet Mickey—Bountiful Valley Farm in "a bug's land"

Ratings are explained on page 86.

RATINGS

Our Value Ratings:		Our Magic Ratings:		Readers' Ratings:
Quality:	8/10	Theme:	8/10	58% fell in love with it
Variety:	8/10	Excitement:	8/10	34% liked it well enough
Scope:	10/10	Fun Factor:	6/10	7% had mixed feelings
Overall Value:	**9/10**	**Overall Magic:**	**7/10**	1% were disappointed

DCA is enjoyed by...		(rated by both authors and readers)	
Younger Kids: ♥♥♥	Young Adults: ♥♥♥♥	Families: ♥♥♥♥
Older Kids: ♥♥♥	Mid Adults: ♥♥♥♥♥	Couples: ♥♥♥♥♥
Teenagers: ♥♥♥♥	Mature Adults: ♥♥♥♥♥	Singles: ♥♥♥♥♥

Charting the Attractions at Hollywood Pictures Backlot

☐ Disney Animation [B-5]   A-ok! | 8 | 8 | 8 |

| | | Jennifer's Rating | Dave's Rating | Readers' Rating |

Animation fans shouldn't miss this walk-through of interactive exhibits and activities. Upon entering, you are in the Animation Courtyard, with huge screens showing famous animated scenes. From here you can visit the Sorceror's Workshop (get to know the characters—and yourself—better), Character Close-Up (meet and greet Disney characters), Animation Academy (learn how to draw a Disney character), and the new **Turtle Talk with Crush** (real-time, voice-activated animation with the laid-back turtle from "Finding Nemo"). Wheelchair accessible. Assistive listening devices. Closed captioning.

Beast's Library in the Sorceror's Workshop

Walkthru/ Show
D-Ticket
All ages
A little dark
Short waits
Allow 45-60 minutes

☐ The Hollywood Backlot Stage [B-6] | 3 | 4 | 5 |

Shows change seasonally at this outdoor stage off Hollywod Boulevard in the Hollywood Pictures Backlot. Generally you can expect to see characters of one sort or another. At the time of writing, "Drawn to the Magic" is performing at this stage several times a day. Wheelchair accessible.

Show
B-Ticket
Ages 3 & up
Length varies

☐ Hyperion Theater showing "Disney's Aladdin" [A-5] | 8 | 7 | 6 |

This beautiful, state-of-the-art, 2,000-seat theater graces the Hollywood Pictures Backlot. Broadway-quality shows are performed here, with "Disney's Aladdin—A Musical Spectacular" as the current show, running since January 2003. Aladdin is a must-see show for all ages—the sets are incredible, with some very cool special effects. There are three levels in this theater—we suggest you sit in the orchestra (for best views of the stage) or the mezannine (for best views of the special effects). These shows are very popular, so arrive early to get the best seats. Wheelchair accessible. Assistive listening devices.

Show
D-Ticket
All ages
Dark and noisy
Medium waits
40-45 min. shows

☐ Monsters, Inc: Mike and Sulley to the Rescue [B-6] | – | – | – |

In January 2006, a new attraction opened starring Mike and Sulley from the hit movie, "Monsters, Inc." This classic dark ride follows Boo through the streets of Monstropolis as Mike and Sulley attempt to catch her and elude the long arm of the Child Protection Agency. At press time, we haven't had a chance to ride it yet, but we hear detail is delighful, and the second-to-last scene is the famous "door warehouse" as Mike and Sulley return Boo to her bedroom. We expect this to be a fun and funny attraction that appeals to all ages. This attraction replaces Superstar Limo, which closed in 2002.

Track Ride
C-Ticket
Ages 5 & up
Short waits
3½ min. ride

Attraction descriptions and ratings are explained on page 93.

Charting the Attractions at Hollywood Pictures Backlot
(continued)

	Jennifer's Rating	Dave's Rating	Readers' Rating

☐ Muppet★Vision 3-D [B-6] A-OK! | 7 | 7 | 9 |

Your 3-D glasses get a real workout as Kermit and his pals show you around the Muppet Labs. The Muppets are at their zany, pun-filled best in a frenetic good time that was Jim Henson's last production. The multi-screen videos and hilarious props shown in the pre-show area deserve your full attention. The theater is very large and air-conditioned, complete with comfy seats. There's no need to sit in front to get a good view. Some effects may be too scary for young children, but this is considerably friendlier to kids than "It's Tough to be a Bug!" in Flik's Fun Fair. Outdoor queue is mostly covered. Wheelchair accessible. Assistive listening. Closed captioning. Reflective captioning.

| 3-D Film |
| E-Ticket |
| Ages 4 & up |
| Intense, loud, a bit violent |
| Long waits |
| 15 min. intro 17 min. film |

☐ Playhouse Disney—Live on Stage! [C-5] A-OK! | 7 | 6 | 8 |

Preschoolers love Bear (and his Big Blue House), and friends like Rolie Polie Olie, Stanley, and JoJo. A pre-show video teaches kids about colors and shapes. For the main production, a cast of costumed characters and puppets gives a live version of Disney Channel favorites. As you can imagine, this is a big hit with young kids. Seating is on a carpeted floor with some benches along the back wall. This attraction replaced the ABC Soap Opera Bistro in April 2003. Outdoor, covered queue. Wheelchair accessible. Assistive listening devices. Closed captioning.

| Live Show |
| C-Ticket |
| All ages |
| Fun for kids! |
| Short waits |
| 21 min. show |

☐ The Twilight Zone Tower of Terror [A-4] FP ♿ | 3 | 9 | 9 |

You'll delight in the delicious spookiness of this new "haunted hotel," long before you ride its legendary "down and up and down and up again" elevator. The gut-wrenching drops are matched by the wonderful visual effects beforehand. When the queue splits in the basement, go left—it's shorter. To enjoy just the fabulous queue and pre-show but skip the ride (Jennifer's preference), take the "chicken exit" before you board the elevator (ask a cast member for assistance). This attraction opened in May 2004. It differs from its Walt Disney World cousin in that you don't move through

Jennifer still refuses to ride the Tower of Terror

| Thrill Ride |
| E-Ticket |
| Ages 8 & up |
| Dark, scary, sudden drops |
| FASTPASS or long waits |
| 10 min. intro 3½ min. ride |

the "Fifth Dimension" scene, and there are three elevator shafts rather than just two. Outdoor queue is mostly covered. Note that you must hold on to your belongings during the ride as there is no on-board storage. 40"/102 cm height restriction. Health warning. Young children should be accompanied by an adult. Must transfer from wheelchair to ride. Closed captioning.

Charting the Attractions at Golden State

	Jennifer's Rating	Dave's Rating	Readers' Rating

☐ The Boudin Bakery Tour [D-3]   A-ok!

	5	5	6

Ever heard of that famous San Francisco sourdough bread? Visit a working bakery where real, soft, sourdough bread is being made with the Boudin family secret recipe. Rosie O'Donnell and Colin Mochrie (from "Whose Line Is It Anyway?") entertain guests in a funny video filled with information on the modern method of baking bread and baking tips. Guests may receive a free sample of bread (subject to availability). If you like the bread, you can purchase a loaf nearby. Wheelchair accessible. Closed captioning.

Walkthru
B-Ticket
Ages 8 & up
Free bread!
Short waits
7 minute tour

☐ Golden Dreams [F-4]

	6	5	7

Explore the rich history of California through this well-made, touching movie. Your host is the Goddess Calafia, the spirit of California (played by Whoopi Goldberg), who introduces you to the many races and ethnicities that have inhabited California through 500 years of history. In the interests of accuracy, the movie is not as cheerful as you might imagine. The 350-seat indoor theater is a cool oasis on hot days. Wheelchair accessible. Assistive listening devices. Reflective captioning.

Show
D-Ticket
Ages 9 & up
Some violent scenes
22-minute show

☐ Golden Vine Winery: Seasons of the Vine [D-4]

	6	7	6

Learn about California winemaking during a short film, "Seasons of the Vine," held in a 50-seat wine barrel room. After a short introduction by a winery worker, the informative film explores the scientific aspects of wine production as vintners go from spring vine cuttings to harvest. Shows are held every 10 minutes. A wine-tasting session is held nearby for $10/adult 21 and over—it includes four half-glasses of wine. Wheelchair accessible. Reflective captioning.

Film
D-Ticket
Ages 9 & up
Short waits
7½ min. film

☐ Grizzly River Run [F-5]   FP 🚶

	8	9	9

Ah, the whitewater beckons you! Grizzly Peak, a large "mountain" shaped like the head of a bear, is home to a thrilling whitewater raft ride—the tallest and fastest in the world. Climb aboard a six-person, circular raft for a fun, wet, and wild ride down the manmade river. Along the way you'll experience a 45-foot climb and two drops—one as far as 22 ft. during which your raft actually spins during its descent! This is a notch above Kali River Rapids at Walt Disney World, being a bit longer and a bit more thrilling. Be aware that you will get wet, perhaps

Grizzly River Run's final descent

Raft Ride
E-Ticket
Ages 8 & up
Sudden drops, and you will get wet!
FASTPASS or long waits
5½ min. ride

even soaked—store your valuables in a locker nearby (free for one hour) and wear a poncho during the ride to stay dry. Outdoor queue is mostly covered. 42"/107 cm. height restriction. Single rider line is faster (when available) if your party is willing to split up. Health warning. Young children should be accompanied by an adult. Must transfer from wheelchair to ride.

Attraction descriptions and ratings are explained on page 93.

Planning | Getting There | Staying in Style | Touring | Feasting | Making Magic | Index | Notes & More

Charting the Attractions at Golden State
(continued)

	Jennifer's Rating	Dave's Rating	Readers' Rating

☐ Mission Tortilla Factory [D-3]   A-ok! | 4 | 5 | 7 |

In the same vein as the Boudin Bakery (see the previous page), you can see how flour and corn tortillas are made in a fully automated factory. The tour is informative with a heart-warming video by tortilla-loving kids. Guests watch the tortilla-making process (producing 25 per minute) through large picture windows that look into the full-scale mock-up kitchen. Live cooking demonstrations. At the conclusion of the tour, you can sample a free, warm tortilla. Wheelchair accessible.

Walkthru
B-Ticket
Ages 8 & up
Free food!
Short waits
7 min. tour

The free tortillas are tasty!

☐ Redwood Creek Challenge Trail [F-5]   A-ok! | 6 | 5 | 7 |

Calling all campers! This 2+-acre playground features storytelling, smoke-jumper cable slide, rock wall, climbing net, and a swaying bridge (see photo below). "The Magic of Brother Bear" show is held here—check your times guide for showtimes. There's a lot of fun stuff to discover here, including Kenai's Spirit Cave. Some challenges are wheelchair accessible, others require that you be ambulatory. Height and age restrictions are also in effect for certain challenges.

Playground
C-Ticket
All ages
Very active!
Allow 60 minutes

☐ Soarin' Over California [E-6]   FP 🧍 | 10 | 9 | 9 |

Get a rush as you "soar" from one end of California to the other on this amazing simulator ride. Guests are strapped into oversized porch swings and rise from the floor for a simulated hang glider tour of the Golden State—you'll see the Golden Gate Bridge, Redwood Country, and San Diego Harbor along the way. An eye-filling, IMAX movie screen, gentle motion, stirring music, and scented breezes combine for an exhilarating journey that ends with fireworks over Disneyland. Be aware that your feet will dangle (you may want to store those flip-flops in the basket underneath) and there's a definite potential for motion sickness if you're prone. Single rider line is faster (when available) if your party is willing to split up. 40"/102 cm height restriction. Must transfer from wheelchair to ride. Closed captioning.

Simulator
E-Ticket
Ages 7 & up
Simulated heights
FASTPASS or long waits
5 min. ride

Attraction descriptions and ratings are explained on page 93.

ⓘ California Kids

Disney's California Adventure caters to toddlers in a way that Disneyland Park doesn't. Not only is the Redwood Creek Challenge Trail a great place to burn off energy and try out recently acquired motor skills, but places like Flik's Fun Fair and "Playhouse Disney—Live on Stage!" are made just for the preschool set. And let's not forget the magic of a ride on King Triton's Carousel, the watery wonder of S.S. rustworthy, and the interactivity of "Turtle Talk with Crush" at Disney Animation.

Exploring Redwood Creek

Charting the Attractions at "a bug's land"

	Jennifer's Rating	Dave's Rating	Readers' Rating

Bountiful Valley Farm [D-4] — A-ok!

2 3 5

Explore a fun "farm" with various interactive exhibits including the Irrigation Station (a water playground), Tractor Yard (farm equipment for kids to climb), and a character meet-and-greet (featuring "a bug's life" characters). Home to the entertaining "Ugly Bug Ball" stage show. Wheelchair accessible.

Playground
A-Ticket
Ages 1 & up
Unlimited

Flik's Flyers [B-4] — A-ok!

5 5 6

Your "honorary bug" will love this simple, spinning ride. Guests climb aboard four-seat "hot-air balloons" fashioned out of fake leaves, twigs, and empty food containers and spin around a pie plate. It doesn't go too high or too fast, though we'd still recommend caution for those prone to motion sickness. Guests must transfer from wheelchair/ECV to ride.

Ride
C-Ticket
Ages 1 & up
Spins!
Short waits
1½ min. ride

Francis' Ladybug Boogie [B-4] — A-ok!

2 5 5

Get dizzy on a spinning car ride—it's a touch tamer than Mad Tea Party's whirling teacups at Disneyland. Each four-person ladybug car spins and twirls in figure-eights around the "dance floor," actually switching tracks throughout the ride. Cars spin toward one another at times, neatly avoiding collisions. No lap-sitting is allowed on this ride. Guests must transfer from wheelchair/ECV to ride.

Ride
C-Ticket
Ages 1 & up
Short waits
1½ min. ride

Heimlich's Chew Chew Train [C-4] — A-ok!

4 4 5

Hop aboard Heimlich as he munches his way through his favorite tasty treats. This miniature train ride has two-person seats and travels at a sedate pace. We recommend you avoid sitting in the very front or back of the train, as you may miss some of the narration. Guests must transfer from wheelchair/ECV to ride.

Train Ride
B-Ticket
All ages
2 min. ride

It's Tough to be a Bug! [C-4]

8 8 9

This humorous show hosted by Flik from "A Bug's Life" features a pint-sized cast of animated and Audio-Animatronics characters. 3-D effects, creepy sensations, and yucky smells can terrify the bug-wary. Look for hilarious movie posters in the "anty room." Air-conditioned, 430-seat theater. Outdoor queue is uncovered. Special effects may be too intense for some (remove the 3-D glasses if scared). Wheelchair accessible. Assistive listening. Reflective captioning.

3-D Show
E-Ticket
Ages 7 & up
Dark, smells, bug noises
8 min. show

Princess Dot's Puddle Park [B-4] — A-ok!

3 3 5

A bug's version of a water playground, complete with a huge, leaky garden hose, a spigot with water cascading down it, and a spraying sprinkler with pop jet fountains. Towering plants provide some shade, and there's seating for the water-wary. Bring a bathing suit or dry clothes. Wheelchair accessible.

Playground
A-Ticket
Ages 1 & up
Unlimited

Tuck and Roll's Drive 'Em Buggies [B-4]

6 4 5

Bumper cars, Disney-style! Each two-person buggy has two gas pedals at different heights for both big and small drivers. The buggies are shaped like pillbugs and the driving arena is under the "big top umbrella" of P.T. Flea's circus. 36"/91 cm. height restriction (children under 48" cannot drive and must be with an adult). Health warning. Must transfer from wheelchair/ECV to ride.

Bumper Cars
D-Ticket
Ages 4 & up
Med. waits
2 min. ride

Charting the Attractions at Paradise Pier

	Jennifer's Rating	Dave's Rating	Readers' Rating

☐ California Screamin' [E-2]   FP 🧍 | 1 | 9 | 9 |

Disney updates the classic roller coaster in this fast-paced, mile-plus-long thrill ride. Your adventure begins with a jet-powered take-off that catapults your 24-seat vehicle from 0 to 55 mph in four seconds. The onboard music soundtrack accompanies you smoothly up to heights of 120 ft., through twists and turns, around a 360° loop in Mickey's "head," and screaming down a 108-foot drop at a 50° angle. The roller coaster is a state-of-the-art steel construction made to look like an old-fashioned wooden coaster from seaside amusement parks. Be aware that both the start and stop are abrupt. A photo is taken during the ride and available for purchase at the exit. Queue is outdoors and mostly covered. Single rider line is faster (when available) if your party is willing to split up. 48"/122 cm. height restriction. Health warning. Guest must transfer from wheelchair/ECV to ride.

Coaster
E-Ticket
Ages 8 & up
Fast start, big drops, 360° loop
FASTPASS or long waits
3 min. ride

☐ Games of the Boardwalk [F-2 & G-2] | 1 | 5 | 7 |

What's a boardwalk amusement park without midway games? Seven old-time pay-for-play games are offered: Boardwalk Bowl (skeeball), Shore Shot (basketball), San Joaquin Valley (ball in a basket), New Haul Fishery (catch a fish), Angels in the Outfield (target knock-out), Dolphin Derby (race), and Cowhuenga Pass (ball in a milk jug). Games are $1–$2 each and prizes are small stuffed toys. It's atmospheric but otherwise pricey. Wheelchair accessible.

Playground
A-Ticket
Ages 5 & up
Money pit!
Unlimited

☐ Golden Zephyr [G-3] | 3 | 7 | 6 |

Ride a Buck Rogers-inspired silver bullet vehicle around a 90-foot tower. Each of the six "galactic gondolas" seats 12 guests and is suspended from above on steel cables. As the vehicles spin, they swing out over the water and walkways of Paradise Pier. This classic attraction was inspired by Harry Traver's Circle Swing which debuted at the turn of the 20th century. Motion sickness warning! Ride during a parade for a shorter wait. Guests must transfer from wheelchair/ECV to ride. Note that this ride may close if winds are greater than 10 mph.

Ride
C-Ticket
Ages 4 & up
Spins!
Med. waits
2 min. ride

☐ Jumpin' Jellyfish [G-3]   🧍 | 5 | 5 | 6 |

This gentle attraction is geared toward kids too small or too timid to do the Maliboomer. Each giant jellyfish seats up to two guests and "jumps" up 40 feet before drifting slowly down again among the kelp. Your feet dangle during the "jump," so avoid loose-fitting footwear. 40"/102 cm. height requirement. 350 lb./159 kg. weight limit per vehicle. Guests must transfer from wheelchair/ECV.

Ride
C-Ticket
Ages 5 & up
Med. waits
1 min. jump

☐ King Triton's Carousel [F-2]   A-ok! | 6 | 5 | 7 |

This enchanting, colorful carousel features 56 hand-sculpted and hand-painted sea creatures that bob up and down as the carousel revolves in time to California-themed calliope music. A "nanny bench" is provided for those who do not wish to ride. The carousel is gorgeous at night (see photo). Take note of the upper panels of the carousel's canopy—they depict scenes from historic seaside piers such as Venice Pier and The Pike. Guests must transfer from ECV to wheelchair to ride.

Carousel
B-Ticket
All ages
Spins!
Short waits
2 min. ride

Attraction descriptions and ratings are explained on page 93.

Attraction descriptions and ratings are explained on page 93.

Charting the Attractions at Paradise Pier

(continued)

	Jennifer's Rating	Dave's Rating	Readers' Rating

Maliboomer [H-2] 🧍

Designed to look like a giant "test-your-strength" hammer-and-bell midway game, the Maliboomer is not for the faint of heart. This ride launches you to the top of a 180-foot tower in just four seconds to "ring" the bell, score 1,000 points, and drop you down again fast. You "bounce" several more times before stopping at the bottom. Note that your feet will dangle during the attraction—avoid loose-fitting footwear. Storage bins are provided for your belongings under each seat. Listen carefully for the fun sound effects at launch and drop. Single rider line is faster (when available) if your party is willing to split up. 52"/132 cm. height restriction. Health warning. Guests must transfer from wheelchair/ECV to ride.

Ratings: 1 7 9

Thrill Ride | E-Ticket | Ages 8 & up | Fast launches and drops | Long waits | 45 sec. ride

Mulholland Madness [H-4] 🅵🅿 🧍

Take a wacky road trip down Los Angeles' infamous Mulholland Drive on this classic "wild mouse" roller coaster. Your "woody station wagon" zips about through switchbacks, tight curves, and mild drops on this rowdy ride through movie-set backdrops depicting the Hollywood Hills and Santa Monica Mountains. Sit in the front of your four-person vehicle for the best ride. Outdoor queue is mostly covered. 42"/107 cm. height restriction. Health warning. Guests must transfer from wheelchair/ECV to ride.

Ratings: 9 7 7

Coaster | D-Ticket | Ages 6 & up | FASTPASS or long waits | 1½ min. ride

Orange Stinger [G-3] 🧍

Hop on the back of a bumblebee and buzz around the inside of a giant, four-story orange on this classic swinging ride. Each of the 48 bees seat just one guest. As the bees begin to "fly" around the orange, they swing out at an angle and the scent of fresh oranges wafts on the air. We do not recommend this ride for those prone to motion sickness or for the bug-wary—there's a realistic buzzing sound effect while you're swinging about. 48"/122 cm. height restriction; 200 lb./91 kg. weight limit. Guests must transfer from wheelchair/ECV to ride.

Ratings: 1 7 6

Ride | D-Ticket | Ages 8 & up | Spins and buzzes | Short waits | 2 min. ride

S.S. rustworthy [H-3] A-OK!

Cool off aboard this old, grounded fireboat full of watery, hands-on fun. You can play with water cannons, ring bells, pull levers, and turn wheels—and you will get wet! There's even an area where you can practice your surfing skills, and opportunities to squirt water at one another and at targets. This attraction is a delight on a hot afternoon, but it can get congested when busy. Wheelchair accessible.

Ratings: 5 5 6

Playground | B-Ticket | Ages 1 & up | Allow about 30 min.

Sun Wheel [G-2] A-OK!

This isn't your daddy's Ferris wheel—it's a 16-story, gold and bronze metal wheel with both stationary and sliding/swinging gondolas that appear to disappear below the water's surface. For a sedate experience, board one of the eight red gondolas that remain in place as the wheel rotates. Thrill-seekers will enjoy one of the 16 other gondolas that swing and slide about as gravity dictates. (The vehicles do not go upside down, however.) This attraction offers spectacular views of the park and surrounding areas. Ride it twice for both experiences! Guests must transfer from ECV to wheelchair to ride.

Ratings: 9 5 7

Ferris Wheel | D-Ticket | All ages | Heights | Med. waits | 10 min. ride

Evening Entertainment
at Disney's California Adventure

Your evening comes to life with **Disney's Electrical Parade**, a "spectacular festival pageant of nighttime magic and imagination" beloved by many. The parade features floats and characters lit with half a million colored, sparkling lights. The rousing "Baroque Hoedown" soundtrack bounces along with the parade in all its electrosynthomagnetic

Staring in awe at Disney's Electrical Parade

musical glory. Among the floats are scenes and/or characters from Alice in Wonderland, Cinderella, Peter Pan, Dumbo, Snow White, and Pete's Dragon. This 15-minute parade generally begins in Sunshine Plaza and ends in Paradise Pier (see parade route on the map on page 112), though the route may be in reverse. This "crown jewel of the summer," as it was known, began its run in Disneyland Park in 1972, leaving in 1996 for a makeover and a transcontinental tour of Walt Disney World in Orlando, Florida, Tokyo Disneyland, Disneyland Paris, and even a brief appearance in New York City, before returning to California in 2001. Some of the best viewing spots are located near Seasons of the Vine and across from Golden Dreams (depicted in the photo above). Or have dinner at either the Wine Country Trattoria or the second-floor Vineyard Room above and then stay for a delightful view of the parade. Reviews of the parade are mixed—we find it utterly charming as do many others, but some feel that it is dated. At the time of writing, the parade only appears on weekend evenings around 8:45 pm—check Disneyland's web site for parade times during your visit.

! Block Party Bash

This new parade isn't typically held in the evenings, but it still deserves a review! The Block Party Bash is a new parade for Disneyland's 50th anniversary and is designed to put you in the middle of an impromptu street party. The parade really does feel like a party—don't be surprised if you're asked to join in or dance. Expect lots of loud music, high energy, and silly sight gags. Be sure to view the parade in one of the Party Zone locations, which is where the floats stop to party down. Of course, the things that make it fun for some may be irritating for others—namely the noise and silliness.

Block Party Bash's first float

Downtown Disney

If "heading downtown" is your idea of rest and recreation, head to the Disneyland Resort's Downtown Disney district. You'll find unique shops, fantastic dining, and super entertainment including top-name bands, street performers, and dancing water fountains.

Downtown Disney is a **destination of its own**. Take a short walk "downtown" from anywhere within the Disneyland Resort and enjoy the friendly urban atmosphere. The pedestrian-only streets, attention to detail, and sprawling layout avoid the "mall" feeling completely. Enjoy one of the brightest, cleanest, safest, and most satisfying downtowns anywhere.

If you can't get your fill of **shopping** inside the theme parks, or if you are looking for just the right gift, come to Downtown Disney. There's no admission charge here, and you'll find much more than Disney merchandise. Shop for collectible figurines and miniature light-up villages at Department 56. Find aeronautically inspired gifts at Island Charters. At Compass Books, you'll find all the latest best-sellers along with a great collection of Disney-related books. Get ready for the California sunshine with sunglasses from the new Sunglass Icon store and the latest in beach gear from Liquid Planet Boardsports. Bring a bit of Hollywood home from Starabilias, where you'll find movie and music collectibles. Try Something Silver for sterling silver jewelry. Pamper yourself with soothing lotions and soaps from Basin, delightful smelling candles and accessories from Illuminations, great skincare products and scents from Sephora, and pre-teen princess fun at Club Libby Lu. For the kid in all of you, shop and play at the Build-a-Bear Workshop, the LEGO Imagination Center, or Anne Geddes, and find a pearl in an oyster at the Pearl Factory. A new Disney's Pin Traders store sells pins and lanyards. There are even carts where you can have a portrait drawn, get your hair wrapped, and buy custom-engraved crystal.

Remember your visit to one of the Downtown Disney eateries with logo merchandise from ESPN Zone, House of Blues, Rainforest Café, and Ralph Brennan's Jazz Kitchen. But don't leave without a visit to World of Disney, the second largest Disney Store in the world, only outdone by the one at Walt Disney World. This is the one-stop shopping spot for all your Disneyland merchandise.

Trying out goodies from the World of Disney

Playing at Downtown Disney

PLAYING

Downtown Disney builds fun into nearly every shop and restaurant, so you don't have to look far for **entertainment**. Sports fans can watch their favorite sporting event on a 16-foot HDTV screen, climb a rock wall, drive a virtual Formula One car, and play the latest sports-related video games at the ESPN Zone Sports Arena. Baseball fans can buy tickets and take a shuttle from the ESPN Zone to see the Anaheim Angels play a home game. Visit http://espnzone.com/anaheim for information on special events and to join the MVP Club for discounts. Pre-teens love Club Libby Lu which offers budding beauties makeovers

Alexander looks for his lost ball outside ESPN Zone

and make-your-own lip gloss—for hours, prices, and reservations, visit http://www.clublibbylu.com. Movie fans enjoy the 12-screen AMC Theaters with loveseat-style stadium seating, movie palace architecture, and bargain shows before 6:00 pm on weekdays. For showtimes, check http://www.moviewatcher.com (use zip code "92802") or check with Guest Relations. Music fans can see top-name performances at House of Blues, or make reservations for the Sunday Gospel Brunch (see page 222). House of Blues shows do sell out, so check http://www.hob.com/venues/clubvenues/anaheim

Jennifer shopped for baby clothes at Downtown Disney during her pregnancy

to see who'll be performing and to purchase tickets in advance. For a little romance, take an evening stroll through Downtown Disney to enjoy live street performers and catch a glimpse of the Disneyland fireworks show. Annual Passholders (see page 82) earn great discounts at many shops and entertainment venues in Downtown Disney, such as AMC Theatres, Basin, Compass Books, ESPN Zone, House of Blues, LEGO, Pearl Factory, Rainforest Cafe, and Starabilias. Just show your annual pass to receive your discount.

Making Your Way at Downtown Disney

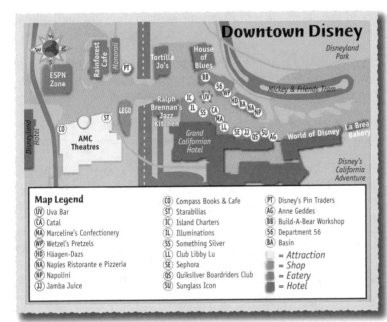

If you are looking for variety, you're sure to find a diverse array of **dining experiences** at Downtown Disney. For a healthy serving of showbiz, head to the House of Blues for down-home cooking and terrific live music from some of the biggest names in blues and rock 'n' roll. If jazz is more your style, Ralph Brennan's Jazz Kitchen has live music nightly along with spicy New Orleans-style food and atmosphere. Margaritas and mariachis add to the south of the border ambiance at Tortilla Jo's. Dine in the tropical jungle at the Rainforest Café with its slightly adventurous menu, or cheer on your favorite team at the ESPN Zone Restaurant with good ol' American food. Catal offers upscale Mediterranean fare in a refined environment. Naples Ristorante e Pizzeria is the choice for casual Italian dining, and its little brother Napolini is great if you're in a hurry or want a more casual meal. If you like people-watching, enjoy patio seating at La Brea Bakery or tapas at the Uva Bar. For a quick meal, try Napolini's pizza slices to go, Wetzel's Pretzels, Jamba Juice's healthy energy drinks, or Tortilla Jo's tacqueria (tacos). Finally, satisfy your sweet tooth at Häagen-Dazs (ice cream) and Marceline's Confectionery (candy). Complete descriptions of these Downtown Disney eateries begin on page 204.

Making the Most of Downtown Disney

TIPS

Avoid the noontime **restaurant crowds** in the parks and take a short walk or monorail ride to Downtown Disney for lunch.

If you plan to eat at the **Rainforest Café**, consider joining their Safari Club. For a small fee you get priority seating and discounts. For details, visit http://www.rainforestcafe.com.

Most shops and restaurants here **stay open late**, so spend more time in the parks, then head "downtown" after the parks close.

Plenty of parking is found in the lot adjacent to Downtown Disney, and the **first three hours of parking are free**. You can get an extra two hours free with validation from table-service restaurants or the movie theater. Valet parking is available after 5:00 pm.

NOTES

Thanks to the parking validation mentioned above, the locals tend to visit Downtown Disney on "date nights," which makes the **weekends very busy** with long waits at eateries.

Disney Dollars are legal tender at all Downtown Disney shops and restaurants. If you're staying at a Disney hotel, purchases can be **delivered to your hotel** (request delivery before ringing up).

Almost of the table-service restaurants here have **priority seating** (Rainforest Cafe is the exception—see page 205). Call 714-781-3463 to make priority seating up to 60 days in advance.

For more information, call **Guest Services** at 714-781-4565, and press 4 for Downtown Disney.

GETTING THERE

By Bus—The Anaheim Resort Transit (ART) offers shuttles from area resorts to Downtown Disney.

By Car—From I-5 South, exit at Disneyland Drive and follow the signs to Downtown Disney. From I-5 North, exit at Katella Avenue, turn left, proceed about 1.5 miles to Disneyland Drive, turn right, and follow the signs.

By Foot—It's a short walk from anywhere within the Disneyland Resort area to Downtown Disney.

By Monorail—Board the monorail at the Tomorrowland station in Disneyland Park, and get off at the Downtown Disney station.

By Tram—From the Mickey & Friends parking structure, the parking tram drops you off across from the World of Disney.

Universal Studios Hollywood

If you've been to the huge Universal Studios Resort in Orlando, you're in for a completely different experience here in Hollywood (well, it's actually in "Universal City"—no kidding!). This 415-acre theme park and production studio (the world's largest) is a movie mecca—you won't find many big roller coasters, just live shows, 3-D films, tame rides, and their famous guided tram tour through the production studios area. The theme park is perched on a terrace that overlooks the studios below, all of which are located in the hills above Hollywood, 35 miles northwest of Disneyland.

Universal Studios Hollywood wants to **immerse you in the movies**, though they come closer to achieving this goal when you're experiencing an attraction, not just walking about. No organized lands or themes dominate this park. The slight attempt at theming is limited to what look like studio backlot sets and carry names such as Old West, Cape Cod, Baker Street, and Moulin Rouge. We found some magic in knowing this theme park was the first of its kind and was the inspiration for other movie-oriented parks like Disney-MGM Studios, Universal Studios Florida, and even parts of Disney's California Adventure. Expect to find a little Hollywood and plenty of entertainment at this park.

You can divide the park into **two major sections**—the upper lot and the lower lot (which is accessible by a series of escalators). The largest of these two is by far the upper lot, which is home to most of the park's signature attractions arrayed around the perimeter. This park grew organically over the years (it began as a simple studio tour in 1964) and structures appear almost randomly placed. We got turned around several times on our first visit. We suggest you study our park map on page 131 prior to your visit. See pages 132–134 for attraction descriptions.

Upper Lot	The original section of the theme park as well as the entrance to the Studio Tram Tour. Popular attractions include Shrek 4-D, Back to the Future—The Ride, WaterWorld, and Terminator 2: 3-D
Headline Attractions:	*Shrek 4-D, Studio Tram Tour, WaterWorld*
Lower Lot	Descend down the Star Way escalators to the smallest part of the park where you'll find two of the most expensive rides available anywhere in the world! This is also the home of Backdraft, Special Effects Stages, and Lucy—A Tribute.
Headline Attractions:	*Jurassic Park River Adventure, Revenge of the Mummy*

AMBIENCE

PARK LAYOUT AND HIGHLIGHTS

Planning

Getting There

Staying in Style

Touring

Feasting

Making Magic

Index

Notes & More

Making Your Way to Universal Studios Hollywood

By Car—Universal Studios Hollywood is 35 miles from the Disneyland Resort, so allow at least 45 minutes driving time (more if you're traveling during peak traffic times). To get from Disneyland Resort to Universal Studios Hollywood by car, take I-5 north to US-101 north and exit at Universal Studios Blvd., turn right onto Universal Studios Blvd. and follow the signs to Universal Studios parking. (For directions from other locations, go to http://www.mapquest.com and use this as your destination address: 100 Universal City Plz, Universal City, CA 91608-1002.) Huge parking structures are available—preferred parking is $17;

A gleaming metal globe stands sentry at Universal Studios

general parking is $10 (cars) and $11 (RVs). Be sure to note where you parked (perhaps tie a scarf to your antenna?)—the parking structure is large and can be confusing.

By Bus—The Disneyland Resort Express bus can get you from Disneyland to Universal Studios (and back) for $27/person (ages 3 & up). For more information, see page 20 or call 800-938-8933. For bus transportation from other points, consider a van service or shuttle (page 20). Some hotels may also offer a free or paid shuttle service.

By Train—Take the Metro Rail Red Line to the Universal City Station. We rode it from Dowtown Los Angeles to Universal Studios Hollywood without a hitch. Right across the street from the Universal City Station is a free shuttle to Universal Studios and CityWalk—shuttles run every 15 minutes between 9:00 am and 7:00 pm (or 8:00 pm on weekends). For more information on Metro Rail, see page 23.

Ratings are explained on page 86.

Our Value Ratings:		Our Magic Ratings:		Readers' Ratings:
Quality:	7/10	Theme:	4/10	28% fell in love with it
Variety:	7/10	Excitement:	5/10	34% liked it well enough
Scope:	6/10	Fun Factor:	6/10	21% had mixed feelings
Overall Value:	**7/10**	**Overall Magic:**	**5/10**	17% were disappointed

Universal Studios is enjoyed by...	(rated by both authors and readers)	
Younger Kids: ♥♥♥	Young Adults: ♥♥♥♥	Families: ♥♥♥♥
Older Kids: ♥♥♥	Mid Adults: ♥♥♥♥	Couples: ♥♥♥
Teenagers: ♥♥♥♥	Mature Adults: ♥♥♥	Singles: ♥♥♥♥

Planning | Getting There | Staying in Style | Touring | Feasting | Making Magic | Index | Notes & More

GETTING THERE

RATINGS

Making Your Way
to Universal Studios Hollywood
(continued)

First, know that **Universal Studios Hollywood is open every day**, except Thanksgiving Day and Christmas Day. Park hours vary—check for hours at http://www.universalstudioshollywood.com or call 800-UNIVERSAL (800-864-8377). The park usually opens between 8:00 am and 10:00 am and closes around 6:00 pm in winter or around 10:00 pm in summer. Generally we suggest you arrive at least 30 minutes before park opening, as the gates may open as early as 15 minutes before the posted time. Like Disneyland, Universal Studios attracts many locals, so it's always best to avoid weekends, holidays, and school vacations. You shouldn't need more than a day to experience this park—estimate seven hours to see most attractions and ten hours to see everything. Note that the ticket window may close earlier than the park (around 5:00 or 6:00 pm), and the last tram of the studio tour leaves about 3–4 hours before the park closes. If you visit the park on a day it receives more than 1/16" of rainfall, you may request a rain check good any time in the following 30 days—see staff at the time of your visit for further details. That said, this isn't a bad park to visit on a rainy day, as many attractions are indoors. If possible, plan to stay until closing at this park so you can enjoy the city lights after dark and/or take advantage of CityWalk in the evening.

Universal Studios Hollywood frequently offers great deals on tickets. Admission for one day is usually **$56 for guests 8 and older** (or 48"/122 cm and taller)—guests ages 3–7 or less than 48"/122 cm. are about $46/day. (Kids under 3 are free.) Tickets with extra perks such as front-of-line passes ($90), eat-for-free ($19.95), and extra days are typically available online if you can purchase in advance. Annual passes are available for about $79 (blockout dates), $99 (no blockout dates), and $129 (no blockout dates plus 10% discounts on food and merchandise, free parking, and "Front of Line" access on Studio Tram Tour). If you want to feel like a star and you've got money to burn, consider the VIP Experience for $149/person—you get a behind-the-scenes guided tour which goes into actual soundstages and sets, a "Front of Line" pass for all attractions, access to a special VIP Lounge, and one day's admission. You must make reservations for the VIP Tour at 818-622-5120 in advance, as space is limited. Universal Studios general admission is included in the Southern California CityPass (see page 10). Discounts on admission may be available in the Entertainment Book, through ARES Travel and AAA (see page 11), and with the Chase Universal MasterCard. For more deals, check MouseSavers.com at http://www.mousesavers.com.

BEST TIMES TO GO

TICKETS

Planning

Getting There

Staying in Style

Touring

Feasting

Making Magic

Index

Notes & More

Making the Most of Universal Studios Hollywood

TIPS

Check the showtimes upon entering the park and plan your day around the shows you want to see. Arrive at least 15 minutes in advance for shows to get a decent seat.

The **Lower Lot typically opens an hour later** than the Upper Lot, so we suggest you do the headliner attractions on the Upper Lot then head down to the Lower Lot.

If you're **visiting during crowded times**, we strongly recommend you purchase the "Front of Line" pass, as lines can be very long.

You cannot view any live movie or TV shoots while at the park, but do check out the in-park **Audiences Unlimited booth** for free tickets to a TV studio audience on a future date. The booth is located just beyond the park's main entrance. Note that most shows do not allow minors. More information and show schedules are available at http://www.tvtickets.com.

NOTES

Universal Studios is **not ideal for preschoolers** as attractions have limited appeal and schlepping a stroller down to the Lower Lot is very difficult. If you visit with a child who needs a stroller, we recommend you rent a stroller ($7) at the park, as you can get a new stroller when you get to the Lower Lot.

Wheelchairs can be rented for $7/day ($20 refundable deposit) just inside the park, along with strollers (also $7/day).

Smoking is permitted only in the **designated smoking areas** indicated on park maps.

A complimentary **kennel service** is available for guests with pets. For more information, call 800-UNIVERSAL (800-864-8377).

Dining is mostly fast food in the park, and no restaurants take reservations. You may enjoy eating at CityWalk instead. Descriptions of eateries at both Universal Studios Hollywood and CityWalk begin on page 211.

Several attractions are **very noisy**, which we note in our attraction descriptions. Bring earplugs if you are noise-sensitive.

⋯⋯⋯➤

Sidebar tabs: Planning · Getting There · Staying in Style · Touring · Feasting · Making Magic · Index · Notes & More

Universal Studios Hollywood
Park Map

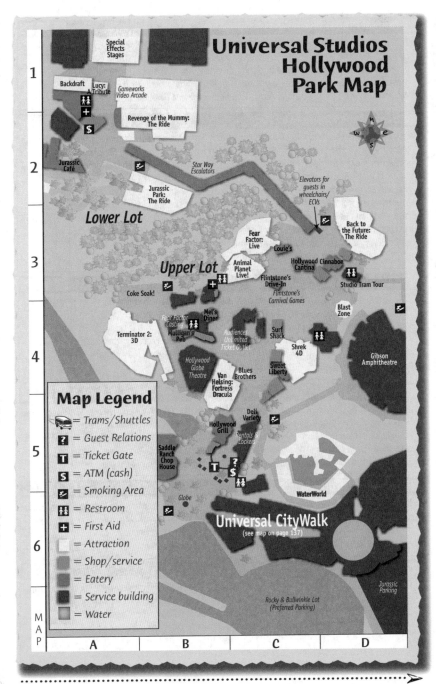

Planning

Getting There

Staying in Style

Touring

Feasting

Making Magic

Index

Notes & More

Charting the Attractions at Universal Studios Hollywood

	Jennifer's Rating	Dave's Rating	Readers' Rating

☐ Animal Planet Live [C-3]

	4	**3**	**6**

This live animal act is mostly a big commercial for the Animal Planet cable channel, but the younger set tends to find it amusing. You'll see animals and birds performing various stunts and a bit of video. The mischievous orangutan is the star of the show and worth visiting. Tip: Bring a dollar bill for the bird act. Wheelchair and ECV accessible. Assistive listening device available.

Live Show
C-Ticket
All ages
25 min. show

☐ Back to the Future–The Ride [D-3] 🚶

	5	**8**	**7**

Doc Brown needs your help chasing that nasty Biff Tannen across time, from the Ice Age to the year 2015. Your eight-passenger, time-traveling Delorean simulator picks up where the "Back to the Future" trilogy left off, deftly dodging a ferocious T-Rex dinosaur and glacial cliffs. Think Star Tours (Disneyland), but wilder and with a huge Omnimax (IMAX) screen. This simulator ride is very bumpy–Jennifer banged her arm hard on the side of the simulator during the ride. Look for the hoverboard in the pre-boarding area. 40"/102 cm. height restriction. Health and motion sickness warning. Guests must transfer from wheelchair/ECV to ride. Closed captioning available upon request. Note that strobe lights and fog are present. Child switch is available.

Thrill Ride
E-Ticket
Ages 6 & up
T-Rex scene is very scary
Medium waits
4 min. ride

☐ Backdraft [A-1]

	6	**7**	**6**

This live show offers a peek at how fire stunts are created. You'll walk from room to room for this show, though most of the time is spent standing. The last scene shows off the power of a 10,000° blast furnace and a "collapsing roof" and it can be both exciting and scary. This show was recently renovated and re-opened in late 2005. Health and noise warning. Guests may remain in wheelchair/ECV/stroller during attraction.

Walkthru
C-Ticket
Ages 9 & up
Short waits
7½ min. film

☐ Blast Zone [D-4]   A-ok!

	5	**5**	**5**

Nickelodeon hosts this 30,000 sq. ft. interactive playground for kids. There's a 500-gallon water play area with soakers, sprayers, and Sponge Bob Square Pants ("Nickelodeon Splash!"), an arena with more than 25,000 foam balls to play in and shoot targets with ("Wild Thornberries Adventure Temple"), and a toddlers play area ("Nick Jr. Backyard"). Guests may remain in wheelchair/ECV.

Playground
A-Ticket
All ages
Allow 30 minutes

☐ The Blues Brothers [C-4]

	3	**5**	**5**

Jake and Elwood Blues impersonators put on a high-octane stage show. Before and after the show, they may travel about in the Blues Mobile with a big speaker on top, or it may simply be parked nearby–be on the lookout for it. As of late 2005, this show is held on weekends only.

Live Show
B-Ticket
Ages 3 & up
Length varies

☐ Fear Factor: Live [C-3] (Seasonal)

	4	**6**	**6**

Prepare to be grossed out at this live version of the popular NBC show. Watch six real contestants compete to be the last one standing as they get dropped from a high-rise platform, locked in a large electrical ball, and have their head stuck in a box with scorpions on top. To be a contestant, register in advance at the Casting Office near Terminator 2: 3-D. Contestants must be 18 or older, between 5 ft. and 6 ft. 2 in., and 100–225 lbs. Rumors say this show may close soon.

Live Show
D-Ticket
Ages 6 & up
Long waits
30 min. show

Charting the Attractions at Universal Studios Hollywood
(continued)

	Jennifer's Rating	Dave's Rating	Readers' Rating

Jurassic Park River Adventure—The Ride [B-2] 👤

	–	7	8

Experience a lovely cruise down a Costa Rican river to an experimental dinosaur refuge. But beware—rafts have been going off course and venturing into the backstage holding pens where the most dangerous dinosaurs are on the loose. This $110 million ride is the second most expensive in the world! Like Disneyland's Splash Mountain, this flume ride is gentle until you get to the big 85-foot drop at the end. Expect to get a bit wet—you may want to wear a poncho to avoid the splashes (a nearby vending machine sells them for $6). The best seats are in the front. Watch for the Mickey ears! 42"/107 cm. height restriction. Health and motion sickness warning. Transfer from wheelchair/ECV to ride. Child switch available.

Thrill Ride
E-Ticket
Ages 9 & up
Steep drop, scary dinosaurs
Medium waits
6 min. ride

Lucy—A Tribute [A-1]

	6	5	6

Delve into the life of America's "Queen of Comedy," Lucille Ball, in this loving tribute. The exhibit displays costumes, scripts, and old home videos of Lucy and her family. "I Love Lucy" fans will also find an interactive trivia quiz about the show. Look for Lucy's Emmys on display, too! Guests may remain in wheelchair/ECV/stroller. Closed captioning provided.

Walkthru
A-Ticket
All ages
Short waits
Allow 20 min.

Revenge of the Mummy—The Ride [B-2] 👤

	2	–	8

Get the daylights scared out of you on this recently built, state-of-the-art indoor roller coaster. Re-creating an Egyptian tomb, this twisted steel coaster features sophisticated Audio-animatronics, holographics, fire, water, and a complex ride system that moves you forward, backward, and upward. Add to this an immersive story, excellent special effects, and a surprise ending, and you've got a real winner with the thrill-seeking set (that's not us, but maybe it's you). Each "mine car" has four rows of four passengers each. 48"/122 cm. height restriction. Health and motion sickness warning. Guests must transfer from wheelchair/ECV. No packs or bags allowed on ride—lockers are nearby if needed.

Thrill Ride
E-Ticket
Ages 9 & up
Dark, fast, goes backwards
Long waits
4 min. ride

Shrek 4-D [C-4]

	9	9	9

In our humble opinion, this is the best attraction in the park and our biggest reason to return. It's in the spirit of Disneyland's "Honey, I Shrunk the Audience" and "It's Tough to be a Bug!" but (dare we say it) even a bit better. After entering via a covered, delightfully themed queue, you experience a 10-minute pre-show and then the 30-minute 3-D movie that artfully bridges the first Shrek movie with the second movie. Without giving too much away, Shrek and his new bride Fiona are pursued by the ghost of Farquaad on their way to their honeymoon—their companion Donkey shows up, of course. The effects are fun, the story is compelling, and the visuals are state-of-the-art. Try to sit in the middle of the theater to get the best 3-D effects. Assistive listening and closed captioning available. Guests may remain in wheelchair/ECV during attraction.

3-D Show
E-Ticket
Ages 4 & up
Dark, sensation of crawling spiders
Medium waits
30 min. show

Special Effects Stages [A-1]

	6	5	7

This three-stage show gives you a glimpse into the making of special effects. Stage One is a virtual studio with "The Mummy," Stage Two is Universal's "Creature Factory" with "The Grinch," and Stage Three is the Sound Lab with Shrek and Scorpion King. Closed captioning. Guests may remain in wheelchair/ECV.

Live Show
B-Ticket
Ages 3 & up
30 min. show

Planning

Getting There

Staying in Style

Touring

Feasting

Making Magic

Index

Notes & More

Charting the Attractions at Universal Studios Hollywood
(continued)

	Jennifer's Rating	Dave's Rating	Readers' Rating

Studio Tram Tour [D-3]

8 | 8 | 9

This is the attraction that spawned the theme park. While the tram tour isn't quite as immersive or "behind-the-scenes" as in the old days, it's still a fun and informative look at movie sets and props. The tour takes you through Universal's backlots, where you'll see sets such as the "Psycho" house, "Jaws," "King Kong" (the original version), and "Jurassic Park." Peeks at more recent movies are included, such as "The Mummy" and "War of the Worlds." There's also a bit of thrill to the tour, such as when your tram "collides" with a big-rig truck that explodes. For the best tour, go Monday–Friday during business hours—this is also your best chance of seeing a celebrity. The last tram leaves around 4:00 pm or 5:00 pm, so do this attraction early on. Closed captioning on request. Guests may remain in wheelchair during attraction.

Thrill Ride
E-Ticket
All ages
Fires, the "Jaws" shark, earthquakes, and King Kong
Medium waits
45 min. tour

Terminator 2: 3D [B-4]

5 | 6 | 7

Mixing a three-screen, 3-D movie with live action, this show propels you into Terminator's future world of robots. The show begins with the unveiling of the new Terminator robots at Cyberdyne Systems Corporation only to be interrupted by a human rebel who starts a cyber war. The effects are excellent, but it's quite violent and may be too scary for some or simply unattractive to those unfamiliar with the "Terminator" movies. This is a very noisy attraction. Also note that strobe lights and fog are present. Assistive listening devices, closed captioning, and reflective captioning available on request. Guests may remain in wheelchair/ECV during attraction. No videotaping allowed.

3-D Show
D-Ticket
Ages 7 & up
Dark, laser fire, large robots, explosions
Long waits
30 min. show

Van Helsing: Fortress Dracula [B-4]

1 | 3 | 4

This is the only PG-13 rated attraction present year-round in a theme park (that we're aware of), but it's more bark than bite. This is your basic "Haunted House" maze complete with live "monsters" that jump out and scare you. And, of course, this maze is filled with props and scenes from "Van Helsing." Before this attraction opened in June 2004, the maze featured props from "The Mummy," so we wouldn't be surprised if this attraction gets a makeover for a new movie in the future. Honestly, we weren't scared and were very underwhelmed by this attraction. Guests may remain in wheelchair/ECV.

Walkthru
C-Ticket
Ages 13 & up
Dark, scary, monsters
Med. waits
Allow 15-30 min.

WaterWorld: A Live Sea War Spectacular [C-5]

8 | 9 | 9

Finally, a theme park attraction that's better than the movie! This is a large-scale spectacular outdoor stunt show featuring water (but of course), fire, shoot-outs, pyrotechnics, breathtaking feats, and a full-scale seaplane. This show is even more spectacular at night. We consider this a must-see attraction. Avoid sitting in the front for a better chance at staying dry. Very noisy. Guests may remain in wheelchair/ECV. Assistive listening devices available.

The WaterWorld set

© MediaMark, Inc.

Live Show
E-Ticket
Ages 4 & up
Loud, explosions, violence
Short waits
16 minute show

Universal CityWalk

Hang out at one of the **"hippest" places in Hollywood** at Universal CityWalk. Wild architecture, blinking neon signs, and street performers create an high-energy urban experience at this shopping, dining, and recreation destination next door to Universal Studios theme park.

A few steps from the entrance to Universal Studios, Universal CityWalk is a great place to experience the street scene in a relatively **safe, clean environment**. It's fun and free to stroll along this pedestrian-only outdoor mall where you can explore shops, restaurants, and nightclubs, as well as spy a 27-foot-tall neon King Kong clinging to the side of a building.

Need a **souvenir** that screams "Hollywood"? This is the place to find it. Wild storefronts, including a smoking alien spacecraft, a giant toucan, and hundreds of PEZ dispensers, welcome you to dozens of unique shops that will appeal to everyone. Film buffs like the Universal Studio Store, with merchandise featuring the latest blockbusters, favorite classics, and theme park souvenirs. Science fiction fans flock to Things From Another World, while horror fans head to THEM! for gifts and collectibles. Hollywood Harley Davidson has branded merchandise and apparel for biker movie fans, and art film lovers can peruse the Martin Lawrence Gallery, featuring creative arts, crafts, and sculpture. If you like westerns, mosey over to Adobe Road for Native American art, instruments, and clothing. Want to dress like a star? Shop for trendy clothing at Abercrombie & Fitch, Hot Topic, and Red Balls, then get outfitted for the beach at Billabong and Quicksilver Boardrider's Club. Go to Fossil for watches, accessories, and T-shirts, and pick up stylish footwear at Skechers. Of course, no Hollywood outfit is complete without sunglasses from Sunglass Hut. Show your team colors with something from The Raider Image, UCLA Spirit, and Team LA, then stop by All Star Collectibles for one-of-a-kind sports memorabilia. Kids and kids at heart alike enjoy the scientific games and educational toys at Awesome Atoms, and stuffed critters that dance and do flips at Captain Coconuts. Find your favorite childhood toys at Sparky's, and every wind-up toy you can imagine at Wound & Wound Toy Co. Visit Dapy for the trendiest toys and gifts, and EB Games for the latest electronic games. Dance to the beat of live bands and browse the huge selection of music and videos at Sam Goody Superstore, then take a quiet break at the Upstart Crow Bookstore and Coffeehouse. After all that, you can escape at Zen Zone, an oxygen bar with one-minute spa products.

Playing at Universal CityWalk

PLAYING

If shopping isn't your thing, CityWalk offers **plenty of entertainment**. Bowl with the stars, dance and play the latest video games at Jillian's Hi Life Lanes (yes, it's actually a bowling alley!), or become a virtual race car driver at NASCAR Motor Speedway. Visit the Saddle Ranch Chop House, where you can try your skill at riding one of the mechanical bulls, sing

Strolling along Universal CityWalk

karaoke, and dance to country music. See the latest movies at the Universal CityWalk Cinemas, including genuine Hollywood red carpet premieres. For movie show times, call 818-508-0711. To see movies on a really big screen, visit the Universal Studios IMAX Theater. Call 818-760-8100 for show times. Enjoy top-name entertainment at the 6,000-seat Universal Amphitheatre. See the calendar and order tickets in advance at http://www.hob.com/venues/concerts/universal. When the sun goes down, head upstairs to CityLoft for more adult entertainment. Sing along with dueling pianos at Howl at the Moon, then take salsa lessons and dance to Latin rhythms at the Rumba

Saddle Ranch Chop House

Room. Listen to great live music at B.B. King's Blues Club. Check their calendar to see who'll be playing at http://www.bbkingclubs.com. Nightclubs have cover charges of $3–$20, so save some money and purchase a Nighttime Party Pass. For $20 you get admission and priority entrance to B.B. King's Blues Club, Howl at the Moon, Rumba Room, and Jillian's Hi Life Lanes, plus two drink coupons, and a $5 Jillian's Hi Life Lanes game card. You can only purchase the pass in advance, and there are some restrictions; call 818-622-7278 for information.

Planning

Getting There

Staying in Style

Touring

Feasting

Making Magic

Index

Notes & More

MAP

DINING

Making Your Way at Universal CityWalk

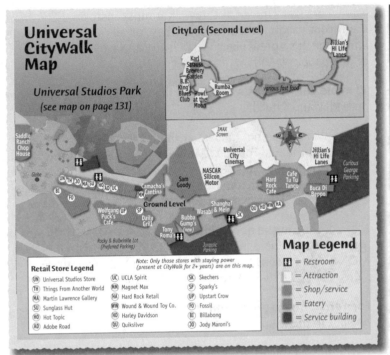

Universal CityWalk Map

Universal Studios Park (see map on page 131)

CityLoft (Second Level)

Karl Strauss Brewery Garden

Jillian's Hi Life Lanes

B.B. King's Blues Club

Bowl Room at the Moon

Rumba Room

various fast food

Saddle Ranch Chop House

IMAX Screen

Universal City Cinemas

Jillian's Hi Life Lanes

Curious George Parking

Globe

NASCAR Silicon Motor

Hard Rock Cafe

Cafe Tu Tu Tango

Buca Di Beppo

Sam Goody

Camacho's Cantina

Ground Level

Wolfgang Puck's Cafe

Daily Grill

Shanghai Wasabi & Mein

Bubba Gump's (new)

Tony Roma's

Rocky & Bullwinkle Lot (Preferred Parking)

Jurassic Parking

Note: Only those stores with staying power (present at CityWalk for 2+ years) are on this map.

Retail Store Legend

UN Universal Studios Store
TH Things From Another World
MA Martin Lawrence Gallery
SU Sunglass Hut
HO Hot Topic
AD Adobe Road
UC UCLA Spirit
MM Magnet Max
HA Hard Rock Retail
WW Wound & Wound Toy Co.
HD Harley Davidson
QU Quiksilver
SK Skechers
SP Sparky's
UP Upstart Crow
FO Fossil
BI Billabong
JO Jody Maroni's

Map Legend

= Restroom
= Attraction
= Shop/service
= Eatery
= Service building

From **casual to elegant dining**, you'll find a good range of eateries at Universal CityWalk. B.B. King's Blues Club has authentic southern cuisine, Buca di Beppo serves family-style Italian food, and Café Tu Tu Tango has international food and tapas. Camacho's Cantina serves Mexican fare. Daily Grill, Hard Rock Café, and the Karl Strauss Brewery Garden all serve traditional American food. Have a steak and make your own s'mores at the Saddle Ranch Chop House, or visit Shanghai and Mein for tea and dim sum. Tony Roma's is the place for ribs, and you'll discover unique sushi at Wasabi at CityWalk. For a quick meal, try The Crepe Café, Pit Fire Pizza Co, Pizzeria Puccino, Jamba Juice, Panda Express, Rubio's Baja Grill, or Wolfgang Puck Café. The Pig offers Memphis-style BBQ, and Versailles has great Cuban food. If you want a little local flavor, head to Dodger Dogs, Jody Maroni's Sausage Kingdom, or Tommy's Hamburgers. Satisfy the munchies at Popcornopolis, Tropic Nut Company, and Wetzel's Pretzels. And for coffee and dessert, visit Starbuck's, Upstart Crow Coffeehouse, Ben & Jerry's, or Cinnabon. Details on these eateries begin on page 213.

Making the Most of Universal CityWalk

TIPS

Many consider Universal CityWalk a **must visit** on a Southern California vacation. It's fun, and best of all, it doesn't charge admission. It's a great place to catch an IMAX movie, enjoy a meal, or just people watch.

To **avoid the crowds**, visit during the week and before 7:00 pm on Friday and Saturday.

If you plan on seeing a movie at the Universal Studio Cinemas, ask at the theater for the **"Movie, Meal, and Parking" deal**. For $19.95/person, you get movie admission, dinner at selected CityWalk restaurants, and free parking. Call the CityWalk hotline at 818-622-4555 for more information.

Many of the **unique neon signs** at CityWalk are historic pieces of art, on permanent loan from the Museum of Neon Art (MONA). MONA gives Neon Cruises that include a walking tour of these signs. Call 213-489-9918 for more information.

For a **great photo opportunity**, pose inside the giant bobble-head doll box in the window of Sparky's.

NOTES

Parking is plentiful but expensive at $10 for an unlimited period of time. Valet parking is available; with validation the cost is $5 for the first 2 hours of parking and $2.50 for each additional half hour up to a maximum of $19.50. Without validation, the cost is $7.50 for the first $1/2$ hour, and $2.50 for each additional half hour up to a maximum of $19.50. Sunday through Thursday after 9:00 pm, valet parking is $3. Validation is available with a purchase at B.B. King's, Rumba Room, Howl at the Moon, Karl Strauss, or Hard Rock Café. Preferred parking is available for $17. Also see page 128 for parking information and driving directions.

Wheelchairs are available for CityWalk visitors at the Universal CityWalk valet areas for a rental fee of $7. Bring valid picture identification, which you'll need to leave while you use the chair.

For **comparison**, CityWalk is an edgy, urban canyon while Downtown Disney is laid-back and low-rise.

For more information, call the CityWalk Information Line at 818-622-4455 or visit http://www.citywalkhollywood.com.

Knott's Berry Farm

Knott's Berry Farm is billed as "America's First Theme Park" and has been a California favorite since the 1940s. A nostalgic part of a classic Southern California family vacation that's now packed with some of the most modern thrill rides to date, Knott's is no longer just a berry farm in a sleepy little town. Knott's Berry Farm is conveniently located just over 5 miles to the northwest of Disneyland Resort.

It all started with a **roadside farm stand** selling rhubarb, asparagus, and of course, berries. The business expanded to jams and jellies, biscuits, and homemade pies. Mrs. Knott served her first chicken dinner in 1934 for a whopping 65 cents! Soon, there were so many folks waiting for the southern fried delicacy that Walter Knott constructed a western ghost town of buildings relocated from real old west towns for diners to wander through for entertainment. From these humble beginnings, it's evolved into a 160-acre amusement park that caters to both thrill-seekers and folks in search of an old-fashioned good time. The park was family-run until 1997, when it was sold to Cedar Fair Amusements (the same company that owns Cedar Point in Sandusky, Ohio—a childhood favorite of Jennifer's).

Knott's Berry Farm is organized into **seven California-themed districts**: California Marketplace, Ghost Town, Wild Water Wilderness, Boardwalk, Fiesta Village, Camp Snoopy, and Indian Trails (see park map on page 143). Below are the districts, clockwise from the entrance, along with descriptions and headline attractions.

California Marketplace Highlights:	A shopping area with a large selection of shops and eateries. Outside the main gates—no admission required. *Independence Hall, Mrs. Knott's Chicken Dinner*
Ghost Town Headline Attractions:	Old-fashioned fun with replica buildings authentically furnished and a craft fair feel. *Ghost Rider, Calico Mine Ride, Timber Mountain Log Ride*
Wild Water Wilderness Headline Attractions:	Rip-roarin' white water and pine woods forest create an outdoorsy feel. *Bigfoot Rapids, Wilderness Scrambler, Mystery Lodge*
Boardwalk Headline Attractions:	Remember old-time amusement park fun while experiencing modern coasters and thrill rides. *Perilous Plunge, Xcelerator, Boomerang, Supreme Scream*
Fiesta Village Headline Attractions:	Come join the party! Stop by the Cantina and enjoy authentic music and food. *Montezooma's Revenge, Jaguar, Merry Go Round*
Camp Snoopy Headline Attractions:	Six acres boasting 30 attractions with kid-style fun in a High Sierra setting. *Charlie Brown Speedway, Timberline Twister*
Indian Trails Headline Attraction:	A tribute to California's native past including handmade crafts, teepees, and other Native American dwellings. *Silver Bullet*

Planning

Getting There

AMBIENCE

Staying in Style

Touring

PARK LAYOUT AND HIGHLIGHTS

Feasting

Making Magic

Index

Notes & More

Planning

Getting There

Staying in Style

Touring

Feasting

Making Magic

Index

Notes & More

Making Your Way to Knott's Berry Farm

GETTING THERE

By Car—It's an **easy drive** to Knott's Berry Farm from the Disneyland Resort area. You don't even have to brave the area's infamous freeways. Just head west on Katella Avenue and then north on Beach Boulevard about 5 miles. Knott's Berry Farm is on your left-hand side. You can't miss it! If you prefer the freeway, try I-5 North to 91 West and take the Beach Boulevard exit (there's a Knott's sign). If you use MapQuest or a similar Internet routing service (which we recommend), the address is 8039 Beach Blvd., Buena Park, CA 90620. Parking is $9/car and $15/bus or RV, or free for three hours to Mrs. Knott's Chicken Dinner/T.G.I. Friday's diners.

Two classic towers at Knott's Berry Farms: Sky Cabin and Supreme Scream

By Bus—If you don't have a vehicle at your disposal, you have several other options for transportation. Knott's Berry Farm Express offers **free round-trip transportation** (in a deluxe motor coach) from the Disneyland Resort Area with full-price paid admission. The service is operated by Pacific Coast/Grayline Sightseeing Tours—call 800-828-6699 for reservations and exact pickup locations. Airport Bus offers transportation on a schedule from shuttle pickup locations—call 714-978-8855 for more information (sometimes a discount is offered for advance purchase of tickets). If you have a large family or group, it might make sense to charter a van through SuperShuttle (714-517-6600) or one of the other airport shuttle companies. Pickup is directly at your hotel at the time you specify. These companies can also arrange limousine service for a fee. And of course, there's always Orange County Transportation Authority (OCTA) with bus stops on almost every corner.

By Taxi—Calling a taxi is another option and may be cost effective with a party of three or more.

Ratings are explained on page 86.

RATINGS

Our Value Ratings:		Our Magic Ratings:		Readers' Ratings:
Quality:	7/10	Theme:	7/10	32% fell in love with it
Variety:	7/10	Excitement:	6/10	30% liked it well enough
Scope:	7/10	Fun Factor:	6/10	23% had mixed feelings
Overall Value:	**7/10**	**Overall Magic:**	**6/10**	15% were disappointed

Knott's Berry Farm is enjoyed by...	(rated by both authors and readers)	
Younger Kids: ♥♥♥♥♥	Young Adults: ♥♥♥♥	Families: ♥♥♥♥♥
Older Kids: ♥♥♥♥	Mid Adults: ♥♥♥♥	Couples: ♥♥♥
Teenagers: ♥♥♥♥♥	Mature Adults: ♥♥♥♥♥	Singles: ♥♥♥♥

Making Your Way
to Knott's Berry Farm
(continued)

As with Disneyland, Knott's tends to be **busiest on weekends**, particularly Saturdays. If you can, visiting mid-week visit is best. Park attendance also swells a bit in the late afternoon and evening hours when it's open late. The reason—drastically reduced admission after 4:00 pm. The crowd changes from the family vacation set to local young people with that admission change as well. Arrive as early as you can for the shortest possible lines for the major attractions. Popular attractions such as the Silver Bullet, Ghost Rider, and Xcelerator can have very long lines (you'll miss Disneyland's FASTPASS). Lines can be quite deceiving, and there is no approximate waiting time posted at the entry of the queue. Families with young children can easily spend an entire day in Camp Snoopy. There are more than 30 attractions available for the younger set. Children (and Western history buffs) may also enjoy the Ghost Town blacksmith, the Old School House, Western Trails Museum, and Ghost Town Jail. There are plenty of attractions for the whole family to enjoy throughout the park. If thrill rides are your thing, you might want to make your way directly to the Boardwalk area at the back of the park—most guests head directly to the Silver Bullet or Ghost Rider first thing because they're closer to the entrance. There are enough thrill rides for even the most daring adventurer. We strongly suggest you shop in the afternoon to avoid crowds. Remember to take breaks regularly throughout the day and drink plenty of water.

Knott's is not organized on a "hub" like Disneyland. It's **easy to become lost** while meandering under all those roller coasters. It's a good idea to consult your map to make sure you see everything you want to see; you may not encounter everything simply by walking in a clockwise or counter-clockwise direction.

Full-day admission at the park's ticket booth is $45.00/adults, $14.95/kids ages 3–11 and seniors ages 62 and older. Southern California residents are $31.00/adults and $14.95/kids and seniors. Advance purchase using Print@Home at http://www.knotts.com is $35.00/adults and $14.95/kids and seniors. Enter after 4:00 pm on any day that Knott's is open until 6:00 pm or later and pay only $22.50/adults and $14.95/kids and seniors. Annual passes are $115.00/adults and $60.00/kids and seniors. A Premium Pass (both the theme park and water park) is $135.00/adults and $75.00/kids and seniors. For more information, visit http://www.knotts.com or call 714-220-5200.

Knott's **shops** specialize in western and Native American-style crafts. You'll also find Peanuts merchandise, famous homemade jams and jellies, and standard theme park souvenirs. Here are some of our favorite themed shops:

Shop	Land	What makes it special
Geode Shop	Ghost Town	Geodes, rocks, and minerals
Snoopy Headquarters	CA Marketplace	The name says it all!
Kid's Crafts	Ghost Town	Create-your-own spin art frisbee!
Bottle House/Indian Trader	Indian Trails	Native American treasures
Girl Power	Boardwalk	Hello Kitty, Powerpuff Girls
Casa California	Fiesta Village	Large selection of Knott's souvenirs
Berry Market	CA Marketplace	World's largest display of signature jams and jellies

Sidebar tabs: Planning · Getting There · Staying in Style · Touring · Feasting · Making Magic · Index · Notes & More

Section markers: BEST TIMES TO GO · TICKETS · SHOPPING

Making the Most of Knott's Berry Farm

TIPS AND NOTES

Theaters, shops, and walk-through attractions are generally **wheelchair accessible**. Some may require assistance. It's a good idea to pick up a copy of the rider safety guide at the Information Center and establish which attractions are safe for people in your party. It lists all services and limitations at the park. Do note that all rides require transfer from wheelchairs.

Rent strollers ($8/single and $13/double + $2 refundable deposit), wheelchairs ($15 + $15 refundable deposit), and ECVs ($17–$34) in Ghost Town next to the Geode Shop. You can reserve ECVs in advance by phoning 714-220-5495.

Just want to pop in to buy something? You can get a **Shopper's Pass** good for 45 minutes by leaving a refundable deposit equal to general admission.

ENTERTAINMENT

Live entertainment comes in two key forms at Knott's Berry Farm. The first are **stage shows**, themed to the area housing the venue and performed on a daily basis. "Knott's Wild West Stunt Show" is the most popular of these shows. Knott's also attracts headline bands and other performers, especially in the summer. Special seasonal performances may be presented in the spacious Charles M. Schulz Theater. Call 714-220-5200 for details on special events or check with the Information Center when you arrive at the park. The other form of live entertainment consists of daily demonstrations of **old-fashioned craftsmanship** such as candle making, horse shoeing, glass blowing, and candy making. Peanuts characters make appearances throughout Camp Snoopy and in front of the main entrance. Performance times vary—your entertainment and show guide lists the day's shows and times.

Show/Entertainment	Land	What makes it special
Knott's Wild West Stunt Show	Ghost Town	Classic western cowboy shoot 'em up
Native American Dancers	Indian Trails	North American and Aztec dancers
Calico Saloon Show	Ghost Town	Music, comedy, and cold beer!
Country Dancin' USA	Ghost Town	Join in the country line-dancin' fun!
Mystery Lodge	Wild Water Wilderness	One-of-a-kind, high-tech Native American storytelling experience
Camp Snoopy Theatre	Camp Snoopy	Lucy, Linus, and Charlie Brown!

Visiting around Halloween? The park becomes **"Knott's Scary Farm"** on select evenings, complete with monsters, mazes, and scare zones. Tickets start at $43.

BEST SPOTS

Best Places to Cool Off—Bigfoot Rapids, Timber Mountain Log Ride, California Marketplace, Perilous Plunge, and Rip Tide.

Best Places to Relax—On a shady bench with the resident cowboys and saloon girls, and in the Calico Saloon with a cold beer.

Best Places to Burn Off Energy—Snoopy's Bounce House, Huff and Puff Mine Cars, and Peanuts Playhouse.

Best Place to Get a Snack—Ghost Town Bakery for Boysenberry Pie and any of the Funnel Cake stands for a best-in-the-west treat.

Best Places for Meals—Mrs. Knott's Chicken Dinner Restaurant (dinner only) and Chow House for chili and beef stew in a sourdough bread bowl. Knott's Berry Farm eateries are described beginning on page 216.

Knott's Berry Farm
Park Map

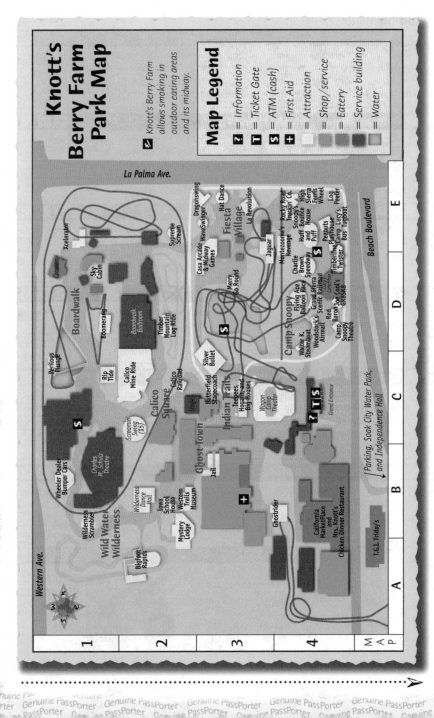

Charting the Attractions at Indian Trails and Ghost Town

	Jennifer's Rating	Dave's Rating	Readers' Rating

Indian Trails

☐ Silver Bullet [C-3]   🧍🚻   1   6   8

Knott's newest, cutting-edge thrill ride debuted in 2004 at a cost of $16 million. With six inversions, including a double corkscrew, this foot-dangling 55 mph steel coaster excites even the most adventurous soul! Avoid loose footwear. Ride duration: 2.5 minutes. Covered outdoor queue. 54"/137 cm height restriction.

Coaster
E-Ticket
Ages 8 & up
Long waits

☐ Teepees, Hogans, and Big Houses [C-3]   3   3   5

Explore authentic Native dwellings of different styles and from many areas of our nation. Also check out the many totem poles in the area, including one custom-made for the Knott family that tells their story. Short waits.

Walk-Thru
A-Ticket
All ages

Ghost Town

☐ Butterfield Stagecoach [C-3]   3   3   5

Hop aboard a raucous stagecoach ride through the park and even back in time. The stagecoach is an authentic, period vehicle and is pulled by a team of four horses. Guests sit on top or inside the coach. Outdoor covered queue. Guests under 46"/117 cm. must be accompanied by a responsible adult.

Coach Ride
D-Ticket
All ages
Med. waits

☐ Calico Mine Ride [C-2]   3   4   6

Train ride into Knott's very own "gold" mine with colorful caverns and simplistic Audio-Animatronics figures. Dated but endearing, this is a classic Knott's attraction. This ride is very dark and may frighten some. Indoor and outdoor queue. Guests under 46"/117 cm. must be accompanied by a responsible adult.

Track Ride
D-Ticket
All ages
Med. waits

☐ Ghostrider [B-4]   🧍🚻   3   6   5

One of the tallest and longest wooden roller coasters anywhere, Ghostrider starts out with a 108-foot drop and just gets better from there. This attraction even has a backstory—legend has it a Union soldier in search of gold ventured into Calico mine one dark night and never returned. Very rough ride. Ride duration: 2.5 minutes. Indoor and outdoor covered queue. 48"/122 cm. height restriction.

Coaster
E-Ticket
Ages 6 & up
Long waits

☐ Ghost Town Calico Railroad [C-2]   3   5   6

Climb aboard an authentic, steam-powered train departing from the Calico Depot for daily trips around the park. Purchased by Walter Knott in 1952, these 1880 beauties are narrow-gauge trains. Look out for train robbers! Outdoor queue. Guests under 46"/117 cm. must be accompanied by a responsible adult.

Train Ride
D-Ticket
All ages
Long waits

☐ Ghost Town Jail [B-3]   3   3   5

Mosey on by this authentic Western "hoosegow" and peek in at shadowy inmate Sad Eye Joe to hear his sad, sad tale. This is an interactive experience, as Sad Eye talks directly to guests—he may even guess your name and hometown! Tip: Send one grown-up to the front window while the rest go to see Joe. Folks tell us this poor guy has been incarcerated since 1941.

Walk-Thru
A-Ticket
All ages

Attraction descriptions and ratings are explained on page

Charting the Attractions at Ghost Town and Wild Water Wilderness

Jennifer's Rating
Dave's Rating
Readers' Rating

Ghost Town (continued)

Iowa School House [B-2]

5 5 5

Original antiques (circa 1875) outfit this full-scale, one-room school replica. Everything is authentic including blackboards, desks, books, and even the potbelly stove. You may even have the chance to sit in on a lesson. Short waits.

Walk-Thru
B-Ticket
All ages

Timber Mountain Log Ride [D-2]

2 6 8

Float swiftly through a dark mountain and past a sawmill on the first flume ride of its kind, and then plummet 38 feet to a gentle splash and classic photo opportunity. Indoor and outdoor queue. Some young children may be frightened by the dark. Guests under 46"/117 cm. must be accompanied by an adult.

Coaster
E-Ticket
Ages 5 & up
Long waits

Western Trails Museum [B-2]

5 4 5

Genuine western artifacts and Knott's memorabilia round out this impressive collection of California historical pieces, including early coins and guns.

Walk-Thru
A-Ticket

Wild Water Wilderness

Bigfoot Rapids [A-2]

6 6 7

Drift along in a High Sierra river complete with rapids and a few splashes along the way. Your free-flowing raft braves whitewater currents, tunnels, geysers, and giant waterfalls. Bigfoot Rapids is the longest man-made whitewater river. Be aware that you will get wet, possibly even soaked. Consider wearing a poncho or storing your valuable items in a locker. Outdoor queue. 46"/117 cm height restriction.

Raft Ride
E-Ticket
Ages 6 & up
Long waits

© MediaMarx, Inc.

Mystery Lodge [B-2]

7 7 7

High tech meets ancient Native American storytelling in this mystical, magical, multi-sensory attraction. The show is a slightly scary but life-affirming story about the important relationships between young and old. The special effect smoke is quite impressive in this award-winning attraction. Twenty-minute shows play hourly on the hour beginning at approximately 11:00 am until park closing. Young children may be frightened by some effects.

Show
C-Ticket
Ages 6 & up
Med. waits

Wilderness Scrambler [B-1]

1 3 7

Classic amusement park spin ride with a wilderness twist. Guests board two-person cars which are suspended from steel arms that whirl about while spinning. Outdoor queue. 42"/107 cm. height requirement. Riders less than 48"/117 cm. must be accompanied by an adult. Previously called Headspin.

Ride
C-Ticket
Ages 6 & up
Long waits

Attraction descriptions and ratings are explained on page 83.

Tip: Knott's Berry Farm has the best posted "Ride Rules" signs of any park that we've visited. Not only do the signs give the health warnings, height requirements, and ride rules, but also a "thrillness rating" ranging from 1 (kiddie ride) to 10 (extreme ride).

Planning
Getting There
Staying in Style
Touring
Feasting
Making Magic
Index
Notes & More

Charting the Attractions at Boardwalk

	Jennifer's Rating	Dave's Rating	Readers' Rating

Boomerang [D-1]   🧍

A short but thrilling coaster that sends you head over heels three times in quick succession. As soon as you catch your breath, you go through the whole thing—backward! Top speed is 48 mph with six inversions. Ride duration: 1 minute, 45 seconds. 48"/122 cm. height requirement. Health warning. Outdoor queue.

Rating	1	5	7

Coaster
E-Ticket
Ages 6 & up
Long waits

Charles M. Schulz Theater [B-1]

A 2,100-seat theater presents a variety of stage shows throughout the year. At press time, "Snoopy's Summer Vacation ... On Ice" was showing here. Check the entertainment and show guide for times. Wheelchair accessible.

Rating	5	3	5

Show
C-Ticket
All ages

Perilous Plunge [C-1]   🧍

Get soaked on a flume ride with a nearly vertical drop—it's the world's tallest and steepest water ride (just 34 feet shorter than Niagara Falls). Those not brave enough to ride can still get drenched on the observation deck. Ride duration: 1.5 minutes. 48"/122 cm. height requirement. Health warning. Outdoor queue.

Rating	1	5	8

Flume Ride
E-Ticket
Ages 6 & up
Long waits

Rip Tide [C-1]   🧍

Soar 59 feet in midair in a floorless gondola and be spun 360 degrees in both directions with 13 inversions. Oh, and you get wet, too—especially if you are seated in the middle of a row! This ride is not for the faint of heart. 54"/137 cm. height requirement. Health warning. Outdoor queue.

Rating	1	6	8

Ride
E-Ticket
Ages 8 & up
Long waits

Sky Cabin [D-1]

Ascend slowly to the top of the 225-foot tower for a view of the entire park and the city beyond. Then float down to earth again. See photo on page 140. This attraction is a great way to cool off and relax. Guests under 46"/117 cm. must be accompanied by a responsible adult. Outdoor queue.

Rating	8	3	4

Ride
C-Ticket
All ages
Med. waits

Supreme Scream [E-2]   🧍

A short, terrifying freefall ride! In three seconds, you're shot straight up to a dizzying height and then plunged downward at more than 50 mph on this extreme thrill ride. The 312-feet-high triple-towers of this monster make it the tallest building in Orange Co. 52"/132 cm. height restriction. Health warning.

Rating	1	5	8

Ride
E-Ticket
Ages 8 & up
Med. waits

Wheeler Dealer Bumper Cars [B-1]   🧍

A classic amusement park ride featuring vintage cars. Watch out for the other drivers! 48"/122 cm. height requirement to ride alone—guests 42"/107 cm. or taller may ride with a responsible adult. Outdoor covered queue.

Rating	3	3	4

Ride
C-Ticket
Ages 6 & up

Xcelerator [E-1]   🧍

This '57 Chevy-themed coaster shoots you almost straight into the air and back down again on just one of its two hairpin curves. It's a real blast to the past! Top speed is a whopping 82 mph, reached during just 2.3 seconds of acceleration. Ride duration: 1 minute. 52"/132 cm. height requirement. Outdoor covered queue.

Rating	1	7	9

Coaster
E-Ticket
Ages 8 & up
Long waits

Note: There's another "attraction" in Boardwalk called Screamin' Swing, but it's an extra $5 to ride due to its low ride capacity. This is basically a gigantic swing that goes more than 90 degrees in each direction as high as 70 feet and as fast as 60 mph. 48 in./122 cm. height requirement.

Charting the Attractions at Fiesta Village

Jennifer's Rating   Dave's Rating   Readers' Rating

Casa Arcade [D-3]
2	3	4

A typical arcade with games ranging from pinball to the latest video craze. Change machines available. A Dance Dance Revolution game is installed here ($1.00 for three stages). This arcade is also sometimes called "Fiesta Village Arcade."

Arcade
A-Ticket
All ages

Dragonswing [E-3]
1	4	6

A rocking swing ride! Will it make a 360-degree swing? Make sure to stow your valuables before your voyage. Don't let this one fool you—those prone to motion sickness should beware. Riders must be at least 42"/107 cm. tall to ride and at least 48"/122 cm. to ride alone. Health warning. Outdoor queue.

Ride
D-Ticket
Ages 6 & up
Med. waits

Fiesta Midway Games [D-3]
2	3	3

What else but games of skill and chance? Winners receive stuffed animals and other souvenirs in varying sizes. Bring plenty of money to play these games.

Arcade
A-Ticket

Hat Dance [E-3]
2	3	6

Spin a sombrero to your heart's content to festive Latin music. Think of Disneyland's teacups but set in Mexico and with more of a kick! Riders must be at least 32"/81 cm. to ride, and 42"/107 cm. to ride alone. Outdoor queue.

Ride
C-Ticket
Ages 4 & up

Jaguar [E-3]
6	5	6

A roller coaster that twists above and through the park's many attractions. The steel track is a half-mile in length, cars go at a top speed of 35 mph, and the drops are no more than 45 feet. Thus, it's one of the tamest coasters in the park. Riders must be 48"/122 cm. tall to ride. Health warning. Outdoor covered queue.

Coaster
D-Ticket
Ages 6 & up
Long waits

Merry Go Round [D-3]
6	5	5

A classic carousel more than 100 years old including authentic organ grinder music with 48 exotic animals and horses to ride. The colorful merry-go-round is sedate, making it popular with younger kids. Outdoor queue. Short waits.

Ride
B-Ticket
All ages

La Revolucion [E-3]
2	3	8

Spin around and up and down and all over again on this brightly colored ride that reminds us of a huge hand-mixer. All thrills, little amusement. Most popular with teens. Riders must be at least 48"/122 cm. tall. Health warning. Outdoor queue.

Ride
D-Ticket
Ages 6 & up

Montezooma's Revenge [E-4]
5	7	8

Blast through a giant seven-story loop at 55 miles per hour and then go through backward again. The steel track is just 800 feet long, and the ride is a mere 30 seconds long. This ride is a classic—it opened way back in 1978. Riders must be 48"/122 cm. tall. Health warning. Outdoor covered queue.

Coaster
E-Ticket
Ages 6 & up
Long waits

WaveSwinger [E-3]
5	4	6

Suspended swings twirl above Fiesta Village, almost appearing to brush the treetops. It's similar to DCA's Orange Stinger, but not as good. Riders must be taller than 48"/122 cm., older than 6, and less than 230 lbs./104 kg. Outdoor queue.

Ride
B-Ticket
Ages 6 & up

Planning   Getting There   Staying in Style   Touring   Feasting   Making Magic   Index   Notes & More

Charting the Attractions at Camp Snoopy

	Jennifer's Rating	Dave's Rating	Readers' Rating

Camp Bus [E-4] — 4 | 4 | 5

Board the camp's bright yellow bus to spin round and round and up high slowly. This is one of the more thrilling rides at Camp Snoopy, rating a "3" on Knott's thrillness scale. Riders less than 42"/107 cm. must be accompanied by a responsible adult. Outdoor queue.

Ride
B-Ticket
All ages
Med. waits

Camp Snoopy Theatre [D-4] — 5 | 3 | 5

This outdoor stage features your favorite Peanuts pals in a foot-stompin' good time! Musical shows vary by season—check the entertainment schedule for performance times. Seating for 200. Wheelchair accessible.

Show
B-Ticket
All ages

Charlie Brown Speedway [D-4] — 6 | 5 | 5

Pint-sized stock cars that go just fast enough! The simple track goes in a circle so it's easy to keep an eye on youngsters. Riders under 42"/107 cm. must be accompanied by a responsible person, and riders over 54"/137 cm. must be accompanied by a person under 42"/107 cm.. Outdoor queue.

Ride
C-Ticket
Ages 2 & up
Med. waits

Flying Ace Balloon Race [D-4] — 5 | 4 | 5

Float high above the trees in your very own balloon. The brightly colored balloons (which aren't actually balloons, of course) drift about in a circle, racing to the finish line. Ballon "baskets" accommodate two persons each. Riders less than 36"/91 cm. must be accompanied by a responsible person. Outdoor queue.

Ride
B-Ticket
All ages
Med. waits

Grand Sierra Scenic Railroad [D-4] — 6 | 5 | 5

A scaled-down steam train ride under the big coasters and around Reflection Lake. This attraction may be re-themed as a Snoopy story adventure during parts of the year. Riders under 46"/117 cm. must be accompanied by a responsible person. Outdoor covered queue.

Train
C-Ticket
All ages
Short waits

High Sierra Ferris Wheel [E-4] — 6 | 4 | 5

Authentic spinning ferris wheel ride high above Camp Snoopy. You'll get a great view of Camp Snoopy from the top. Each of the 12 cars seats 2-3 persons. Riders under 46"/117 cm. must be accompanied by a responsible person. Outdoor queue.

Ride
C-Ticket
All ages
Med. waits

Huff and Puff [E-4] — 5 | 4 | 5

These kid-powered mini mine cars get pushed and pumped around the track. It doesn't take much to get these cars going, but we think kids should be able to ride a tricycle before they try this ride (the hand/eye coordination is similiar). Riders must be under 52"/132 cm. to ride. Outdoor covered queue.

Ride
B-Ticket
Ages 3-8
Med. waits

Joe Cool's GR8SK8 [D-4] — 5 | 5 | 6

Slide around on Snoopy's giant skateboard. Guest sit in seats on the huge, eight-person skateboard, which then rolls back and forth smoothly on its pivoting, 40-foot track. Riders must be between 36"/91 cm. and 80"/203 cm. tall to ride. Outdoor queue.

Ride
B-Ticket
Ages 3-8
Med. waits

Charting the Attractions
at Camp Snoopy
(continued)

	Jennifer's Rating	Dave's Rating	Readers' Rating

Log Peeler [E-4]
| | − | − | 5 |

Kid-sized version of the classic scrambler spinning ride. While it is more gentle than Wilderness Scrambler on page 145, this is still not a good ride to go on after a meal. Riders must be between 32"/81 cm. and 48"/122 cm. to ride. Outdoor queue.

Ride
B-Ticket
Ages 2–6

Lucy's Tugboat [E-4]
| | 6 | 3 | 5 |

Cute little back and forth, up and down nautical adventure for the tiny ones. The tugboat reaches heights of 21 feet, and no water is involved. This ride opened in 2004, making it the newest ride in Camp Snoopy at the time of writing. Riders under 42"/107 cm. must be accompanied by a responsible person. Outdoor queue.

Ride
A-Ticket
All ages
Short waits

Peanuts Playhouse [E-4]
| | 6 | 5 | 5 |

A Peanuts-themed play area perfect for blowing off some steam. The two-story "camp headquarters" playground contains several rooms filled with interactive fun. Little ones under 36"/91 cm. must be accompanied by a responsible person.

Ride
B-Ticket
Ages 2–8

Red Baron [D-4]
| | 5 | 5 | 5 |

Pilot your own biplane with World War I flying ace, Snoopy. Each "Sopwith Camel" style plane seats two persons. Riders must be between 32"/81 cm. and 54"/137 cm. tall. Outdoor queue. Medium waits.

Ride
B-Ticket
Ages 2–8

Rocky Road Truckin' Company [E-4]
| | 5 | 4 | 5 |

Ten-four, good buddy! Toot the air horn as you motor your own mini 18-wheeler around the track. Kids can "drive" in the cab while grown-ups ride in the back. Riders under 42"/107 cm. must be accompanied by a responsible person. Outdoor covered queue.

Track Ride
B-Ticket
Ages 2 & up
Med. waits

Snoopy's Bounce House [E-4]
| | 3 | 4 | 4 |

A huge Snoopy-shaped bounce house. Fun for jumping around, of course. Now that the similiar Goofy's Bounce House at Disneyland is gone, this attraction may be popular. Riders must be under 54"/137 cm. Outdoor queue. Long waits.

Playground
A-Ticket
Ages 2 & up

Timberline Twister [D-4]
| | 5 | 5 | 6 |

Just-right pint-size thrill for kids. Twist and turn through the Camp Snoopy Wilderness on this junior steel coaster. The "big drop" is just 10 feet. Riders must be between 36"/91 cm. and 69"/175 cm. to ride. Outdoor queue. 50-second ride.

Coaster
C-Ticket
Ages 3 & up

Walter K. Steamboat [D-4]
| | 6 | 5 | 5 |

Relaxing cruise of Reflection Lake departing daily from Knott Landing. The steamboat makes a leisurely circuit around the lake, going under the Grand Sierra Scenic Railroad drawbridge. Riders under 36"/91 cm. must be accompanied by a responsible person. Outdoor covered queue.

Ride
C-Ticket
All ages
Short waits

Woodstock's Airmail [D-4]
| | 5 | 4 | 5 |

Kid-sized version of the Supreme Scream. The ride is 1/14th the scale of its elder sister, and the 20 ft. "drop" is more of a bounce. Riders must be 36"/91 cm. or taller. Outdoor queue.

Ride
B-Ticket
Ages 3 & up

Planning
Getting There
Staying in Style
Touring
Feasting
Making Magic
Index
Notes & More

Cooling Off at Knott's Soak City Water Park

Hey, dudes, d'ya need to cool off? Right next door to Knott's Berry Farm is Knott's Soak City, a clean, **13-acre water park** open in late May through September. Note that there are two more Soak City parks in San Diego and Palm Springs, but this description refers only to the park in Orange County. The water park, which opened in June 2000, is themed after California's surfing culture of the 1950s. While its slides are thrilling, they are not extreme, and we think this family-friendly park caters more towards kids, young teens, and adults who don't mind getting wet. Follow the directions on page 140 or use a routing service such as MapQuest. com with this as your destination address: 8039 Beach Blvd., Buena Park, CA 90620.

Old Man Falls and Tidal Wave Bay

Knott's Soak City features **22 different slides and water attractions**. The new Pacific Spin (opening May 2006) is a six-story funnel tube slide. Old Man Falls is a set of three, high-speed slides that start from a platform 62 feet high. Malibu Run and Laguna Storm Water Tower are multi-slide tube slides. Banzai Falls is a set of six speed lanes which guests slide down on mats. Beyond the slides, the park features Tidal Wave Bay (750,000-gallon wave pool), Sunset River (1/3-mile-long lazy river), Gremmie Lagoon (children's pool and activity area), and Toyota Beach House and Slides (a four-story family funhouse and body slides for the younger kids).

Food is available in several counter-service spots (including Mrs. Knott's Fried Chicken Express). There are also several picnic areas available.

Changing rooms are available free of charge. Lockers are $5–$10, plus a $3 deposit.

Swimwear with rivets, buckles, metal, or plastic ornamentation is not allowed on the body slides. We also suggest one-piece suits for modest females who want to slide.

You may rent **inner tubes** for use in the wave pool. Life vests are provided at no charge.

The slides have minimum height requirements between 42" and 48".

You can rent **semi-private cabanas** starting at $70/day. The cabanas includes a patio table, umbrella, four chairs, four lounge chairs, four inner tubes, and private food service (the food itself is extra, of course). Prices are higher on weekends and holidays. For reservations, call 714-761-6268.

Having a birthday? Birthday "Splash Bash" deals include party invitations, admission, lunch, and cake in a reserved party area, plus a gift for the birthday boy or girl. Call 714-220-5298.

Shade is scarce here, so bring appropriate cover-ups, sunscreen, and hats.

Water park admission is $25.95/adults and $14.95/kids ages 3–11. Discounts are available for S. California residents and admission after 3:00 pm.

Six Flags Magic Mountain

Each of these Southern California theme parks has its own personality: Disney is quality and theming, Universal Studios is movies, Knott's Berry Farm is Western charm and thrills, and Six Flags Magic Mountain is coasters. That's right—Six Flags Magic Mountain is the place for roller coasters—there are 17 coasters in this one park at last count (a Guinness world record). Its arsenal of coasters is about the only thing going for it—we do not feel it is a very family-friendly park. But if you're a coaster enthusiast, we suspect you'll be in heaven at Six Flags Magic Mountain.

Six Flags Magic Mountain feels and looks like your **basic amusement park** with a paper-thin veneer of theming. Built in the 1970s by the folks who created Sea World, originally Magic Mountain had just one roller coaster and 29 other attractions ranging from a simple monorail to a bumper boats ride. Ah, such innocence! Many roller coasters were added over the years, as much as one a year. While attractions geared toward families have been added, the park is very popular with local teens, who tend to roam around in groups and affect the park experience negatively for others. It's also not the cleanest place, thanks in large part to the teens. But if you're here for the coasters, who's worried about that stuff? Do note that all guests must pass through metal detectors as they enter the park.

This 260-acre park is nestled in the mountains (hence the name) and its terrain is quite hilly. The park is divided into ten sections, in counter-clockwise order:

Six Flags Plaza *Headline Attraction:*	The entrance plaza with services, eateries, and shops. *Grand Carousel*
High Sierra Territory *Headline Attractions:*	California's High Sierras are loosely evoked in this wooded land with a good eatery—Mooseburger Lodge. *Log Jammer, Sierra Twist, Granny Grand Prix*
Bugs Bunny World *Headline Attractions:*	Children's ride area with the world's largest man-made tree. *Goliath Jr., Canyon Blaster, Sylvester's Pounce & Bounce*
Colossus County Fair *Headline Attractions:*	It's huge! It's giant! It's colossal! Well, at least its coasters are big and hugely popular. *Goliath, Colossus, Scream!*
Gotham City Backlot *Headline Attractions:*	Enter a large, gritty city—this is the realm of Batman! Gray never looked so good. *Batman The Ride, Atom Smashers, Grinder Gearworks*
The Movie District *Headline Attractions:*	More Batman in a show and coaster, plus family rides. *Riddler's Revenge, Batman Begins, Goldrusher*
Cyclone Bay *Headline Attractions:*	No hills to climb here other than the coaster hills. *Deja Vu, Psyclone*
Samurai Summit *Headline Attractions:*	Under renovation for a new ride—the name could change. *Tatsu (summer 2006), Ninja, Superman The Escape*
Rapids Camp Crossing *Headline Attraction:*	Hike up the hill lined with tall trees to a small area with just one ride, Katy's Kettle eatery, and arcade games. *Roaring Rapids*
Baja Ridge *Headline Attractions:*	Mexican-Baja California with the infamous X coaster. *X, Revolution, Viper*

Planning · Getting There · Staying in Style · Touring · Feasting · Making Magic · Index · Notes & More

AMBIENCE

PARK LAYOUT AND HIGHLIGHTS

Making Your Way to Six Flags Magic Mountain

Planning
Getting There
Staying in Style
Touring
Feasting
Making Magic
Index
Notes & More

GETTING THERE

By Car—Six Flags is about 60 miles northwest of Disneyland. To get there from Anaheim, take I-5 north, exit at Magic Mountain Parkway, turn left at the bottom of the ramp, and follow signs to parking ($10). If you need directions from another point, use a routing service such as MapQuest.com with this as your destination address: 26101 Magic Mountain Parkway, Valencia, CA 91355.

By Bus—No wheels of your own? Magic Mountain is off the beaten path, so alternate transportation is more of a challenge. We do know of one tour company that picks you up at your Los Angeles-area hotel, takes you to the park in a motor

Six Flags Plaza

coach—the price of the tour includes park admission. For more information, visit http://la.com.toursandshows.com/Body.asp?Page=TourDetails&tour=LAX-B0016 or call 888-609-5665.

BEST TIMES TO GO

Unlike most other S. Calfiornia parks, Magic Mountain is **not open year-round**. It tends to close on weekdays in the colder months (October–March), though it is open daily during the last two weeks of December. On operating days, the park opens at 10:00 am and closes as early as 6:00 pm in the off-season and as late as 10:00 pm or even midnight on summer weekends. You can get the operating hours for your visit at their web site (http://www.sixflags.com/parks/magicmountain) or by phoning 661-255-4100. As with most parks, you'll encounter fewer crowds if you avoid the summer and holidays. Our most recent visit was in November, and while the crowds were light, we were still astounded by the number of teens in the park. But assuming you're here for the adrenaline rush, arrive early to beat the crowds on a busy day. If you're traveling in the off-season, many coasters may not even be open until 11:00 am.

Ratings are explained on page 86.

RATINGS

Our Value Ratings:		Our Magic Ratings:		Readers' Ratings:
Quality:	4/10	Theme:	3/10	22% fell in love with it
Variety:	5/10	Excitement:	6/10	20% liked it well enough
Scope:	5/10	Fun Factor:	6/10	33% had mixed feelings
Overall Value:	**5/10**	**Overall Magic:**	**5/10**	25% were disappointed

Six Flags is enjoyed by...		(rated by both authors and readers)
Younger Kids: ❤❤	Young Adults: ❤❤❤❤❤	Families: ❤❤
Older Kids: ❤❤❤❤	Mid Adults: ❤❤❤	Couples: ❤❤❤
Teenagers: ❤❤❤❤❤	Mature Adults: ❤❤	Singles: ❤❤❤

Making Your Way
to Six Flags Magic Mountain
(continued)

Full-day admission at the park's ticket booth is $59.99/adults, $29.99/kids 48"/ 122 cm. and under as well as seniors aged 55 and older. Kids age two and under are free of charge. You can save significantly on your admission if you buy online—at press time, a one-day ticket is just $29.99/adults online. Season passes may be a good deal if you plan a multi-day visit or think you'll return again soon—prices range from $59.99 for a "Play Pass," which gives you admission year-round to all Six Flags theme parks. Something else to consider, especially in the busy season, is a Fast Lane pass, which reduces your wait time for select attractions. Fast Lane resembles Disneyland's FASTPASS, but the price is $15 for four tickets (one ticket per person per attraction), and there are a limited number of Fast Lane passes available each day, so arrive early if you're interested.

Try to visit the water-based attractions **earlier in the day**, when lines are shorter. Coaster lines get shorter in the afternoons.

The new attraction of 2006 is **Tatsu**, which strives to give riders a sense of flight as they are suspended below the track. Open in spring 2006.

Here's a fun bit of trivia: Six Flags Magic Mountain was the infamous **"Wally World"** in the movie "National Lampoon's Vacation," which came out in 1983.

Some attractions **ban backpacks**. Consider using lockers for your stuff instead— you'll find lockers near the park entrance and at attractions that have backpack restrictions or are water-based.

Thanks to the park's hilly terrain, you'll be **walking up and down inclines** throughout your visit. Plan to take it a little slower to avoid getting overly tired.

At **900 feet above sea level**, this park is hot during the summer. It's also relatively unshaded, even in many of the queue lines. Your sun exposure increases by 4% here compared to a location at sea level. Be sure to bring hats and waterproof sunscreen, but be sure to stow your hat when you ride a coaster. That said, this park can get cool in the evenings, even during the summer, thanks to its location. Be sure you've got a light jacket if you plan to stay late.

This is **not the best park for little ones**. More than 60 percent of the rides have height restrictions, and those that don't just aren't that great. Besides, the thought of pushing a stroller up those hills makes our backs hurt.

Why are we so **negative** about this park? It simply doesn't appeal to us. We're spoiled by Disney's quality and attention to detail. And as we're not coaster fans or thrill-seekers, this park has little to tempt us. If, however, you are really interested in this park and just aren't finding enough information, please let us know (see page 246) and we'll consider expanding this section in the future.

For more information about Six Flags Magic Mountain, call 661-255-4100 or visit their web site at http://www.sixflags.com/parks/magicmountain. For an unofficial look at the park, visit http://members.tripod.com/heylownine/sfmm.htm.

TICKETS

TIPS/NOTES

Planning

Getting There

Staying in Style

Touring

Feasting

Making Magic

Index

Notes & More

Cooling Off at
Six Flags Hurricane Harbor

After sweating at Six Flags Magic Mountain (be it due to the heat or the thrills), you can cool off next door at the 12-acre Hurricane Harbor water park. It's open daily from 10:00 am to 6:00 pm in June–August, as well as on weekends in May and September. To get to the water park, follow the directions on page 152.

We liked the Six Flags water park better than its sister theme park—it was clean and had plenty of **activities for various ages**. On the other hand, its attempt at a "treasure island" theme falls short (again, we're too spoiled by Disney's water parks in Florida) and there's a serious lack of shade. Still, if you want to have fun in the water, this is hydromania heaven.

*Black Snake Summit and
Forgotten Sea Wave Pool*

Hurricane Harbor features **13 different slides and water attractions**. The new Tornado slide is a six-story, 132-foot-long swirling raft ride. Arrowhead Splashdown is a set of three tube slides. Bamboo Racer is a six-lane toboggan race slide. Black Snake Summit is the big daddy of the slides, with five different speed body slides. Reptile Ridge has five tamer body slides. Taboo Tower features three speed body slides. Tiki Falls is a tamer raft ride. Lost Temple Rapids is a family raft ride. Forgotten Sea Wave Pool is a largish wave pool with two-foot-high waves. Castaway Cove is a water play area with little slides and a fortress to play in. Lizard Lagoon is a 3-acre play area for teens and adults with basketball hoops, water volleyball, and bamboo shade structures. River Cruise is a 1/3-mile-long lazy river. Shipwreck Shores is a family activity pool.

Food is available in several counter-service spots, such as Red Eye's Kitchen, Tradewind Treats, and Paradise Snacks. There are also several picnic areas available.

Changing rooms are available free of charge. Lockers are $5.

Swimwear with rivets, buckles, metal, or plastic ornamentation is not allowed on the body slides. We also suggest one-piece suits for modest females who want to slide.

You may rent **rafts** for the day at Captain Buoy Raft Rentals. Life vests are provided at no charge.

Many of the slides have a **48"/122 cm. minimum height requirement**.

Shade is scarce here, so bring appropriate cover-ups, sunscreen, and hats.

Water park admission is $29.99/adults and $20.99/kids 48"/122 cm. and under, as well as seniors 55+. Combo tickets may be available for Magic Mountain and Hurricane Harbor. Parking is $10 (same parking lot as Magic Mountain). Season passes also available.

For more information, visit http://www.sixflags.com/parks/hurricaneharborla or call 661-255-4100.

LEGOLAND

Fifty miles south of Disneyland, just off I-5, is a charming, 128-acre theme park called LEGOLAND, billed as a "country just for kids." Its slower-paced rides, pleasant landscaping, and occasional glimpses of the nearby Pacific Ocean make LEGOLAND a relaxing respite from the more "thrilling" theme parks in Southern California. LEGOLAND opened in 1999 and is located between Los Angeles and San Diego.

AMBIENCE

Invented in 1932, the word "Lego" combines two Danish words ("leg" and "godt") meaning "play well," which is what you'll do at LEGOLAND, where creativity and imagination flourish. Colorful LEGO® models are everywhere—on the water, in the trees, and in unexpected hideaways. Even the attraction vehicles are large-scale versions of LEGO® models. Unique rides encourage active participation: pedaling a sky cruiser, using a pully to hoist your chair up a tower, searching for hidden keys. These attractions and an abundance of LEGO® building opportunities keep visitors engaged and involved, awakening the "master builder" in everyone. Younger pre-teens often rate LEGOLAND as the highlight of their Southern California trip. Children ages 2–12 are sure to love the kid-sized attractions, and adults will marvel at the detailed and humorous LEGO® models. Teens and young adults, however, might not want to stick around due to the lack of "thrill" rides. LEGOLAND is the most "Disney" of any non-Disney park. They really "get it."

PARK LAYOUT AND HIGHLIGHTS

The areas in LEGOLAND are divided into six play themes that follow the different lines of LEGO® toys. Below are the areas, along with descriptions and headline attractions. See pages 160–166 for attraction details.

The Beginning	LEGOLAND's entry plaza with guest services, shops, and eateries. No attractions are here.
Dino Island *Headline Attraction:*	Dig for dinosaurs and ride through prehistoric jungles under the watchful eye of full-size LEGO® dinosaur models. *Coastersaurus*
Miniland USA *Headline Attraction:*	Billed as the "heart" of LEGOLAND, Miniland USA has seven U.S. regions built with more than 20 million LEGOs®. *Coast Cruise*
Fun Town *Headline Attractions:*	Drive cars, boats, helicopters, planes, and fire engines in this LEGO® town designed and sized especially for kids. *Sky Cruiser, Volvo Driving School*
Knight's Kingdom *Headline Attractions:*	Imagine a time when kings ruled the land and knights rescued fair princesses from fire-breathing dragons. *The Dragon, Knight's Tournament*
Imagination Zone *Headline Attractions:*	Oversized LEGO® models welcome visitors to build LEGO® robots, play video games, and ride big LEGO® vehicles. *AQUAZONE Wave Racers, LEGO® TECHNIC Test Trac*
Explore Village *Headline Attractions:*	Geared toward the younger set, every attraction here, from safaris to musical fountains, is loved by little ones. *Fairy Tale Brook, Safari Trek*

Planning

Getting There

Staying in Style

Touring

Feasting

Making Magic

Index

Notes & More

Planning

Getting There

Staying in Style

Touring

Feasting

Making Magic

Index

Notes & More

Making Your Way to LEGOLAND

GETTING THERE

By Car—Southern California freeways are legendary for being crowded and difficult to navigate, but getting to LEGOLAND by car is relatively easy; just be sure to allow extra time for traffic. Located just off I-5 in Carlsbad, LEGOLAND is about 50 miles south of Disneyland and 25 miles north of San Diego. Take the Cannon Road exit and go east (away from the ocean), following the signs. Plenty of parking is available at the park ($8 cars, $11 campers/RVs, $5 motorcycles, $15 preferred parking). A drop-off area is on the left before the parking toll booths. Look for the big WELCOME structure made of LEGOs®!

Jennifer with a fellow LEGO traveller at the Adventurers' Club

By Bus—If driving sounds stressful, check with your hotel to see if there is a shuttle service available to LEGOLAND. Another option is public transportation, which can be a fun adventure as long as you plan ahead and know your route. North County Transit District (NCTD) Route 344 picks up passengers at the Carlsbad Village Coaster Rail Station and stops right in front of the ticket booths at LEGOLAND. For fares, schedules, and more information, call the NCTD at 760-722-6283. If traveling from Los Angeles County, contact the Metro system (see page 23).

BEST TIMES

LEGOLAND is open every day except Tuesday and Wednesday when schools are in session. As long as the park is open, almost any day is a good day to visit—it doesn't see the huge crowds that other parks get. The park opens at 10:00 am and stays open until 5:00 pm, staying open as late as 6:00 pm or 7:00 pm on weekends and/or holidays. To beat the crowds, plan to arrive about 10 to 15 minutes before opening. This allows time to purchase park tickets and have any children measured for wristbands. Once the park opens, most rides will have no lines for the first hour.

Ratings are explained on page 86.

RATINGS

Our Value Ratings:		Our Magic Ratings:		Readers' Ratings:
Quality:	8/10	Theme:	8/10	38% fell in love with it
Variety:	7/10	Excitement:	6/10	33% liked it well enough
Scope:	7/10	Fun Factor:	8/10	17% had mixed feelings
Overall Value:	**7/10**	**Overall Magic:**	**7/10**	12% were disappointed

LEGOLAND is enjoyed by...		**(rated by both authors and readers)**
Younger Kids: ♥♥♥♥♥	Young Adults: ♥♥	Families: ♥♥♥♥♥
Older Kids: ♥♥♥♥	Mid Adults: ♥♥♥	Couples: ♥♥
Teenagers: ♥♥	Mature Adults: ♥♥♥♥♥	Singles: ♥♥

Making Your Way to LEGOLAND

One-day admission to LEGOLAND is $49.95/adults and $41.95/kids ages 3–12 and seniors ages 60+. Children two and under are free of charge. Two-day tickets are available for $57.95/adults and $49.95/kids and seniors. An annual pass, called LEGOLAND Membership, is $89/adults and $69/kids and seniors. The LEGOLAND Membership Plus pass adds free parking, a free one-day pass, and various discounts

Dave enjoys Miniland USA

to the annual pass for $119/adults and $99/kids and seniors. And then there's the Ambassador Membership Program with lifetime admission and bunch of other perks for a mere $1,000/member. To get discounts on regular admission, look for deals at Costco, AAA, ARES Travel, and through Entertainment Book. You may also find coupons or free passes in special LEGO® brick buckets.

Even though the focus is on building and playing, LEGOLAND also stimulates visitors with some **fun and imaginative entertainment**. While the characters may not be quite as familiar as those you'll run into at the Disneyland Resort, there are opportunities for kids to meet their favorite LEGO® heroes. And there are several live shows throughout the day. To get the most out of LEGOLAND's unique entertainment, visit during one of the many seasonal special events. During the Mini-Renaissance Faire (usually held in June), kids can participate in the Knight's Quest, listen to bagpipers, enjoy special food and drink, and watch a blacksmith practice his trade. Generally, LEGOLAND closes before dark, but during summer months when the park is open later, there are usually fireworks shows Thursdays–Saturdays. At Halloween time, the Brick-or-Treat Celebration brings extra haunted surprises to visitors, including Howlin' Howlie, the wandering werewolf. And during the Holiday Block Party (December 21–30, 2006), kids can sit with LEGO® Santa and marvel at the 30' LEGO® Christmas tree. Check the LEGOLAND web site at http://www.lego.com/legoland/california for special events and park hours.

After spending the day playing with seemingly endless piles of LEGO® bricks, it's nearly **impossible to leave the park without taking a few bricks home**. Whether you are the casual builder or a LEGO® aficionado, the shops at Legoland will fulfill all your building needs. For everything from individual LEGO® bricks to entire kits, LEGOLAND is the place to shop. The park even offers a shopper's pass, which allows you up to one hour of shopping time without paying for park entry. And if you spend more than $20 with your pass, parking will be refunded. For those spending the day in the park, ask for package pickup and purchases will be waiting at the park exit when you leave. Below is a list of favorite shops at LEGOLAND:

Shop	Play area	What makes it special
LEGO® Club House	Fun Town	Bulk LEGOs®, Make & Create Kits
The King's Market	Knights' Kingdom	Costumes and accessories
The Big Shop	The Beginning	Largest selection of LEGO® products
Brick Brothers Trading Co.	Fun Town	Adventure theme LEGO® toys
Clickits Corner	Explore Village	LEGO® toys for pre-teen girls

Planning · Getting There · Staying in Style · Touring · Feasting · Making Magic · Index · Notes & More

TICKETS · ENTERTAINMENT · SHOPPING

Making the Most of LEGOLAND

Planning
Getting There
Staying in Style
Touring
Feasting
Making Magic
Index
Notes & More

TIPS AND NOTES

Families with younger children should **head toward the left** after entering the park, to take advantage of Dino Island and Explore Village. If there are older kids in your group, head toward the right and start your day in the Imagination Zone. If you're really eager to ride the new attraction Knight's Tournament, go right upon entering the park and cut through Miniland USA to get to the attraction early.

Summer 2006 welcomes **Pirate Shores**, a new $10 million area of the park with four water play attractions. This is the park's largest expansion since 1999.

Dining options inside the park are pretty good. Granny's Apple Fries ($3.75) are delicious, as are the pizzas at Ristorante Brickolini. You'll also find barbecue over at Knight's Table. Inquire about a "Brickfest" Buffet at Sports Cafe—at press time it was offered every morning at 9:00 am, $15/adults and $7/kids. Bonus: Several nearby attractions are opened early for Brickfest diners, too.

Consider joining **AAA**. In addition to receiving discounts at many area hotels, AAA members receive discounts on admission, food, and merchandise at LEGOLAND.

Sign up as a **LEGO Brickmaster** for $39.99 and receive a free child's admission to LEGOLAND, a LEGO® set, and more. Call 800-651-0323 for more information.

Most attractions have a **34"/86 cm. minimum height requirement**, but while very young children may not be able to experience the attractions, there are still plenty of play areas they are likely to enjoy.

LEGOLAND never has the crowds Disneyland Resort does, so even the busiest summer weekends are **relatively uncrowded and comfortable**. Tuesdays and Wednesdays during the summer are best for the lightest crowds.

Most people think of LEGOLAND as a kid's park, but we must confess we've visited sans children and still enjoyed ourselves. It's so well-constructed, with Disney-like attention to detail, that we were **utterly charmed and delighted**. We imagine bringing a child is even more fun and rewarding, and we really look forward to our next visit with our son Alexander.

For more information about LEGOLAND, call 760-918-5346 or visit http://www.lego.com/legoland/california. LEGOLAND is located at One LEGOLAND Drive, Carlsbad, CA 92008.

Fun details include this abandoned boot and lioness, which tell a story

BEST SPOTS

Best Places to Cool Off—Water Works, Adventurers' Club, AQUAZONE Water Racers

Best Places to Relax—Miniland, Coast Cruise

Best Places to Burn Off Energy—The Hideaways, Playtown, Fun Town Fire Academy, Dig Those Dinos

Best Place to Snack—Granny's Apple Fries

Best Places for a Meal—Sports Cafe, Knight's Table

LEGOLAND
Park Map

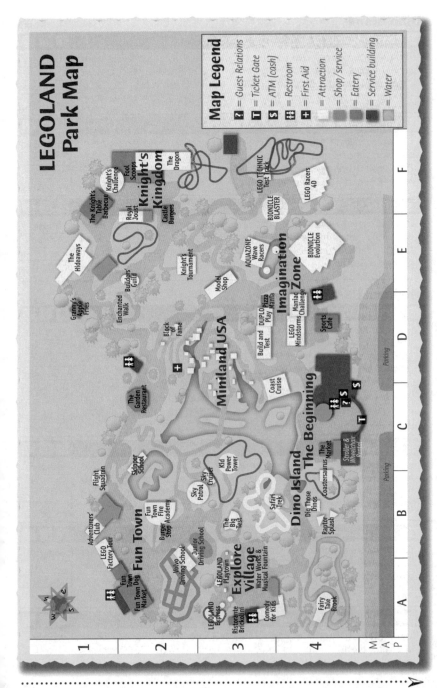

LEGOLAND Park Map

Map Legend

? = Guest Relations
T = Ticket Gate
$ = ATM (cash)
🚻 = Restroom
+ = First Aid
☐ = Attraction
☐ = Shop/service
☐ = Eatery
☐ = Service building
☐ = Water

Knight's Kingdom
- Foot Scoops
- The Dragon
- The Knights' Table Barbecue
- Knight's Challenge
- Castle Burgers
- Royal Joust
- LEGO TECHNIC Test Track
- LEGO Racers 4D
- BIONICLE BLASTER
- The Hideaways
- Builders' Guild
- Knight's Tournament
- Granny's Apple Fries
- Enchanted Walk
- Model Shop

Imagination Zone
- AQUAZONE Wave Racers
- BIONICLE Evolution
- Block of Fame
- Build and Test
- DUPLO Play Mania
- Pizza Mania
- LEGO Mindstorms Maniac Challenge
- Sports Cafe

Miniland USA
- The Garden Restaurant
- Coast Cruise

The Beginning
- The Market
- Stroller & Wheelchair Rental

Fun Town
- Adventurers' Club
- LEGO Factory Tour
- Flight Squadron
- Skipper School
- Fun Town Fire Academy
- Burger Stop
- Fun Town Dog
- Fun Town Market
- Junior Driving School
- Volvo Driving School

Dino Island
- Sky Patrol
- Sky Cruiser
- Kid Power Tower
- Safari Trek
- Big Those Dinos
- Coastersaurus
- Raptor Splash

Explore Village
- The Big Test
- LEGOLAND Playtown
- Water Works & Musical Fountain
- Comedy for Kids
- Fairy Tale Brook
- LEGOLAND Express
- Ristorante Brickolini

Parking

MAP

1 2 3 4
A B C D E F
N S E W

Charting the Attractions at Dino Island and Miniland USA

Rating columns (left to right): Jennifer's Rating, Dave's Rating, Readers' Rating

Dino Island

Coastersaurus [B-4] 🧍 — 7 7 6

This kid-sized coaster speeds up to 21 mph as it climbs, curves, and dips in and around a prehistoric jungle of animated and life-sized dinosaurs. When lines are short, operators may send passengers around twice. Larger riders should sit in the right-hand seat. Minimum height: 36"/91 cm., 48"/122 cm. to ride alone.

Coaster	
D-Ticket	
Ages 6 & up	
1 min. ride	

Dig Those Dinos [B-4] — *A-ok!* — 6 6 6

Kids become junior paleontologists as they dig for the "skeletal remains" of dinosaurs buried in sand! Excavate claws, teeth, bones, and full-sized skeletons. For a small fee, rent paleontologist tools, including bucket, shovel, and fossil brush. Return the tools and get a Dino egg to keep. No minimum height.

Playground	
B-Ticket	
Ages 1 & up	
Allow 30 min.	

Raptor Splash [B-4] — 4 5 5

Pick one of four Raptor battle stations about 25 feet apart from each other, pay a little money, and get ready for a high-tech water balloon battle using a slingshot launcher. Just aim, launch, and splash! A great way to cool off on a sunny day. Seasonal.

Game	
B-Ticket	
Ages 6 & up	
10 min. game	

Miniland USA

Miniland USA [C-3] — 8 9 9

From sea lions barking on Pier 39 in San Francisco to a Presidential motorcade in Washington DC, the sights and sounds of seven regions in the United States have been captured by master LEGO® builders with millions of LEGO® bricks. Look for the space shuttle ready to take off from Cape Canaveral and the newly constructed Freedom Tower in New York City. And if you look closely, there are some funny and realistic LEGO-sized vignettes waiting to be discovered. Head to Miniland later in the day, when lines are long elsewhere in the park. Outdoor pathways. Wheelchair accessible.

Walkthru	
C-Ticket	
All ages	
No wait	
Allow at least 30 min.	

Block of Fame [D-2] — 6 6 7

Stroll through this LEGO® version of an art gallery where master LEGO® builders have re-created the works of master painters and sculptors, including The Thinker by Rodin and Van Gogh's Starry Night. Peruse busts of famous people, including William Shakespeare and Arnold Schwarzenegger. Wheelchair accessible.

Walkthru	
B-Ticket	
All ages	
Allow 10 min.	

Coast Cruise [C-4] 🧍 — 8 6 7

Climb aboard and enjoy a grand tour of Miniland USA from the water, hosted by a LEGOLAND "Model Citizen." Wait until afternoon to take a ride when lines are shorter and your tired feet will enjoy a break. Watch out for water "bombs" activated by mischievous park guests. 48"/122 cm. minimum height to ride alone.

Boat ride	
D-Ticket	
Ages 6 & up	
Long waits	

Model Shop [E-3] — 7 6 7

Take a peek inside the workshop of LEGO® master builders. Relax on a bench and watch builders at work, constructing and renovating the LEGO® creations that adorn LEGOLAND. Wheelchair accessible. No height minimum.

Walkthru	
A-Ticket	
Allow 10 min.	

Charting the Attractions at Fun Town

	Jennifer's Rating	Dave's Rating	Readers' Rating

☐ Adventurers' Club [B-1] *A-ok!* — 7 6 6

Search for the Seven Keys on this mysterious journey featuring inhabitants of the Amazon rainforest, ancient Egypt, and the Arctic—all made of LEGO® bricks. This attraction can be scary for smaller children with dark places, strobe lights, and shaking ground, and older kids may find the keys to easy to spot.

Walkthru
B-Ticket
All ages
Allow 20 min.

☐ The Big Test [B-3] — 5 5 6

Join a bumbling team of firefighter recruits as they discover how to work together to learn fire safety rules, overcome their fears, and finally pass The Big Test to become certified Fun Town firefighters. This show features a working fire truck—so be prepared, you might get wet!

Live Show
C-Ticket
All ages
20 min. show

☐ Flight Squadron [B-1] 🧍 — 6 5 6

Climb aboard these two-seater bi-planes and take flight over Fun Town. Aviators young and old can spin around and up and down this Dumbo-style ride using a simple control lever. Minimum height: 34"/86 cm., 48"/122 cm. to ride alone. Guests must transfer from wheelchair to ride.

Ride
C-Ticket
Ages 2 & up
2 min. flight

☐ Fun Town Fire Academy [B-2] 🧍 — 8 8 9

Test your family's fitness, imagination, and speed. Four teams of up to four people race LEGO® fire trucks across a straightaway, pump water, and aim to put out a "burning" building, then race back to the starting line. Have the littlest ones steer the truck and aim the hoses while the bigger kids (or adults) do the pumping work. Minimum height 34"/86 cm., 48"/122 cm. to ride alone.

Ride
D-Ticket
Ages 3 & up
Medium waits

☐ Kid Power Towers [C-3] 🧍 — – – 7

Discover the magic of pulleys and use "kid power" to raise yourself up in special seats to the top of these towers where the reward is a panoramic view of the Park and the Pacific Ocean. Then "free fall" back to the bottom, as gently as you like. Minimum height 36"/91 cm., 48"/122 cm. to ride alone. 170 lb./ 77 kg. weight limit. Must transfer from wheelchair.

Ride
C-Ticket
Ages 4 & up
Long waits

LEGO Wolf in Adventurers' Club

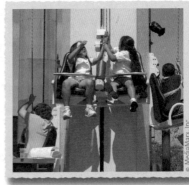

Kid Power Towers

Planning · Getting There · Staying in Style · Touring · Feasting · Making Magic · Index · Notes & More

Planning | Getting There | Staying in Style | Touring | Feasting | Making Magic | Index | Notes & More

Charting the Attractions at Fun Town
(continued)

	Jennifer's Rating	Dave's Rating	Readers' Rating

☐ LEGO® Factory Tour [B-1]

		6	5	6

Tour through a simulated LEGO® factory where automated machinery demonstrates molding, decorating, assembling, and packing of LEGO® products. Interactive displays and videos reveal interesting LEGO® trivia. Wheelchair friendly.

Walkthru
B-Ticket
All ages
Allow 15 min.

☐ Skipper School [C-2]　　🏃

	8	7	7

Pilot a two-seater LEGO® boat along a water course with no track. Keep an eye out for LEGO® brick characters along the way, like the Skipper floating in a bath tub. This is a popular ride, so get in line early or at the end of the day. The Interactive Queue Line allows kids to play with LEGOs while the grown-ups wait in line. Minimum height: 34"/86 cm., 48"/122 cm. to ride alone. Must transfer from wheelchair.

Boat Ride
D-Ticket
Ages 3 & up
Long
waits
3-5 min. ride

☐ Sky Cruiser [B-3]　　🏃

	8	5	6

On a track high above Fun Town, unique and colorful LEGO® pedal cars provide riders with a bird's eye view of Fun Town at a leisurely pace. Energetic drivers can use pedal power to speed up a bit. Each car holds two people and has two sets of pedals. Go first thing in the morning to avoid the lines. If there is a line, kids can play with LEGO® bricks within eyesight of the adults who wait in the line. Minimum height: 36"/91 cm., 48"/122 cm. to ride alone.

Ride
E-Ticket
Ages 4 & up
Long
waits
2 min. ride

☐ Sky Patrol [A-2]　　🏃

	7	6	7

Climb aboard and pilot your own LEGO® helicopter! Using a simple control, small pilots can make the spinning propeller move the helicopter up, down, and around a pole. Minimum height: 34"/86 cm., 40"/102 cm. to ride alone. Must transfer from wheelchair.

Ride
C-Ticket
Ages 3 & up
2 min. ride

☐ Volvo Driving School [A-2]

			9

Learn basic traffic safety like signaling, turning, stopping, going, and sharing the road, then head out in single-seat cars to take a drive and earn a LEGOLAND Driving License. With no rails, it's up to the kids to navigate through intersections, stop lights, and traffic signs on a city grid without running into each other. Sorry grown-ups, this is a "kids only" attraction for ages 6–13 only. Must transfer from wheelchair and be able to operate steering wheel and foot pedals.

Driving School Car

© MediaMarx, Inc.

Ride
D-Ticket
Ages 6-13
Long waits

☐ Volvo Junior Driving School [B-2]

			9

Smaller cars and a simple oval track give the younger set an opportunity to try their hand at driving and earning their own driver's license. Ages 3–5.

Ride
C-Ticket

Charting the Attractions at Knight's Kingdom

	Jennifer's Rating	Dave's Rating	Readers' Rating

Builder's Guild [E-2]

	5	5	6

This shady spot with tens of thousands of LEGO® bricks and plenty of room for playing beckons young builders, and benches provide an inviting spot to relax and watch the action. Wheelchair friendly.

Playground
A-Ticket
All ages

The Dragon [E-2] 🧍‍♂️📏

	8	7	8

Merlin the Magician hosts this animated ride which starts quietly, weaving through the enchanted LEGO® castle and down to the cave of a fire-breathing LEGO® dragon before heading outside on an exhilarating coaster ride with wonderful views of the park. Minimum height: 40"/102 cm., 48"/122 cm. to ride alone. Must transfer from wheelchair.

Coaster
E-Ticket
Ages 4 & up
Long waits

Enchanted Walk [D-2]   A-OK!

	6	6	7

Stroll through this enchanted garden setting, and have fun finding and identifying life-like LEGO® models of animals native to the area including bears, fish, and insects. Wheelchair friendly.

Walkthru
A-Ticket
Allow 20 min.

The Hideaways [E-1]   A-OK!

	5	5	6

Climb rope ladders, brave wooden catwalks, slide down tunnels, and have a grand time on this multi-level play structure. Parents can follow children through or can walk on paths and stairs built parallel to the obstacle courses.

Playground
C-Ticket
All ages

Knight's Challenge: By the Code We Serve [F-2]

	6	6	6

At the Courtyard Theater, watch as the Brave Knights of Morcia compete to defend their code of honor, settle knightly disputes, and help defeat the Dark Knight. Arrive early for a chance at a starring role in the show. Wheelchair seating available.

Live Show
C-Ticket
All ages

Knight's Tournament [E-2] 🧍‍♂️📏

	–	–	7

Become a knight in training and tame the dragon of the Knights' Kingdom. The newest attraction in LEGOLAND and the first coaster of its type in North America. Riders get to choose their destiny and the intensity of the ride experience. Cross a medieval moat and get ready for plenty of twists and turns aboard one of six passenger-carrying robotic arms. Be aware that intensity levels 4 and 5 (the two highest) are relatively extreme and are not for those prone to motion sickness. Minimum height 36"/91 cm., 48"/122 cm. to ride alone.

Coaster
E-Ticket
Ages 4 & up
Long waits
2 min. ride

Royal Joust [E-2] 🧍‍♂️📏

	–	–	6

Mount your very own kid-sized LEGO® horse and ride through an enchanted forest, complete with jousting LEGO® knights. Horses trot along a track and even whinny occasionally. This line can get long, but it is covered. Like the Driving Schools, this ride is for children only. Minimum height: 36"/86 cm. Maximum age: 12. Maximum weight: 170 lbs/77 kg.

Track Ride
D-Ticket
Ages 3-12
Med. to long waits

Side tabs: Planning · Getting There · Staying in Style · Touring · Feasting · Making Magic · Index · Notes & More

Charting the Attractions at Imagination Zone

	Jennifer's Rating	Dave's Rating	Readers' Rating

☐ AQUAZONE Wave Racers [E-3] 🧍 | 8 | 8 | 8

Expect to get wet as you power ski through waves and dodge surprise water blasts triggered by mischievous park visitors. AQUAZONE Wave Racers are two-person vehicles that you stand on. An adaptive vehicle is available for guests with special needs. Assume that you WILL get wet! Minimum height: 40"/102 cm., 48"/122 cm. to ride alone.	**Boat Ride** C-Ticket Ages 4 & up Med. to long waits

☐ BIONICLE Blaster [E-3] 🧍 | 2 | 5 | 7

LEGOLAND's version of Disney's Mad Tea Party. Climb in one of 12 BIONICLE cars that twist and spin—the faster you spin the wheel, the wilder the ride. If you don't like getting dizzy, keep your hands off the wheel or sit this one out. Minimum height: 42"/107 cm., 52"/132 cm. to ride alone.	**Ride** C-Ticket Ages 5 & up Short waits

☐ BIONICLE Evolution [E-4] | 6 | 6 | 6

Find out the story of BIONICLE, a popular LEGO® comic book series, at this exhibit. Afterwards, you have the opportunity to be a part of the story and build a BIONICLE creation using hundreds of different elements.	**Walkthru** A-Ticket Allow 20 min.

☐ Build and Test [D-3] | 6 | 6 | 6

Become an automotive engineer! Find out what makes a car go fast, then build your own car and test it against the competition on the racetrack. Who will cross the finish line first? This attraction is subject to closure on weekdays from 10:00 am to 2:00 pm to accommodate Education Program classes.	**Playground** B-Ticket All ages Allow 30 min.

☐ DUPLO Play [D-3]   *A-ok!* | 5 | 5 | 6

Toddlers love this free-play area filled with extra large LEGO® bricks specially designed for little hands. While the youngest explore, there are comfortable benches for adults to relax.	**Playground** A-Ticket Ages 2-5

☐ LEGO® Mindstorms [D-4] | 6 | 7 | 6

Learn about robotics, then build and program a cutting-edge, computerized LEGO® Mindstorms robot in this hands-on classroom experience. Finally, compete in a contest to collect foam balls in a plastic box. Reservations are required to participate in this program, and they fill up quickly. Wheelchair friendly.	**Live Show** D-Ticket Ages 10 & up 45 min.

AQUAZONE Wave Racers

DUPLO Play

Charting the Attractions at Imagination Zone
(continued)

	Jennifer's Rating	Dave's Rating	Readers' Rating
LEGO® Racers 4D [F-4]	8	7	8

Buckle up as animated racecar driver Max Axel invites everyone in the theater to join in the racing action! Wearing special 3-D glasses, you'll dodge smoke, wind, snow, and water and speed into the wild world of racecar driving. Save this show for the afternoon when everyone is tired and lines are long elsewhere. There is plenty of room in the 400-seat theater. In May 2006, a new show, "Spellbreaker 4D," will alternate with performances of "Racers 4D."

- 3-D Show
- D-Ticket
- All ages
- No wait
- 12 min. show

LEGO® TECHNIC Test Track [F-4]	🚶	5	7	8

Climb into a life-sized LEGO® TECHNIC ride vehicle and feel the powerful acceleration, braking, and maneuverability of these cars while riding on the fastest and biggest roller coaster track at LEGOLAND. Minimum height 40"/102 cm., 48"/122 cm. to ride alone. Must transfer from wheelchair.

- Coaster
- E-Ticket
- Ages 6 & up
- Med. waits

Maniac Challenge [D-4]	6	5	7

When kids can't get their fingers off their Gameboys, send them into the Maniac Challenge where 40 Alienware desktop personal computer systems await, fully loaded with state-of-the-art LEGO® PC games including BIONICLE, Drome Racers, Islands 2, Racers 2, LEGO® Friends, Chess, and Soccer Mania. This attraction is subject to closure on weekdays from 10:00 am to 2:00 pm to accommodate Education Program classes. Wheelchair friendly.

- Arcade
- B-Ticket
- Ages 6 & up
- Short waits

LEGO TECHNIC Test Track

⚠ Wild Woods Golf: A Kid-Sized Golf Course

In July 2005, a new golf course—created just for kids—opened at LEGOLAND. The 23,000 sq. ft. course features 18 holes filled with 40 LEGO models and a variety of interactive experiences. Sounds like mini golf, doesn't it? Yes and no. It does bear a resemblance, but it's lacking those traditional mini golf features—it takes itself more seriously. Special clubs were designed for kids and adults that are supposed to help golfers improve (or learn) their game. Wild Woods is $5/person, but the price is half off with a Membership Plus pass.

Planning
Getting There
Staying in Style
Touring
Feasting
Making Magic
Index
Notes & More

Planning

Getting There

Staying in Style

Touring

Feasting

Making Magic

Index

Notes & More

Charting the Attractions
at Explore Village

| | Jennifer's Rating | Dave's Rating | Readers' Rating |

☐ Fairy Tale Brook [A-4]　　　🚶 A-OK!

	7	5	8

Climb aboard a leaf-shaped boat and sail gently through different LEGO® fairy tale scenes like the Three Little Pigs and the Three Billy Goats Gruff. Watch for unexpected twists to the familiar tales! Guest must be more than 48"/122 cm. to ride alone.

Boat Ride
D-Ticket
All ages
Long waits

☐ LEGOLAND Express [A-3]　　　🚶 A-OK!

	5	5	6

All aboard this LEGO® choo-choo train designed with the young engineer in mind. Take a short trip through Playtown, enjoying the ride and the view. Guests must be 36"/86 cm. to ride alone.

Track Ride
B-Ticket
All ages

☐ LEGOLAND Playtown [A-3]　　　A-OK!

	7	7	7

Become a resident of Playtown, a play area geared toward younger guests complete with a kid-sized fire station, police station, and other buildings. Lots of structures and slides for kids to explore. Wheelchair accessible.

Playground
C-Ticket
Ages 1-6

☐ Comedy for Kids Starring Kevin Johnson [A-3]

	6	6	8

Master Ventriloquist Kevin Johnson takes the stage along with his puppets Clyde and Matilda. This show is popular among adults and kids, with comedy, impersonations, a little bit of magic, and a whole lot of fun. Sit near the front for a chance to be part of the show.

Live Show
D-Ticket
All ages
20 min. show

☐ Safari Trek [B-4]　　　🚶

	7	6	7

Venture into the wilds of Africa in animal-print Jeeps on a safari trek to discover wild LEGO® animals, including life-sized gorillas, giraffes, elephants, and crocodiles. While the trip is short, the lush landscaping and impressive models are worth the wait. Minimum height: 34"/86 cm., 48"/122 cm. to ride alone.

Track Ride
D-Ticket
Ages 4 & up
Med. waits

☐ Village Theater [B-3]

	6	5	8

Watch a short show that introduces several LEGO® characters, then stick around for an opportunity to meet and get your picture taken with characters like LEGO® adventurers Johnny Thunder and Miss Pippin Reed, and BIONICLE hero Tahu Nuva.

Live Show
C-Ticket
All ages
30 min. show

☐ Water Works and Musical Fountain [A-3]　　　A-OK!

	8	7	9

Get creative and get wet in this interactive water play area, where kids can play with water and music. Water Works includes the Magical Fountain, the Zany Zoo, Rain Maker, and the Stomp and Spritz. Hop up and down at the Musical Fountain to make larger-than-life LEGO® instruments play. Large fans coming out of the ground can help wet guests dry off.

Playground
C-Ticket
All ages
No wait
Allow 20 min.

SeaWorld San Diego

Located on Mission Bay about 90 miles southwest of Disneyland, SeaWorld is **San Diego's main "theme park,"** showcasing the aquatic life of the nearby Pacific and oceans around the world. There's a great mix of hands-on experiences, detailed exhibits, and entertaining shows, but the animals take center stage at SeaWorld.

SeaWorld San Diego features three major types of attractions: interactive exhibits, shows, and rides. **Popular animal exhibits** include Penguin Encounter with a moving walkway, as well as a stationary viewing area inside the exhibit (sometimes you can find an expert outside the exhibit with South American Magellenic penguins, answering questions and feeding the birds); Shark Encounter, where you can take a look at the sharks from above, then walk through the tank and let the sharks surround you; and Manatee Rescue, where Florida manatees glide and flip in a tank with a large underwater viewing area.

If you'd really like to get **up-close and personal with sea creatures**, visit the Forbidden Reef and Tide Pools to touch starfish and hermit crabs, or even feed a moray eel! Or just take a leisurely stroll through the two large aquariums, housing both fresh and saltwater fish.

SeaWorld is known for its shows, starring fan favorites orcas (killer whales), dolphins, and sea lions. The park's most popular show, **Shamu Adventure**, features Shamu, baby Shamu, and grandbaby Shamu, as well as some of their friends, jumping, playing, and of course, splashing the guests in the lower rows of the huge stadium. There are two glass-enclosed walkways above both sides of the seven-million-gallon tank, as well as an underwater viewing area for a closer look at these graceful animals. For true Shamu fans, take advantage of the "Dine with Shamu" program for breakfast or dinner, where you can eat literally right next to the killer whale habitat with no need to worry about getting soaked! In spring 2006, the new "Believe" show with Shamu opens—it will feature a two-story stage, a huge water fountain, underwater cameras, and four LED screens.

During the **Dolphin Discovery Show**, watch bottlenose dolphins and pilot whales perform in a high-energy show complete with flips, jumps, and splashes. You can also view San Diego sea lions and otters (and some interesting human characters) act out a humorous love story set in a submarine at Clyde and Seamore in Deep, Deep Trouble. And at the new Pets Rule! show, dogs, cats, and pigs prove that land animals can do tricks, too!

A **great way to cool off** without getting soaked by Shamu is R.L. Stine's Haunted Lighthouse, a 4-D show featuring a spooky film based on the popular kids' "Goosebumps" series, complete with special effects. Or enjoy Euro-style acrobatics and music at Cirque de la Mer, located in the Amphibitheater on Mission Bay.

SeaWorld's newest ride, **Journey to Atlantis**, is half rollercoaster, half flume ride, and takes you through the mythical lost city of Atlantis. Because portions of the ride are outside, hop on again after dark for a completely different experience.

Rounding out the rides in the park are **Shipwreck Rapids**, a river-rapids ride through the South Seas, and Wild Arctic, a combination helicopter-simulator ride and Arctic research exhibit with polar bears, walruses, and beluga whales.

AMBIENCE

PARK HIGHLIGHTS

Planning

Getting There

Staying in Style

Touring

Feasting

Making Magic

Index

Notes & More

Planning

Getting There

Staying in Style

Touring

Feasting

Making Magic

Index

Notes & More

Making the Most of SeaWorld

TICKETS

Full-day admission is $53/adult and $43/kids ages 3–9 (kids under 3 are free). Two-day passes and annual passes are also available. Choose your admission ticket carefully. There are several options available, as well as combination tickets that include behind-the-scenes tours, the Skyride and Skytower rides, or admission to other San Diego area attractions. You can view the ticket options online at http://www. seaworldsandiego.com.

SeaWorld is **open year-round**, starting at 9:00 am or 10:00 am. Park closing can be as early as 5:00 pm in the off-season, or as late as 11:00 pm in busy season.

Walking through the Shark Encounter

TIPS AND NOTES

The Skytower offers **fantastic panoramic views** of Mission Bay from more than 300 feet and the Bayside Skyride takes you over Mission Bay and part of the SeaWorld park; both of these rides are available at an additional cost.

The **Splash Zone** is well marked in all of the stadiums. If you do not want to get wet during the shows, be sure to move to higher seating.

All of the shows, especially Shamu Adventure, are popular, and stadiums fill up quickly, so **arrive early** to stake out great seats.

The **weather in San Diego**, particularly on the coastline, can be cooler in the early morning and evening, and warm during the day, so dress in layers, and bring a change of clothing if you plan to get wet during the animal shows. Note also that the outdoor performances are for the most part uncovered—sit by the water to get a nice breeze and remember your sunblock!

Most of the exhibits include animal-themed gift shops, so if you are looking for merchandise featuring a **specific animal**, you will find the best selection at the exhibits' shops.

If you love a particular animal (say, penguins or beluga whales), book a SeaWorld **behind-the-scenes tour** for a once-in-a-lifetime interactive experience.

Dining options are mostly the standard fast-food fare, but the variety is good. If you prefer to tour the park rather than spend time eating, consider the Showtime Picnic—it gives you a reserved seat for the Shamu Adventure and a meal delivered to you to eat during the show. Price is $12/adults and $7/kids, plus tax. You must reserve online at http://www.seaworldsandiego.com.

For **driving directions**, visit the SeaWorld San Diego web site, call 800-25-SHAMU (800-257-4268), or use a trip routing service such as MapQuest.com (destination address: 500 SeaWorld Drive, San Diego, CA 92109).

San Diego Zoo

No trip to San Diego is complete without a visit to the San Diego Zoo, about 95 miles southwest of Disneyland. Located on 100 acres in San Diego's historic Balboa Park, the zoo is **home to more than 4,000 animals and 700,000 plants**, and most of its residents are rare or endangered.

Arguably, the most popular animals at the zoo are the panda family (including mother, father, and son) on exhibit at the **SBC Giant Panda Research Station**. Visit this exhibit early for more time to watch these animals eat, play, and interact with each other.

Animals of the Arctic, including polar bears and Siberian reindeer, spend their days in a two-acre exhibit including an underwater viewing area, where you can get up-close and personal with the playful polar bears. The Ituri Forest showcases four acres of African jungle animals, including visitor favorites hippopotamuses and otters (both of which have underwater viewing areas). Gorilla Tropics houses western lowland gorillas, as well as several monkey and chimp species in a habitat filled with lush greenery and waterfalls. And the newest exhibit, "Monkey Trails and Forest Tails," opened in June 2005, giving monkey lovers a place to watch their favorite animals in a beautifully re-created rainforest. Australia is represented as well, with kangaroos, koalas, and wallabies from "down under," and all of the eucalyptus leaves that the koalas nibble on are grown right in San Diego.

Scripps Aviary features more than 200 African birds in a rainforest environment. The Owens Rain Forest Aviary is one of the world's largest walk-through aviaries showcasing more than 200 bird species from Southeast Asia and Australia. These and smaller exhibits throughout the park keep bird-lovers walking on air.

The San Diego Zoo isn't all about exhibits! Take a break and enjoy some of the **informational and fun shows** that the zoo puts on, where you can get to know the birds, sea life, or primates a little better. And kids of all ages love lingering around the Children's Zoo, to pet an animal or get a close look at tiny insects.

For an **overview of the zoo and its inhabitants**, we recommend you purchase a Guided Bus Tour ticket ($10.00/adult; $5.50/children; bus tickets are included in some admission tickets, so check yours carefully), valid for the 35-minute tour of the park with a well-informed driver/guide. Bus ticket holders have unlimited use of the Express Buses, which will shuttle you to five various stops throughout the zoo, saving on walking time and energy.

The **Skyfari Aerial Tram** ($3 per person, one-way) transports guests from the Children's Zoo area near the entrance of the zoo to the Polar Bear Plunge exhibit area, saving you a long hike. The Skyfari also gives you a great overview of the zoo and the San Diego downtown area, and is especially beautiful during the twilight and evening hours.

A view of the San Diego Zoo from the Skyfari Aerial Tram

© MediaMarx, Inc.

PARK HIGHLIGHTS

Planning

Getting There

Staying in Style

Touring

Feasting

Making Magic

Index

Notes & More

Making the Most of San Diego Zoo

TICKETS

One-day admission is $22.00/adults and $14.50/kids ages 3–11 (kids under 3 are free). Several other admission options are available, including a Best Value (admission plus Guided Bus Tour, Express Bus, and Skyfari), a two-park ticket that includes admission to Wild Animal Park, etc. You can purchase tickets online at http://www.sandiegozoo.org or by calling 619-718-3000. Note that military guests are free if they arrive in uniform, and October is Kids Free days (kids are free with paying adult). Parking is free.

Giant Panda Research Station

TIPS AND NOTES

The best way to see the zoo is on foot, of course, so that you can take your time at your favorite exhibits, and bypass those that may not interest you as much. The zoo is **built on hilly land**, and certain areas are more difficult for those with limited mobility to reach. Moving walkways and escalators are available in a handful of locations in the zoo, so take advantage of these whenever possible to help you get from one exhibit to the next. If walking will present problems for you, make sure you get admission that includes use of the Express Bus.

Don't try to see everything in one day. The **San Diego Zoo is very large**, covering 100 hilly acres, and features more than 4,000 animals. Take time to take breaks at the exhibits, rest at the shows, and utilize the escalators and other transportation when possible.

Visit the park **early in the morning**, as viewing areas will be less crowded, and the animals are usually more active before it begins to heat up. The San Diego Zoo is also a popular attraction for locals, so it's best to stay away on weekends.

Take advantage of **"Nighttime Zoo"** during the summer, where the zoo offers special evening shows and extended hours, and where you can see nocturnal animals at their most active.

Don't forget your camera and plenty of film, memory, and batteries. (Note that flash photography is prohibited at the Giant Panda exhibit.)

Guided tours and themed sleepovers are also available for the true zoo lover, at an additional cost, offered to both adults and children.

San Diego Zoo is **open year-round**. During the traditional school months, the park is typically open from 9:00 am to 4:00 pm. Summer sees typical park hours of 9:00 am to 8:00 pm. Check the web site or call 619-234-3153 for hours.

For **driving directions**, visit the San Diego Zoo web site, call 619-234-3153, or use a trip routing service such as MapQuest.com (destination address: 2920 Zoo Drive, Balboa Park, San Diego, CA 92101).

San Diego Zoo's Wild Animal Park

If an African safari isn't in your plans, or your budget, the next best thing is a visit to the San Diego Wild Animal Park. Located about 35 miles north of the San Diego Zoo and 85 miles from Disneyland, the park is home to more than **3,500 animals and 1.5 million plants** throughout its 1,800 acres.

The busiest area in the Wild Animal Park is **Nairobi Village**, just past the entrance, where you will find most of the shopping and dining, as well as several exhibits, including the Gorilla Habitat and aviaries containing everything from bee-eating birds to storks. Kids and adults alike will marvel at the unique animals available for personal attention in the Petting Kraal, including impalas and sika deer. Steps away are the Nursery Kraal and Animal Care Center, where the park's newest arrivals and any sick or injured animals are cared for.

For an overview of the park, catch a ride on the **Wgasa Bush Line Railway** (no extra charge). This hour-long, five-mile tour takes you through the expansive African and Asian field exhibits that make the Wild Animal Park so unique, where animals roam freely amongst each other, just as they would in their native habitats. Be prepared to see hundreds of animals, including elephants, zebras, giraffes, gazelle, and more. Each time you ride will be different—you may be lucky enough to catch antelope sparring, or rhinos stampeding across the savanna—so keep your camera ready and your eyes open, and make time to ride more than once during your visit. (Your guide will point out animals and provide information for you, and can slow down if something interesting is happening.) This aging railway will be rebuilt soon, but it will keep operating on a modified route during construction.

If you'd like to tour on your own, set out on the **two-mile Kilamanjaro Safari Walk**, which will take you past the lions, tigers, and elephants. Make sure to stop at Kilima point for a breathtaking view of the East Africa exhibit. Or head down to the Heart of Africa to see the cheetahs, giraffes, and warthogs.

While the large field exhibits focus on Africa and Asia, **Condor Ridge** highlights endangered animals of North America, including California condors, desert bighorn sheep, and black-tailed prairie dogs. Also take time to experience the Hidden Jungle, home to butterflies, hummingbirds, and insects native to the rainforest.

For a uniquely up-close experience, stop at **Lorikeet Landing**, where rainbow lorikeets (also known as brush-tongued parrots), native to Australia and New Guinea, fearlessly land on your arms (or shoulders, or even your head!) and drink nectar straight out of your hand. There is a small fee for a cup of nectar, but the experience is well worth the minimal cost.

The Wild Animal Park does have a **handful of daily shows**—Frequent Flyers (featuring 20 species of birds) and the Elephant Show, as well as various animal encounters throughout the park. There are also a couple of rides available for an additional fee, but the focus of this park is animals and plants in their natural habitats, so the shows and rides are more of an afterthought, and your experience will not suffer if you skip these extras.

Making the Most of Wild Animal Park

TICKETS

One-day admission to the Wild Animal Park is $28.50/adults and $17.50/kids 3–11. If you will be spending several days exploring attractions in the San Diego area, it will be more cost-effective to purchase admission in combination with admission to other area attractions, including the San Diego Zoo and Sea World San Diego.

TIPS AND NOTES

This park is located further inland, and it **tends to get warm quickly** and stay that way throughout the day. There is very little shade here, so be sure to wear sunscreen, sunglasses, and a hat to protect yourself. And because the Wild Animal Park is so expansive, wear comfortable shoes and breathable clothing. If you will be staying at the park during one of the nighttime events, bring along a sweatshirt for the cool nighttime breezes.

A giraffe and two zebras spotted on the Wgasa Bush Line Railway at the Wild Animal Park

The Wild Animal Park also provides **Photo Caravan Safari Tours**, where you can join a handful of other guests as you embark on a truly memorable experience. You will board an open-air vehicle and head into the field exhibits, just like a genuine African safari. Not only will you be able to get fantastic photographs, but you may also be able to feed a rhinoceros or giraffe! Prices vary depending on the length of the tour.

For the most adventurous, book a **Roar and Snore Experience**, where you will camp out among the stars, the trees, and most importantly, the animals! Tents, meals and snacks, and activities are included in the themed sleepovers, and the programming can be tailored to families or adults, depending on the evening. Reservations are required, and availability is limited, so book early.

The Wild Animal Park **opens at 9:00 am daily** and closes at 4:00 pm (fall, winter, and spring months) or 8:00 pm (summer months). Open 365 days a year.

If you've been to **Disney's Animal Kingdom park** at Walt Disney World, you may be struck by some similarities, as we were. There's a familiar African theme and even a couple of familiar names. Of course the two parks are vastly different in scope, but we think the Disney folks took a cue from the successful Wild Animal Park when they designed their theme park.

For **driving directions**, visit http://www.wildanimalpark.com, call 760-747-8702, or use a trip routing service such as MapQuest.com (destination address: 15500 San Pasqual Valley Road, Escondido, CA 92027).

Planning | Getting There | Staying in Style | Touring | Feasting | Making Magic | Index | Notes & More

Balboa Park

In the heart of San Diego lies Balboa Park, the **largest urban cultural park** in America with a 1,200-acre collection of culture, gardens, and activities. The Park was established in the late 1800s as City Park, and later renamed for the Spanish explorer Vasco Núñez de Balboa. Many buildings were originally built for the Panama-California exposition of 1915–16, a celebration of the completion of the Panama Canal, and now house an amazing variety of museums and cultural attractions.

If museums are your passion, you've just hit the jackpot! Balboa Park is home to a **variety of museums**, including the San Diego Museum of Art, San Diego Aerospace Museum, San Diego Natural History Museum, San Diego Museum of Man, Veterans Museum, and the San Diego Model Railroad Museum, just to name a few. Whether it is art, history, or science you are interested in, Balboa Park has a museum to suit your interests—see page 185 for more details.

For those interested in the **visual arts**, the San Diego Art Institute, Museum of Photographic Arts, and the Timken Museum of Arts are must-sees. Various craft and art shows are also held periodically at Balboa Park.

The most visited attraction at Balboa Park is the "World Famous **San Diego Zoo**" (see pages 169–170 for more detailed information).

Music lovers can marvel at the **world's largest outdoor pipe organ** at the Spreckles Organ Pavilion. The organ was first played at Balboa Park in 1914, and performances are still free. The Tony award-winning Old Globe Theater hosts more than 500 performances each year, ranging from Shakespeare classics to Broadway-style musicals. Musical theater is also showcased at Starlight Theater, home to opera, musicals, and concerts by popular artists, and the San Diego Youth Ballet holds performances throughout the year as well. Or treat the little ones to a show at the Marie Hitchcock Puppet Theatre.

Another unique attraction at Balboa Park is the **antique carousel**, which has been a mainstay at the Park since 1922. A gem of quality craftsmanship, most of the animals on the carousel are hand-carved, and the murals on the carousel are hand-painted. The carousel also still has the brass ring game!

There is no shortage of **flora and fauna** in Balboa Park, which contains more than 15,000 trees and several beautifully manicured gardens. One of the most popular is the Inez Grant Parker Memorial Rose Garden, containing more than 2,400 rose bushes and recently named one of the top 12 public rose gardens in the world, and the Japanese Friendship Garden, a tranquil area amidst the hustle and bustle of the city, complete with koi ponds and waterfalls. Admission to most of the gardens is free.

Diversity is celebrated at several of the attractions, including Centro Cultural de la Raza, the Japanese Friendship Garden, and WorldBeat Center. Cultural events are held throughout the year; check Balboa Park's schedule for up-to-date information at http://www.balboapark.org.

PARK HIGHLIGHTS

Planning
Getting There
Staying in Style
Touring
Feasting
Making Magic
Index
Notes & More

Planning

Getting There

Staying in Style

Touring

Feasting

Making Magic

Index

Notes & More

Making the Most of Balboa Park

TICKETS

It's **free to enter the park** and walk around. Museums and attractions have seperate costs, but parking is free in various lots throughout the park. For specific museum admission prices, visit http://www.balboa.org, where you'll find web site links and phone numbers for the park's museums. If you are planning to visit several of the museums during your time in San Diego, consider purchasing the **Passport to Balboa Park**, available at any participating museum or the Visitors Center. It includes admission to 12 of the museums, as well as the Japanese Friendship Garden, and is valid for one week of use.

TIPS AND NOTES

Budget-seekers can take advantage of one of the free guided walking tours, for a closer look at what the park has to offer.

The California Tower viewed from the Alcazar Garden in Balboa Park

A **free tram** shuttles visitors around the expansive area seven days a week from 8:30 am to 6:00 pm (with expanded hours in the spring and summer). Free admission to the park's popular museums and other select attractions is offered during "Free Tuesdays," on a rotating schedule throughout the month. (Special exhibits at the museums may still be subject to an admission fee on Free Tuesdays.) Also inquire about discounts for AAA members and military, if appropriate.

Don't try to see everything in one day; **reserve at least one full day** to tour the park, and set aside time to see the attractions that interest you most.

Park your car in one of the **free parking lots**, then take advantage of the free transportation to get you from place to place within the park.

Pack a picnic lunch, enjoy the beautiful San Diego weather in one of the numerous gardens, and let the kids burn off some energy at a playground.

Don't miss any **special events or performances**! Check the schedule on the Balboa Park web site at http://www.balboapark.org.

You can download a **high-resolution map** of Balboa Park from its web site.

For **driving directions**, visit the web site mentioned above, call 619-239-0512, or use a trip routing service such as MapQuest.com (destination address: 1549 El Prado, San Diego, CA 92101).

More Southern California Attractions

Southern California really has it all—if an international visitor could only visit one region on the U.S., we would recommend Southern California. Of course, we can't possibly include information on every attraction in this guide—a book with all that would require Dr. Wayne Szalinski's shrinking machine! Instead, we present the most popular sites that we think will interest you:

Anaheim Area Attractions

❏ **Discovery Science Center** is full of hands-on exhibits—at last count, there are 120 exhibits here! You can rock climb, create a 19-foot tidal wave in a wave pool, and experience what a 6.3 earthquake feels like. And let's not forget the 3-D laser adventure shows, safe activities for those under 5 at the Kidstation, and more. The Center is open 10:00 am–5:00 pm, daily except Thanksgiving and Christmas Day. General admission is $11.00/adults, $8.50/kids ages 3–17 and seniors 55+. Children under 3 are free, but there is a $1.00 charge for all age groups for the 3-D Laser Theater. Discovery Science Center is located at 2500 N. Main St., Santa Ana, CA 92705. Phone: 714-542-2823. Web: http://www.discoverycube.org.

❏ **Crystal Cathedral** is a spectacular, world-renowned church. It's the largest glass building in the world (more than 12,000 panes) and resembles a four-pointed star. It is open daily for free public tours, as long as no events are planned. Tours are informal with limited access every half-hour, Monday–Saturday, 9:30 am–3:30 pm. Sunday services for 3,000 are held at 9:30 am and 11:00 am, with an evening service at 6:30 pm. The Glory of Christmas Pageant runs November–December and The Glory of Easter Pageant runs March–April. The Drs. Schuller I & II officiate the morning services. The church's denomination is Reformed Church of America. Crystal Cathedral, 13280 Chapman Ave., Garden Grove, CA 92840. Phone: 714-971-4000. Web: http://www.crystalcathedral.org.

❏ **The Los Angeles Angels of Anaheim baseball team** was once owned by the Walt Disney Company (who called it the "Anaheim Angels"), but is now owned by Arte Moreno. The Angels home is Angel Stadium of Anaheim, known as a power hitter's park because the ball carries well. It boasts three full-service restaurants, a family-oriented seating section, an interactive area (The Perfect Game Pavilion), and the Outfield Extravaganza area. Modeled after the California coastline, the stadium has a 90-foot geyser, fireworks, and pyrotechnics to celebrate great plays. Home games run through the end of September. Seating, ticket information, and a pricing chart can be viewed at their web site. Angel Stadium is located at 2000 Gene Autry Way, Anaheim, CA 92806. Phone: 888-796-4256. Web: http://www.angelsbaseball.com.

❏ **The Mighty Ducks of Anaheim hockey team** is one of Southern California's most popular professional sports teams. The Walt Disney Company recently sold the team to the owners of Arrowhead Pond Arena. The season runs October–April. Ticket prices range from $15 to $75 and parking is $7. Home ice is at Arrowhead Pond, 2695 E. Katella Ave, Anaheim, CA 92806. Phone: 877-945-3946. Web: http://www.mightyducks.com.

❏ **Medieval Times Dinner and Tournament** is a popular dinner show. Go back in time and watch a "medieval" jousting tournament with amazing horsemanship and pageantry. All this while you enjoy a four-course meal inside a faux 11th century castle. Prices are $47.95/adults, $33.95/kids ages 12 and under, and $42.06/seniors 55+. 7662 Beach Blvd., Buena Park, CA 90622. Phone: 714-521-4740. Web: http://www.medievaltimes.com.

••➤

More Southern California Attractions

(continued)

Anaheim Area Attractions *(continued)*

❏ **Anaheim GardenWalk**, a proposed shopping/dining area within walking distance of Disneyland, is resuming construction and is scheduled to open October 2007.

❏ **Pirate's Dinner Adventure** is a new dinner show in Buena Park along the same lines as Medieval Times (previous page). Prices are $48.95/adults and $31.99/kids ages 3–11. 7600 Beach Blvd., Buena Park, CA 90620. http://www.piratesdinneradventure.com.

❏ **Wild Rivers Waterpark** is a large, 21-acre water park with 40 water-based attractions, two huge wave pools, and a giant children's area called Explorer's Island. The park has lush tropical foliage, beach huts, and island décor. You can rent a cabana for $50 with waitress service, lounge chairs, and shade! The park is generally open weekends 11:00 am–5:00 pm and 10:00 am–8:00 pm during the hot summer months. Prices are $24.95/adults and $18.95/kids under 48"/122 cm. Rentals are $7/single tube, $8/double tube, and $5/body board. Parking is $6. Wild Rivers is located at 8770 Irvine Center Dr., Irvine, CA 92618. Phone: 949-788-0808. Web: http://www.wildrivers.com.

Beaches and Pacific Coast Highway (from North to South)

❏ **Malibu** has a road sign that reads, "Malibu, 27 miles of scenic beauty." Wide, sandy beaches and rugged rural beauty are reasons why Malibu is a favorite location for the film industry. A great place to view spectacular sunsets is at Paradise Cove. There is a parking fee of $25, but you can get it validated if you eat at the Paradise Cove Beach Café on Paradise Cove Pier located at 28128 Pacific Coast Highway. Malibu's colorful history is on display at the Malibu Lagoon Museum. The museum contains photographs and artifacts from the Chumash Indian era through the Spanish California culture. It is located at 23200 Pacific Coast Highway. Admission is free. Next door you can visit the Adamson house decorated with Malibu tiles that were produced by Malibu Potteries (1926–1932). It contains the original 1929 furnishings. From the house and grounds, you can view Malibu Beach, Lagoon, and Pier. It affords one of the most beautiful beach locations in Southern California. The guided house tour schedule is Wednesday–Saturday, 11:00 am–3:00 pm. Admission is $5/ages 17 & up, $2/ages 6–16, and under 5 free.

❏ **Santa Monica** is known as a "beachopolis"—part city and part beach town. This city has the beach, shopping at its best, and culture. On the beach, you can sunbathe, surf, bike, rollerblade, jog, or have fun at Pacific Park on Santa Monica Pier with amusements in a carnival atmosphere, including a towering Ferris wheel. Admission is free, but if you choose to park under the pier, there is a charge. The rides and games are pay as you go. The park is open every day and is located at Colorado Blvd. and Ocean Ave. The Third Street Promenade is a three-block, pedestrian-only shopping and dining district with a variety of street performers, pushcarts, kiosks, and colorful individuals. Here you will find some of Los Angeles' finest restaurants—this could be your best bet to spot a celebrity. The Promenade is located between Wilshire and Broadway.

❏ The **Getty Museum** is one of the best museums in California. It is a complex of five interconnected buildings with courtyards and terraces. This cultural center contains European paintings, drawings, sculpture, illuminated manuscripts, decorative arts, and European and American photographs. Admission is free, parking is $5/car, and reservations may be required on weekdays (inquire at 310-440-7300). The museum (which is closed on Mondays and major holidays) is located at 1220 Getty Drive, Los Angeles, CA 90049.

More Southern California Attractions
(continued)

Beaches and Pacific Coast Highway (continued)

❏ **Venice** is home to the world famous "Muscle Beach." The phenomenon of Muscle Beach began a long time ago in Santa Monica. It started out in the 1930s, 40s, and 50s with acrobats—young men and woman doing somersaults and handstands and building human towers. Later, Muscle Beach moved to Venice with the focus on bodybuilding. Large crowds gather particularly in the summer months to watch the muscle men and women conduct their workouts. Known for its eccentricity, Ocean Front Walk is home to many shops and street performers. In the summer months, crowds gather along the promenade to watch the various unscheduled activities by local street performers.

❏ **Marina del Rey** is a community with a small beach, but it has the largest man-made marina in the world. Marina del Rey's identity is tied to boating. It also boasts more restaurants in one square mile than any other city except New York City. Visit Fisherman's Village at 13715 Fiji Way for shopping, eateries, boat rentals/tours, and sport fishing.

❏ **Redondo Beach** is a typical California beach community. It has the pier for sport fishing; marinas for charters, tours, and rentals; two miles of beaches to sunbathe, swim, or surf; bike rentals and roller skating/rollerblading; The Fun Factory amusement park; Riviera Village—a six-block hamlet of unique, independently owned boutiques, gift shops, arts & craft galleries, restaurants, and cafes; Seaside Lagoon—a heated salt water, sand-bottom pool; Veterans Park and Czuleger Park for picnicking; and SEA Lab Aquarium, where you can learn about the marine environment.

❏ **Long Beach** offers more than just a beach. The Aquarium of the Pacific in Rainbow Harbor focuses on the Pacific. The aquarium contains 500 species, 19 major habitats, 30 exhibits and is one of the largest in the United States. Hours are 9:00 am–6:00 pm daily, but it is closed December 25 and a weekend in April during the Long Beach Grand Prix. Price is $18.95/adults, $14.95/seniors 60+, and $10.95/ages 3-11. The aquarium is located at Shoreline Drive and Aquarium Way, Long Beach. Across the harbor you will find The Queen Mary. Under British Registry, the historic, "grandest ocean liner ever built" was hostess to the rich and famous in the 1930s and was a troop transport during WWII as the "Grey Ghost" before it returned to peacetime service in 1947. Ownership was turned over to Long Beach in 1967. The Queen Mary is a museum and a hotel with authentic period staterooms, restaurants, banquet rooms, guided and unguided tours, and fireworks displays every Saturday during the summer. Past sightings of ghosts and paranormal activity are part of the ship's charm. You can purchase a general admission passport which includes the Ghosts & Legends Tour and the self-guided ship walk tour. Prices are $24.95/adults, $22.95/seniors and military, and $22.95/ages 3-11. You can add a Behind the Scenes Tour for an additional $5/adults and $3/ages 5-11. We enjoyed our overnight stay on the Queen Mary, but spotted no ghosts (thankfully). The Queen Mary is located at 1126 Queens Highway. For some quaint, intimate charm, travel a few miles to the community of Naples. Navigate the canals surrounding Naples Island in a gondola with an authentically clad gondolier, gentle music, brie, French bread and your own wine.

Dave explores our stateroom on the Queen Mary

More Southern California Attractions
(continued)

Beaches and Pacific Coast Highway (continued)

❑ **Catalina Island** is a unique California getaway. If you have the time, money, and want to get away from the Los Angeles traffic, this is the place to go. As you pull into Avalon Cove in a high-speed catamaran ($40 roundtrip), you get a glimpse of the million dollar yachts and the landmark, historic Casino Building which is now a museum. Day trips are popular, but overnight accommodations make for a more relaxing visit. Things to do are endless: a sandy beach, boat and land tours, snorkeling, scuba diving, horseback riding, golf, shopping, and more. Rent a golf cart and travel up the winding, narrow roads to get breathtaking views of the city of Avalon, Avalon Cove, and the Pacific Ocean. Catamaran and helicopter departures and more of what Catalina has to offer can be found at http://www.ecatalina.com. This site also has a great photo gallery to give you a good view and feel of the Island.

❑ **Newport Beach** has small community beaches for swimming or sunbathing, and it is the "in" place to go. It is one of the smallest large boat harbors in the world. You can go sport fishing or rent boats, skates, bikes, and boards. A jetty called "The Wedge" makes the surfing awesome. You can get a real feel for how the "rich and famous" live on a narrated boat tour around Newport, sailing by homes previously owned by John Wayne, Roy Rogers, Dale Evans, and George Burns. The Balboa Fun Zone is a small pay-as-you-go amusement area. Fashion Island Shopping Center is one of the nicest outdoor malls in Southern California. The Newport Beach Ferry will take you between Newport Beach Peninsula and Balboa Island. Part of Newport Beach, Balboa is man-made and jam-packed with quaint homes and unique shopping on Marine Avenue.

❑ **Laguna Beach** is a seaside artist haven with seven miles of scenic coastline. Laguna has its beaches, but also Dolphin and Whale Safaris and many art festivals that run July into October. Climb the coastal bluff (via stairs) just north of Main Beach to view the breathtaking beauty of the coastline. The area has diverse offerings for dining—choose American, French, Mediterranean, Greek, Italian, Japanese/Sushi, Mexican, or Thai.

❑ **Dana Point** was founded by seaman and author Richard Dana. This natural cove offers panoramic views and great whale watching (http://www.danapointharbor.com). Mariner's Village and Dana's Wharf have numerous restaurants and shops in a scenic setting. The Marine Institute is an educational experience that studies marine life in the Institute and offshore on a 70' research vessel, the "Sea Explorer." Doheny State Park has more than a mile of whitewashed beaches. Within the Park, Doheny State Beach offers 5 acres of lawn for picnicking, a sandy beach with restrooms, showers, volleyball, and snack bars.

❑ **San Clemente** is built into the hillsides overlooking the Pacific. There's a 1,200-ft. pier, a number of beaches including popular North Beach and a "naturist beach," (sorry, no photo). Many restaurants, shops, and parks with bluff-top picnic areas. About 10 miles northwest is Mission San Juan Capistrano. The mission is a cultural, historical, and educational center. The annual return of the swallows occurs every March 19. Self-guided tours are free. Hours are 8:30 am–5:00 pm daily, except Thanksgiving Day, Christmas Day, and Good Friday.

*Dave and Alexander
play in the sand*

More Southern California Attractions
(continued)

Pasadena Area

❏ **The Gamble House**, located in Pasadena, is a National Historic Landmark. The house is deemed a "masterpiece of the American Arts and Crafts movement" and was built by Charles and Henry Greene in 1908 for David and Mary Gamble of the Procter and Gamble Company. It's now owned by the City of Pasadena and operated by the University of Southern California. When you visit, you will know what inspired the architecture of Disney's Grand Californian Hotel. Public guided one-hour tours are available Thursday–Sunday, 12:00 pm–3:00 pm (last tour begins at 3:00 pm). Tickets are on sale in the bookstore the day of the tour starting at 10:00 am on Thursday–Saturday and 11:30 am on Sundays. Tour fees: $8/adult; $5/ages 65+ and full-time students with ID; kids under 12 are free of charge. The Gamble House is located at 4 Westmoreland Place, Pasadena, CA 91103. Phone: 626-793-3334. Web: http://www.gamblehouse.org.

❏ **The Huntington Library, Art Collections, and Botanical Gardens**, situated 32 miles from Disneyland in San Marino, is home to one of the world's largest and most widely used rare book and manuscript collections in America. The Library, Art Collections, and Botanical Gardens are a "collections-based research and educational institution" founded in 1919 by Henry E. and Arabella Huntington. Huntington was an avid collector of rare books, manuscripts, art, and plants. The focus of the collection is on American and British history, literature, and art, as well as rare plant specimens. Famous paintings here include "The Blue Boy" and "Pinkie." The Botanical Gardens are on 150 acres divided into "multiple thematic areas." Open to the public: Tue.–Fri.: 12:00 pm–4:30 pm; Sat.–Sun.: 10:30 am–4:30 pm. Closed on Mondays. Admission: $15/adult; $12/ages 65+; $10/students (ages 12–18 or with student ID); $6/ages 5–11; free for kids under 5. The Huntington Library is at 1151 Oxford Road, San Marino, CA 91108. Phone: 626-405-2100. Web: http://www.huntington.org.

❏ **Old Pasadena** is the site of the famous New Year's Day parade, The Tournament of Roses. Colorado Boulevard is the main thoroughfare of Old Pasadena, lined with more than 80 restaurants and clubs and 120 stores and shops. Old Pasadena is a great destination if you are looking for a charming town center to window-shop, dine, or for some evening entertainment at many theaters, cinemas, and art galleries.

❏ **The Rose Bowl Stadium** is home of the famous Rose Bowl Game. The Rose Bowl is the oldest college football bowl game in existence, held on New Year's Day since 1923 at the Rose Bowl Stadium. Though the Rose Bowl is mainly known for the New Year's Day football game, other events are hosted at the Rose Bowl. For instance, it's home to UCLA football, Major League Soccer team LA Galaxy, and various prestigious world cup and professional sporting events. The Rose Bowl is at 1001 Rose Bowl Drive, Pasadena, CA 91103. Phone: 626-577-3100. Web: http://www.rosebowlstadium.com.

❏ **The Norton Simon Museum of Art** is recognized as one of Pasadena's landmarks. It houses private collections of European, American, and Asian art covering more than 2,000 years. The Norton Simon Museum includes rare works by artists such as Rembrandt, Goya, and Picasso. Museum hours: Mon. and Sat.: 12:00 pm–6:00 pm; Tue.: closed; Wed.–Thu.: 12:00 pm–6:00 pm; Fri.: 12:00 pm–9:00 pm. Admission: $8/adult; $4/ages 62+; under 18 is free (admission is free for all on the first Friday of every month from 6:00 pm to 9:00 pm). The Norton Simon Museum of Art, 411 West Colorado Blvd., Pasadena, CA 91105. Phone: 626-449-6840. Web: http://www.nortonsimon.org.

Planning

Getting There

Staying in Style

Touring

Feasting

Making Magic

Index

Notes & More

More Southern California Attractions
(continued)

Hollywood/Beverly Hills

❑ The **El Capitan Theatre** was recently restored by the Walt Disney Company. It has the original grandeur of the classic movie palaces with a glittering marquee, a box office with ornate, gold woodwork, a plush interior with gold, rococo ceilings, and opera boxes. Colored spotlights illuminate the three layers of glittering curtains. Disney movie presentations are often preceded by a live stage show, but the prices are high: $20/adults and $10/kids. Regular movie price is $9.50/adults; $5.75/seniors and kids under 12; $20/VIP admission (includes balcony seats and popcorn). Close parking lots and garages cost $3-$8. El Capitan is located at 6838 Hollywood Blvd. Phone: 800-347-6396. Web: http://www. elcapitantheater.com. While you're there, check out Disney's Soda Fountain and Studio Shop next door (see page 219).

❑ The **George C. Page Museum of La Brea Discoveries** can be found at the Rancho La Brea Tar Pits. View extinct ice age plants and animals, learn about the Los Angeles of 40,000 years ago, and view bones being cleaned and repaired. Could these be bones from a saber-toothed cat or mammoth? Price is $7/adult, $4.50/seniors (62+) and students with ID, $2/ages 5-12. Admission is free the first Tuesday of the month. Parking is $8 or $6 with validation. The museum is located at 5801 Wilshire Blvd., Los Angeles, CA 90036. Phone: 323-934-7243. Web: http://www.tarpits.org.

❑ **Grauman's Chinese Theatre** with its hands and footprints of the stars forecourt is the most famous movie theater in the world. The theater opened in 1927 and has been the site of more gala movie premieres than any other theater. The exterior is an ornate Chinese pagoda and the interior has many exotic Asian motifs. Movie tickets prices are $10/adult and $7/senior (60+) and kids under 12. A half-hour walking tour is $5 with kids under 5 free. There is no charge to explore the forecourt. The Chinese Theatre is located at 6925 Hollywood Blvd., Hollywood, CA 90028. Phone: 323-464-8111. Web: http://www.manntheatres.com.

❑ The **Hollywood Walk of Fame** runs for 18 blocks on both sides of Hollywood Blvd. from Gower St. to La Brea Ave. It also runs for three blocks along Vine St. between Sunset Blvd. and Yucca St. Bronze star-

Grauman's Chinese Theatre

plaques are embedded in pink and charcoal terrazzo, which you can see in the photo below of Mickey Mouse's star. These stars honor movie stars, directors, singers, songwriters, TV and stage performers ... and the occasional mouse!

❑ The **Hollywood Sign** is a Hollywood landmark atop Mount Lee in Griffith Park. To get an up-close view of the sign, drive up Beachwood Drive. If you are lucky enough to have a clear day, the sign can also be seen from the Beverly Center Mall, the Hollywood (101) Freeway, the Hollywood Bowl, and the Griffith Park Observatory.

More Southern California Attractions
(continued)

Hollywood/Beverly Hills *(continued)*

❏ The **Kodak Theatre** has the elegance of a European opera house with state-of-the-art capabilities. The theater opened in 2001 and is now the Home of the Academy Awards ceremonies. You can tour the theater seven days a week from 9:30 am to 2:30 pm. Tour prices are $15/adult; $10/kids under 12, seniors, and students with ID; and kids under 3 are free. Hours are subject to change, and there are no tours for one month prior to the Academy Awards. The Kodak Theatre is located at the Hollywood & Highland Center at 6801 Hollywood Blvd., Hollywood, CA 90028. Phone: 323-308-6300. Web: http://www.kodaktheatre.com.

❏ The **Pantages Theatre** was built in 1930 and was once owned by Howard Hughes. The theater has been the site of the Academy Awards ceremonies, the Emmy Awards, movie locations, and many live stage shows. The Lion King ran here from October 2000 to January 2003, prior to which it underwent a $10 million renovation. The new interior will take your breath away! The Pantages is located at 6233 Hollywood Blvd., Hollywod, CA 90028. Phone: 323-468-1770. Web: http://www.broadwayla.org/pantages/history.asp.

❏ **Rodeo Drive**, the most famous shopping district in America, is only three blocks long. Most of Rodeo Drive is nondescript unless you venture inside the small shops. There is however, a newer portion, "Two Rodeo," built at a cost of more than $200 million. Two Rodeo is two parallel streets with Spanish steps, sparkling fountains, old-world cobblestones, romantic archways, and charming balconies. The most expensive restaurant in Southern California, Ginza Sushi-Ko, has sushi flown in from Tokyo. It has a ten-seat bar and costs $200/person. Two Rodeo even has a posh underground parking garage. Every Father's Day, Rodeo Drive is carpeted for the "Concours on Rodeo," a vintage car show free to the public. Rodeo Drive runs between Wilshire Boulevard and Santa Monica Boulevard.

❏ **Red Line Tours** offers several guided tours, including Hollywood Behind-the-Scenes, Walk of Fame, Downtown L.A., and the Sony movie studio. We tried the Hollywood Behind-the-Scenes tour, which provided an excellent overview of several famous Tinseltown spots such as Grauman's Chinese Theatre, Kodak Theatre, Hollywood Walk of Fame, Egyptian Theater, Roosevelt Hotel, and an old speakeasy. We really liked the fact that it was a walking tour, and our guide spoke into a microphone which allowed us to hear him on our own headsets. The Hollywood Movie Star Experience Tour combines a bus tour that takes you inside the working Sony Pictures Studios and gives you a tour of movie stars' homes, as well as a walking tour of Hollywood. Tour prices range from $20 to $72/adults and $15 to $56/kids. For more information, call 323-402-1074 or visit http://www.redlinetours.com.

❏ **Beverly Hills Tours** are available on the Beverly Hills Trolley. Professional guides on the tram show you some of the luxury neighborhoods and the posh downtown area. The 40-minute tour starts at the corner of Rodeo Drive and Payton Way. The tour costs $5/adults and $1/kids under 12. The trolley operates May–Labor Day and Thanksgiving–New Year's Eve. For more information, call 310-285-2438.

Planning

Getting There

Staying in Style

Touring

Feasting

Making Magic

Index

Notes & More

More Southern California Attractions

(continued)

Downtown Los Angeles

❑ **Dodger Stadium**, home of the Los Angeles Dodgers, is in Chavez Ravine overlooking downtown Los Angeles. Dodger Stadium is a classic pitcher's park and claims to be the cleanest park in the major leagues. Schedules and tickets are available at http://www.dodgers.com. 1000 Elysian Park Ave., Los Angeles, CA 90012. Phone: 323-224-1500.

❑ **Exposition Park** is a cultural center with a number of sites: California Science Center, California African-American Museum, Exposition Park Clubhouse, IMAX Theatre at California Science Center, Los Angeles Memorial Coliseum, Los Angeles Memorial Sports Arena, Los Angeles Swimming Stadium, Natural History Museum of L. A. County, and the Rose Garden. Located at 701 State Drive, Los Angeles, CA 90037.

❑ The **California Science Center** has more than 1,000 interactive exhibits. Guests are encouraged to touch just about everything. There is a working hovercraft, an earthquake demonstration, a drunken-driving simulator, a wind machine, echo chairs, and a 50-foot animatronics model that comes to life to explain how the body works. You can ride a bicycle suspended on a 40-foot-high wire and build an igloo. The Science Center makes science fun! Go weekdays after 1:30 pm to avoid the crowds of school groups or on weekends. Admission is free, but there is a charge for the High Wire Bicycle, the Motion Based Simulator, and the Cave Climb. Parking is $6/car. The center is located at 700 State Drive, Los Angeles, CA 90037. Phone: 323-724-3623. Web: http://www.californiasicencecenter.org.

❑ The **Natural History Museum of Los Angeles County** has a mission "to inspire wonder, discovery, and responsibility for our natural and cultural world." Just a few of the exhibits include complete dinosaur skeletons, Navajo textiles, 2,000 gems and minerals, an insect zoo, a hall of birds, and dioramas of California marine life. Collections include 25,000 fish species and moths and butterflies. Admission is $9.00/adult; $6.50/senior (62+), students with ID, and kids 13–17; $2/kids 5–12; and kids under 5 are free. Hours are 9:30 am–5:00 pm on Monday–Friday and 10:00 am–5:00 pm on Saturday, Sunday, and holidays. The museum is closed Independence Day, Thanksgiving Day, Christmas Day, and New Year's Day. Parking is $5–$10. The museum is located at 900 Exposition Blvd., Los Angeles, CA 90007. Phone: 213-763-3466. Web: http://www.nhm.org.

❑ The **Music Center** is a performing arts center in downtown Los Angeles. The venues include the beautiful Walt Disney Concert Hall, the Dorothy Chandler Pavilion, the Ahmanson Theatre, and the Mark Taper Forum. Resident companies are the Los Angeles Philharmonic, the Center Theatre Group, the Los Angeles Opera, and the Los Angeles Master Chorale. Performances and tours are available. 135 North Grand Ave., Los Angeles, CA 90012. Phone: 213-972-7211. Web: http://www.musiccenter.org.

❑ The **Staples Center** is home to the Los Angeles Lakers, the Los Angeles Kings, the Los Angeles Clippers, the Los Angeles Avengers, and the Los Angeles Sparks. Schedules and ticket information at http://www.staplescenter.com. 1111 S. Figueroa St., Los Angeles, CA 90015. Phone: 213-742-7340

Walt Disney Concert Hall

➤

More Southern California Attractions
(continued)

Movie Studios

❏ **Paramount Studios** is the longest continually operating studio in Hollywood. In fact, it's the only major motion picture studio left in Hollywood. Paramount Pictures has produced 3,000 pictures since its beginning on July 12, 1912. Among those pictures are 17 Dean Martin and Jerry Lewis comedies, many of Elvis Presley's movies, Citizen Kane, Saturday Night Fever, Forrest Gump, Star Trek, and the Indiana Jones adventures. The landmark Bronson Gate can be seen at the north end of Bronson Avenue. If you wish to take the two-hour walking tour, advance reservations are required (call 323-956-1777). Paramount Studios is located at 5555 Melrose Ave., Hollywood, CA 90038. Phone: 323-956-5000. Web: http://www.paramount.com/studio.

❏ **Sony Pictures Studios** is the old, grand MGM studio that was purchased by Sony Entertainment of Japan. Along with the purchase, Sony acquired MGM's library of films. This is the biggest library of color films in the world. Pictures produced at MGM include James Bond, The Pink Panther, and Rocky. Newer releases include A Few Good Men, Men in Black II, Jumanji, Sleepless in Seattle, As Good As It Gets, and Spiderman. Two-hour walking tours are available Monday–Friday for $25/person (must be at least 12)—reserve at 323-520-8687. Get tickets to watch a taping of a show at http://www.audiencesunlimited.com. Sony Pictures Studios is located at 10202 W. Washington Blvd., Culver City, CA 90232. Phone: 310-244-4000. Web: http://www.sonypicturesstudios.com.

❏ **Warner Brothers Studios** is one of Hollywood's most famous studios. The first "talkie" with Al Jolson was produced at Warner Bros in 1927. Some of their other films include Casablanca, the Batman series, Rebel Without a Cause, the Harry Potter series, and Lord of the Rings. VIP Studio Tours are offered via a tour cart—get options, prices, and hours at http://www2.warnerbros.com/vipstudiotour. Information about attending a free taping is at http://www.audiencesunlimited.com. The studio tour is located at 3400 Riverside Drive, Burbank, CA 91522. Phone: 818-972-8687. Web: http://www.wbsf.com.

❏ **Universal Studios** is the largest film and television studio in the world. Films produced by Universal include E.T., Jurassic Park, Schindler's List, Frankenstein, The Birds, and Back to the Future. Many of the rides and attractions at Universal Studios theme park (see pages 127–138) are themed after these and other films. At Universal Studios park you can take a studio tram tour, enjoy rides, shop, dine, or be entertained at CityWalk. Universal Studios is located at 100 Universal City Plaza at Lankershim, Universal City, CA 91608. Phone: 818-622-3801. Web: http://www.universalstudios.com.

❏ The **Walt Disney Studios** and its subsidiaries, Touchstone Pictures, Hollywood Pictures, and Miramax Films, have released some of the most popular films in recent years, including "Pirates of the Caribbean," "Pearl Harbor," and "Chicago." The Walt Disney Studios began in 1923 in a tiny studio in L.A. In 1937, with the profits from Snow White, Walt bought 51 acres in Burbank and built a state-of-the-art animation building. The large glass-and-brick company headquarters sports seven, 19-foot-tall Dwarfs. Tours are not available, but you can get tickets for a taping at http://www.audiencesunlimited.com. The studio is located at 500 S. Buena Vista St., Burbank, CA 91521. Phone: 818-560-1000.

Planning

Getting There

Staying in Style

Touring

Feasting

Making Magic

Index

Notes & More

More Southern California Attractions

(continued)

San Diego

❑ **Beaches** are popular in San Diego, which has more than 70 miles of coastline, encompassing 30 individual beaches. Some of the most beautiful include Coronado Beach (and the adjacent Silver Strand) on Coronado Island, Mission Beach (a popular spot for the locals), Ocean Beach (great for surfing), and La Jolla Cove (some of the calmest and clearest water on the coast). For visitors who are used to the warm Atlantic or Caribbean water, keep in mind that the water temperature in the Pacific tends to be cooler, averaging in the 50s and 60s year-round.

❑ **Birch Aquarium at Scripps** offers some of San Diego's best views of the Pacific, as well as a more intimate look at Pacific sea life. This aquarium and research center is the educational arm of the Scripps Institution of Oceanography, part of the University of California at San Diego. With tanks filled with everything from sharks to seahorses, including a huge kelp forest and large interactive tidepool, and an adjacent museum with exhibits on oceanography and weather, the Birch Aquarium is a great place for educational fun. Address: 2300 Expedition Way, La Jolla, CA 92037 Phone: 858-534-3474. Web: http://aquarium.ucsd.edu.

❑ **Harbor tours** take place on the bay of San Diego, either on a one- or two-hour tour, or an excursion including brunch or dinner. It is the best way to see the Navy ships in port, the Coronado Bay Bridge, and America's Cup Harbor, as well as San Diego's famous seals. Two of the most popular tour companies are Hornblower Cruises (888-467-6256, http://www.hornblower.com/port.asp?port=sd) and the San Diego Harbor Excursion (619-234-4111, http://www.sdhe.com).

❑ **Mission Bay** is the largest man-made aquatic park in the United States and a great place to spend a day enjoying beautiful San Diego weather. SeaWorld is here, and visitors can enjoy water sports including windsurfing, waterskiing, and boating of all kinds or just pack a picnic and fly a kite. For more family fun, visit Belmont Park (858-488-1549, http://www.belmontpark.com), an amusement park located on Mission Beach, featuring carnival favorites bumper cars, tilt-a-whirl, and carousel, as well as the 1925 Giant Dipper wooden roller coaster, and FlowRider, an "endless wave" for bodyboarding.

❑ **Old Town San Diego State Historic Park** offers a rare glimpse into the past with a re-creation of life in the 1800s in the Mexican-owned California territory. A mix of original and replicated buildings house exhibits and shops, ranging from a working blacksmith to San Diego's first public schoolhouse. Also in the park is Bazaar del Mundo, a bright and colorful marketplace, with Mexican-style shopping and authentic Mexican dining. If you find yourself in the San Diego area on Cinco de Mayo, this is the place to celebrate it! Address: San Diego Avenue at Twiggs Street, San Diego, CA, 92110. Phone: 619-220-5422. Web: http://www.parks.ca.gov (search on "Old Town San Diego").

Old Town San Diego

More Southern California Attractions
(continued)

San Diego (continued)

❏ **Old Town Trolley Tours** are a fun way to see Old Town as well as several other points of interest we've recommended, like Balboa Park, Seaport Village, San Diego Zoo, and the Aerospace Museum. You can get on and off at several locations as you make a complete loop with your narrating tour conductor. Prices are $30/adult and $15/child. Phone: 619-298-8687. Web: http://www.historictours.com/sandiego.

❏ **Reuben H. Fleet Science Center**, located in Balboa Park and a favorite among kids and adults alike, boasts interactive exhibits, the first IMAX Dome Theater in the world, and exciting experiences in motion simulators and virtual reality. Don't miss the simulated space missions in the Nierman Challenger Learning Center. You'll have so much fun, you'll forget that you're learning at the same time! Prices are $6.75/ages 13+, $5.50/ages 3–12, and $6.00/ages 65+. Address: 1875 El Prado, San Diego, CA 92101. Phone: 619-238-1233. Web: http://www.rhfleet.org.

❏ **San Diego Aerospace Museum** is one of the country's best aerospace museums, located in Balboa Park. The museum showcases everything from hot air balloons to modern combat airplanes, replicas of Apollo, Gemini, and Mercury spacecraft, and an International Aerospace Hall of Fame, as well as interactive exhibits and short films to entertain and educate. Prices are $9/adult, $4/kids ages 17 and under. Address: 2001 Pan American Plaza, Balboa Park, San Diego, CA 92101. Phone: 619-234-8291. Web: http://www.aerospacemuseum.org.

❏ **San Diego Maritime Museum** has one of the best collections of historic ships, including the world's oldest active ship, the Star of India. You can also explore exhibits showcasing sailing, steam ships, commercial fishing, and the U.S. Navy. Prices are $10/adults, $8/ages 13–17 and ages 62+, $7/ages 6–12 (kids 5 and under are free). Address: 1492 North Harbor Drive, San Diego, CA 92101. Phone: 619-234-9153. Web: http://www.sdmaritime.com.

❏ **Seaport Village** is a charming waterfront collection of one-of-a-kind shops and restaurants close to downtown. This is a great place to spend a lazy afternoon. Little ones enjoy a ride on the antique carousel, and adults enjoy some of the best views of the bay. Parking is limited—you may need to park and walk several blocks. Address: 849 W. Harbor Drive, San Diego, CA 92101. Phone: 619-235-4014. Web: http://www.seaportvillage.com.

❏ **Sporting events** give you the chance to spend a beautiful afternoon enjoying a baseball or football game in an open-air stadium. San Diego is home to the 2004 AFC West Division Champions San Diego Chargers, as well as the San Diego Padres baseball team, giving visitors great options for watching two of America's favorite pastimes.

❏ **USS Midway** was the longest-serving aircraft carrier in the U.S. Navy, seeing action from World War II through Operation Desert Storm. The ship has been converted to a museum, showcasing the history of naval aviation. The flight deck is also a unique place to watch fireworks over the bay on the Fourth of July. Prices are $15/adults, $10/ages 62+ and students with ID, $8/ages 6–17 (kids 5 and under are free). Address: 910 N. Harbor Drive, San Diego, CA 92101. Phone: 619-544-9600. Web: http://www.midway.org.

Planning
Getting There
Staying in Style
Touring
Feasting
Making Magic
Index
Notes & More

Planning

Getting There

Staying in Style

Touring

Feasting

Making Magic

Index

Notes & More

Deciding What To Do

Whew! We bet you're now wondering how in the world you'll find the time to **fit everything** into your vacation. It's simple: you can't do it. Even a month-long stay wouldn't be enough to do and see everything we've recommended in this chapter. Rather than try to fit everything into your vacation, make a practical plan that includes the places of most importance to you and your traveling party.

Naturally, you can't plan everything in advance, nor should you try—spontaneity and discovery are two elements of a great vacation. Yet it is a good idea to get a feeling for the parks, attractions, and activities before you go and to make a note of the ones you simply "must" do. This helps you **create an itinerary** and keeps you from missing the things you've got your heart set on.

First, read the preceding pages carefully to gain a solid idea of what attractions are available in Southern California. Next, **make a list** of all the things you'd like to see and do. This can be a great family activity. Make it a free-for-all, no-holds-barred event—what we call a "blue-sky session." List everything, no matter how impractical, silly, or expensive. Once you've got a good list, pare it down to the things that are most important and copy them to the worksheet on the next two pages. List the activity, where it is located (i.e., which park, town, or area), its approximate cost, and any notes (including why it's on the list).

When you're done with the list, take a good look at the locations. Are several located in the same area? If so, can you do them all on the same day? Go through the list and note other patterns. With luck, you'll have a better sense of where you're headed. Next, **assign the activities** to specific days of your vacation, using the Day/Date column on the far right. For example, on a recent trip, we wanted to visit Hollywood's Walk of Fame, see a movie at Grauman's Chinese Theater, and eat dinner at Universal CityWalk. Two of those activities are in Hollywood, with a third a short subway ride away, so we grouped them together on our third day. We wrote a "3" next to each of those items, but you could write "Wed" or the date instead. If you've planned too much for one day or place, your Cost and Notes columns may help you decide which activities to keep and which to throw out or schedule for another day.

Not all activities can be decided this way, nor should they. Some choices should be **spur of the moment**. Be sure to "schedule" some free time in your trip—preferably a whole day or two. Use these techniques as a general game plan to a great vacation!

Sample Touring Plans

Looking for some guidance on where to go when? Here are some of our **favorite touring plans** for various ages and interests:

Play Your Way Vacation (one full week)
Day One: Knott's Berry Farm
Day Two: Disneyland Park
Day Three: Disneyland Park
Day Four: Disney's California Adventure
Day Five: Disney's California Adventure
Day Six: Universal Studios
Day Seven: LEGOLAND (if you have young kids) or SeaWorld San Diego

California Dreamin' Highlights Vacation (one four-day weekend)
Day One: Balboa Park in San Diego
Day Two: California Beaches
Day Three: Disneyland Resort
Day Four: Hollywood

Major Movie Buff Vacation (five days)
Day One: Universal Studios
Day Two: Disneyland Park
Day Three: Disney's California Adventure
Day Four: Hollywood and Grauman's Chinese Theater
Day Five: Sony Pictures Studios Tour and Warner Bros. Studio Tour

Love to Learn Vacation (four days)
Day One: Discovery Science Center and Natural History Museum
Day Two: San Diego Zoo and Balboa Park
Day Three: The Mission San Juan Capistrano and The Marine Institute at Dana Point
Day Four: Disneyland Resort (focusing on its edutainment offerings)

Ultimate Blow-Out Vacation (two full weeks)
Day One: Knott's Berry Farm
Day Two: Universal Studios
Day Three: Six Flags Magic Mountain and Hurricane Harbor
Day Four: Disneyland Park
Day Five: Disneyland Park
Day Six: Disney's California Adventure
Day Seven: Disney's California Adventure
Day Eight: Downtown Los Angeles and Hollywood
Day Nine: California Beaches
Day Ten: Balboa Park
Day Eleven: San Diego Zoo
Day Twelve: San Diego Wild Animal Park
Day Thirteen: LEGOLAND
Day Fourteen: SeaWorld San Diego

Planning
Getting There
Staying in Style
Touring
Feasting
Making Magic
Index
Notes & More

Touring Worksheet

Use this worksheet to figure out the things you want to do most on your trip. Match up attractions and activities to determine the parks and areas you want to visit, noting the day/date. Fill in the schedule grid at the bottom of the next page once you've picked days—park schedules can help you complete your itinerary and choose eateries (in the next chapter).

Activity	Area	Cost	Notes	Day/Date

Useful Abbreviations:

DLP (Disneyland Park)	DLA (Downtown L.A.)	SW (SeaWorld)
DCA (Disney's California Adv.)	DSC (Discovery Sci. Ctr.)	SDZ (San Diego Zoo)
DD (Downtown Disney)	CI (Catalina Island)	WAP (Wild Animal Park)
KBF (Knott's Berry Farm)	PA (Pasadena)	BP (Balboa Park)
USH (Universal Studios)	MA (Malibu)	LL (LEGOLAND)
CW (CityWalk)	VE (Venice)	SDB (San Diego Beaches)
SFMM (Six Flags)	LB (Long Beach)	BA (Birch Aquarium)
HW (Hollywood)	SM (Santa Monica)	MB (Mission Bay)
	WR (Wild Rivers Waterpark)	FH (Friend/Family's House)

Activity	Area	Cost	Notes	Day/Date

Write your schedule in this calendar grid—note the date in the corners.

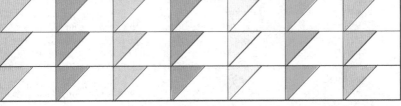

Planning

Getting There

Staying in Style

Touring

Feasting

Making Magic

Index

Notes & More

It's Not Such a Small World After All

If you've read this chapter, you know that touring Southern California is no simple walk in the park. Here are some tips and tricks to help you:

- Write down the **number printed on the back of your Disney pass** in your PassPorter and on a separate sheet of paper that stays in your room. If you lose your passes, this number allows Disney to void and reissue them.

- If you need to **keep in touch with others** while touring a park, consider two-way radios, cell phones, or pagers. You may even be able to rent them for the duration of your stay from local companies.

- Southern California is diverse, with **many cultural differences**. What is polite or rude to you may be different here. Be tolerant of the differences and you'll find yourself well-rewarded!

Magical Memories

"We spent a wonderful day in July celebrating the 50th anniversary of Disneyland. Our group of 20, including Grandma and Grandpa, siblings and 11 cousins, had many magical moments ... but one stands out as about the most incredible Disney moment of my life. Our kids were getting tired at Disneyland and we decided that instead of staking out spots for the fireworks, we would head for the monorail to go home. But as we passed the Matterhorn, we could see that the lines were short. We hopped in line, and just as the first fireworks exploded overhead, our bobsled pulled away. We zoomed in the mountain, my daughter squealing gleefully. But I was not prepared for the amazing images we were about to encounter. There are several points during the ride that the sleds come out of the mountain. We were treated to the most amazing views of the park, lit up like I have never seen it by the exploding fireworks. At several points, it seemed as if we were on the same level as the fireworks. We were zooming around inside the mountain, with the noises and squeals of the other riders, and then would come out for 2-3 seconds of relative quiet, with the amazing fireworks bursting in our view. It was, by far, the most memorable ride I have had at Disney. Maybe because it was so unexpected, maybe because of my daughter's joy, maybe because of the softly lit park of dreams below us. By the end of the ride I was crying! I felt a little silly, but as we joined up with the rest of our party, I discovered that everyone felt as I did."

...as told by vacationer Katie Gilbert

"Disneyland is beautiful by night and also quite busy! Want some time to enjoy a little peace and quiet? Late at night, close to closing, head over to Critter Country and ride on Winnie the Pooh. After the last ride, Critter Country is usually pretty isolated. On our most recent trip, my hubby actually danced with me with the stars shining brightly as we listened to the music. Our daughter just looked on happily. We then all walked back to Main Street hand-in-hand at a very leisurely pace and enjoyed the deserted pathways. It was very serene and peaceful. It's a great way to end the evening after all the hustle and bustle of the day."

...as told by vacationer Kristen Lamb

Feasting and Snacking

You can't have a good vacation without a good meal (or two), and your Disney vacation is no exception. Disney knows how to make your mealtimes as entertaining, adventuresome, and satisfying as the rest of your vacation experience. Disney eateries go out of their way to give everyone a unique and delicious dining experience, so you'll find that even the most exotic restaurant can please any taste, including the finicky eaters in your family. From the atmosphere to the service to the food itself, it has all been created to fill your imagination as well as your belly.

The choices can be awesome, ranging from basic hot dogs and burgers to exclusive elegance, from ultra-romantic dinners for two to foot-stompin' family fun, and from exotic samplings of far-off places to the magic of a breakfast hug from Goofy himself. One thing's for sure—you can't say, "There's nothing to eat around here!"

For us, meal planning is more important than choosing which attractions to visit. It's easier to jump in an unexpectedly short line at Space Mountain than it is to get a table at the better eateries.

The six basic types of Disneyland Resort meals are table-service restaurants, counter-service cafes, quick-service snack shops, "special experiences" (such as character meals), room service, and meals you fix yourself. We devote most of the space here to table-service and special dining experiences, which are more costly and require the most planning. We also include details on the counter-service eateries and snacks in the parks. Room service is mentioned in the "Staying in Style" chapter. We can't say much about your home cooking until we're invited over, though.

The chapter begins with a meal planning guide, then moves to mealtime tips, park-by-park and hotel-by-hotel eatery reviews, the low-down on the big shindigs, and ends with worksheets to plan your meals.

Bon appetit!

Planning

Getting There

Staying in Style

Touring

Feasting

Making Magic

Index

Notes & More

Planning

Getting There

Staying in Style

Touring

Feasting

Making Magic

Index

Notes & More

Deciding on Dining

If you thought selecting a restaurant in your hometown was tough, it doesn't get any easier at Disneyland. There are **more than 70 eateries** in the Disneyland Resort alone, and that doesn't count the almost endless options beyond Disney's gates. But before you go running for the exit, take heart. We've been to every eatery on Disney property at least once and we offer easily digestible descriptions and yummy ratings in this chapter.

First things first: decide **how often** you want to eat out. Many folks (including ourselves) bring or buy some food for in-room snacks or meals, with light breakfasts being the most practical choice. Most hotels can supply a refrigerator (sometimes for an additional fee), some include a coffeemaker, and a few even have kitchen facilities, too. You can, of course, eat out every meal. We like to eat a light breakfast in our room with food we've packed or purchased, such as peanut butter and jelly on English muffins. We then do one or two special breakfasts "out" (such as a character breakfast—see pages 220–221). We often eat lunch and dinner at the parks, hotels, or Downtown Disney. Some vacationers prefer to eat a big meal mid-morning and another mid-afternoon to save time and money. More money-saving ideas are on page 195.

Once you have an idea of how often you want (and can afford) to eat out, your next task is to decide **when and where**. Revisit your Touring Worksheet (pages 188–189) and check the parks you want to visit—it is much easier to choose a restaurant in or near your day's destination. Every Disney park offers table-service restaurants, and all theme parks offer counter-service eateries, snack shops, and carts. To help you choose from the overwhelming number of dining choices, this chapter offers descriptions of all eateries at the Disneyland Resort, Universal Studios, Universal CityWalk, and Knott's Berry Farm. We've also included a selection of other area eateries outside the parks. Descriptions are organized alphabetically within each park and hotel to help you focus on your choices. Pick the eateries that fall within your budget, tastes, and needs—you may find it helpful to highlight or circle those eatery descriptions that interest you.

As you make decisions about your meals and the eateries you want to visit, jot them down on your **Meal Worksheet** at the end of the chapter on page 224. Make note of those table-service eateries for which advance seating arrangements (called "priority seating" at Disneyland) or reservations may be made. To learn about the priority seating system at Disneyland Resort, continue on to the next page.

Disney's Priority Seating

Virtually every table-service restaurant within Disneyland Resort (parks, hotels, and Downtown Disney) allows **advance seating arrangements**, known as "priority seating" ("PS" for short). If you're familiar with Walt Disney World, you may know that they changed their term from "priority seating" to "advance reservations," but Disneyland has not (yet) followed suit. And it's important to note that priority seating arrangements are not reservations. Rather, priority seating gives you the first available table upon arrival at your specified time. This system works better than traditional reservations, which require that guests wait while there is a table free because of latecomers and no-shows. The Rainforest Cafe is the only table-service restaurant that is not hooked into Disney's priority seating system, but you can make reservations for this eatery by phoning 714-772-0413. Note that the Plaza Inn, which is often mistaken for a table-service restaurant but is in fact a buffeteria eatery, does not accept priority seatings (it does take reservations for its birthday parties however—see page 222).

Priority seating can be made in **advance of your arrival** by calling 714-781-DINE (714-781-3463) between 8:00 am and 9:00 pm Pacific time. Call up to 60 days in advance for priority seating at most restaurants. Arrangements can also be made the same day at the parks, and by touching *86 on any Disney pay phone or "55" on your Disney resort phone.

When you call, you may be asked to supply the name of the Disney hotel at which you are staying and your date of arrival—you can record this information at the top of your **Priority Seating Worksheet** on page 225. If you aren't staying at a Disney hotel, no problem—you'll simply need to provide a daytime phone number. You will receive a **confirmation number** for each successfully arranged priority seating. Record this in your worksheet, and later transfer it to your daily PassPockets.

If you later decide not to eat at a particular restaurant, just call Disney again and **cancel your priority seating**. If you are unable to get a priority seating, call back about one week before the desired date.

Due to the nature of priority seating arrangements, you should plan to **check in at the restaurant's podium 15 minutes before** your seating time. You may also need to wait anywhere from 5 to 30 minutes for a table to become available, depending on how busy it is. Some restaurants issue a pager, and most have a comfortable waiting area or bar.

All About Disney Eateries

Alcoholic Beverages—Many eateries serve alcoholic drinks, with the notable exception of those in the Disneyland Park, which is alcohol-free. Bars and lounges are located around the Disneyland Resort. Legal drinking age is 21, and they do check your identification.

Character Dining—Dine with Disney characters! See pages 220–221.

Children's Meals—Nearly every eatery has a children's menu at parent-friendly prices. Kid-staples like macaroni & cheese and chicken tenders can usually be had at the most exotic of restaurants—ask your server. Note that at Disneyland and most other Southern California eateries, kids can order off the kids menu (or get the kids price at a buffet) if they are ages 3–11. Walt Disney World recently changed their kids menu ages to 3–9, however, so it seems possible that Disneyland could follow suit at some point in the future. Adults with light appetites or on a budget can generally order kids meals at counter-service eateries, but not at table-service restaurants.

Counter Service—Most food at Disneyland is sold fast-food style. The quality does vary, but on the whole it's better than fast food sold in other parks. At Disneyland Park, we like Rancho del Zocalo, Plaza Inn, and French Market. At Disney's California Adventure, we prefer Pacific Wharf Cafe or Taste Pilot's Grill. Downtown Disney's Tortilla Jo's and La Brea Bakery are good, as is White Water Snacks at the Grand Californian Hotel.

Coupons/Discounts—Don't plan on finding coupons for in-park restaurants, but you may find them for some restaurants in Downtown Disney. Discounts for AAA members, Annual Passholders, and Disney Visa cardholders are common—see our list below, and be sure to ask your server. See the money-saving tips on the following page for more information on available discounts.

> *Eateries with AAA discounts at press time: 10% off Plaza Inn, Wine Country Trattoria, Ariel's Grotto, PCH Grill, and Goofy's Kitchen*
>
> *Eateries with Annual Pass discounts at press time: 10% off at virtually all eateries (Premium Annual Passholders get 15% off at virtually all in-park and hotel eateries). Note that there is a $10 minimum purchase to receive discount.*
>
> *Eateries with Disney Visa discounts at press time: 10% off Rancho del Zocalo, Carnation Cafe, Redd Rockett's Pizza Port, Pizza Oom Mow Mow, Wine Country Trattoria, The Vineyard Room, Granville's Steakhouse (dinner only), Yamabuki, and PCH Grill*

Dietary Requirements—Low-cholesterol, low-salt, low-fat, and/or vegetarian meals are a regular part of the menu in most restaurants. Special dietary needs, such as food allergies, vegetarian, and medically restricted diets, can be accommodated at most table-service eateries—contact Disney at least 24 hours in advance at 714-781-3463. Plaza Inn and Blue Bayou in Disneyland Park have pre-packaged kosher meals on request, as do most of the restaurants at the Disney hotels, but kosher meals are not currently an option at Disney's California Adventure. To request a kosher meal, inform the cast member when you make your priority seating arrangements (see previous page)—it's important to give the restaurant advance notice.

Dress—Casual clothing is appropriate for all eateries, though you may wish to dress up a bit for special restaurants like Napa Rose. In general, we suggest "business casual" dress for upscale eateries, which means forego the shorts, t-shirts, hats, swimsuits, swim coveralls, tank tops, torn clothing, or flip-flops.

Menus—All menus can be previewed at each eatery. We also offer selected menu items and prices in our eatery descriptions in this chapter. For more complete menus, see Deb Wills' AllEarsNet.com web site (http://www. allearsnet.com), which has started an excellent collection of Disneyland menus.

Money—Cash, Disney Dollars, Disney gift cards, traveler's checks, Disney Visa Reward Vouchers, MasterCard, Visa, American Express, JCB, Discover, and Diner's Club. Disney Resort room charge cards are welcomed in most places. Sales tax is 7.75%. Gratuities may be applied automatically to large parties.

Personal Food—Disneyland policies prohibit bringing food into the parks unless you have specific dietary restrictions. In practice, however, it is rare for Disney cast members to confiscate personal food items. We suggest that if you need to bring your own snacks, be subtle about it—no coolers or huge grocery bags.

Smoking—California law prohibits smoking in all enclosed restaurants, lounges, and other indoor public spaces. For more details on smoking, see page 208.

Contributor and peer reviewer LauraBelle Hime at Pacific Wharf Cafe at Disney's California Adventure

---

⚠ Time- and Money-Saving Dining Tips

✔ At counter-service eateries, there are usually several lines. The line farthest from the entry is often shorter. Look before you leap. In addition, quick-service eateries have lines on <u>both</u> sides of the cash register. If you see a short or nonexistent line on one side of an open register, jump in!

✔ Consider eating earlier or later than traditional mealtime hours. You'll be more likely to get a seat (if you haven't arranged priority seating) or simply find the restaurant less crowded and noisy.

✔ Every item at counter-service restaurants can be ordered a la carte. If you don't want fries with that burger "meal," just ask, and you'll pay a reduced price.

✔ At table-service restaurants, consider ordering two appetizers rather than one appetizer and one entree. It saves both money and calories.

✔ The Rainforest Cafe offers discounts through its Safari Club and an e-mail list—get details at http://www.rainforestcafe.com. Safari Club members may also be able to get the next available table even without a priority seating.

✔ Disney hotel eateries are frequently less crowded than those in the parks. Consider a visit to a nearby hotel, such as the Grand Californian, before, during, or after a park visit.

✔ Check MouseSavers.com for dining deals at Disneyland before you leave.

Understanding and Using the Eatery Descriptions and Ratings

PassPorter's popular capsule reviews of eateries cover all table-service restaurants, as well as counter-service eateries in the parks. We even include snack carts. Our reviews include all important details, plus ratings by us and fellow vacationers. Below is a key to our eatery charts. Dig in!

Description Key

Ratings[7]

[1] Eatery Name [D-2[2]] (Bar Color[3]) B/L/D/S[4] $[5] ♀[6] # # #	
Description offering an overview of the eatery, including comments on the theming, quality, and menu range. We try to give you an idea of what sort of foods you'll find at a particular eatery, along with typical prices and our recommendations. We also include information on the availability of lighter fare, children's meals, and alcoholic beverages. Whenever possible, we describe the type of seating (tables, booths, etc.) and whether it is indoor or outdoor.	Type[8]
	Cuisine[8]
	Noise Factor[8]
	Reservations[8]
	Avg. Wait[8]
	Hours[8]

[1] Each chart has an empty checkbox in the upper left corner—use it to check off the eateries that interest you (before you go) or those at which you ate (after your return).

[2] Map coordinates—match them up to park maps in "Touring the Lands" for locations.

[3] The **bar color** indicates the eatery's main draw, as follows:

Gourmet Tastes	Eateries for Everyone	Fun Food	Character Meals

[4] Meals are indicated by letters: B (breakfast), L (lunch), D (dinner), and S (snack).

[5] Dollar signs represent the average cost of a full adult dinner. Table-service meal costs include appetizer, entree, dessert, soft drink, tax, and tip. Average counter-service meal costs include entree (with fries when appropriate), dessert, soft drink, and tax. Average counter-service snack prices include a snack, soft drink, and tax.

$$$$	$30 or more per person
$$$	$20–$30 per person
$$	$10–$20 per person
$	$10 or less per person

[6] Eateries with a reasonable selection of healthy items (low-fat/low-sodium/low-calorie) are indicated with a tape measure symbol. These are also friendly to weight watchers!

[7] The three white boxes on the right show ratings on a scale of 1 (poor) to 10 (loved it!). The first rating is Jennifer's, the second is Dave's, and the third is our Readers' rating. We offer our personal ratings to show how opinions vary, even between two like-minded people. You can also use our ratings as a point of reference—Jennifer likes eateries with extensive theming and well-prepared foods that aren't too exotic or spicy. Dave has more cultured tastes, enjoys unusual, spicy, and barbecue dishes, and loves seafood!

[8] The boxes on the right beneath the numeric ratings give basic information: eatery type (Table, Counter, or Buffet); cuisine; noise factor (from quiet to very noisy); seating (if reservations are accepted, needed, suggested, recommended, or required, and how many days in advance you can call); average wait time; and the eatery's hours.

Disneyland Park Eateries

	Jennifer's Rating	Dave's Rating	Readers' Rating

Bengal Barbeque [C-5, Adventureland]   L/D/S $ | 5 | 7 | 7 |

This unique eatery serves spicy meat ($3.29-$4.29) and grilled vegetables ($2.99) on skewers. Limited patio seating. Rumor has it this eatery will close in Oct. 2006 to make room for a River Belle Terrace expansion (see page 200).

Counter
American
11 am-10:30 pm

Blue Bayou [B-5, New Orleans Square]   L/D $$$ | 8 | 6 | 7 |

It's always evening on the bayou at this ultimate Disney dining experience located inside Pirates of the Caribbean—diners are actually a part of the attraction! Dine on lavish selections such as the famous Monte Cristo sandwich ($12.99, lunch only), roast prime rib of beef ($17.99 lunch, $26.99 dinner), and Caribbean crab cakes ($24.99). Kids meals ($6.99) and vegetarian menu are available. You can even get a Mint Julep drink (non-alcoholic, of course). In all honesty, you're mostly paying for the delightful atmosphere here—the food is good, but not amazing. Priority seating is a must and can be made up to 60 days in advance. A perfect spot for a quiet, romantic meal. Ask for a table by the water to get the most out of this enchanting restaurant.

Sipping a Mint Julep at the Blue Bayou

Table
Creole
Quiet
Priority seats strongly recommended
Call 60 days
Long waits
11:30 am–10:00 pm

Blue Ribbon Bakery [D-5, Main Street]   B/S $ | 5 | 6 | 7 |

Tasty baked goods and sandwiches, served to go. Very little seating available. Popular for a quick breakfast and pre-parade dining. Baked goods $1.29-$3.19, sandwiches $6.59. Specialty coffees also on the menu ($1.99-$4.29).

Counter
American
All day

Café Orleans [B-5, New Orleans Square]   L/D/S $$ | 7 | 7 | 9 |

A quaint French cafe on the banks of the Rivers of America. Table seating on a beautiful shady terrace provides a lovely view. This restaurant is closed at press time; when it reopens, we expect a new menu and different style of seating (perhaps table service rather than counter service).

Counter
Creole
Med. noise
~11 am-10 pm

Carnation Cafe [D-5, Main Street]   B/L/D $$ | 8 | 6 | 7 |

This classic Main Street eatery offers table service on a street-side terrace—all table seating, all outdoors. This is the quintessential spot for a Disney breakfast with Mickey Mouse waffles ($6.29) or croissant Benedict ($7.89). Salads (chicken Caesar, $8.79), sandwiches (veggie medley, $8.29), and pot roast ($11.29) round out lunch and dinner options. Kids can choose from two mini hot dogs, a peanut butter sandwich, or macaroni and cheese ($5.99). No priority seating.

Table
American
Med. noise
Long waits
~8 am-1 hour before closing

Clarabelle's Frozen Yogurt [E-1, Toontown]   S $ | 5 | 5 | 7 |

While you're pondering how Clarabelle the Cow got so cold in California, enjoy chocolate or vanilla frozen yogurt ($2.49 or $3.49) with a variety of toppings ($0.89). Sundaes ($3.99) and baked goods also available. Seating nearby.

Counter
American
11 am-8 pm

Planning
Getting There
Staying in Style
Touring
Feasting
Making Magic
Index
Notes & More

Disneyland Park Eateries
(continued)

	Jennifer's Rating	Dave's Rating	Readers' Rating

☐ **Club Buzz** [F-4, Tomorrowland] L/D/S $ | 7 | 6 | 8 |

To lunch... and beyond! This large outdoor restaurant in Tomorrowland serves fast-food quality meals with a little entertainment on the side. The intergalactic menu offers standard fare (burgers $6.19–$6.69, fried chicken $8.99, fish basket $8.99, and roast beef & cheddar sandwich $6.99). Kids can choose from chicken nuggets, PB&J, or mini corn dogs ($4.99–$5.99). All seating is outside on the covered, multi-level terrace. A large stage rises out of the ground. Seating is at a premium just before and during the performances.

Counter / American / Very noisy / No priority seats / ~8:00 am–park closing

☐ **Conestoga Fries** [C-4, Frontierland] S $ | 2 | 3 | 5 |

This Frontierland covered wagon ("Westward Ho!") serves McDonald's French fries ($2.75) and pricey soft drinks (ubiquitous Coke products at $2.70–$2.75). Soft drinks are 15–20 cents cheaper at nearby Rancho del Zocalo.

Counter / American / 10 am–closing

☐ **Daisy's Diner** [E-1, Toontown] L/D/S $ | 6 | 5 | 5 |

This eatery is everything it's "quacked" up to be! Part of a mini food court area in Toontown, this little place is named after Donald's girlfriend and offers pizza and salad combos ($5.99–$6.19) and a variety of desserts. All seating is outside at patio tables at nearby Toontown City Hall.

Counter / American / Very noisy / 11 am–8 pm

☐ **The Enchanted Cottage** [E-2, Fantasyland] S $ | 8 | 6 | 5 |

Open just before and during the Snow White musical, this sweet little snack stand offers treats with a Bavarian twist. Bratwurst and knockwurst sandwiches and chips ($6.59) and kids meals ($5.99) are on the menu, as are Bavarian pretzels ($2.99) and Diamond Mine Delight (cinnamon crisps with whipped cream and candy for $5.69). Only a few tables are available nearby.

Counter / American / Noisy / 11:30 am–6:45 pm

☐ **French Market Restaurant** [B-5, New Orleans Square] L/D/S $$ | 7 | 7 | 5 |

A live jazz band and shaded patio dining really set this eatery apart. The food's good too! Sample tasty Cajun/Creole dishes such as jambalaya ($11.99), fried chicken with rice and beans ($10.99), and fettucino with ham-crawfish cream ($9.49). Soup and stew served in bread bowls ($7.99–$10.79) are a favorite here. Salads range from $2.99 to $8.99. Kids' choices are mac & cheese and chicken nuggets ($5.99). Patio tables are outside under trees. Musicians may perform on busy afternoons.

Counter / Creole / Medium noise / 11:00 am–park closing

☐ **Gibson Girl Ice Cream Parlor** [D-5, Main Street] S $ | 7 | 6 | 5 |

A real old-fashioned "scoop shop." Single scoops are $2.99, milkshakes are $3.99, and sundaes $5.49. Toppings are $0.89. Frozen yogurt is also available. This eatery was originally called the Puffin Bakery back in Walt's day. Note that the signature Fantasia ice cream (banana/cherry/pistachio) is now gone.

Counter / American / Very noisy / 11 am–closing

☐ **The Golden Horseshoe** [C-4, Frontierland] L/D/S $ | 7 | 5 | 5 |

Usually open just prior to and during shows at the Golden Horseshoe Stage, this venue shares a kitchen and a menu with the Stage Door Café (see page 200 for menu offerings). Eat your vittles at tables inside while you enjoy the show.

Counter / American / 11 am–closing

Eatery descriptions and ratings are explained on page 196.

Disneyland Park Eateries
(continued)

Jennifer's Rating · Dave's Rating · Readers' Rating

Harbour Galley [B-4, Frontierland]   S $ | 4 | 4 | 5 |

McDonald's French fries ($2.75) and the usual drinks ($2.70-$2.75) are offered at this nautically themed snack stand. Just want a drink? Save 15-20 cents by purchasing at Hungry Bear instead. A few outdoor tables are available.

Counter
American
10 am-closing

Hungry Bear Restaurant [B-3, Critter Country]   L/D $$ | 7 | 6 | 7 |

Standard but satisfying burger combos ($6.19-$6.69), fried chicken sandwiches ($6.49), and barbeque chicken salads ($6.99) are served at this counter-service spot. Desserts include Apple Pie Pop-Ins with caramel dipping sauce ($2.99) and Fantasy Funnel Cake ($5.49). This eatery is possibly the most peaceful place to dine at Disneyland Park, overlooking the Rivers of America.

Counter
American
Med. waits
~10:30 am-
4:00 pm

Main Street Cone Shop [D-5, Main Street]   S $ | 5 | 5 | 5 |

Tucked down a side street, this often-overlooked snack stop is famous for its huge ice cream sandwiches ($4.49). Also Mickey bars ($3.29), sundaes ($4.99), and, of course, ice cream cones ($2.99-$3.69). Seating is at nearby patio tables.

Counter
American
Seasonal

Mint Julep Bar [B-5, New Orleans Square]   S $ | 4 | 6 | 5 |

Enjoy fritters ($3.69), mint juleps ($2.19), coffees ($1.99-$3.49), and baked goods ($2.29) from this "little hole in the wall" facing the train station. The mint juleps—a minty drink with a hint of lime—are loved by some, hated by others.

Counter
American
11 am-closing

The Plaza Inn [E-4, Main Street]   B/L/D $$ | 8 | 6 | 7 |

Located on the border of Main Street, U.S.A. and Tomorrowland, this beautifully appointed (originally designed by Walt's wife) food court-style restaurant serves classic American fare in oversized portions. Fried chicken ($12.99), pot roast ($13.99), and penne pasta ($11.99) are the favorites here. Kids meals are $5.99. Breakfast is an all-you-care-to-eat buffet with Minnie and friends ($23.63 for adults, $12.92 for kids). Tables and half-booths are available inside, and an outdoor patio provides a view of the castle and is sometimes a quieter locale for your meal. Guests with birthdays can have a "My Disneyland Birthday Party" here on the patio, complete with a guest appearance by Mickey and Minnie, cake decorating, and music—see page 221 for more information.

Counter
American
Med. noise
Priority
seating at
breakfast
Short waits
8 am-11 am,
noon-1 hour
before closing

Pluto's Dog House [E-1, Toontown]   L/D/S $ | 5 | 5 | 5 |

Just as the name says, it's all about the dogs at this eatery. Hot dogs, that is! Foot-long combos are $5.39 and mini hot dog meals for kids are $5.49. Shares seating with Daisy's Diner at Toontown City Hall. Very noisy.

Counter
American
11 am-8 pm

Rancho del Zocalo [C-4, Frontierland]   L/D/S $$ | 9 | 7 | 7 |

Hola! You'll find a little bit of Mexico at this themed eatery with two distinct menus. You can enjoy especiales del Norte with such delights as citrus fire-grilled chicken ($9.99), red chile enchilada platter ($8.99), carne asada and enchilada platter ($10.99), burrito Sonora ($9.99), tacos Monterrey ($8.99), and tostada salad ($9.99). Kids enjoy bean and cheese burritos, tacos, or chicken nuggets ($5.99). Seating is at tables on a partially covered patio.

Counter
Mexican
Med. noise
Med. waits
~10:30 am-
park closing

Side tabs: Planning · Getting There · Staying in Style · Touring · Feasting · Making Magic · Index · Notes & More

Planning
Getting There
Staying in Style
Touring
Feasting
Making Magic
Index
Notes & More

Disneyland Park Eateries
(continued)

	Jennifer's Rating	Dave's Rating	Readers' Rating

☐ Redd Rockett's Pizza Port [F-5, Tomorrowland]   L/D $ | 7 | 6 | 7 |

A spacious Italian eatery offering traditional favorites such as pizza (by the slice is $5.99, a whole 16" pie is $29.99), pasta (chicken fusilli is $7.99), and salads (planetary pizza salad is $7.49). A variety of salads are also available for $6.49-$8.29. Ample indoor and outdoor seating. Kids meals feature cheese ravioli or "Space-getti" (spaghetti) for $5.99. Large portions are the norm here, so this is a great place to share.

Counter / Italian / Very noisy / Med. waits / ~11:00 am–park closing

☐ Refreshment Corner [D-5, Main Street]   L/D/S $ | 6 | 7 | 5 |

A simple spot for foot-long hot dogs ($5.39), chili in sourdough bread bowls ($7.99), and soft Mickey Mouse pretzels ($2.99). Limited table seating is available inside, but there's ample seating outside with a ragtime piano player in the evening. A great place to satisfy those evening munchies!

Counter / American / 10:30 am–park closing

☐ River Belle Terrace [C-5, Adventureland]   B/L/D/S $$ | 8 | 6 | 7 |

Located at the meeting point of Adventureland and Frontierland, this classic Disneyland restaurant is the only place in the park that serves Mickey Mouse pancakes ($5.49). Egg platters ($6.49) and fruit plates round out the breakfast menu. Aunt Polly's chicken ($9.99) and sandwiches are good choices for lunch and dinner. Seating inside at half-booths and tables, or sit on the outside terrace for a view of Fantasmic! This eatery may close in fall 2006 for expansion.

Counter / American / Med. noise / Med. waits / ~8:00 am–park closing

☐ Royal Street Veranda [C-5, New Orleans Square]   L/D/S $ | 6 | 6 | 5 |

Soups in bread bowls ($7.49), fritters ($3.69), and specialty coffees are served at this small but satisfying eatery. Limited patio seating. Open 11 am–10 pm.

Counter / American

☐ Stage Door Cafe [C-4, Frontierland]   L/D/S $ | 5 | 5 | 5 |

Chicken strips ($7.99), fish and chips ($8.99), and mozzarella sticks ($7.49) are the mainstays of this western counter-service locale. Outdoor table seating with a view of Rivers of America is available nearby.

Counter / American / 11 am–closing

☐ Tiki Juice Bar [C-4, Adventureland]   S $ | 9 | 7 | 5 |

This is where you can get those famous pineapple Dole Whips ($2.50), which are delicious, refreshing, and dairy-free! Also available are pineapple spears ($2.25), floats ($4.50), juice ($2.00), and fruit bowls ($2.50).

Counter / American / 10 am–closing

☐ Village Haus [D-3, Fantasyland]   L/D/S $ | 7 | 6 | 5 |

Pizza/salad combos and burger combos ($6.19-$6.99) top the menu at this Pinnochio-themed eatery in Fantasyland. Turkey sandwiches with chips ($6.99) and fresh fruit salad ($6.99) are lighter alternatives. Kids can munch Mickey-shaped chicken nuggets ($5.99) or two mini hot dogs ($5.49). Plenty of indoor and outdoor table seating in delightfully detailed surroundings, as seen in the photo to the right.

Counter / American / 10:30 am–park closing

Eatery descriptions and ratings are explained on page 196.

Disney's California Adventure Eateries

	Jennifer's Rating	Dave's Rating	Readers' Rating

Ariel's Grotto [F-2, Paradise Pier]   L/D $$ | 6 | 6 | 7

The only character dining in Disney's California Adventure features Ariel and her fellow princesses such as Snow White, Belle, Sleeping Beauty, and Cinderella. Lunch is $17/adult and $12/child 3-11, while dinner is $21/adult and $14/child. Price includes one appetizer (cheesy onion soup, chicken noodle soup, or salad) and one entree (fish & chips, burger, penne pasta, B.L.T., chicken pot pie, Caesar salad, or cobb salad). Desserts and beverages are extra. Kids meals include a beverage, an appetizer (chicken soup or veggie sticks) and an entree (mac & cheese, fish sticks, spaghetti, chicken nuggets, or mini corn dogs). Enjoy the undersea décor in the downstairs dining room or sit on the waterfront patio. Lighter fare is available in the upstairs Cove Bar.

Table / American / Noisy / Priority seats strongly suggested / Med. waits / 11:30 am–1 hour before closing

Award Wieners [C-5, Hollywood Pictures]   L/D/S $ | 6 | 6 | 5

Feeling like a star? Award yourself by trying some "Hollywood-themed" hot dogs with fries ($5.69-$6.59), sausages with fries ($6.59), chili fries ($3.99), and assorted baked goods. This is a popular place to dine with its location just inside the entrance to the Hollywood Pictures Backlot. Outside seating.

Counter / American / 11 am–1 hour before closing

Baker's Field Bakery [D-6, Sunshine Plaza]   B/L/D/S $ | 8 | 6 | 7

All aboard the California Zephyr—destination Yummyville. This patisserie is housed within the gleaming silver replica train at the edge of Sunshine Plaza. Inside you can purchase a variety of baked goods, specialty coffee ($2.19-$4.99), turkey, roast beef, or ham sandwiches ($6.59), and salads which may include Caesar ($7.29) or Cambria classic ($7.29). All seating is outside at patio tables, most under shade (alas, no highchairs are available here).

Counter / American / Med. waits / 10:00 am–1 hour before closing

Between Takes Catering Co. [B-5, Hollywood Pictures]   L/S $ | 5 | 5 | 7

Take five at this catering truck across from the Hyperion Theater. Stop here for some chili and cheese nachos ($7.49), chili in a sourdough bread bowl ($7.49), or a dessert of cinnamon-apple nachos ($5.69). Microbrew beer (Karl Strauss—$5.19) is also available, as are soft drinks ($2.49). Outside seating nearby. Note that this snack stand may only be open on weekends and during peak times.

Counter / Mexican / Med. waits / 11:00 am–1 hour before closing

Bountiful Valley Farmers Market [D-4, Golden State]   L/D/S $ | 7 | 6 | 7

This eatery is a great choice for those looking for a healthy selection or picnic favorites. Choose from a fruit salad or vegetable basket ($7.29), BBQ or country roasted chicken with sides ($7.99), or turkey leg with sides ($7.99). And for the young ones, a PB&J wrap with a surprise inside (OK, it's a gummy worm, but don't tell). Open seasonally; closed at press time. Outside seating available.

Counter / American / Med. waits / 11 am–1 hour before closing

Bur-r-r Bank Ice Cream [D-6, Sunshine Plaza]   S $ | 6 | 7 | 5

This little shop has the best ice cream in the park! You can get single scoops ($2.99-$4.39) and double scoops ($3.69-$4.69) in nine flavors. Fabulous flavored waffle cones (made on premises) are available, as are toppings (.89 each) and sundaes ($5.29-$7.99). Outdoor, shaded seating nearby.

Counter / American / 11:30 am–park closing

Planning · Getting There · Staying in Style · Touring · Feasting · Making Magic · Index · Notes & More

Disney's California Adventure Eateries
(continued)

	Jennifer's Rating	Dave's Rating	Readers' Rating

Burger Invasion [H-3, *Paradise Pier*]   L/D/S $ | 2 | 5 | 7 |

Serving McDonald's burgers ($5.69–$5.79), fries ($2.59), salads ($2.99–$5.99), shakes ($3.79), and other favorites. Happy Meals for the little ones are $4.99. You can't miss this 45' spaceship disguised as a hamburger on Paradise Pier. Outside seating nearby.

Counter
American
11 am–1 hour before closing

Catch a Flave [G-2, *Paradise Pier*]   S $ | 3 | 5 | 5 |

Prefer soft-serve ice cream? This snack stand on Paradise Pier has vanilla swirl ice cream (cone or cup, $2.49–$3.19)—swirl flavors range from bubblegum to butter pecan. Floats ($3.19) and soft drinks ($2.49) also available.

Counter
American
2 pm–closing

Cocina Cucamonga Mexican Grill [D-3, *Golden State*]   L/D $ | 7 | 6 | 7 |

Chicken tacos ($6.49) and carne asada nachos ($7.49) served with a blend of California and Mexican flavors. Other choices include a child's meal of bean and cheese burrito ($4.99) or cinnamon rice pudding ($2.99) for dessert. Curious how tortillas are made? Check out the Mission Tortilla Factory next door (see page 118). Outside seating.

Counter
Mexican
Med. waits
11 am–1 hour before closing

Corn Dog Castle [C-5, *Paradise Pier*]   L/D/S $ | 6 | 6 | 5 |

Calling all corn dog fans! Here you will find them plump and hand-dipped. The limited menu includes hot-link corn dog with a bag of chips ($5.39), corn dog with a bag of chips, ($4.99), cheddar cheese stick ($4.99), and a cheesecake brownie ($2.99). Outdoor seating.

Counter
American
11 am–1 hour before closing

Fairfax Market [B-5, *Hollywood Pictures*]   L/S $ | 6 | 6 | 5 |

You'll feel like you are in "Hollywood" with the beautiful people when you order up these healthy choices. Fruit, veggies with dip, deli-style sandwiches, and even strawberries with chocolate dipping sauce. May be open only on weekends and during peak periods. Open seasonally; closed at press time.

Counter
American
10:00 am–6:00 pm

Pacific Wharf Cafe [E-3, *Golden State*]   B/L/D/S $ | 7 | 7 | 7 |

Ever wonder how sourdough bread is made? Take a quick tour and see at the Boudin Bakery next door (see page 117). Afterward, try a yummy sourdough bread bowl filled with soup or salad. Soup choices are clam chowder, corn chowder, broccoli and cheese ($6.99). Salads include nicoise, apple & chicken ($7.99), or shrimp louie ($9.99). Outside seating.

Counter
American
Med. waits
11 am–1 hour before closing

Pizza Oom Mow Mow [H-3, *Paradise Pier*]   L/D $ | 7 | 6 | 7 |

This menu will get you "California Dreamin'" with Cowabunga Pizza by the slice ($5.69) or 16" ($29.99), far-out chicken fusilli ($7.99), totally marinara pasta ($8.29), and more. The kids can get a stringer spaghetti meal ($5.99) or PB&J meal ($5.99). Outside seating. Vegetarian and healthy selections.

Counter
American
11 am–1 hour before closing

Eatery descriptions and ratings are explained on page 196.

Disney's California Adventure Eateries
(continued)

Eatery				Jennifer's Rating	Dave's Rating	Readers' Rating

Sam Andreas Shakes [F-4, *Golden State*] S $ — **4 5 5**

Cool off with an ice cream shake ($4.49) made with extra-rich vanilla ice cream, your choice of flavor and candy toppings, and a dollop of whip cream. Try the date shake—a California original! Shakes without the candy are $3.99.

Counter
American
Noon–7 pm

Schmoozies [B-5, *Hollywood Pictures*] S $ — **5 6 6**

What's more California than a smoothie? Choose from Mango Madness, Make Mine Mocha, Dynamic Duo, or Three Berries and a Banana—each at $4.99. Fruit juices ($2.49) and specialty coffees ($1.99–$3.49) are also available.

Counter
American
Noon–7 pm

Strips, Dips, n' Chips [F-1, *Paradise Pier*] L/D/S $ — **6 6 7**

Just what the name suggests…some chicken strips with your choice of dippin' sauce with fries ($5.99), zucchini strips with fries ($5.99), or some good ol' fish 'n' chips. Sweet tooth? Try some apple wedges with caramel ($2.99). Decent size portions—enough to share. Outside seating available.

Counter
American
11 am–1 hour before closing

Taste Pilots Grill [D-6, *Golden State*] L/D/S $ — **7 6 8**

Soar in for some fly-by food! Hearty menu choices include a hamburger (pick your own toppings, $8.29), ribs with coleslaw ($9.99 & $12.49), and a B-2 BBQ chicken sandwich ($8.29). Other choices include popcorn chicken salad ($7.49), onion rings ($2.00), beer, shakes, and baked goods. Kids meals are $5.99 for two mini-burgers or popcorn chicken (plus potatoes and a drink). Plenty of seating is available both inside and outside at patio tables. Full toppings bar.

Counter
American
Med. waits
11 am–1 hour before closing

Terrace Wine Tasting [D-4, *Golden State*] S $ — **9 7 7**

Here's another California tradition—wine tasting! Join a "wine country ambassador" for a tasting of three selections for $10. Different tastings are available at different times. Watch for the port and blue cheese tasting!

Counter
11:30 am–1 hr. before closing

The Vineyard Room [D-4, *Golden State*] D $$$ 🎀 — **9 8 9**

Experience California's wine country without leaving Disney property. Enjoy the meticulously prepared menu combining the finest foods with some of California's most superb wines. The three-course menu is $43 (add $19 for wine pairings) and the four-course menu is $56 (add $29 for wine parings). A $15 cheese course can be added. The first course includes items like parma prosciutto and poached pear salad. The optional second course brings salmon carpaccio and duck confit salad. Entrees range from lamb shank to wild king salmon. White chocolate mint mousse and strawberry parfait are two of the tempting desserts. No kids menu. This eatery was modeled after the private dining room at the Robert Mondavi winery.

Table
California
Quiet
Priority seats strongly recommended
5:00 pm–8:30 pm (closed Mon.)

Wine Country Trattoria [D-4, *Golden State*] L/D $$ — **7 7 8**

Sit outside on the spacious patio or inside for a delightful Italian meal including such favorites as lasagna ($12.59), grilled sandwiches ($9.79–$9.99), and entree salads ($9.79–$10.79). Desserts are $4.99 and include tiramisu and chocolate creme. If you plan your meal time right, you can have a lovely place to sit on the patio to enjoy Disney's Electrical Parade. Some splendid California wines are available, naturally. Vegetarian selections.

Table
Italian
Priority seats suggested
11:30 am–1 hour before closing

Planning

Getting There

Staying in Style

Touring

Feasting

Making Magic

Index

Notes & More

Downtown Disney Eateries

| | Jennifer's Rating | Dave's Rating | Readers' Rating |

Catal Restaurant   B/L/D $$$$ 🏆 | 9 | 8 | 8 |

An exceptional upscale dining experience featuring Chef Joachim Splichal that specializes in wines paired with appetizers such as escargot ($7.50) and marinated olives ($3.50). Large full-course meals are also available—entrees include osso bucco ($16.25) and ribeye steak ($19.25). An elegant location for a special evening out. Catal is short for Catalonia, a region in Spain. Two private rooms are available for special events—the Rotunda Room seats 40 and the Picola Room seats 20. The more casual Uva Bar out in the plaza (see page 206) is a nice place to wait for your table. For more information, menus, and online reservations, visit http://www.patinagroup.com/catal.

Table
Mediterranean
Quiet
Priority seats strongly recommended
5-10 pm (open to 11 pm on weekends)

Compass Books Cafe   S $ | 5 | 5 | 5 |

Themed after New York's Explorers Club, this cozy bookstore offers coffees, teas, smoothies, Italian and French sodas, sandwiches, salads, pastries, Krispy Kreme doughnuts, and cakes. Seating outside. Open to midnight on weekends.

Counter
American
8 am-11 pm

ESPN Zone   L/D/S $$$ | 5 | 6 | 6 |

This upscale sports-themed restaurant and bar comes complete with live talk-radio broadcasts and a 16-ft. high-definition TV. The standard sports bar menu includes chicken wings ($8.49), burgers ($8.99), cheese fries ($7.79), and a good selection of entrees as well. Baby back ribs ($19.49) and Atlantic salmon ($15.99) are just some of the choices. Meal-sized salads and pasta also available. Save some time and money to play in the "Sports Arena" arcade located here on the second floor above the dining room. The Screening Room sports bar is restricted to guests 21 and older after 5:00 pm. On busy game days, a $10 food/beverage minimum (per person, per hour) may be required. For more information, visit http://www.espnzone.com/anaheim.

Table
American
Very noisy
No priority seats
11:30 am-midnight (1:00 am on Fri.- Sat.)

Haagen-Dazs   S $ | 7 | 7 | 7 |

A traditional ice cream shop located right in the center of Downtown Disney. On the menu is ice cream and frozen yogurt ($4.95) as well as smoothies ($5.25) and malts ($4.95). Open to midnight on weekends.

Counter
American
9:30 am-11 pm

House of Blues Restaurant   L/D $$$ | 7 | 7 | 8 |

The musical acts are the real attraction on this menu, but you won't leave hungry. There are enough Cajun and Creole dishes to chase the blues away. The fried catfish starter ($9.95), gumbo ($3.95/5.25), and seafood jambalaya ($17.95) are two beats ahead of any place similar in Disneyland, and you can get fine burgers ($9.95), Cajun meatloaf ($15.95), steaks ($24.95), ribs ($23.95), salads ($5-$13), and sandwiches ($9.95), too. Live blues bands keep the joint cookin' (and make conversation difficult). Headliners play at the concert hall next door. A Gospel Brunch is held every Sunday (see page 222 for details).

Table
Southern/ Cajun
Priority seats for hotel guests only
11:30 am-11:30 pm

Jamba Juice   S $ | 8 | 7 | 8 |

Go healthy with the offerings from this little shop. You can get fruit juices and smoothies for $3.50-$4.70 (each providing 3-6 servings of fruit) and pretzels made with vitamin- and mineral-enriched grains.

Counter
American
Hours vary

Eatery descriptions and ratings are explained on page 196.

Downtown Disney Eateries
(continued)

		Jennifer's Rating	Dave's Rating	Readers' Rating

☐ La Brea Bakery Cafe — B/L/D/S — $$ — 7 7 8

Tasty soups ($6), salads ($8), and panini ($12) make most of the offerings at this busy little spot with indoor and patio seating. It's the closest Downtown Disney eatery to Disney's parks, making it a convenient stop for breakfast in the morning or a snack break during the day. Ahi tuna ($17), and lamb, sausage, and sirloin stew ($18) make for some interesting dinner choices. Next door is a quick-service counter (8:00 am–10:00 pm) that serves specialty coffees, pastries, and gourmet sandwiches. Kids ($4) are offered a choice of grilled cheese, chicken nuggets, or peanut butter and jelly. Breads are baked on the premises and are amazingly delicious. Open to 11:00 pm on Saturday (Express counter) and to 11:00 pm on weekends (full-service dining). More information is available at http://www.labreabakery.com.

Counter
American
8:00 am–10:00 pm (Express);
11:00 am–9:00 pm (full-service)

☐ Naples Ristorante e Pizzeria — L/D — $$$ — 6 7 7

Antipasti ($7.50–$10.95), unique pasta dishes ($14.50–$19.95), and gourmet personal-size pizzas fired in a wood burning oven ($13.50–$14.95) are the highlights of this menu. Authentic Italian Ice and espresso concoctions make dessert a real treat ($6.95). Right next door is Napolini, the quick-service counter offering a scaled-down menu and outside seating. Like Catal, Naples is owned by the Patina Group and you can view menus and make online reservations at http://www.patinagroup.com/naples.

Table
S. Italian
Very noisy
11:00 am–10:00 pm
(11:00 pm on weekends)

☐ Napolini — B/L/D — $ — 7 6 7

This Italian deli beside Naples Ristorante offers grab-and-go salads ($8.50), soups ($3.50–$6.50), pastas ($6.00–$9.00), pizza slices ($5.00), and panini sandwiches ($5.95–$7.25). The pizza slices are huge! Look for the "Slice and a Soda" deal at lunchtime. Limited indoor seating is available. The breakfast menu changes daily and usually offers pastries and various hot breakfasts.

Counter
S. Italian
Closes one hour later than Naples

☐ Rainforest Cafe — L/D/S — $$$ — 6 6 7

Impressive indoor and outdoor theming make this more of an adventure than a meal! The menu is extensive with everything from appetizers (Coastal Calamari, $8.99; Big Blue Crab Delight Dip with chips, $7.99), salads (China Island Chicken Salad, $11.99), sandwiches (Bamba's BBQ Beef Wrap, $10.99; Rain Forest Burger, $8.99), pasta (Mogambo shrimp with Penne, $13.99), pizza (BBQ chicken, $12.99), fish (Parmesan crusted snapper, $19.99), chicken and beef entrees (mixed grill, $20.99; Primal steak, $20.99) to desserts (Bananas Foster, $6.99). Smoothies and specialty adult beverages are a favorite here. An extensive gift shop carries many eco-friendly and logo items. The breakfast menu offers standard American fare with "wild" names. Get more information at http://www.rainforestcafe.com.

Table
American
Very noisy
Call 714-772-0413 for reservations
8:00 am–11:00 am,
11:00 am–12:00 am

🔔 Ch-Ch-Ch-Changes

Don't be surprised if Downtown Disney's line-up of restaurants changes by the time you read this. Due to its nature, its eateries are more likely to swap out with others than those in the theme parks. For the latest list of Downtown Disney eateries, visit http://www.downtowndisney.com, click on "Anaheim," and then "Dining."

Sidebar tabs: Planning · Getting There · Staying in Style · Touring · Feasting · Making Magic · Index · Notes & More

Downtown Disney Eateries
(continued)

	Jennifer's Rating	Dave's Rating	Readers' Rating

Ralph Brennan's Jazz Kitchen B/Brunch/L/D $$$ | 8 | 8 | 8 |

Enter this two-story, French Quarter-inspired restaurant for some Louisiana home cooking and live jazz. The restaurant offers three dining areas with very similar menus. Flambeaux's offers table service on the ground floor and a delightful patio—it features live Jazz nightly along with its gumbo ya-ya ($7.50), jambalaya skewers ($18.75), and other southern entrees. The Carnival Club (dinner only) is located upstairs and focuses on fine dining—it has a "jazz balcony" overlooking Downtown Disney. Jazz Kitchen Express is the take-out window offering po' boys ($10.00) and crawfish pie ($4.00)—it's sometimes open for beignets and coffee at 8:00 am. The restaurant hosts a Zydeco Jazz Brunch on Sundays—see page 222. For more information, menus, performance calendars, and online reservations, visit http://www.rbjazzkitchen.com.

Table
Southern
Noisy
Priority seats recommended
714-776-5200
11 am-10 pm
(11:00 pm on weekends)

Tortilla Jo's L/D $$$ | 9 | 7 | 8 |

Casual inside and outside dining featuring Mexican favorites such as quesadillas ($8.25) and made-to-order guacamole with chips ($6.50). Combination plates feature their famous cone-shaped tacos, enchiladas, and tamales ($11.95-$13.95). An abbreviated menu is available at the Taqueria take-out window located next door. The Cantina is open daily from 3:00 pm to 1:00 am and serves more than 100 different tequilas. Live mariachi bands play Wednesday–Sunday evenings in the Cantina. More information, menus, and online reservations are available at http://www.patinagroup.com/tortillajos.

Table
Mexican
Quiet
Priority seats recommended
11 am-10 pm
(11:00 pm on weekends)

Uva Bar and Cafe S $$$ | 6 | 7 | 6 |

This funky gathering spot offers tapas ($5.50-$9.50), salads ($10.50-$16.75), entrees ($9.50-$18.95), and desserts ($5.25-$6.95) from the Catal Restaurant kitchen (see page 204). Excellent wine list also available ("uva" means "grape" in Spanish). Outdoor seating. Great place for people watching.

Table
12 pm-10 pm
(11 pm on weekends)

Wetzel's Pretzels S $ | 6 | 6 | 6 |

Former Disneyland cast member Rick Wetzel is king of the gourmet soft pretzel. This shop offers fresh, hand-rolled soft pretzels, dips, "pretzel dogs" (pretzel dough-wrapped weiners), fresh-squeezed lemonade, and fruit drinks. More details at http://www.wetzelspretzels.com.

Counter
10 am-10 pm
(11 pm on weekends)

Eatery descriptions and ratings are explained on page 196.

Marceline's Confectionery

If the parks aren't stimulating enough, you can get a sugar fix at this nostalgic little confectionery at Downtown Disney. You'll find plenty of fine candies, chocolates, fudge, cookies, caramel apples, and other sweets ($2 and up). You can even watch the confectioners make Jennifer's favorite treat, choclate-covered strawberries, on the weekends. The shop aims to evoke a turn-of-the-century shop, like one you may have found in Marceline, Missouri (Walt's hometown). Open 11:00 am-10:00 pm (until 11:00 pm on Fridays and Saturdays).

Disneyland's Hotel Eateries

Disneyland Hotel

				Jennifer's Rating	Dave's Rating	Readers' Rating

Captain's Galley — L/D/S — $ — 6 6 7

Spending the afternoon by the pool? The poolside Captain's Galley has something for everyone. Menu items include sandwiches (roast beef, turkey, tuna, or vegetable at $5.25) and salads (garden, chef, chicken, Caesar, or Chinese chicken at $2.95-$5.95). If you have a taste for sushi, grab some California rolls ($5.95). Looking for just a snack? Choose a specialty coffee ($3.70), bakery items ($1.95-$3.10), or ice cream novelties ($2.10). Poolside seating. Vegetarian/healthy choices also available. Open seasonally.

Counter
American
Hours vary by season

The Coffee House — B/S — $ — 5 5 7

If you want to grab a quick continental breakfast before the park, this is the place. Bakery items include a scone, bagel, croissant, Danish, bear claw, muffin, or cinnamon roll ($1.95-$3.10). Healthier choices include assorted cereals and fresh apples, oranges, and bananas ($1.00-$1.35). Enjoy a coffee, cappuccino, juice, or soda ($1.60-$3.70). After 11:30 am, sandwiches and salads are also available. Outside seating is nearby.

Counter
American
6:00 am-9:00 pm

Croc's Bits 'n' Bites — L/D/S — $ — 5 5 5

There's no croc here, but there are bits and bites for lunch or a light dinner. The short menu consists of chicken tenders ($7.49), BBQ chicken sandwich ($7.29), cheeseburger ($6.25), and nachos ($7.49). Kids meal choices are a cheeseburger or chicken tenders ($5.99). Outside or covered open-air seating.

Counter
American
11:30 am-10:00 pm

Goofy's Kitchen — Brunch/D — $$$ — 7 6 7

Join Goofy and four of his friends for a lively, fun time. The kids can even get up and dance with Goofy! This is a great place to celebrate a birthday. The buffet has something for everyone, including omelets made to order, Mickey pancakes and waffles, a carving station, sliced fresh fruit, salads, sandwiches, meaty lasagna, peanut butter and jelly pizza, and Goofy's hot chocolate cake. Vegetarian and healthy choices are also available. Brunch prices are $27.25 for adults and $14.86 for kids 3-11; dinner is $35.92 for adults and $14.86 for kids (prices include tax and tip). Note that brunch hours are 7:00 am-2:00 pm on weekends. Characters come out about every 15 minutes.

Buffet
American
Noisy
Priority seats strongly suggested
Med. waits
7 am-12 pm, 5 pm-9 pm

Granville's Steak House — B/D — $$$$ — 9 9 9

This fine dining restaurant features steak specialties and a wine cellar with California's finest wines. Appetizers, soups, and salads include broiled portobello mushroom ($8.00), Granville's signature seven-onion soup ($7.00), and baby spinach with warm applewood smoked bacon vinaigrette ($9.00). Entrees include Angus beef cuts ($26.00-$32.00), Shelton free-range double breast of chicken ($22.00), Australian lobster tail (market), and prix-fixe ($28.00). Vegetable sides are extra ($5.00/$6.00). Breakfast choices include buttermilk pancakes or French toast with bananas foster or warm berries ($9.39), New York steak and eggs ($14.99), and an egg white omelet ($9.89). Kids enjoy a Mickey pancake ($5.29) or scrambled eggs with Mickey toast ($5.29).

Table
American
Quiet
Priority seats recommended for dinner
7:00 am-11:30 am, 5:30 pm-10:00 pm

Eatery descriptions and ratings are explained on page 196.

Side tab navigation: Planning · Getting There · Staying in Style · Touring · Feasting · Making Magic · Index · Notes & More

Disneyland's Hotel Eateries
(continued)

Disneyland Hotel (continued)

		Jennifer's Rating	Dave's Rating	Readers' Rating

Hook's Pointe — D — $$$ 🎀

	9 7 7

This cozy, unique casual restaurant has views of the Never Land Pool. The décor is reminiscent of Captain Hook's pirate ship. The extensive menu changes seasonally. Appetizers, soups, and salads include bruschetta ($6.79), fried calamari ($9.99), roasted garlic ($8.99), seafood chowder ($6.79), wild mushroom soup ($5.79), C-Zar salad ($7.19), and vine-ripened tomatoes ($7.49). Entrees to choose from include sea bass ($21.99), Pacific salmon ($19.99), grilled prawns ($19.99), Kansas City pork chops ($19.99), Black Angus New York steak ($27.99), firecracker fettuccini ($16.89), and vegetable pasta ($16.89). The children's menu lists a hot dog with fries, Mickeroni and cheese, meat lasagna, or chicken strips ($5.79).

Table
American
Quiet
Priority seats strongly recommended
5:00 pm–10:00 pm

The Lost Bar — S — $

3 5 7

Sit back, relax, order your favorite drink, and enjoy yourself in the middle of the Disneyland Resort. Sit inside in the open-air bar if you are in the mood to watch sports on one of nine screens, or sit outside for a quieter atmosphere. The bar menu is the same as Croc's Bits 'n Bites on the previous page.

Lounge
American
11:30 am–1:30 am

Top Brass — L/D — $

3 6 7

If you are looking for a quiet, comfortable place to relax, this is the spot. The bar menu can fill the bill for a light, late dinner. Choose from chips and homemade salsa ($2.95), California cheeseburger ($6.60), 9" pizzas made with homemade dough, or create your own ham or turkey sandwich ($6.95). Add a tropical drink ($7.95–$9.95) or wine by the glass ($5.00–$8.50).

Table
American
11:00 am–9:00 pm

The Wine Cellar — S — $$

3 7 7

Tucked under Hook's Pointe is this cozy little wine bar. Appetizers served here are the same as on Hook's Pointe menu (see above), which can be accompanied by many fine California wines by the glass or bottle. The wine bar also offers free cheese and crackers to go along with your drinks.

Lounge
American
5:00 pm–10:00 pm

Eatery descriptions and ratings are explained on page 196.

Smoking

Smokers, take note: California has a widespread ban on smoking—you can't light up in restaurants, bars, or the majority of public indoor places. Some hotels, including every Disneyland-owned hotel and the Westin chain, permit no smoking at all. Even beaches are getting into the act these days. If you're a smoker, come prepared. Study the Disney park maps in chapter 4 for smoking-allowed areas—the rest of the parks are smoke-free. Bring your own smokes—the gift shops don't sell them. You may even want to consider bringing nicotine patches and/or gum in the event you're stuck without a smoking area. But here's some good news for smokers: The outdoor areas at Downtown Disney have no smoking ban (yet), and you'll find ashtrays built into the tops of many of their trash cans. Peer reviewer Lani Teshima has a very informative article on smoking in Disneyland at MousePlanet.com—read it at http://www.mouseplanet.com/lani/tp030827lt.htm.

Disneyland's Hotel Eateries
(continued)

Disney's Grand Californian

	Jennifer's Rating	Dave's Rating	Readers' Rating

Hearthstone Lounge   S $$ | 5 | 7 | 7 |

Get away from it all in this delightful nook. Specialty coffees and fresh pastries and muffins can be had in the mornings. Later in the day, sit by the fire inside or by the cozy fireplace on the porch outside. The lounge serves signature starters inspired by other Disneyland Resort restaurants, such as tuna Takaki (Yamabuki, $13.99), chicken quesadilla (Storyteller's Café, $9.59), or BLT pizzetta (Golden Vine, $10.59). Desserts served are warm chocolate brownie ($6.59) or New York-style cheesecake ($7.59). Dessert wines, turn-of-the-century cocktails, specialty martinis, specialty hot drinks, and espresso drinks, too.

Counter
American
Quiet
6:00 am–
9:00 am,
12:00 pm–
12:00 am

Napa Rose   D $$$$ | 9 | 9 | 9 |

Every visit to Napa Rose is memorable with seasonal offerings inspired by California's Napa Valley. Starters include pheasant and dumplings ($13) and Baja California white shrimp ($10). How about Kenter Canyon field greens ($10) or Portobello mushroom cappuccino bisque ($9) as a second course? Main course selections include honey-glazed duck ($27), roasted rabbit ($28), and skillet-roasted beef ribeye ($36). A prix-fixe meal is also available ($65) to which you can add a flight of four wines ($45). Desserts choices may be a strawberry-lemon-almond cake tart or crème brulee. Napa Rose has a unique children's "fine dining" menu with items like grilled filet of prime beef tenderloin ($13), sautéed Pacific salmon, and a dessert of Balboa "beach sand."

Table
American
Quiet
Priority seats
strongly
recommended
5:00 pm–
10:00 pm

Storyteller's Cafe   B/L/D $$$ | 7 | 7 | 8 |

A great spot for breakfast, lunch, or dinner! You will be fascinated by the murals of tall tales from early California. For breakfast you can join Chip, Dale, and Brother Bear's Koda and Kenai for a character buffet ($27.25/adults and $12/kids ages 3-11) or order off the menu. The buffet offers pastries, Mickey waffles, French toast, eggs Benedict, fresh fruit, and asparagus. Menu choices include an American breakfast ($9.59) and Huevos rancheros ($9.79). Lunch and dinner menu items include "Introductions" of fire-roasted vegetable soup ($5.59) and Storyteller's salad ($7.29). "Chapter One" selections include grilled NY steak sandwich ($18.99) and honey-glazed chicken breast ($13.29). For "Chapter Two," a four-cheese ravioli ($13.79) or a 9" pizza ($12.29). "Chapter Three" offers up spicy swordfish ($20.99) or linguini with prawns ($21.99). "Sweet endings" include a cobbler ($7.59) or strawberry ice cream cake ($7.59). Dinnertime also brings a buffet option ($27/adults and $12/kids ages 3-11) with herb/pepper crust prime rib, chicken, salmon, pasta, corn chowder, mac and cheese, mixed greens, and yummy desserts. Kids meals and light and healthy selections available, too.

Buffet
American
Noisy
Priority
seating
strongly
suggested
Med. waits
7:00 am–

White Water Snacks   B/L/D/S $ | 4 | 7 | 7 |

Tucked in a corner by the pool, you'll find a convenient spot to have a quick meal before or after the park or while at the pool. Breakfast items are California burrito ($4.99) and French toast sticks ($3.99). The all-day menu (after 10:30 am) offers a classic French dip ($8.99), char-broiled cheeseburger ($6.99), chicken sandwich ($7.29), or tuna salad sandwich ($6.99). Healthy selections are available. Your choice of inside or outside seating.

Counter
American
7:00 am–
9:00 pm

Planning
Getting There
Staying in Style
Touring
Feasting
Making Magic
Index
Notes & More

Disneyland's Hotel Eateries
(continued)

Jennifer's Rating
Dave's Rating
Readers' Rating

Disney's Paradise Pier Hotel

☐ PCH Grill   B/D $$$ | 6 | 7 | 7 |

Join Lilo and Stitch for an all-you-care-to-eat Aloha Breakfast with French toast, fresh fruit, bacon, sausage, omelet station, chicken flautas, huevos rancheros, beignets, and other pastries ($22/adults and $12/kids ages 3–11). You can also order off a complete menu with choices such as "626's Cinnamon French Toast" or Lilo's Mickey-shaped pancakes ($7.29). In addition to Lilo and Stitch, you may see Minnie, Daisy, Pluto, and/or Max as they make the rounds or dance to Hawaiian music. Dinner is a quieter affair without characters but with plenty of menu options: try crab Louis salad ($9.99), a PCH club ($8.49), or a grilled New York steak ($21.49). There's an excellent kids menu here—kids can even create their own pizzas. PCH Grill has many yummy desserts—we dare you to try "The Whole PCH Grill & Kitchen Sink" (10 scoops of ice cream with your choice of toppings for a mere $21.99). Vegetarian and healthy choices are also available. This recently renovated restaurant has an open kitchen, a pizza oven, and bright, vibrant tilework. This restaurant was known as Summertree up until Disney's acquisition in 1996.

Table
American
Noisy
Priority seating strongly suggested
Med. waits
6:30 am–11:00 pm

☐ Surfside Lounge & Coffee Bar   S $ | 4 | 6 | 7 |

Comfortable chairs and a wide-screen TV just off the Paradise Pier Hotel lobby make this a relaxing spot to enjoy coffee or a drink. The snack menu offers specialty coffees, ice blended drinks, yogurt, fruit cups, and pastries. Limited seating includes some booths. This little cafe was previously called simply The Coffee House. It's a good place to grab a light breakfast before heading out to the parks.

Lounge
American
6:00 am–12:00 am (open to 1:30 am weekends)

☐ Yamabuki   L/D $$$ 🍴 | 9 | 8 | 8 |

Named after a beautiful Japanese flower, Yamabuki serves traditional and contemporary Japanese dishes. The extensive menu offers authentic meals of teriyaki, tempura, sukiyaki, and a full sushi bar. Choose from beef, chicken, fish, and vegetarian dinners ($18–$26). Appetizers include fresh squid ($7.75), salmon roe ($8.75), and two of Jennifer's favorites: hiyayakko tofu ($6.25) and yakitori chicken ($7.25). Dave's favorites—sushi and sashimi dinners—are also available for $28–$35. Wash it all down with Japanese beer or sake. Children's selections include chicken or beef teriyaki ($6.59/$7.59), tempura ($9.59), or

Good Japanese = Happy Dave

© MediaMarx, Inc.

Table
Japanese
Quiet
Priority seats strongly recommended
11:00 am–2:00 pm, 5:30 pm–10:00 pm

chicken nuggets ($6.29). Vegetarian and healthy selections available. We consider ourselves extremely experienced when it comes to Japanese cuisine, and Yamabuki does not disappoint. Seating is at regular tables and chairs, but we noticed a tatami room with sunken tables off to the side, too.

Eatery descriptions and ratings are explained on page 196.

Universal Studios Eateries

			Jennifer's Rating	Dave's Rating	Readers' Rating

Cantina [C-3]	L/D	$	**4**	**5**	**5**

Hollywood's version of a Mexican cantina serves your Mexican favorite combinations alongside El Pollo Loco flame-broiled chicken. Menu items include chicken enchilada ($6.99), 4-piece chicken ($7.99), soft taco ($6.99), grande burrito ($7.99)—each of these are served with rice and beans. A kids meal with a taco or quesadilla, plus rice and beans, is $4.99. A toppings bar is available, too. Margaritas are $5.79. Open seasonally.

Counter
Mexican
Med. waits
11:00 am–5:30 pm

Cinnabon [D-3]	B/S	$	**5**	**6**	**5**

This popular cinnamon bun chain has proven to be a winner inside Universal Studios. Stop by for a Cinnabon Classic ($2.89), Caramel Pecanbon ($3.79), or a MochaLatta Chill ($3.29/$3.59). Be prepared for long lines early in the day. For more information on Cinnabon, visit http://www.cinnabon.com.

Counter
American
Hours vary by season

Dodger Dogs [A-2]	L/S	$	**3**	**4**	**4**

Hot dogs, get yer hot dogs here! Here's another chain that's come to the park, but with more mixed results. Dodger Dogs, named after the Los Angeles-based baseball franchise, sells foot-long, 100% pork wieners ($4), pretzels, and soft drinks. Some love these dogs, but we prefer kosher dogs (which these aren't).

Counter
American
Hours vary by season

Flintstone's Drive-In [C-3]	L/D/S	$	**3**	**5**	**6**

Yabba dabba doo! Flintstone's fans may remember how Fred's vehicle tipped over onto its side when the car hop brought him a huge slab of beef. Well, don't expect the same thing here. Despite the cute faux rock architecture, this is a simple amusement park snack concession stand with hot dogs, turkey legs, sandwiches, and ice cream. This location was previously known as The River Princess snack bar. Outdoor seating.

Counter
American
Hours vary by season

Hollywood Grill [B-5]	L/D/S	$	**5**	**4**	**7**

Conveniently located near the park entrance, this eatery touts its pizza, burgers, and chicken. Its pizza is from Pizza Hut Express. Funnel cakes are also on the menu. Outside seating is nearby.

Counter
American
Hours vary

Jurassic Cafe [A-2]	L/D/S	$	**6**	**6**	**7**

A pleasant spot for lunch or an early dinner down on the Lower Lot. Menu items include family pleasers like burgers, chicken, pizza (again, from Pizza Hut Express), Chinese (from the Panda Express chain), and specialty coffees (from Starbucks). Salads and fruit bowls are also available for the health-conscious, while chocolate cake and cookies please your sweet tooth. Indoor seating is available here, unlike many other eateries at this theme park.

Counter
Various
Open same hours as the Lower Lot

Escape If You Can

Sorry, but Universal's in-park food is nothing but tummy filler, in our opinions. If it's possible, escape to CityWalk (see page 213) for better food and real service.

(side tabs:) Planning · Getting There · Staying in Style · Touring · Feasting · Making Magic · Index · Notes & More

Universal Studios Eateries
(continued)

	Jennifer's Rating	Dave's Rating	Readers' Rating

Louie's Italian Pizza and Pasta [C-3]   L/D/S $ | 3 4 6

If you've been to New York's Little Italy for their pizza and pasta, this fake Italian food knock-off will disappoint you. But it does offer pizza slices and simple pasta dishes ($7.50) for the hungry. Food is served cafeteria-style, portions are small, and quality is poor. We recommend you look elsewhere for your food, if possible. Outdoor seating.

Counter
Italian
Hours vary by season

Mel's Diner [B-4]   L/D/S $ | 6 6 8

This 1950s-style diner offers—surprise, surprise—your basic diner fare. Menu items include the classic burger ($4.79), cheeseburger ($5.19), jumbo hot dog ($3.99), grilled chicken club ($6.99), grilled cheese sandwich ($5.29), chicken tenders ($6.99), Caesar salad ($4.99), onion rings ($3.79), and kids meals with a burger or chicken tenders ($4.99). More interesting are the soda fountain chocolate, strawberry, and vanilla shakes. Indoor and outdoor seating.

Counter
American
Hours vary by season

Mulligan's Pub [B-4]   S $ | 2 3 3

This "pub" near Terminator 2: 3-D serves beer and spirits along with basic park fare. Alas, this imitator is nothing like John Mulligan's Pub in Dublin.

Lounge
Hours vary

Popcornopolis [C-4]   S $ | 6 6 6

Gourmet popcorn from the Popcornopolis company. This isn't your basic popcorn—a variety of flavors are available, from caramel and cheddar to almond and Rocky Road. For more popcorn details, or if you enjoyed it at the park and want to mail order, visit http://www.popcornopolis.com or call 800-POP-CITY.

Counter
American
Hours vary by season

Surf Shack Sweets [C-4]   S $ | 3 4 4

Yet another snack stand—you won't have a problem snacking in this park. Offers candy apples, fudge, and other sweets. Previously called Shore Shack Snacks.

Counter
American

Sweet Liberty [C-4]   S $ | 6 5 4

A quaint little sweet shop brimming with fudge, chocolate, salt-water taffy, and other candies. Hours vary by season.

Counter
American

Eatery descriptions and ratings are explained on page 196.

All You Can Eat Pass

In press time, Universal Studios Hollywood offers an "All You Can Eat Pass" for a mere $20/adult and $12/kids 48" or less. The deal gives guests a wristband that allows them to order a complimentary entree, side, and dessert at selected eateries throughout the day. Want more food? Just get back in line and order again. Beverages are not included. No sharing allowed, either. Eateries included in the deal at press time are Mel's Diner, Jurassic Cafe, and Louie's Itlian Pizza and Pasta. Note that this deal disappeared for a while recently, so don't assume it'll be always be available.

Universal CityWalk Eateries

			Jennifer's Rating	Dave's Rating	Readers' Rating

B.B. King's Blues Club — D — $$ — 8 7 5

Head on up to CityLoft (second level) for blues, booze, and black beans. The menu of Creole cuisine includes gumbo, BBQ ribs, and blackened catfish. A gospel brunch may be held on Sundays. Live music is played every night, but a cover is required and some events require tickets. Open to 2:00 am on Fri.-Sat. Menus and calendars at http://www.bbkings.com, or call 818-622-5464.

Table / Creole / Noisy / 4:00 pm–midnight

Ben & Jerry's — S — $ — 5 6 4

Bring your Chunky Monkey over to Ben & Jerry's for ice cream favorites, smoothies, shakes, and sundaes. Need we really say more?

Counter / Ice Cream

Buca di Beppo — L/D — $$ — 6 7 7

Hearty food and a warm atmosphere at this popular family eatery serving what they term "immigrant Southern Italian food" (basically meaning popular Italian dishes you're probably familiar with). Food is served family-style in large portions for sharing. Our meal was was huge and could have easily fed twice the people. Menu and more details at http://www.bucadibeppo.com. Tip: Check out the photographs in the restrooms for a chuckle.

Table / S. Italian / 11:00 am–11:00 pm (midnight on Fri.-Sat.)

Cafe Puccino — B/L/D/S — $ — 3 6 4

This little cafe that serves European favorites like pizza, Italian salads, sandwiches, baked goods, and cappucinno. Huge cups of coffee are a big draw here.

Counter / European

Cafe Tu Tu Tango — L/D — $$ — 6 7 6

A Spanish artist's loft is the setting for this funky restaurant with an international flair. Menu items include dips, spreads, soups, and entrees like seared tuna sashimi, cuban grilled steak skewers, and kim chee glazed ribs. On the walls are artwork from local artists—artists may even be present working on their latest canvas.

Table / International / 11:00 am–12:00 am

Camacho's Cantina — Brunch/L/D — $$ — 5 6 7

Mariachi bands, familiar Mexican dishes, and killer margaritas make the cantina a lively place. Mariachi performs on Fri.-Sat. evenings and during Sunday brunch. View their menu at http://www.camachosinc.com.

Table / Mexican / 11 am–11 pm

Cinnabon — B/S — $ — 5 6 5

Another installation of the popular cinnamon bun chain. It offers basically the same items (baked on premises) as the theme park's outlet (see page 211).

Counter / American

Crêpe Cafe — S — $ — 6 6 4

Traditional French crepes prepared to order, which you can watch through the eatery's front window. Salads also available. Indoor/outdoor seating.

Counter / French

Daily Grill — L/D — $$ — 5 6 7

American comfort food reigns here—pot pie, meatloaf, mashed potatoes, skirt steak, and spaghetti are all on the crowded menu. Leave room for the fruit cobbler. Reserve tables at 818-760-4448. Open to 11:00 pm on Fri. and Sat.

Table / American / 11 am–9 pm

Planning
Getting There
Staying in Style
Touring
Feasting
Making Magic
Index
Notes & More

Universal CityWalk Eateries
(continued)

				Jennifer's Rating	Dave's Rating	Readers' Rating

Dodger Dogs   S $ | 3 | 4 | 4 |

More Dodger Stadium hot dogs like those in the theme park (see page 211). Also cheesesteaks, hamburgers, buffalo wings, ice cream, and soft drinks.

Counter
American

Hard Rock Cafe   L/D $$ | 5 | 6 | 6 |

With more than 120 Hard Rock Cafes around the world, chances are you've been to one (and in our opinion, the only reason to visit again is to collect a new t-shirt). The menu has basic American fare and the walls are covered with music memorabilia, including a 78-foot neon green stratocaster guitar at the entrance. Get on the list for the next available table at http://www.hardrockcafe.com.

Table
American
Noisy
11:00 am–
10:00 pm

Jamba Juice   S $ | 8 | 7 | 8 |

Like its sister location at Downtown Disney (see page 204), this little spot sells healthy smoothies and juices.

Counter
American

Jody Maroni's Sausage Kingdom   B/L/D/S $ | 4 | 7 | 4 |

Gobble up a gourmet sausage (is that an oxymoron?) in flavors like Hot Italian, Louisiana Boudin, chicken apple, and Cubana. Breakfast burritos also sold.

Counter
Various

Karl Strauss Brewery Garden   L/D $$$ | 5 | 6 | 6 |

Raise your beer stein and toast one of the largest beer towers of Southern California. The draw here are the 8-10 handcrafted beers. You'll need to eat too, and their menu includes items like firecracker sirloin strips and ginger salmon. Try a keg-tapping party the first Thursday of each month at 10:00 pm. Open 11:00 am to 9:00 pm on Sundays, and to midnight on Fridays and Saturdays.

Table
American
Noisy
4:00 pm–
9:00 pm

Panda Express   L/D $ | 3 | 4 | 5 |

This chain eatery serves Chinese-American fare with old standbys like Mandarin chicken, sweet and sour pork, egg rolls, and fried rice. Kids menu available.

Counter
Chinese

Popcornopolis   S $ | 5 | 4 | 4 |

Another camp-out of the cool corn store (see page 212). This is the best place for caramel corn—it stays fresh for six months, even after opening and resealing.

Counter
American

Rubio's Baja Grill   L/D $ | 6 | 7 | 8 |

Want Mexican without the mariachi bands and higher prices of Camacho's? Rubio's has great prices and decent food. Menu at http://www.rubios.com.

Counter
Mexican

Saddle Ranch Chop House   Brunch/L/D $$$ | 6 | 5 | 7 |

Yee-haw! This huge lodge just outside Universal's park gates has all you'd expect from a tinseltown version of a Texas chop house: mechanical bulls, big dance floor, large TV screens, and an outdoor patio with campfire pits. Brunch is served daily (try the Johnny Appleseed Pancakes), along with lunch and dinner. Full menu, events, and floor plan at http://www.srrestaurants.com.

Table
Western
Noisy
8:00 am–
2:00 am

Tip: AAA members may get discounts at some CityWalk eateries—ask about discounts! Also inquire with your human resources dept. at work about Universal Fan Club membership—it's only available to U.S. companies and it offers discounts at Universal, including CityWalk.

Universal CityWalk Eateries
(continued)

				Jennifer's Rating	Dave's Rating	Readers' Rating

☐ **Shanghai and Mein**	L/D	$$		5	7	7

Like its name, this eatery is a crossroads between urban decor and traditional Chinese-American cuisine. Dim sum and noodles are also served. Check out the extensive tea menu, too. Seating is limited here.

Table
Chinese
11 am–9 pm

☐ **Starbucks**	B/S	$		5	5	5

The ever-present coffeehouse is here at CityWalk, too. Specialty coffees and pastries are on the menu, which you can view at http://www.starbucks.com.

Counter
American

☐ **Subway**	L/D	$		6	5	6

We love Subway—when you need a filling meal on a shoestring, grab a sub sandwich here. Menu at http://www.subway.com.

Counter
American

☐ **Tommy's Hamburgers**	L/D/S	$		5	5	5

Tommy's began in Los Angeles in 1946 and became popular for its chili-topped burgers. You can also get hot dogs, tamales, and fries—fast! Large portions.

Counter
American

☐ **Tony Roma's**	L/D	$$		5	6	7

B.B. King's isn't the only place for ribs at CityWalk—Tony Roma's specializes in ribs in a variety of flavors and styles, along with steaks, chicken, seafood, and burgers. Open to midnight on Fridays and Saturdays.

Table
American
11 am – 10 pm

☐ **Upstart Crow Coffeehouse**	L/D/S	$		5	6	7

Upstart Crow (another name for Shakespeare) is a little cafe among the shelves of the bookstore by the same name. Order espresso, English tea, sandwiches, and fresh pastries while you peruse the latest bestseller or a classic.

Counter
American
Hours vary

☐ **Versailles Restaurant**	S	$		3	6	5

Cuban comes to CityWalk, with menu items like roast pork, beef tongue, sautéed oxtail, and halibut in garlic sauce. http://www.versaillescuban.com.

Counter
Cuban

☐ **Wasabi at CityWalk**	L/D	$$		7	6	7

This is the hot sushi joint with imaginatively named sushi, such as T-Rex Roll (soft-shell crab, $9.95) and Gotta Rock n' Roll (tempura roll, $7.95). Traditional items like chicken teriyaki also available. Limited seating inside and outside.

Counter
Japanese
Hours vary

☐ **Wetzel's Pretzels**	L/S	$		6	6	5

Rick Wetzel does Universal in addition to his Disney location (see page 206). We recommend one of the sweet pretzels with cream cheese. Yum!

Counter
American

☐ **Wolfgang Puck Cafe**	L/D	$$$		7	7	6

Southern California's golden boy Puck is famous for nearly single-handedly popularizing California cuisine and for putting wood-fired, individual pizzas on the map. Menu favorites include Chinois Chicken Salad ($10.95) and Pad Thai noodles ($12.95–$16.95). Reservations accepted Mon.–Thu. at 818-985-9653.

Table
Californian
11:00 am–
9:00 pm

Eatery descriptions and ratings are explained on page 196.

Planning · Getting There · Staying in Style · Touring · Feasting · Making Magic · Index · Notes & More

Knott's Berry Farm Eateries

Knott's Berry Farm lists 22 eateries in its theme park and another six just outside its gates in the California Marketplace. Rather than reviewing all 28 eateries, some of which are seasonal, we've focused on popular table-service and larger counter-service eateries.

	Jennifer's Rating	Dave's Rating	Readers' Rating

Angel's Diner [D-1]   L/D/S $ 5 · 5 · 7

The winged-bun sign on this eatery certainly doesn't mean "fast food" as the line here is quite daunting. The menu offers burgers ($3.95), hot dogs ($3.50), sweet BBQ pork ($4.25), personal pizzas ($4.50–$4.95), and malts ($3.50).

Counter
American
Hours vary

Auntie Pasta's Pizza Palace [C-3]   L/D/S $ 5 · 5 · 7

Hungry? This buffeteria has all-you-can-eat pizza, as well as pasta, salads and sandwiches. Snoopy cartoons play on the TV.

Counter
American

Bigfoot Broiler [B-2]   L/D/S $ 6 · 6 · 8

A basic burger joint with walk-up service. Menu items include a 1/3 lb. burger ($3.95), cheeseburger ($4.35), 1/4 lb. hot dog ($3.40), chili cheese fries ($4.25), ice cream sandwich ($1.95), soft drinks ($2.95/$3.50), and a frozen lemon icee ($3.75). Outdoor seating nearby.

Counter
American
Hours vary by season

Chow House [B-3]   L/D/S $ 5 · 6 · 6

Nachos, hot dogs, pizza slices, plus dessert and ice cream. Look for the sourdough bread bowls with soup for a filling meal.

Counter
American

Coasters [D-1]   L/D $ 6 · 6 · 7

Knott's '50s-style diner serves up the usual cheeseburgers ($4.25–$5.25), fries ($3.25–$4.25), and extra-thick shakes ($3.75) amidst tabletop jukeboxes with golden oldies. You can also get salads and sandwiches. This eatery is a Cedar Fair signature and is also found at Cedar Point, Dorney Park, etc. Jukeboxes can make this a noisy place. Indoor seating at booths and outdoor seating at patio tables.

Counter
American
Hours vary by season

Comidas Fritas [D-3]   L/D/S $ 7 · 7 · 6

Hola! Finally ... something other than basic American food! This Mexican counter offers big burritos (dry or wet—$4.95–$6.85), taquitos with salsa ($4.25), rice pudding ($2.25), nacho basket ($6.25), and boysenberry punch ($2.95/$3.50).

Counter
Mexican
Hours vary

Fireman's Brigade Barbecue [B-3]   L/D $$ 7 · 6 · 7

Grab an outdoor picnic table and put out the fire in your belly with decent barbecue chicken, ribs, and baked potatoes. The 1/4 chicken meal with potato, cole slaw, and garlic toast is $9.50. Menu also has pork ribs, beef ribs, and fresh fruit. A Jr. Fireman kids meal is $5.95 and includes chicken, chips, cookie, and kid's drink.

Counter
American
Hours vary by season

Funnel Cake Kitchen [B-3]   L/D/S $ 7 · 5 · 8

Knott's Berry Farm's famous funnel cakes are still as hot, sweet, and tasty as ever! Your choice of boysenberry, apple, or chocolate topping.

Counter
American

Eatery descriptions and ratings are explained on page 196.

Knott's Berry Farm Eateries
(continued)

	Jennifer's Rating	Dave's Rating	Readers' Rating
Ghost Town Grill [B-3] L/D/S $$	7	7	9

The only table-service restaurant actually inside the park offers burgers, steaks, chicken, fajitas, chili, hot wings, and salads. Huge portions are served here. And the restaurant is nicely themed, too. A fan favorite!

Table
American
Hours vary

Hollywood Hits [D-1] L/D/S $	6	6	8

Another walk-up counter-service spot with a varied menu. Items include Italian sausage ($4.35), corn dog ($3.95), guacamole burger ($4.95), Mrs. Knott's two-piece chicken box ($7.95), individual pizzas ($4.50-$4.95), and kids meals ($7.95—yikes!). Outdoor patio tables with some shade nearby.

Counter
American
Hours vary by season

Lucy's Lunchbox [D-4] S $	6	6	7

This two-story, indoor eatery features the basic fare found throughout the park: burger ($3.95), cheeseburger ($4.95), hot dog ($3.50), chicken tenders ($2.95-$4.95), personal cheese pizza ($4.50), junior camper kids meals ($2.25-$5.95), fries ($2.50-$3.25), and green salad ($3.95). Nice place to cool off and relax.

Counter
American
Hours vary by season

Mrs. Knott's Chicken [B-4] B/Brunch/L/D $$	8	7	9

It all started with a chicken! Cordelia Knott began selling her famous fried chicken from a five-table tearoom back in 1934. It was popular back then, and it's still widely popular today. Along with your fried chicken, you can get buttermilk biscuits, mashed potatoes, chicken gravy, veggies, and boysenberry pie—all made from Mrs. Knott's original recipes. If you're not in the mood for chicken, the menu also includes pork ribs, turkey, and sandwiches. Call 714-220-5080 for reservations for parties of 12 or more. A Sunday champagne brunch is held from 9:30 am to 2:00 pm (reservations accepted). Next door is Chicken To Go with many of the same favorites served in the restaurant, including pies.

Table
American
7:00 am-8:30 pm (open to 9:00 or 9:30 pm on weekends)

Señora Knott's Fried Chicken Express [D-3] L/D/S $$	6	6	8

More of Mrs. Knott's fried chicken in a quaint courtyard. Menu items include the traditional 3-piece chicken meal ($9.75), a two-piece chicken plate ($7.95), chicken snack plate ($5.95), kids meal ($5.95), chicken on the side ($0.85-$2.05), corn ($1.75), beer ($4.00), and frozen wine margaritas ($4.50).

Counter
American
Hours vary by season

Sharky's Cafe [D-1] L/D/S $	6	6	8

This finger-food spot offers all the favorites: chicken tender baskets ($4.25-$7.95), chicken wings (hot, BBQ, or teriyaki—$3.95-$7.25), hot dogs ($2.25-$4.50), spicy chicken sandwich ($4.95), kids meals ($5.95), jumbo pretzel ($2.75), cotton candy ($2.75), and caramel apple ($2.95). Outdoor seating nearby. Long lines.

Counter
American
Hours vary by season

Sutter's Fine Family Fare [B-3] S $	6	6	7

Ghost Town is home to a counter-service food court offering hot wings, pizza, hot dogs, hamburgers, Navajo tacos, more of Mrs. Knott's chicken meals, and funnel cakes.

Counter
American
Hours vary

Tip: A new Johnny Rockets eatery is opening in the Boardwalk section of the park in June 2006. For details, visit http://www.johnnyrockets.com.

Planning
Getting There
Staying in Style
Touring
Feasting
Making Magic
Index
Notes & More

Other Area Eateries

Jennifer's Rating
Dave's Rating
Readers' Rating

If you don't already have enough choices, here are some eateries to choose from outside the parks. For each area below, we include at least one cheap eat, one family restaurant, one with entertainment, and one for fine dining (listed in that order, too).

Disneyland Area

McDonald's	B/L/D/S	$	3	4	5

We're not suggesting you come all the way to Disneyland to eat at the Golden Arches, but it works if you're on a tight budget or need a Big Mac fix. The McDonald's across from Disneyland Resort on 1500 S. Harbor Blvd. is convenient and cheap–prices are not inflated just because it's near Disneyland.

Counter
American
5:30 am–11:00 pm

Millie's Restaurant	B/L/D	$	5	5	5

This inexpensive, family restaurant offers basic American comfort food like burgers, meatloaf, and steaks. (Note that they no longer have a buffet here.) It's within walking distance of Disneyland Resort, just across the street at 1480 S. Harbor Blvd. More information at http://www.millies.com.

Table
American
6:00 am–midnight

Tiffy's Family Restaurant	B/L/D	$	5	6	5

This simple ice cream parlor is also an affordable family restaurant. Beyond the ice cream, you'll find breakfast treats like strawberry Belgian waffles and lunch/dinner staples like soup, salads, and a variety of burgers. Located at 1060 W. Katella Ave. Phone: 714-635-1801.

Table
American
6:00 am–11:00 pm

Dave & Buster's	L/D/S	$$	6	6	5

A massive complex that combines food and fun is the idea behind Dave & Buster's. In other words, it's a grown-up Chuck E. Cheese–complete with games that spit out redemption tickets. Food is decent but pricey. The games are fun, but also pricey. But it does seem to offer something for everyone. Located at 20 City Blvd., Orange, CA. Phone: 714-769-1515. Note: 21 and older after 10:00 pm.

Table
American
Very noisy
11:00 am–1:00 am

See also Medieval Times on page 175 and Pirate's Dinner Adventure on page 176.

Anaheim White House	L/D	$$$$	9	–	5

A grand 1909 home is the setting for this acclaimed, award-winning restaurant. Relax in one of the eight lovely dining areas while you enjoy menu items such as linguini putanesca ($23), rack of New Zealand lamb ($37), and salmon chocolat ($28). Extensive wine list. Dress code is business casual (see page 194). Reservations are recommended–call 714-772-1381 or visit http://www.anaheimwhitehouse.com. 887 S. Anaheim Blvd., Anaheim, CA.

Table
N. Italian
11:30 am–2:30 pm, 5-10:00 pm

Chains

For those who want to know what chain restaurants are in the area: Denny's (714-776-3300), Tony Roma's (714-520-0200), HomeTown Buffet (714-539-2234), El Pollo Loco (714-776-7195), Kentucky Fried Chicken (714-635-7830), Baker's Square (714-750-2661), IHOP (714-635-0933), Benihana (714-774-4940), Joe's Crab Shack (714-703,0505), Little Caesar's Pizza (714-991-3190), and Taco Bell (714-563-2477).

Other Area Eateries
(continued)

Greater Los Angeles Area

				Jennifer's Rating	Dave's Rating	Readers' Rating

Pink's Hot Dogs — L/D/S — $ — 6 7 7

A "Hollywood Legend" since 1939 serving chili dogs ($2.65), pastrami dogs, and Ozzy Osbourne spicy dogs. Long waits at this popular spot. Free parking behind the eatery. 709 N. La Brea; 323-931-4223. http://www.pinkshollywood.com.

Counter · American · 9:30 am–2 am

Bob's Big Boy — B/L/D/S — $ — 7 7 7

This isn't your typical Big Boy—it's one of the originals and a national landmark! They even have car hop, drive-in service on weekends, 5:00–10:00 pm. Excellent food, good prices. 4211 Riverside Dr., Burbank; 818-843-9334.

Table · American · 24 hours

Disney's Soda Fountain — B/L/D/S — $ — 8 6 5

Next door to the El Capitan Theater is Disney's take on an old-fashioned ice cream parlor, complete with soda jerks and Dewar's ice cream. Menu has sundaes, shakes, malts, cones, freezes, phosphates, sodas, waffles, and sandwiches. 6834 Hollywood Blvd., Hollywood, CA; 818-845-3110; http://www.disneysodafountain.com.

Table · American · 9:00 am–10:00 pm

Fabiolus — L/D — $$$ — 8 8 5

This little trattoria is the perfect spot for dinner before a show at the Pantages Theater (been there, done that). The food here is delightful—menu items include penne alla vodka ($9.75), pollo dijone ($14.45), and sogliola miranese ($19.00). You can sit indoors or out, but we think the patio in the back is best. 6270 W. Sunset Blvd., Hollywood; 323-467-2882; http://www.fabiolus.org.

Table · Italian · 5:30 pm–midnight

San Diego Area

Rubio's Fresh Mexican Grill — L/D/S — $ — 6 7 7

Rubio is credited with introducing fish tacos—a San Diegan food if there ever was one. And his eateries were voted the #1 cheap eat in San Diego. More than 40 locations in San Diego—visit http://www.rubios.com or call 760-929-8226.

Counter · American · Hours vary

Brians' American Eatery — B/L/D — $ — 6 6 7

This family-friendly, all-American diner offers a huge menu—you want it, they probably have it. Hearty portions are served inside in the comfy booths or on the outside patio. Open 24 hours on weekends. 619-296-8268

Table · American · Hours vary

Corvette Diner — L/D — $$ — 8 6 5

Kids and grown-ups alike enjoy this '50s-style diner with a DJ booth, a soda fountain, and Elvis. The servers get into the act, cracking gum and blowing straws at diners. We loved our onion rings ($5.95/basket) and meatloaf ($8.95). It's very noisy, but tons of fun. http://www.cohnrestaurants.com. 619-542-1476

Table · American · 11:00 am–10:00 pm

The Prado at Balboa Park — L/D — $$$$ — 8 7 5

Top off your day at Balboa Park (see pages 173–174) with an elegant meal admist romantic Spanish architecture and verdant gardens. The menu features seasonal dishes such as grilled swordfish, wild mushroom risotto, and bouillabaisse. Be sure to try a mojito! Reservations suggested—call 619-557-9441.

Table · Italian · 11:30 am–9:00 pm

Side tabs: Planning · Getting There · Staying in Style · Touring · Feasting · Making Magic · Index · Notes & More

Character Meals

The number of character meals at the Disneyland Resort may be limited, but the **character interaction is hard to beat** and provides a great experience no matter what your age. The characters don't actually sit with you, but they roam around the restaurant and give your table individual attention for short interludes. The characters stay true to their roles, whether it's Goofy or a princess, interacting with you in their own personal style. This provides some great photo opportunities, and in some cases, that's the main focus of the character's visit.

Character meals are generally **more expensive** than regular meals (usually $18–$36/adults and $12–$15/kids), but the chance to meet the characters in an unhurried atmosphere is well worth it. Even if characters aren't at the top of your menu, the price of these buffets and family-style meals can be less than a comparable full-service meal when you factor in all the costs. Priority seating arrangements are recommended, but walk-up seating may be available. Call Disney Dining at 714-781-3463 up to 60 days in advance for priority seating arrangements.

Character Meal Tips:

✔ The parks and resorts are all within easy walking distance. Even so, do allow for enough travel time before your seating time.

✔ For the best character experience, dine off-hours or off-season. While the characters may give you a quick visit during busy mealtimes, you might end up with a close personal relationship when tables are empty.

✔ Be careful of counting on specific character appearances. Disney characters may get swapped out with a different Disney friend due to scheduling conflicts. The exceptions are the "headline" characters: Ariel at Ariel's Grotto, Goofy at Goofy's Kitchen, Lilo and Stitch at PCH Grill, Minnie at Plaza Inn, and Chip and Dale at Storyteller's Cafe. Don't expect to see Mickey Mouse frequently either—he's usually otherwise engaged in important park business (he's the Big Cheese, after all).

✔ Don't be shy, grown-ups! Even if you aren't dining with kids, the characters visit your table. If you would rather sit things out, they will simply give you a nod and a handshake.

✔ The "head" characters don't speak, but that doesn't mean you have to keep quiet. Talk to them and they'll pantomime and play along!

✔ Bring your cameras and autograph books!

✔ Collecting tip: Some character meal prices include a souvenir button—if you aren't given a button, inquire about it.

Dave's cousins Andrea and Bradley get a special hug at Storyteller's Cafe

Character Dining Locations

Ariel's Disney Princess Celebration (Ariel's Grotto at Disney's California Adventure)

Ariel and your favorite princesses are your royal hosts for this three-course meal. The princesses may include Snow White, Cinderella, Belle, and Sleeping Beauty. Lunch (11:30 am–3:30 pm) is served at your table and includes a starter, entrée, dessert, and one soft drink. Cost (including tax) is $22.62/adults and $15.07/kids ages 3–11. Dinner starts at 3:30 pm with the last seating about one hour before park closing. Note: You'll be meeting Ariel as a human rather than as the Little Mermaid, so expect her to wear a dress and walk about on those ... what do you call them? ... feet! Jennifer and Dave's Rating: 6/10

Goofy's Kitchen (Disneyland Hotel)

Goofy's Kitchen serves breakfast, lunch, and dinner and is the most expensive of the character meals. Don't let this scare you away as Goofy, Pluto, and friends make this a rockin' good time with song and dance. The lunch/brunch buffet is amazing; it's a feast for the eyes as well as your appetite. If you are celebrating a birthday during your stay, Goofy's can make your birthday special with a Birthday Bag (see details on next page). Cost (including tax) for breakfast is $27.25/adults and $14.86/kids ages 3–11. Cost with tax for dinner is $35.96/adults and $14.86/kids ages 3–11. Breakfast hours are 7:00 am to 12:00 pm on weekdays, and until 2:00 pm on weekends; dinner hours are 5:00–9:00 pm. Jennifer and Dave's Rating: 8/10

Lilo & Stitch Aloha Breakfast (PCH Grill at Paradise Pier Hotel)

Who can resist Lilo and the ever rascally Stitch? Kahuna Kali serves as your human host and other characters may include Minnie, Daisy, Pluto, and Max. The characters not only greet you at your table, but encourage kids to participate at interactive "show" locations surrounding the restaurant. The buffet menu has a definite Mexican flavor, but more traditional items are available, as well as an a la carte menu. The cost (including tax) is $23.69/adults and $12.92/kids ages 3–11. The meal includes a complimentary Character Breakfast button. Hours are 7:00–11:00 am on weekdays and until 1:00 pm on weekends and holidays. Jennifer and Dave's Rating: 8/10

Breakfast with Minnie & Friends (Plaza Inn at Disneyland Park)

Enjoy a delicious buffet meal while Disney characters cavort around you. You'll certainly meet Minnie and many of her friends, who may include Pooh, Tigger, Eeyore, Chip, Dale, Goofy, and/or Pluto. (Sorry, Mickey is busy over in Toontown and can't make it.) Cost is $23.63/adults and $12.92/kids ages 3–11. The meal includes a Breakfast button. The first seating typically begins at park opening with the last seating at 11:00 am. Priority seating arrangements are definitely recommended for this popular breakfast. Note that this character meal was princess-themed in its previous incarnation, but word has it that this new meal is much better. Jennifer and Dave's Rating: 9/10

Storyteller's Café Breakfast with Chip 'n Dale (Grand Californian Hotel)

This very popular character breakfast is hosted by pals Chip and Dale and Brother Bear's Koda and Kenai. The Storyteller's Café is well known for its delicious, "more than you can eat" buffets. Add to this some zany adventures, sing-and-dance-a-longs, and you are in for a "nutty" good time. Note, however, that the characters do not visit the tables as frequently as other Disney character meals. Cost is $23.69/adults and $12.92/kids ages 3–11. The meal includes a Character Breakfast button. Breakfast seating starts at 7:00 am and ends at 10:30 am. Jennifer and Dave's Rating: 7/10

Special Disney Dining Opportunities

The Disneyland Resort boasts some of finest chefs in the world. Try one of these distinguished restaurants for a romantic/fine dining experience: Catal or Ralph Brennan's Jazz Kitchen in Downtown Disney, Granville's Steak House at the Disneyland Hotel, The Vineyard Room in Disney's California Adventure, or Napa Rose at the Grand Californian Hotel. Remember it's Disney, so a quiet table may not always be possible. Call 714-781-DINE to arrange priority seating for all of the above restaurants.

Birthdays

So you say it's your birthday? Good news! Disneyland has a special birthday party spot at the Plaza Inn in Disneyland Park. "**My Disneyland Birthday Party**" is hosted by the zany Pat E. Cake with guest apperances from Mickey, Minnie, or other Disney friends. Add in some music, a party hat, cake decorating (and cake), punch, and a special Happy Birthday cup and Mickey Mouse plate for the birthday person, and you've got 40 minutes of fun! Parties are held at 2:00 pm and 3:00 pm daily and cost $10 per guest. Reserve your party up to 30 days in advance at 714-781-DINE. Note that park admission is required for this event, and be aware that a number of other guests will be celebrating their birthday at the same time (it's not a private event).

For an extra cost you can purchase a special **Birthday Bucket** at most Disneyland resort restaurants. For $20 the birthday kid receives a Sorcerer Mickey, Princess, Buzz Lightyear, or Winnie the Pooh Birthday Bucket topped with a mini cake plus stickers, a birthday pin, and a toy. You can also buy the buckets through room service at the Disney hotels.

Or how about a **Goofy's Kitchen Birthday Bag** filled with a balloon, party hat, Goofy pen, toy maraca, and a puzzle? Birthday Bags are an extra $5/person—be sure to request this when you make your priority seating for Goofy's Kitchen.

For a **more personal celebration**, choose one of the Disneyland Resort's full-service restaurants and be sure to let the server know it's your birthday! More tips on celebrating birthdays at Disneyland are on page 238.

Holidays

Holidays are always special at the Disneyland Resort. The parks and resorts overflow with special entertainment and decorations that vary from season to season and year to year. The Christmas and New Year's season is especially magical, with all kinds of celebrations throughout the property. Holiday dinners at the hotels and selected theme park restaurants are not advertised. You can be fairly certain that the Disney hotels will have something on Easter Sunday, Mother's Day, Father's Day, Thanksgiving Day, Christmas Day, and New Year's Eve. In fact, Disney Dining won't always know if something special is planned at the hotels, so call the hotels direct for special holiday dining opportunities.

House of Blues

House of Blues has a concert hall separate from its restaurant (see page 204) that features performances by top musicians. On Sundays at 10:00 am and 1:00 pm, they serve an all-you-care-to-eat Gospel Brunch with soul food and glorious gospel music—price is $33.00/adults and $16.50/kids 3–9 (children under 3 are free but you still need to reserve a place for them). Reservations can be made up to a month in advance at the House of Blues box office (or call 717-778-2583). Tickets for evening performances are available through the box office or Ticketmaster, and range from $15 to $30. The House of Blues is located at Downtown Disney, 1530 S. Disneyland Dr., Anaheim, CA 92802. More information at http://www.hob.com.

Planning

Getting There

Staying in Style

Touring

Feasting

Making Magic

Index

Notes & More

Zydeco Jazz Brunch at Ralph Brennan's Jazz Kitchen

On Sundays from 11:00 am to 4:00 pm, Ralph Brennan's Jazz Kitchen puts on its Zydeco Jazz Brunch with a special brunch menu and live jazz. Diners order off the menu—there's no special price for the brunch. Note that the music typically begins at 11:30 am and ends at 3:00 pm. For more information on Ralph Brennan's Jazz Kitchen, see page 206.

Disney's Electrical Parade Viewing at Wine Country Trattoria

Enjoy a meat and cheese appetizer tray and a beverage when you reserve premier seating for Disney's Electrical Parade at the Wine Country Trattoria in Disney's California Adventure. Cost is $56/adults and $46/kids. Reserve up to 30 days in advance at 714-781-4400.

Fantasmic! Balcony Dessert Buffet

Sit on the balcony of the Disney Gallery for the performance of Fantasmic! while you enjoy a dessert buffet. Sounds divine, doesn't it? This buffet is pricey ($56/person), but it offers an amazing view for Fantasmic! The seating is limited (only 21 guests) on the balcony overlooking New Orleans Square, providing an up close and personal viewing of Fantasmic! The price reserves your spot and includes the dessert buffet and a beverage, but does not include park admission. Reserve up to 30 days in advance at 714-781-4400 (a credit card is required). Note that this is very popular and you should be prepared to call at 8:00 am PT (11:00 am ET) exactly 30 days beforehand if you hope to secure reservations.

Fantasmic! Premium Seating

Can't get onto the Disney Gallery balcony to see Fantasmic? Consider the premium seating option—it's not as cool and the view is a tad obstructed by poles and railings, but you get a chair to sit in, your choice of desserts in a keepsake box, and a beverage. Seating is a on a first-come, first-serve basis—arrive at least an hour ahead of time and sign in with the cast member. The seating area is located in front of Haunted Mansion (look for the roped off area with folding chairs). Price is $56/adults, $46/kids 3–9, and kids under 3 are free if they sit on your lap.

Toll House Cookie Junior Chef

Children can visit the Plaza Pavilion kitchen and make their own chocolate chip cookie creation free of charge.

Large Groups

Since Disneyland Resort is in a heavily populated area, large groups and businesses are offered special dining opportunities. For a price, Disneyland will customize and cater events at a variety of venues in the parks and hotels. Events can accommodate group sizes from 40 to 7,000 guests! For more information, call 714-956-6556 or visit http://www.disneylandmeetings.com.

Have a smaller group? Napa Rose at the Grand Californian has a **private dining room** with a fireplace that seats up to 30 guests. Call 714-300-7170 for more information.

Club 33

This very special dining opportunity is only for members and their guests. It's not unusual for a non-member to get invited by one of their connections, however, so if you do get an invitation from a friend or business associate, don't turn down this rare and special opportunity. We had the good fortune to be invited by colleagues (see photo on right) and had a memorable meal here with them. This club has no formal dress code, but guests generally dress up for the occasion—slacks and a polo shirt or sportscoat for gentlemen, a sundress or slacks for the ladies. More information on Club 33 is on page 96.

Jennifer and Dave at Club 33

Meal Worksheet

The first step is to determine your needs. Start by checkmarking the meals you'll need in the worksheet below. Next, write down where you would like to eat your meals—be specific ("cereal in room" or "Blue Bayou at Disneyland"). Circle the meals that need priority seatings/reservations, then use the worksheet on the next page to make the arrangements.

Meal	Location	Meal	Location
Day One–Date:		**Day Six–Date:**	
❑ Breakfast		❑ Breakfast	
❑ Lunch		❑ Lunch	
❑ Dinner		❑ Dinner	
❑ Other		❑ Other	
Day Two–Date:		**Day Seven–Date:**	
❑ Breakfast		❑ Breakfast	
❑ Lunch		❑ Lunch	
❑ Dinner		❑ Dinner	
❑ Other		❑ Other	
Day Three–Date:		**Day Eight–Date:**	
❑ Breakfast		❑ Breakfast	
❑ Lunch		❑ Lunch	
❑ Dinner		❑ Dinner	
❑ Other		❑ Other	
Day Four–Date:		**Day Nine–Date:**	
❑ Breakfast		❑ Breakfast	
❑ Lunch		❑ Lunch	
❑ Dinner		❑ Dinner	
❑ Other		❑ Other	
Day Five–Date:		**Day Ten–Date:**	
❑ Breakfast		❑ Breakfast	
❑ Lunch		❑ Lunch	
❑ Dinner		❑ Dinner	
❑ Other		❑ Other	

Planning · Getting There · Staying in Style · Touring · Feasting · Making Magic · Index · Notes & More

Priority Seating/Reservations Worksheet

Once you've determined what meals you plan to eat in table-service restaurants, note them in the chart below along with your preferred dining time. Next, call 714-781-DINE to make Disney priority seatings (check non-Disney eatery descriptions for reservation details and numbers). Note the actual meal time and confirmation number below. When dining arrangements are finalized, transfer the information to your PassPockets.

		Before calling, fill in everything
Our Hotel:		← to the left of this line.
Our Arrival Date:		

Date	Restaurant Name	Preferred Time	Actual Time	Confirmation Number

Planning

Getting There

Staying in Style

Touring

Feasting

Making Magic

Index

Notes & More

A Recipe for Fun

Make the most of your dining experience at Disneyland and in Southern California with these tips and tricks we've collected over the years:

"If you like the food at the **Rainforest Cafe** but don't like the loudness of the restaurant, ask to be seated on the top floor, outside. We did this one year and it was fabulous. Of course, kids like eating outside to begin with, so they didn't mind missing the jungle atmosphere. It was really peaceful—there's even a small waterfall so you can hear the trickling of the water vs. the elephants and gorillas."
— Contributed by peer reviewer Tina Peterson

"Here are two great **money-saving meal ideas**: 1. Eat for less at Redd Rockett's Pizza Port in Tomorrowland. The pasta dishes are very generously portioned, big enough for my daughter and me to split one dish, especially if we add an order of garlic bread. At $7.50 for the pasta and $4-ish for bread, you get a tasty and inexpensive Disney meal! 2. Share at the Blue Bayou. On our trip we each got a bowl of clam chowder and split a blackened chicken salad (fairly large), getting out of there for around $25. We even had mint juleps to drink and ice cream for dessert!" *— Contributed by vacationer Susan Billings*

"For Universal Studios Hollywood, I've always found the restaurants are overpriced and the food quality is poor. A great option is to get your hand stamped and stroll over to **CityWalk**. You can eat at a table-service restaurant like Hard Rock Cafe, Buco di Beppo, or Cafe Tu Tu Tango for roughly the same price as a counter-service restaurant in the park. Or you can get fast food at Panda Express, Dodger Dogs, or the best chili burgers in Southern California at Tommy's and save money." *— Contributed by vacationer Keith Burrus*

Magical Memory

"During a Disneyland visit with my husband and our close friends last year, we experienced a wonderfully unplanned, blissful moment. We all ordered Dole Whip Floats from the Tiki Juice Bar. Sitting on a shaded bench in the hub, we enjoyed our delicious treats. When we finished, as if by consensus, we all relaxed and closed our eyes and just rested for a moment. The breeze gently washed over us, and the sounds of the people all around us faded. After a short while, we all 'woke up' feeling refreshed and incredibly relaxed. It was like a mini-vacation within our vacation. Sometimes in the midst of all our planning and strategizing, it's good to just let the day unfold and allow the magic to appear out of nowhere."
...as told by Disney vacationer Nicola Winkel

Making More Magic

You're bold. You're daring. You're a traveller. Now, here's your passport to an even more magical Disneyland Resort vacation!

Once you've tasted Southern California, you'll hunger for more. Most visitors can only *nibble* at the many wonders this region holds. There is much, much more that can be done to make your vacation magical. We've been to Southern California more than most and yet there are *still so many* things we haven't done, and we add new discoveries to the wish list after every trip. It can all be a bit overwhelming, not to mention habit-forming.

If you tried to keep up with each new activity on the horizon, you'd have a full-time job on your hands. So we've narrowed things down a bit to the Disneyland Resort and a few choice locations. And to help you undertake your own magical explorations, we present a collection of useful information about some of Disneyland's lesser-known aspects and attractions. This is our "everything else" chapter.

To begin, we give you a backstage pass to the guided tours that Disney offers. Then it's on to recreational pursuits in and near Disneyland. From there, we lead you on a treasure hunt for fun tucked away inside the parks—both real "treasure hunts" and hunts for items you'll treasure. We've even added a mini worksheet for those of you who love to shop! Next we share our special tricks for feeling and looking like a VIP on your trip—a little extra-special attention can go a long way! Then we give you the low-down on childcare. Special occasions and events aren't forgotten either, with ideas, tips, and details on celebrating birthdays, engagements, honeymoons, anniversaries, holidays, and more. Before we say goodbye, we'll leave you with information for explorations beyond the Disneyland Resort at other Disney vacation spots—from exotic ports of call, to foreign lands, to home lands.

So get out that pixie dust and don your sorcerer's hat—we're making magic, Disney-style!

Sidebar tabs: Planning · Getting There · Staying in Style · Touring · Feasting · Making Magic · Index · Notes & More

Disney's Guided Tours

Disney does such a good job of hiding the figurative ropes and pulleys that you'll be disappointed if you hope to catch a glimpse of what makes Disney really work. To meet the growing demands of interminably curious guests, Disney offers tours and programs that satisfy the need for more knowledge, more trivia, more history, and more fun!

Unless otherwise noted, advance reservations may (and should be) made up to 30 days in advance by phoning 714-781-4400 or by visiting Guest Services (hotels) or Guest Relations (parks). Some discounts are available to Annual Passholders, Disney Visa cardholders, and AAA members. Note that to get the Disney Visa discount you must actually pay for the tour with your Disney Visa card. Foreign language and American Sign Language tours may be available with advance notice. Many tours require substantial walking and most are wheelchair accessible. Tours depart from the Tour Garden, located beside City Hall on Main Street U.S.A. (Disneyland Park). Cancel 48 hours in advance to avoid penalties. Tours that require regular park admission are noted with the ticket (🎟️) icon. Important: Bring photo ID with you for tour check-in.

■ Welcome to Disneyland [Both Parks] 🎟️

This 2 ½-hour tour introduces the magic of Disneyland to first-time guests, those who have not visited the park in recent years, and those with limited time to visit. The tour includes a park overview, trivia, history, tips, and suggestions designed to help you make the most of your visit. Tour participants receive a complimentary priority seating at a selected stage show or parade. Participants receive instructions on using the FASTPASS system plus two bonus FASTPASS tickets. Participants may also receive special access to at least one attraction. Note that the tour length may vary depending on wait time for attractions visited on the tour. Note also that this tour does not include backstage peeks. Times: Usually 10:00 am daily. Discounts: AAA members and Disney Visa cardholders receive 20% off this tour. Formerly called the "Red Carpet Experience" prior to mid-2004. Wheelchair accessible.	**$25** All ages On-stage only (no backstage peeks)

■ Discover the Magic [Disneyland Park] 🎟️

This fun, three-hour treasure hunt through the Disneyland Park is designed especially for families. Guests join forces with Disney characters to dig up musical clues and uncover hidden treasure on their adventure to help Mickey Mouse. There's plenty of character interaction, including a run-in with a Disney villain and a visit with a Disney princess! The hunt covers a lot of ground in the park, including Tom Sawyer Island, so be sure to wear those comfortable shoes! Lunch at Rancho del Zocalo is included in the tour, as is an exclusive souvenir gift. Pricing: $49/person for the first two tickets (there is a two-ticket minimum); $39/person for each additional ticket. Guests ages 18 and under must be accompanied by an adult. All ages may participate, but Disney feels kids ages 5-9 (and their watching parents) are likely to get the most from the experience. Times: 10:30 am and 2:00 pm daily. Discounts: Disney Visa cardholders receive 20% off this tour; Disneyland Annual Passholders save $10 per person on this tour.	**$49** All ages. No strollers are allowed on tour and guests 18 and under must be with an adult On-stage only (no backstage peeks)

Planning   Getting There   Staying in Style   Touring   Feasting   Making Magic   Index   Notes & More

☐ A Walk in Walt's Footsteps [Disneyland Park]

Enjoy a 3½-hour tour filled with park facts, trivia, and an exploration of Walt's personal vision and challenges while developing the world's original theme park. Includes a private lunch on the balcony of the Disney Gallery—the menu changes, but usually includes an entree (such as a salad or sandwich), a canned beverage, and a dessert. Guests also receive an exclusive collectible trading pin and a peek in the lobby of the private Club 33. There's even the possibility of a VIP ride in the Disneyland Railroad's presidential car ("Lilly Belle"). Tour participants also ride the Disneyland Railroad and enjoy a unique visit to the Enchanted Tiki Room. This tour is not recommended for toddlers as they'll probably lose interest quickly. Times: Typically 9:00 am and 2:30 pm daily. Discounts: AAA members and Disney Visa cardholders receive 20% off this tour; Disneyland Annual Passholders save $10 per person on this tour. We really enjoyed this tour and highly recommend it to anyone who wants a deeper look at Disneyland's history.	**$49** Ages 8 & up Peek inside Club 33

☐ From Imagination to Celebration [Disneyland Park]

This 3½-hour tour of each of Disneyland's decades leads guests through the park to experience representative attractions and lands in celebration of Disneyland's 50th Anniversary. The tour visits three of these five attractions: Storybook Land Boats, Pirates of the Caribbean, Big Thunder Railroad, Splash Mountain, and Buzz Lightyear's Astro Blasters. Guests wear special headphones that allow them to hear the tour guide regardless of group size or other noise. Tour participants enjoy reserved seating for a parade or fireworks. Additional goodies are several bonus FASTPASS tickets, a snack (chips, cookie, fruit, and water), souvenir group photograph, collectible pin, and replica Disneyland ticket book. Times: 10:00 am, 3:15 pm, and 5:00 pm (Monday–Thursday); 9:00 am, 12:15 pm, 4:00 pm, and 5:40 pm (Friday); and 8:00 am, 12:15 pm, 4:00 pm, and 5:40 pm (weekends). Discounts: Disney Visa cardholders receive 20% off this tour.	**$55** All ages On-stage only (no backstage peeks)

☐ Cruzin' Disney's California Adventure Tour

Beginning in early 2006, this new two-hour tour offers a unique opportunity to ride a Segway (a self-balancing, two-wheeled "vehicle"). Learn to use the Segway for the first hour, then practice riding around Disney's California Adventure over a variety of terrains. Max. weight is 250 lbs.; pregnant and special needs guests may not participate. Guests receive a special trading pin. Interesting photo opportunities also available on this tour. Discounts and other details not yet known.	**$75** All ages On-stage only (no backstage peeks)

☐ Holiday Tour [Disneyland Park]

Usually offered during the holiday season (mid-November through the first week of January), this tour teaches guests about Disneyland's holiday traditions. Guests also experience the holiday-themed attractions (Haunted Mansion Holiday and "it's a small world holiday"), a priority seating for the holiday parade, and a sweet treat.	**$49** All ages On-stage only

☐ VIP Tours

VIP tours (sometimes called Premiere Tours) can be booked exclusively for your group. These excursions include a knowledgeable host or hostess who helps plans your day, accompanies your group around the park(s), and offers Disney trivia and historical facts. A four-hour minimum is required. Not recommended for children. Prices start at $75/hour for up to ten guests and do not include admission. Parties with more than ten guests can arrange for a second tour guide. Arrangements must be made at least 48 hours in advance—call 714-300-7710.	**$75/hour** All ages On-stage only (no backstage peeks)

Recreation and Sports

Ready to work off all that delicious vacation food? Here's the skinny on recreation and sports at the Disneyland Resort and Southern California:

Fitness Centers—Each of the three Disney hotels (Grand Californian, Disneyland Hotel, and Disney's Paradise Pier) have fitness centers. Guests staying at these hotels have access to these fitness centers, which is included in the mandatory resort fee; non-guests cannot enter Disney's fitness centers. Details on each hotel's fitness centers are on pages 40, 44, and 48. Many other hotels have fitness centers—check with your hotel for fitness center availability, hours, and pricing. And if you are a member of a national fitness chain, check to see if they have branches in the area.

Team Mickey's Workout II at Paradise Pier

Tennis—Alas, no tennis courts exist at any of the three Disney hotels. If playing tennis is important, consider staying at one of the Good Neighbor Hotels that has a tennis court (see pages 51–64). The City of Anaheim has more than 50 public tennis courts—call 714-765-5233 for locations.

Swimming—Beyond the swimming pools at hotels (almost every hotel and motel has one, and they are almost always exclusively for hotel guests), there are several water parks (see pages 150, 154, and 176) and beaches (see pages 176–178).

Jogging—The Disneyland Resort is a fun place to jog—jogging paths are available through the hotels' grounds and you can venture into Downtown Disney in the early mornings when crowds are light. Several other hotels have jogging trails, too. The sidewalks around and near the Disneyland Resort are wide and well-lit, making for easy jogging, too. If you're serious about running, check out the inaugural Disney Half Marathon in September 2006—see page 239 for more details.

Golf—Again, no Disney golf at Disneyland, but there are plenty of other golf courses in the area. Nearest is probably Coyote Hills Golf Course (714-672-6800)—its championship course is just 7 miles from Disneyland. Black Gold Golf Course (714-961-0060) has great views and is 10 miles away. Tustin Ranch Golf Course (714-730-1611) has a four-star-rated course just 12 miles away. And Anaheim Hills Golf Course (714-998-3041) is 13 miles from Disneyland, but is the most affordable of those mentioned here.

Spa Treatments—The new Mandara Spa at Disney's Grand Californian Hotel (scheduled to open in early- to mid-2006) is a full-service spa with treatment rooms, a couples suite, steam rooms, and a "nail spa." For a look at Mandara's approach, see http://www.mandara.com. Other day spas in Anaheim and Orange County include the Burke Williams Day Spa (714-769-1360, http://www.burkewilliamsspa.com), The Spa and Fitness Club (714-850-0050, http://www.thespaandfitnessclub.com), and Glen Ivy Hot Springs Spa (909-277-3529, http://www.glenivy.com).

Sporting Events—See pages 175, 179, and 182 for stadiums and venues.

Treasure Hunts

There is hidden treasure at the Disneyland Resort. While it may not consist of golden doubloons, it is every bit as priceless. There are countless sets of often-hidden and always-valuable Disneyesque items for you to find during your vacation. Sometimes these items are purposely hidden; other times they are out in plain view for all to see but few to notice. Hunting for your favorite item can add a new dimension to your vacation! Here are our favorite things to collect:

Disney Characters and Autographs

Live Disney characters abound, and kids of all ages delight in spotting them. You can discover where some characters are "hiding" by checking with Guest Relations at both parks. If you want to "bag your catch," take photographs—and try to get yourself or your family in the picture! Keep in mind that characters are popular and crowds will form. If you know when your characters will appear, show up early to greet them. (Tip: Ask a Disney cast member about character appearances for the day.) You can also collect autographs from characters who are able to sign their name. Special autograph books are available at most shops, or you can bring your own. Or use the PassPorter's autograph space on pages 274–276. Try to bring a wide-barreled pen or marker so the character can hold it easily—their costumes may cover their fingers. You can also have the characters sign hats or shirts (which must be Disney or non-commercial), but shirts cannot be worn while they are being signed and you need something to slip under the fabric to provide a writing surface.

Pressed Pennies and Quarters

One of the least expensive souvenirs at the Disneyland Resort is pressed coins. Souvenir Pressed Coin machines, found throughout the resort, press different Disney designs onto pennies or quarters. Cost is 51 cents for a pressed penny and $1.25 for a pressed quarter. Designs differ from machine to machine, making a complete collection a worthy achievement. Bring rolls of shiny pennies and quarters along with you—the hunt for a money-changing machine isn't as much fun. While there are good lists of pressed coin machine locations on the Internet (try http://www.parkpennies.com), finding them is half the fun! **Tip**: Buy a keepsake book at Disney's gift shops to store your coins.

Free Stuff

Disney may seem to be a mecca to capitalism, but there are still free things for the taking, and they make great souvenirs! Some may even become collector's items one day. You can collect guidemaps, brochures, napkins, paper cups and plates, containers, bags, menus, and more.

Planning

Getting There

Staying in Style

Touring

Feasting

Making Magic

Index

Notes & More

Hidden Mickeys

Believe it or not, Disney intentionally hides "Mickeys" all over the place! The internationally recognized Mickey Mouse head (one big circle and two smaller circles for the ears) has been discovered hidden in murals, fences, shows—you name it, you can probably find a Mickey hidden somewhere in it! Disney fans maintain lists of these hidden Mickeys at Disneyland—try http://www.hiddenmickeys.org/disneyland. We made a list of our favorite Hidden Mickeys for a rainy day activity—how many hiding places can you find? Write your answers below.

# Location	Hint	Hiding Place
1. General	When parking on Daisy level 2, look between 3A and 3B for a clue!	
2. General	Ka-ching! Look at what you get when the cash register rings!	
3. General	The esplanade's benches are wide, but who's lying on their side?	
4. Disneyland Park	Visit Main Street Cinema today, and Mickey will light your way	
5. Disneyland Park	If you cruise the jungle a lot, a shield with Mickey you will spot.	
6. Disneyland Park	Go sailing with pirates and we'll bet you'll see lily pads that're all wet	
7. Disneyland Park	Peter Pan hopes you don't fall when you check the nursery wall.	
8. California Adventure	Across the road from Grizzly Peak is a strange cactus that you seek.	
9. California Adventure	Mulholland Madness is so cool— dive into a Mickey-shaped pool!	
10. California Adventure	Scooter the Muppet does a test but that pattern is no pest!	
11. California Adventure	Behind the big "R" I run, look to the ground for the fun.	
12. Disney's Grand Californian Hotel	Look to the branches, just below, on the tree of the hotel's logo	
13. Disney's Grand Californian Hotel	The Great Hall's clock case hides his head in the face	
14. Disneyland Hotel	As you check in, look to your feet for the swirls and circles oh-so-neat!	
15. Disney's Paradise Pier Hotel	The lamp's lifeguard is of fame, now that's the end of this game!	

Hidden Mickey hiding places are found on page 242.

Photographs and Memories

Many vacationers bring a camera or a camcorder to record their trip. Most seem content to simply take pictures as the mood strikes them, but you can also "collect" pictures as well! Here are some ideas for fun photograph collections: Disney puns and visual gags that often go unnoticed (try "holding up" the monorail track in your photos); your favorite spot at different times of the day; all of the "Kodak Picture Spot" signs; and pictures through the eyes of your children (give them their own camera). How about a photo of each family member next to their favorite attraction? If you take these same photos on return trips, you can make a "growth chart" over time. Another idea is to hold a family photo scavenger hunt for fun things and places around Disneyland.

Souvenirs

If you enjoy taking home souvenirs but you're tired of the usual T-shirts or postcards, consider beginning a new collection. Chances are that if you can collect it, Disney and every other attraction has it in their stores. Here are favorite collectibles: trading pins (see page 236 for details), patches (you can sew them onto your packs), figurines, hats, clothing, stuffed animals, mini bean bags, antenna balls, and themed toys. Love shopping? Here's a mini worksheet to help you organize the items you want to purchase for yourself and others in Southern California!

Who	What	Size/Color	$$	✔

PassPorter's Photographs

Ever wonder why we put ourselves in the photos that appear in these pages? Here's the story: Back in the early days of our first guidebook, "PassPorter Walt Disney World," we were the first to include actual photos of the parks in our book. Once other books caught up with us, we realized how boring it was to have a photo of just an empty room, or (even worse) nameless models. So we decided to make ourselves (and our friends and family members) models for our publication's photos. The feedback has been tremendous—our readers love seeing "real people" having fun on their vacations. We encourage you to try to duplicate our fun photos with your own friends and family!

In Search Of...

Quite often we're on the lookout for specific items, whether they be souvenirs or necessities. To help hunt down your treasures, here is a partial list of places to find some of the more commonly sought items:

Alcohol—You can buy a mixed drink, beer, or wine at any of the hotels, Downtown Disney, and Disney's California Adventure park. The only place that prohibits the sale or consumption of alcohol is Disneyland Park. There are also several liquor stores within walking distance of Disneyland on Harbor Blvd. Supermarkets (see Groceries below) also sell beer, wine, and liquor in California.

Baby Needs—The baby care centers in the two Disney parks sell common baby items, such as diapers, wipes, and formula. Your hotel's gift shop may stock these items as well.

Groceries—Snacks are available at most of the hotel shops. For more serious shopping, visit Wal-Mart or Target (see hours, phone numbers, and directions on page 27)—other options include Albertson's (810 S. State College, 714-533-4820) and Vons (130 W. Lincoln, 714-535-2288).

Gum—Gum is not sold on Disney property to avoid messes. If you need it, bring it with you or buy it off-property.

Lost Items—Lost and Found centers are located everywhere you go—generally near the front of the park or complex. You can also call Disney Lost and Found at 714-817-2166. Lost and found items are kept at each park only until closing. After that, they're transferred to Central Lost and Found to the left of the main entrance of Disney's California Adventure.

Medicine—Get prescription and over-the-counter medicines from these nearby drugstores: Sav-On (1 mile east of Disneyland, 1660 W. Katella, 714-530-0500), Rite Aid (3 miles south of Disneyland, 12897 Harbor Blvd., 714-636-1143), Walgreens (3 miles north of Disneyland, 1720 W. La Palma Ave., 714-991-3082), and CVS (7065 La Palma Ave., 714-228-2085). Walgreens is the only 24-hour drugstore in Anaheim.

Missing or Lost Persons—Should you become separated, immediately alert a cast member or go to Guest Relations. Teach kids how to recognize cast members. A message book is available at Guest Relations to help coordinate hook-ups, even if you aren't lost (yet). It's a good idea to choose a meeting place each day in the event you are separated from your family or friends. You may also find it helpful to give each member of your party a two-way radio or cell phone to stay in touch with one another. We also suggest you take a digital photo of kids each morning—this will help you if a child is lost. Consider using "Who's Shoes ID" tags (http://www.whosshoesid.com), too!

Money—ATMs (cash machines) are located in all the parks and resorts. See our park maps or Disney's guidemaps for locations. The Disneyland Resort accepts American Express, MasterCard, Visa, Discover, JCB, Diner's Club, traveler's checks, cash, Disney Dollars, and Disney Visa Reward Vouchers (see page 10 for details on the Disney Visa card). Personal checks are also accepted (with two forms of identification) in most spots.

Rain Gear—If you didn't bring an umbrella or poncho along, Disney will sell you one at virtually any shop. You may need to ask, but chances are they'll have something. Tip: If your poncho rips, bring it back to any shop and they'll replace it.

Souvenirs—Need a Disneyland souvenir before you go or after you return home? Call Disneyland DelivEARS at 800-362-4533 for mail-order shopping.

VIP Tips

Wake-Up Call
If you're staying at a Disney hotel, start your day with a call from Mickey. Just use the phone system to arrange a wake-up call, and when the phone rings, Mickey welcomes you to the new day! When your wake-up call comes in, press the speakerphone button so everyone in the room can hear it!

Disney's Walk of Magical Memories
Next time you're at Disneyland, look down at the esplanade (the plaza between Disneyland Park and Disney's California Adventure) and you'll see it is paved in personalized, hexagon-shaped bricks. You, too, can have your name, hometown, and special date engraved on a brick for $150. For an extra $35, you can buy an acrylic or wood replica of your brick to display at home. At press time, it takes about five months for your brick to appear in the esplanade after

Our "brick" at Disneyland

ordering. We have our own brick to commemorate our wedding (see photo). For more information and to order, call 800-760-3566. Discounts may be available for annual passholders—inquire at time of order.

Personalized Vacation T-Shirts
In recent years we've spotted families and groups of vacationers wearing t-shirts personalized with their name and/or vacation dates. Not only is this fun and celebratory, but having your group wear the same shirt makes it easier to spot each other in the crowds. Some vacationers make the shirts themselves using a computer and iron-on, inkjet transfer sheets available at most office supply stores. You can also order personalized shirts with Disney images at http://www.disneyinkshop.com.

Disney Shopping Service
Want a gift basket or stuffed Mickey delivered to your room? Disney hotel guests can call 714-300-7526 to order special items.

Planning

Getting There

Staying in Style

Touring

Feasting

Making Magic

Index

Notes & More

Disney Trading Pins

Colorful, enameled commemorative pins are a favorite Disney collectible, available at nearly every shop. Disney designs thousands of these colorful, cloisonné pins, which commemorate the theme parks, resorts, attractions, characters, and events. Over the years, Disney stepped up pin trading activity by introducing Pin Trading Stations at the parks and the Disney's Pin Traders shop at Downtown Disney, where you can buy and swap pins. Bring (or buy) your own Disney pins, and trade pins with other guests and with cast members wearing special pin-trading lanyards around their neck. Note that cast members wearing green lanyards trade only with children, and cast members

Jennifer displays trading pins on her hat and lanyard

can only trade metal pins that have "© Disney" stamped on the back. Pin trading is a fun way to meet fellow vacationers and learn more about the world of Disney. Buy a Disney pin lanyard, or display your pins in a scrapbook, or on a vest or hat (see photo above). We've collected hundreds of trading pins and proudly display them in our home on black felt squares attached to a corkboard. For more information, news, and an online pin store, visit http://eventservices.disney.go.com/pintrading/index. You may also enjoy this unofficial site with an index of known Disney pins, events, and message boards: http://www.dizpins.com.

Name Badges and Pins

Show everyone how special you are with an oval Disney name badge, personalized with your first name. The badges make great conversation starters—you may even get more personal attention from cast members while wearing one. You can purchase badges in the parks and at Downtown Disney for $6. Have an unusual name? Visit the engraving shops at these locations: Guide 2 Kiosk (to the right of the Opera House on Main Street), Pioneer Mercantile (Frontierland in Disneyland Park); Le Petit Chalet (Fantasyland in Disneyland Park), Souvenir 66 (near entrance of Disney's California Adventure), or World of Disney (Downtown Disney). You can also order Disney name badges in advance through the LaughingPlace.com store at http://www.laughingplacestore.com/badges. Another option is our own PassPorter Badge, which our readers requested to help them spot fellow fans in the parks. PassPorter Badges are $4 and also come with free personalization. You can order PassPorter Badges at our web site. We also issue our own collectible, cloisonné PassPorter Pins each year for $6 each—see page 279).

Childcare

"We're going to Disneyland. Why would we need childcare?" The Disneyland Resort is an adult playground, too. And as parents ourselves, we know there are times when the **grown-ups need alone time** or it's just not appropriate to drag along the kids. If you're looking for childcare (and you're not bringing along a nanny or grandparents), you can get private, in-room babysitting. And if you're a guest of a Disney hotel (Disneyland Hotel, Disney's Grand Californian, or Disney's Paradise Pier), you can use the services of Pinocchio's Workshop. Here are the details on both:

In-Room Childcare

Fullerton Child Care Agency has sitters who will come to your hotel room with age-appropriate toys and activities. The professional sitters will not take kids to the theme parks, but they will watch infants and children with some special needs. They are well-trained, bonded, and insured. Basic rates are $48 for the first four hours and $10 for each hour thereafter. We used their services when our son Alexander was 9 months old and it worked well for us. You can make reservations at 714-528-1640 at least 24 hours in advance. We suggest you bring a cell phone—and give the number to the sitter—so you can be within easy reach in the event there is a question or problem.

Pinocchio's Workshop

Disney's Grand Californian offers the Pinocchio's Workshop childcare program for guests of Disney's hotels. Pinocchio's Workshop is a good bit like daycare, but unlike daycare, their "day" usually starts at 5:00 pm and runs until midnight. The workshop—which is themed after a European carpenter's workshop—offers a variety of structured activities and entertainment, such as storytelling, board games, computer games, and videos. Snacks of fresh fruit are provided and you can pre-purchase a meal for $5 if your child is staying more than four hours. The program accepts children from 5 to 12 years of age, and all children must be potty-trained. Rates are $9/hour with no minimum stay. The program also has an overtime rate—the kids won't be evicted if your coach turns into a pumpkin on the way back from Sleeping Beauty Castle. Parents are given pagers, too. We recommend you call well in advance and ask plenty of questions. Reservations can be made at Pinocchio's Workshop itself or by phoning—guests staying at Disney's Grand Californian may reserve up to two months in advance; guests at Disneyland Hotel and Disney's Paradise Pier may only make same-day reservations. Cancel at least 24 hours in advance to avoid a $27 fee.

Special Occasions

It seems natural to celebrate a special occasion at Disney. It's designed for fun and comes predecorated! So whether you plan a trip around a special day or want to celebrate one that falls during your vacation, you can do it at Disney! Here are our tips and tricks for a magical celebration:

Birthdays—What better place to celebrate a birthday than at Disney? Be sure to request a birthday sticker at City Hall at Disneyland Park and at Guest Relations at Disney's California Adventure. Disneyland Hotel guests can visit the front desk for birthday button, too! Wear your sticker/button all day so cast members can wish you a "Happy Birthday!" While you are at City Hall, ask a cast member about a birthday call from Goofy—the cast member can dial a special extension so the birthday person can listen to Goofy wish them a happy day. Also at the Disneyland Park, there may be a "birthday cart" outside the Plaza Inn that sells commemorative birthday souvenirs, such as pins, balloons, Birthday Buckets, and birthday party tickets (see page 222). And let's not forget the birthday parties at Plaza Inn (see page 222). You can also pre-order a birthday cake if you're dining at a Disney restaurant—call 714-781-3463 at least 48 hours in advance.

Engagements—Disney is a magical place to propose to a loved one. Alas, you'll have to devise your own scheme as Disney does not offer official assistance.

Weddings—Of course you can get married at Disney! From intimate to traditional to themed, Disney's Fairy Tale Weddings have something for virtually every budget. Visit http://www.disneylandweddings.com or call 714-956-6527.

Honeymoons—The Disneyland Resort is a popular honeymoon destination. Not only are romantic spots found around virtually every corner, but Disney goes out of its way to make newlyweds welcome. Special vacation packages, romantic rooms, candlelit dinners, and adult-oriented entertainment abound. Even if you do nothing more than mention that it is your honeymoon to cast members, you may be in for a special treat. For details, call Disney at 800-854-3104. We honeymooned at Disneyland in May 2004—see the photo of our commemorative wedding brick on page 235.

Jennifer and Dave share a Mickey Rice Krispie Bar on their honeymoon

Anniversaries—Like birthdays, anniversaries are always in style at the Disneyland Resort. You can plan a special night out at a romantic restaurant or shape an entire vacation around your special day. Be sure to mention your anniversary when making priority seating arrangements.

Group Events—With all the conventions they host each year, Disney is a pro at group parties and functions. You can have a private party virtually anywhere in the resort for small or large groups. For information, call 714-956-6556 or visit http://www.disneyland.com and click on "Special Occasions." Restaurants at Downtown Disney can host private functions, too—contact them directly for details. Fan groups also like to gather for group events at Disneyland, such as MousePlanet.com's MouseAdventure, which is a fun, in-park game that takes place every six months (visit http://www.mouseplanet.com and click on "MouseAdventure" for details).

Special Events and Holidays

Disney really knows how to celebrate. Nearly every holiday seems to have at least one event, and Easter, Halloween, Christmas, and New Year's Eve spark extended festivities. Disney also is a master at battling periods of slow attendance with specially themed events throughout the year. Call Disneyland's main information line at 714-781-4565 for more details.

Festivals and Fun
Grad Nites party down at Disneyland Park from 11:00 pm to 5:00 am during the high school graduation season—for details, visit http://www.disneylandgradnite.com. Late June/early July should see the world premiere of the second "Pirates of the Caribbean" movie (debuts July 7, 2006) and there may be some fun events associated with that. The inaugural **Disneyland Half Marathon Weekend** is September 15-17, 2006—for details visit http://www.disneylandhalfmarathon.com and click on Special Events.

Easter (April 16, 2006)
Spring crowds reach a peak during Easter week, and some Disney park and hotel restaurants offer special Easter dinners (see page 222).

Mother's Day (May 14, 2006)
In addition to special Mother's Day menus at some Disneyland restaurants, each adult female who entered the park on Mother's Day 2005 received a free carnation!

Independence Day (July 4, 2006)
Disneyland Park traditionally puts on a spectacular fireworks show for park guests.

Halloween (October 31, 2006)
The Haunted Mansion gets its "Haunted Mansion Holiday" facelift with Jack Skellington and other characters and decor from movie "The Nightmare Before Christmas." This holiday makeover is very detailed and very well done—it's frightfully good! There's also a great chance that the Halloween party held at Disney's California Adventure in 2005 (called "Mickey's Halloween Treat") will return in 2006. The not-so-scary party proved very popular—all dates sold out. Here's what it was like in 2005: kid-friendly spookiness invaded Disney's California Adventure for six nights from 7:30 pm to 10:30 pm in late October (the weekend before Halloween and the four days leading up to Halloween, but not Halloween night). Guests enjoy trick-or-treating around the park at 13 stations (each with candy or a Halloween sticker), Halloween-themed character greetings, face painting, Halloween crafts, live entertainment (Monster Mash Bash, Hokey Pokey Hoedown, and Boogieman Boogie), free Boardwalk games, and a character farewell at the end of the night. Tickets were $20/person (or $15 to annual passholders and Disney Visa cardholders). Each guest received a plastic treat bag and a special Halloween guidemap with space for the Halloween stickers. Most of the park was open, with the notable exception of Golden State. Special note: While guests of all ages may wear costumes during Mickey's Halloween Party, adults are not otherwise allowed to wear costumes in Disneyland's parks, even on Halloween (so costumed grown-ups should bring a change of clothes if they want to go over to Disneyland Park after the party). To find out what, if anything, is happening for Halloween in 2006, keep an eye on Disneyland's web site or call Disneyland in the summer (tickets for the 2005 event went on sale September 15, 2005).

Tip: Knott's Berry Farm becomes Knott's Scary Farm around Halloween (see page 142).

Special Events and Holidays *(continued)*

Thanksgiving *(November 23, 2006)*

Crowds take a bump up for this All-American holiday. Disney's holiday decorations are on their way up, and a number of the full-service restaurants at the parks, almost all of the Disney hotels, and many Downtown Disney eateries host special holiday dinners.

Christmas *(December 25, 2006)*

Christmas is a special time, with delightful decorations, holiday entertainment, and countless ways to enjoy the season. Decorations go up around Thanksgiving, so there's more than a month of merriment. Try to come during the first two weeks of December when the crowds are (slightly) thinner, the party is in full swing, and the resort is decked with holiday cheer. A tree-lighting ceremony takes place daily in Disneyland Park and "it's a small world" (see page 101) gets dressed up for the holidays. Big Thunder Ranch (see page 98) transformed into Santa's Reindeer Round-Up in 2005 and may do so again in 2006. The Christmas Fantasy Parade may also make an appearance at Disneyland Park. Snow falls on Main Street, U.S.A. after the nightly fireworks. The traditional **Candlelight Processional** has been running since 1958 and features a celebrity narrator, chorus, and orchestra presenting the Christmas tale. The show is performed inside Disneyland Park, and no extra admission (beyond regular park admission) is required. A special dinner package offers reserved seating (call 714-781-3463 in early November for details). In 2005, the Candlelight Processional was held on December 3 and 4, hosted by Dick Van Dyke, and the dinner packages were available for $60/adult and $15/kid at Storyteller's Cafe and Napa Rose and for $40/adult and $15/kid at Granville's and Hook's Pointe.

New Year's Eve *(December 31, 2006)*

Both Disneyland Park and Disney's California Adventure host big New Year celebrations. The theme parks overflow during the Christmas-New Year's week, and reservations at hotels are hard to get. Disney charges regular admission to the parks on New Year's Eve, but it is very crowded and the park is likely to impose admission restrictions due to large crowds.

Other Holidays and Observances

Of most significance is **The Happiest Homecoming on Earth**, which runs through 2006—see page 108. The **Unofficial Gay Days** group has a "Mini Gay Day" on April 1, 2006, and a longer event on the first long weekend in October (October 6–8, 2006)—for more information, visit http://www.gayday2.com). The Unofficial Gay Days event drew about 25,000 attendees in 2005 (most of them wearing red shirts).

"it's a small world holiday" shines merrily on a wet winter evening

More Disney Destinations

Like any other forward-thinking organization, The Walt Disney Company has expanded into other locales. Here are the details:

Walt Disney World Resort (Florida)— Forty-seven square miles of fun are packed into Disney's flagship resort in Florida, complete with four major theme parks, two water parks, several more minor parks, and more than 20 Disney resort hotels. You can learn more about the resort at http://www.disneyworld.com. We cover the entire Walt Disney World Resort in our bestselling guidebook, "PassPorter® Walt Disney World® Resort." For more details and to order a copy, visit http://www.passporter.com/wdw (see page 280).

Disney Cruise Line (Caribbean and Beyond)—"Take the magic of Disney and just add water!" The Disney Cruise Line set sail in 1998 with the same enthusiasm and energy you find at the other Disney resorts. Learn more at http://www.disneycruise.com. Pick up a copy of our popular guidebook, "PassPorter's Field Guide to the Disney Cruise Line and Its Ports of Call" (available in bookstores or order online at http://www.passporter.com/dcl—more details on page 281).

Disneyland Paris Resort (France)—The first (and only) Disney resort in Europe, the park has a similar layout to Disneyland, with the major change being a substitution of the Jules Verne-styled Discoveryland for Tomorrowland. The new Walt Disney Studios theme park opened across the plaza in 2002. Visit http://www.disneylandparis.com for more details. We visited Disneyland Paris in late February 2005 and experienced real snow on Main Street. Brrrr!

More Disney Destinations (continued)

Tokyo Disney Resort (Japan)–Disney, Japan-style! Tokyo Disney Resort is located in Urayasu, just outside Tokyo. It is similar to Disneyland in California, incorporating the quintessential "American" things. When Jennifer visited, she found it squeaky clean and definitely Disney, with just a touch of Japanese peeking through. In 2001, Tokyo DisneySea theme park opened immediately adjacent to Tokyo Disneyland. The aquatically themed park has seven lands and a deluxe resort, Hotel MiraCosta. Visit http://www.tokyodisneyresort.co.jp and click "English."

Hong Kong Disneyland–Just opened in September 2005, this new theme park overlooks the water of Penny's Bay, Lantau. The park has just four lands—Main Street, U.S.A., Adventureland, Fantasyland, and Tomorrowland—but the park is already proving popular! For details, visit http://www.hongkongdisneyland.com and click "English."

Disney's Vero Beach Resort–Vero Beach, Florida, is Disney's first oceanside resort, a two-hour drive from Walt Disney World. Relaxing and definitely laid-back compared to the parks, Vero Beach Resort offers the chance to get some real rest. But there's also plenty to do nearby—nightclubs, theater, movies, restaurants, cultural events, recreation, and of course, walking on the beach (very important). Call 561-234-2000 for more information, or visit http://www.disneyvacationclub.com and click Resorts.

Disney's Hilton Head Island Resort–For southern grace and charm, experience the Carolina Low Country lifestyle at Disney's Hilton Head Island Resort. Hilton Head is a golfer's nirvana, boasting 12 nearby golf courses. The tennis and beaches are also big draws. It's an ideal spot for small group retreats. For more information, call 843-341-4100.

DisneyQuest–This is a large, indoor theme park located at Downtown Disney at Walt Disney World. Visit http://www.disneyquest.com.

Hidden Mickey Hiding Places (from list on page 232)

1) Between poles 3A and 3B on the second level (Daisy) of the Mickey & Friends parking structure; 2) On cash register receipts; 3) The concrete supports on the ends of benches in the esplanade; 4) The shape of the lights in the steps leading into the Main Street Cinema; 5) On a shield on the other side of the river as you board your Jungle Cruise boat; 6) The lily pads in the water as you pass Blue Bayou on Pirates of the Caribbean; 7) Mickey picture on the nursery wall during Peter Pan's Flight; 8) The Mickey-shaped cactus across from Grizzly Peak Recreation Area; 9) The Mickey-shaped pool on the billboard for Mulholland Madness; 10) Mickey appears in the test pattern on the TV screen during Muppet*Vision 3-D's pre-show; 11) A Mickey-shaped piece of rock or glass behind the big "R" that forms the "CALIFORNIA" signs in front of the park; 12) At the bottom of the branches in the redwood tree of the Grand Californian Hotel's logo; 13) In the face of the grandfather clock across from the fireplace in the Great Hall; 14) The carpet in the Disneyland Hotel lobby has Mickey-shaped swirls; 15) The lamps in the guest rooms have Mickey perched on a lifeguard stand.

Beyond This Book

Like us, many other people love to write about Disneyland and Southern California. And, happily, we all love to read about it! We know many fascinating topics fall outside the scope of this guidebook, but we can at least guide you to the better books and web sites. Enjoy!

Our Favorite Disneyland Books

Disneyland Detective by Kendra Trahan ($19.95; ISBN: 0-9717464-0-0; Permagrin Publishing) is a treasure trove of nearly hidden details at Disneyland. The book is filled with fascinating trivia, locations of Hidden Mickeys, historical lore, and delightful sketches of Disney imagineers, legends, and other heroes. This is essentially a guided tour in a neat little book. It's great for armchair travel enthusiasts, too.

Magic Quizdom by Kevin Yee and Jason Schultz ($17.99; 0-9728398-0-1; Zauberreich Press) is stuffed with Disneyland trivia questions in three levels of difficulty. The answers are in separate sections with nice, long explanations. Use the book as a trivia game or just read the answer sections to gain a fascinating peek into the history and magic of Disneyland.

101 Things You Never Knew About Disneyland also by Kevin Yee and Jason Schultz ($14.95; 0-9728398-1-X; Zauberreich Press) is a collection of lesser-known stories and tributes, many of which were learned directly from Disney Imagineers. Among the 101 gems in this book, you'll learn about the special palm tree in Adventureland, a pumpkin that honors a Disneyland official, and a special appearance by Eeyore at Indiana Jones.

Mouse Tales: A Behind-the-Ears Look at Disneyland ($13.95; 0-9640605-6-6; Bonaventure Press) and *More Mouse Tales: A Closer Peek Backstage at Disneyland* ($14.95; 0-9640605-8-2; Bonaventure Press). Author David Koenig presents a less squeaky-clean version of Disneyland in these semi-exposés. Even so, you're more likely to find dust bunnies than real dirt in this book—the author is still a Disney admirer. This is fascinating reading if you're interested in peeking behind the scenes.

Unofficial Guide to Disneyland by Bob Sehlinger ($15.99; 0-7645-8342-5; Wiley Publishing) is a great source for advice on touring Disneyland. It offers more than ten touring plans, plus really solid information on reducing wait times in Disneyland. It's an excellent companion to PassPorter.

Welcome Aboard the Disneyland Railroad by Steve DeGaetano ($64.95; 0-9758584-0-9; Steam Passages) is an hefty book in size, price, and content. If you love railroads, you'll adore this book filled with elaborate detail, in-depth histories, and more than 100 color photographs.

Planning

Getting There

Staying in Style

Touring

Feasting

Making Magic

Index

Notes & More

Beyond This Book (continued)

For those who venture beyond Disneyland, here are several titles on Southern California we find helpful when we travel:

NFT Not For Tourists Guide to Los Angeles by Jane Pirone ($21.95; 0-9758664-8-6; American Map) is a huge compendium of practical information on Los Angeles. Despite its name, we find it an extremely handy reference to have on our trips, and its many, many maps are clear, concise, and easy to read. It helps you find most anything in the area!

Free Orange County ($12.95; 0-970642-2-0; CorleyGuide) and *Free L.A.* ($12.95; 0-9706242-1-2; CorleyGuide), both by Robert Stock, are guides to all the free things to do near Disneyland (Orange County) and in Los Angeles. For example, the Oak Canyon Nature Center in Anaheim is a 58-acre park that offers free admission and free nature programs on Saturday mornings at 10:00 am (714-998-8380).

Our Favorite Disneyland Web Sites

Yes, we know this book is filled with web sites we enjoy, but several of them deserve special mention.

MousePlanet.com (http://www.mouseplanet.com) is where we go to learn about the latest buzz at Disneyland. Beyond its many informative columns and articles on Disneyland, it also produces a weekly update with exhaustive details on what's new and changed. Bookmark this site!

AllEarsNet.com (http://www.allearsnet.com), best known for its unparalleled information on Walt Disney World, it has recently begun expanding its coverage to Disneyland with excellent results. Beyond the informative attraction guides, you'll also find most Disneyland eatery menus listed here (and they're up-to-date, too).

LaughingPlace.com (http://www.laughingplace.com) is produced by two die-hard Disneyland fans and includes guides to Disneyland's attractions and events, complete with photos and ratings.

MiceAge.com (http://www.miceage.com) offers timely, in-depth articles on Disney parks, with a distinct focus on Disneyland. Its discussion area—MiceChat—has a very active Disneyland message forum.

MouseSavers.com (http://www.mousesavers.com) may not offer a lot of information or advice on Disneyland in general, but it is packed full of really useful tips on saving money and timely deals. Everyone going to Disneyland should do a thorough scan of this site.

IntercotWest.com (http://www.intercotwest.com) offers news bites and reviews on Disneyland, but it really shines with its popular discussion forums categorized into more than 10 sub-forums devoted to Disneyland.

ThemeParkInsider.com (http://www.themeparkinsider.com) offers basic information and vacationer ratings and reviews for Disneyland attractions (among many other theme parks). We found it to be quite comprehensive, though perhaps not as detailed as we like.

Yesterland.com (http://www.yesterland.com) takes you back in time to discontinued Disneyland attractions, complete with photos, delightful detail, and trivia. If you've been to Disneyland before, you'll love finding and touring your old favorites on this site.

VisionsFantastic.com (http://www.visionsfantastic.com) is a relative newcomer on the Disneyland web scene, offering gorgeous multimedia content with rich photos and informative updates. While some of the content requires registration (free), this site is really a treat for the eyes and food for the brain.

MouseInfo.com (http://www.mouseinfo.com) began as an information site but has really found its calling in its much-frequented message boards that focus on Disneyland.

WestCoaster.net (http://www.westcoaster.net) is an irreverent site with the latest news, photos, and technical specs on West Cost thrill rides.

ColdDeadFish.com (http://www.colddeadfish.net/csdlr.html), despite its unusual name, contains plenty of in-depth articles on Disneyland, including select reviews of eateries, attractions, events, and guided tours, plus trip reports.

DISboards.com (http://www.disboards.com) has an extremely active dicussion forum for Disneyland, including a large repository of Disneyland trip reports. This is where you'll learn what fellow vacationers think of vacationing in Disneyland.

Doug's Disneyland Page (http://www.pacificsites.com/~drhoades) is a fan site with an in-depth tour of Disneyland Park.

The Sounds of Disneyland (http://gwensmith.com/dland) is fun for your ears, offering clips from Disneyland attractions and environs.

Iago & Zazu's Attraction of the Week (http://aotw.figzu.com) conveys amazing details about Disney's attractions in the form of hilarious conversations between Iago ("Aladdin") and Zazu ("The Lion King").

Your Own Disneyland

These tips and memories show how Disneyland can be your playground!

"In order to help find each other if you are separated for any reason, **carry walkie talkies** (we found ours at the Disney Store). Also plan to wear matching shirts—on our trip we all wore red one day, blue the next day, etc."—*Contributed by Disney vacationer Kristine Chase*

Write to us and **share your experiences, memories, and tips**. If we use them, we'll credit you in PassPorter and send you a copy! Drop us a note at P.O. Box 3880, Ann Arbor, Michigan 48106 or e-mail us at memories@passporter.com.

Magical Memories

"For weeks before we took our 18-month-old (now 17-year-old) daughter to Disneyland, my husband would say, 'When you see Mickey, are you going to give him a kiss on the nose?' They rehearsed HOW she would do this every day. Finally we arrived at Disneyland, and lo and behold, there was Mickey on Main Street. While many children were scared by Mickey's size (he's much bigger than on television), my daughter took one look and made a beeline to him with her arms outstretched. Mickey bent down, and our daughter put one hand on either side of his nose, making sure there was no way she could miss giving Mickey his "kiss on the nose." We got the impression that even Mickey was surprised by this tot. Last year, we were at Disney's California Adventure and found Mickey. My teenager made sure she was able to once again kiss Mickey on the nose ... perhaps to show her Dad that she does listen to him at times."

...as told by Disney vacationer Debbie Mekler

"For a special birthday treat for my seven-year-old niece Mary Graves, we dined at Goofy's Kitchen with hopes of seeing Cinderella. Not only was she there, but she carried out Mary's birthday cake and sang to her along with Snow White, Jasmine, and Aladdin. Mary (a frequent guest of Walt Disney World and Cinderella's Royal Table) is not often silenced by Disney characters, but this special treat left her speechless. She couldn't even answer Cinderella when asked how old she was. The characters are more interactive, and different characters kept appearing. We counted nine different characters in one dinner. When Mary returned home, NO ONE was allowed to wish her a happy birthday because it might erase Cinderella's special birthday wish!"

...as told by Disney vacationer Mary Karlo

"My husband surprised me with an 18th anniversary trip to Disneyland! We got engaged there and then moved across the country. (While we adore Disney World, the intimate spaces at Disneyland just cry out for romantic moments.) With the help of Disney cast members, my husband placed small red hearts just outside of various rides, and I collected these as we walked. The hearts were like a treasure hunt, with each one a clue to the next location! My last heart was an invitation to dinner at the Grand Californian, where he had prearranged a bottle of the same wine we had our engagement Disney dinner and had ordered a small duplicate of the top of our wedding cake. It was truly a magical evening, and although we were in a place full of other Valentine's couples and families, I felt like we were all alone in the most magical place on earth!"

...as told by Disney vacationer Jane Peters

Index

We feel that a comprehensive index is very important to a successful travel guide. Too many times we've tried to look something up in other books only to find there was no entry at all, forcing us to flip through pages and waste valuable time. When you're on the phone with a reservation agent and looking for that little detail, time is of the essence.

You'll find the PassPorter index is complete and detailed. Whenever we reference more than one page for a given topic, the major topic is in **bold** to help you home in on exactly what you need. For those times you want to find everything there is to be had, we include all the minor references. We have plenty of cross-references, too, just in case you don't look it up under the name we use.

P.S. This isn't the end of the book. More nifty features begin on page 265!

Planning

Getting There

Staying in Style

Touring

Feasting

Making Magic

Index

Notes & More

Planning

Getting There

Staying in Style

Touring

Feasting

Making Magic

Index

Notes & More

Planning
Getting There
Staying in Style
Touring
Feasting
Making Magic
Index
Notes & More

Planning

Getting There

Staying in Style

Touring

Feasting

Making Magic

Index

Notes & More

Planning

Getting There

Staying in Style

Touring

Feasting

Making Magic

Index

Notes & More

Planning

Getting There

Staying in Style

Touring

Feasting

Making Magic

Index

Notes & More

Web Site Index

Planning

Getting There

Staying in Style

Touring

Feasting

Making Magic

Index

Notes & More

Web Site Index (continued)

Planning

Getting There

Staying in Style

Touring

Feasting

Making Magic

Index

Notes & More

Web Site Index (continued)

Planning · Getting There · Staying in Style · Touring · Feasting · Making Magic · Index · Notes & More

Notes & Photos

Whether you run out of space somewhere else or want to get your favorite character's autograph, these pages stand ready! Among these note pages we've included a small photo gallery with images we didn't have room to include earlier. Enjoy!

The Matterhorn, Monorail, and Club Buzz

Planning

Getting There

Staying in Style

Touring

Feasting

Making Magic

Index

Notes & More

Notes & Photos

The 50-ft. titanium gold sun at
Disney's California Adventure

Notes & Photos

Planning

Getting There

Staying in Style

Touring

Feasting

Making Magic

Index

Notes & More

Downtown Disney during the holidays

© MediaMarx, Inc.

Notes & Photos

California Screamin' and Sun Wheel

Notes & Photos

Planning

Getting There

Staying in Style

Touring

Feasting

Making Magic

Index

Notes & More

A hideaway in New Orleans Square

Notes & Photos

Haunted Mansion during the holidays

Notes & Photos

Planning

Getting There

Staying in Style

Touring

Feasting

Making Magic

Index

Notes & More

Jumpin' Jellyfish

Notes & Photos

Bur-r-r Bank Ice Cream at Disney's California Adventure

Notes & Photos

Planning

Getting There

Staying in Style

Touring

Feasting

Making Magic

Index

Notes & More

The Golden Zephyr

Planning

Getting There

Staying in Style

Touring

Feasting

Making Magic

Index

Notes & More

Autographs

Kids and kids-at-heart love to get autographs from Disney characters! These two pages beg to be filled with signatures, paw prints, and doodles from your favorite characters. We've even provided places to write the actual name of the character (they can be hard to read—they are autographs, after all), plus the location you discovered the character and the date of your find. Even if you bring or purchase an autograph book, use these pages when you fill it up or just plain forget it. (Been there, done that!) Be sure to see page 231 for tips and tricks on how to get character autographs, too!

Character: *Location:* *Date:*

Character: *Location:* *Date:*

Character: *Location:* *Date:*

Autographs Anonymous

We know. We understand. Bouncing tigers and giant mice can be intimidating. After several months of research and development, we came up with the following system that can help both the interminably shy and the overly stimulated. Just write your name in the blank below, take a deep breath, and hold out your book. Now, wasn't that easy?

Hi, my name is _____. **May I have your autograph?**

(write your name here)

Character:
Location: Date:

Character:
Location: Date:

Character: Location: Date:

Character: Location: Date:

Planning

Getting There

Staying in Style

Touring

Feasting

Making Magic

Index

Notes & More

More Autographs

Character: Location: Date:

Character: Location: Date:

Character: Location: Date:

Character: Location: Date:

PassPorter Online

A wonderful way to get the most from your PassPorter is to visit our active web site at http://www.passporter.com. We serve up valuable PassPorter updates, plus useful Disneyland and S. California information and advice we couldn't jam into our book. You can swap tales (that's t-a-l-e-s, Mickey!) with fellow vacationers, play contests and games, find links to other sites, get plenty of details, and ask us questions. You can also order PassPorters and shop for PassPorter accessories and travel gear! The latest information on new PassPorters to other destinations is available on our web site as well. To go directly to our latest list of page-by-page PassPorter updates, visit http://www.passporter.com/customs/bookupdates.htm.

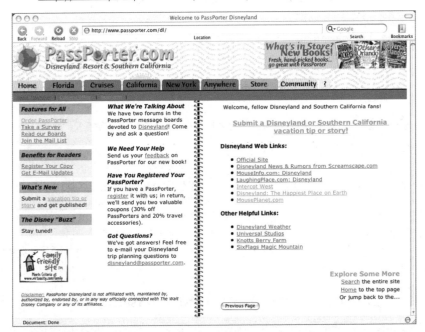

PassPorter Web Sites	Address (URL)
Main Page: PassPorter Online	http://www.passporter.com
Disneyland Forum	http://www.passporter.com/dl
PassPorter Message Boards	http://www.passporterboards.com
Book Updates	http://www.passporter.com/customs/bookupdates.htm
Luggage Log and Tag Maker	http://www.passporter.com/wdw/luggagelog.htm
Rate the Rides, Resorts, Restaurants	http://www.passporter.com/dl/rate.htm
Register Your PassPorter	http://www.passporter.com/register.htm
PassPorter Deluxe Edition Information	http://www.passporter.com/wdw/deluxe.htm

Planning

Getting There

Staying in Style

Touring

Feasting

Making Magic

Index

Notes & More

Register Your PassPorter

We are <u>very</u> interested to learn how your vacation went and what you think of the PassPorter, how it worked (or didn't work) for you, and your opinion on how we could improve it! We encourage you to register your copy of PassPorter with us—in return for your feedback, we'll send you **two valuable coupons** good for discounts on PassPorters and PassHolder pouches when purchased directly from us. You can register your copy of PassPorter at http://www.passporter.com/register.htm, or you can send us a postcard or letter to P.O. Box 3880, Ann Arbor, Michigan 48106.

Report a Correction or Change

Keeping up with the changes at Disneyland and S. California is virtually impossible without your help. When you notice something is different from what is printed in PassPorter, or you just come across something you'd like to see us cover, please let us know! Report your news, updates, changes, and corrections at http://www.passporter.com/dl/report.htm.

Contribute to the Next Edition of PassPorter

You can become an important part of the next edition of PassPorter Disneyland and Southern California! The easiest way is to rate the hotels, rides, and/or restaurants at http://www.passporter.com/dl/rate.htm. Your ratings and comments become part of our reader ratings throughout the book and help future readers make travel decisions. Want to get more involved? Send us a vacation tip or magical memory—if we use it in a future edition of PassPorter, we'll credit you by name in the guidebook and send you a free copy of the edition!

Get Your Questions Answered

We love to hear from you! Alas, due to the thousands of e-mails and hundreds of phone calls we receive each week we cannot offer personalized advice to all our readers. But there's a great way to get your questions answered: ask your fellow readers! Visit our message boards at http://www.passporterboards.com, join for free, and post your question. In most cases, fellow readers and Disney fans will offer their ideas and experiences! Our message boards also function as an ultimate list of frequently asked questions. Just browsing through to see the answers to other readers' questions will reap untold benefit! This is also a great way to make friends and have fun while planning your vacation. But be careful—our message boards can be addictive!

PassPorter Goodies

PassPorter was born out of the necessity for more planning, organization, and a way to preserve the memories of a great vacation! Along the way, we've found other things that either help us use the PassPorter better, appreciate our vacation more, or just make our journey a little more comfortable. Others have asked us about them, so we thought we'd share them with you. Order online at http://www.passporterstore.com, call us toll-free 877-929-3273, or use the order form below.

PassPorter® PassHolder is a small, lightweight nylon pouch that holds passes, I.D. cards, passports, money, and pens. Wear it around your neck for hands-free touring and for easy access at the airport. The front features a clear compartment, a zippered pocket, and a velcro pocket; the back has a small pocket (perfect size for FASTPASS) and two pen slots. Adjustable cord. Royal blue. $4 \frac{7}{8}" \times 6 \frac{1}{2}"$

Quantity:
____ x $7.95

PassPorter® Badge personalized with your name! Tour Southern California in style with our lemon yellow oval pin. Price includes personalization with your name, shipping, and handling. Please indicate badge name(s) with your order.

Quantity:
___ x $4.00

Name(s): _____

PassPorter® Pin is our collectible, cloissone pin. The current version depicts our colorful PassPorter logo, the pages of a book, and the words, "The World is an Open Book." The pin measures nearly $1 \frac{1}{2}$ in diameter. Watch for new pins to be introduced each year!

Quantity:
___ x $6.00

Please ship my PassPorter goodies to:

Name ....

Address...

City, State, Zip...

Daytime Phone...

Payment: ❏ Check (make payable to "MediaMarx")

❏ MasterCard ❏ Visa ❏ American Express ❏ Discover

Card number ....Exp. Date. ....

Signature ....

Sub-Total:

Tax*:

Shipping**:

Total:

* Include 6% sales tax if you live in Michigan.
**Shipping costs are:
$5 for totals up to $9
$6 for totals up to $19
$7 for totals up to $29
$8 for totals up to $39
Delivery takes 1–2 weeks.

Send your order form to P.O. Box 3880, Ann Arbor, MI 48106, call us toll-free at 877-WAYFARER (877-929-3273), or order online http://www.passporterstore.com/store.

Planning

Getting There

Staying in Style

Touring

Feasting

Making Magic

Index

Notes & More

More PassPorters

You've asked for more PassPorters—we've listened! We now publish five PassPorter titles, all designed to make your Disney vacation the best it can be. And if you've wished for a PassPorter with all the flexibility and features of a daily planner, check out our Deluxe Editions (described below). To learn more about new PassPorters and get release dates, please visit us at http://www.passporter.com.

PassPorter Disneyland Deluxe Edition

Design first-class vacations with this loose-leaf ring binder edition. The Deluxe Edition features the same great content as the PassPorter Disneyland spiral guide. Special features of the Deluxe Edition include ten interior storage slots in the binder to hold guidemaps, ID cards, and a pen (we even include a pen). The Deluxe binder makes it really easy to add, remove, and rearrange pages ... you can even download, print, and add in updates and supplemental pages from our web site, and refills are available for purchase. Learn more at http://www.passporter.com/wdw/deluxe.htm. The Deluxe Edition is available through bookstores by special order—just give your favorite bookstore the ISBN for the 2006 Deluxe Edition (1587710056).

PassPorter Walt Disney World Resort

It all started with Walt Disney World (and a mouse)! Our Walt Disney World guidebook covers everything you need to plan a practically perfect vacation, including fold-out park maps, resort room layout diagrams, KidTips,

descriptions, reviews, and ratings for the resorts, parks, attractions, and restaurants, and much more! This edition also includes 14 organizer pockets you can use to plan your trip before you go, hold papers while you're there, and record your memories for when you return. Learn more and order at http://www.passporter.com/wdw or get a copy at your favorite bookstore. Our Walt Disney World 2006 edition is available in a spiral-bound edition (ISBN: 1587710277) and a Deluxe Edition (ISBN: 1587710285)—both have 14 PassPockets. Our 2007 edition will be available in November 2006—ISBN-13 codes are 978-1-58771-033-9 (spiral edition) and 978-1-58771-034-6 (deluxe starter kit). You can order any of these editions on our web site or through a bookstore.

Even More PassPorters

PassPorter's Field Guide to the Disney Cruise Line and its Ports of Call—Fourth Edition

Completely updated for 2006! Get your cruise plans in shipshape with our updated field

guide! Authors Jennifer and Dave Marx cover the Disney Cruise Line in incredible detail, including deck plans, stateroom floor plans, original photos, menus, entertainment guides, port/shore excursion details, and plenty of worksheets to help you budget, plan, and record your cruise information. Now in its fourth edition, this is the original and most comprehensive guidebook devoted to the Disney Cruise Line! Learn more and order your copy at http://www.passporter.com/dcl or get a copy at your favorite bookstore (paperback, no PassPockets: ISBN: 1587710307). Also available in a Deluxe Edition with organizer PassPockets (ISBN: 1587710315).

PassPorter's Walt Disney World For Your Special Needs

It's hardly a one-size-fits-all world at Disney's Orlando resort, yet everyone seems to fit. And Walt Disney World does more to accommodate their many needs than just about anyone. You'll see more wheelchairs and electric scooters in Disney parks than you're likely to see anywhere else. If you know to ask, Disney has devices to help a hearing- or vision-impaired guest, park maps and translation devices, "Special Assistance" passes for children with autism or ADD, chefs and waiters schooled to serve a wide spectrum of special dietary needs, rides sized to fit guests of various abilities and dimensions ... you could fill a book, and indeed, that's what authors Deb Wills and Debra Martin Koma have done! They've prepared more than 400 pages of in-depth information for Walt Disney World vacationers of all abilities, delivering in-depth coverage of every ride, attraction and resort on Walt Disney World property from a distinctive "special needs" perspective. Learn more and order your copy at http://www.passporter.com/wdw/specialneeds or get a copy at your favorite bookstore (ISBN: 1587710188).

PassPorter's Treasure Hunts at Walt Disney World

Have even more fun at Walt Disney World! Jennifer and Dave's treasure hunts have long been a favorite part of PassPorter reader gatherings at Walt Disney World, and now you can join in the fun. Gain a whole new appreciation of Disney's fabulous attention to detail as you search through the parks and resorts for the little (and big) things that you may never have noticed before. Great for individuals, families, and groups, with hunts for people of all ages and levels of Disney knowledge. Special, "secure" answer pages make sure nobody can cheat. Prepared with plenty of help from Jen and Jeff Carter, famous for their all-day, all-parks scavenger hunts. Learn more at http://www.passporter.com/wdw/hunts or get a copy at your favorite bookstore (ISBN: 1587710269).

To order any of our guidebooks, visit http://www.passporterstore.com or call toll-free 877-929-3273. PassPorter guidebooks are also available in your local bookstore. If you don't see it on the shelf, just ask!

Note: The ISBN codes above apply to our 2006–2007 editions. For the latest edition, ask your bookstore to search their database for "PassPorter."

Vacation At-A-Glance

Create an overview of your itinerary on the chart below for easy reference. You can then make copies of it and give one to everyone in your traveling party, as well as to friends and family members who stay behind.

Name(s):	
Departing on: Time: #:	
Arriving at:	
Staying at: Phone:	

Date:	Date:
Park/Activity:	Park/Activity:
Breakfast:	Breakfast:
Lunch:	Lunch:
Dinner:	Dinner:
Other:	Other:

Date:	Date:
Park/Activity:	Park/Activity:
Breakfast:	Breakfast:
Lunch:	Lunch:
Dinner:	Dinner:
Other:	Other:

Date:	Date:
Park/Activity:	Park/Activity:
Breakfast:	Breakfast:
Lunch:	Lunch:
Dinner:	Dinner:
Other:	Other:

Date:	Date:
Park/Activity:	Park/Activity:
Breakfast:	Breakfast:
Lunch:	Lunch:
Dinner:	Dinner:
Other:	Other:

Date:	Date:
Park/Activity:	Park/Activity:
Breakfast:	Breakfast:
Lunch:	Lunch:
Dinner:	Dinner:
Other:	Other:

Departing on: Time: #:	
Returning at:	

Side tabs: Planning · Getting There · Staying in Style · Touring · Feasting · Making Magic · Index · Notes & More